# ELECTRONIC PROCESSES
## IN
# IONIC CRYSTALS

BY

N. F. MOTT, M.A., F.R.S.

AND

R. W. GURNEY, M.A., Ph.D.

SECOND EDITION

DOVER PUBLICATIONS, INC.
NEW YORK

Published in the United Kingdom by Constable
and Company, Limited, 10 Orange Street, London
W.C.2.


This new Dover edition, first published in 1964,
is an unabridged and unaltered republication of the
second edition (1948) of the work first published by
Oxford University Press in 1940.

This edition is published by special arrangement
with Oxford University Press.


*Library of Congress Catalog Card Number 64-18650*


Manufactured in the United States of America


Dover Publications, Inc.
180 Varick Street
New York 14, N.Y.

## PREFACE TO THE SECOND EDITION

THE first edition has been changed only by the addition at the ends of Chapters V, VII, and VIII of paragraphs on rectifying contacts, photographic emulsions, and the theory of oxidation. It was felt that recent advances in the subject have changed the theory very little, and most of the book is still well suited for the interpretation of experimental phenomena. The experimental side of the subject is advancing very fast, and the present moment would be rather inopportune for a review of all of it in the light of the theory.

For this reason we felt that the time had not yet come for any extensive revision.

N. F. M.
R. W. G.

# PREFACE

THIS book was written in order to develop the theory of the movement of electrons in ionic crystals. One of the authors had studied for some years the behaviour of electrons in metals, the other the properties of ions in solutions; we were thus able to approach the problems of the conduction of electricity in ionic crystals from somewhat different points of view. We were first attracted to the subject by the very detailed and complete experimental investigations of the properties of alkali-halide crystals with colour centres which have been carried out in recent years; we have found that an explanation based on quantum mechanics can be given of the great majority of these properties. We found, moreover, that the phenomena observed in alkali-halides shed a great deal of light on the more complex behaviour of substances of greater technical importance, such as semi-conductors, photographic emulsions, and luminescent materials. These are described and interpreted in the later chapters of this book, and a final chapter touches the fringes of the large subject of reactions in solids.

It is a pleasure to thank those of our friends and colleagues who have helped us to prepare the book. Dr. W. F. Berg, Dr. H. Fröhlich, Professor P. Gross and Dr. J. T. Randall have read all, or part, of the book in proof. Dr. H. W. B. Skinner and Dr. J. T. Randall have given us information about their work prior to publication, and to Dr. Skinner we owe the preparation of the diagrams on pp. 76 and 79. Finally we should like to thank the staff of the Oxford University Press for their unfailing skill and courtesy.

N. F. M.
R. W. G.

*January* 1940

# CONTENTS

## VI. LUMINESCENCE AND THE DISSIPATION OF ENERGY

## VII. PHOTOCHEMICAL PROCESSES IN SILVER HALIDES AND THE PHOTOGRAPHIC LATENT IMAGE

## VIII. PROCESSES INVOLVING THE TRANSPORT OF BOTH IONS AND ELECTRONS

# INTRODUCTION

THE optical and the electrical behaviour of electrons in ionic crystals are intimately related. One can only hope to unravel the underlying mechanisms if one studies each complex process in the light of as many allied phenomena as possible. In this book we have, therefore, attempted to correlate all the principal types of electronic behaviour—optical, electrical, and chemical—and to show that a unified interpretation, based on quantum mechanics, is possible.

Many of the most striking properties of ionic crystals depend mainly on small quantities of some impurity or on lattice imperfections of a particular kind. For only one type of crystal imperfection, however, has the experimental investigation been at all exhaustive—that is, for the so-called colour centres in coloured alkali-halide crystals. We hope that the thorough discussion of this field, given in Chapter IV, will be of assistance in understanding the not dissimilar properties of substances of greater technical importance, some of which are discussed in later chapters. Out of the enormous mass of experimental material we have selected only the most recent results, which seemed susceptible to theoretical discussion.

As the title suggests, the book is not directly concerned with the structure or the static properties of ionic crystals, but rather with phenomena which occur in them. Nevertheless, a knowledge of the inter-ionic forces, the lattice vibrations, and the dielectric constants in perfect crystals is necessary, and in Chapter I some account of these has been given. Chapter II deals with the Wagner-Schottky theory of lattice defects existing in pure crystals in thermal equilibrium. Chapter III begins the theoretical discussion of electrons in ionic crystals, and examines their motion and interaction with the lattice. Chapter IV deals with polar crystals containing a stoichiometric excess of either constituent, and in particular the properties of the colour centres ($F$-centres) in alkali-halides; a general discussion of the behaviour of primary photoelectric currents is also included. Chapter V deals with semi-conductors, including the action of oxide rectifiers, and also with secondary photoelectric currents and currents in insulators in strong fields. Chapter VI is concerned with luminescent materials, and the general problem of the dissipation of the energy absorbed by an insulator. Chapter VII discusses the photochemical reduction of silver halides, and the behaviour of photographic emulsions. Chapter VIII is concerned with other problems in which both ions and electrons move in crystals, in particular with Wagner's theory of the tarnishing and oxidation of metals, and with certain processes involving the reduction of metallic salts.

# I

## THE PERFECT IONIC LATTICE

## 1. Introduction

ONE of the aims of theoretical physics is to discover the properties of atoms. A complementary aim is to deduce from the properties of atoms the properties of matter as we know them. A theory of solids must therefore enable the crystal form, elastic properties, and so on, of any solid substance to be deduced from the properties of the atoms of which it is built up. Ionic crystals, in particular the alkali-halides, were the first solids to be treated in this way. The alkali-halides were among the first crystals whose structure was worked out by means of X-rays; and Born,[†] assuming them to be built up of positively and negatively charged ions, was able to give a detailed quantitative account of their lattice energies and elastic properties.

In each ion the electrons are normally in their lowest energy levels. In discussing the properties of ionic crystals it is therefore convenient to make a distinction between phenomena in which the ions remain unexcited and those in which some of the ions become excited or ionized by the removal of an electron. In the latter class are included the absorption of visible and ultra-violet light, photo-conductivity, luminescence, and properties of semi-conductors. They are treated in Chapters III–VIII of this book. To the former class belong the energy of the crystal, its elastic properties and dielectric constant, its absorption of infra-red rays, and its electrolytic conductivity. All these phenomena may, for the alkali-halides at any rate, be discussed by treating the crystal as a simple assembly of polarizable ions; though we shall see that for other salts and for certain properties even of the alkali-halides a rather more sophisticated model is necessary.

## 2. Cohesive forces in ionic crystals; theory

A number of accounts of the theory of cohesive forces in ionic crystals have been published[‡] and only an outline will be included here. Theoretical calculations of the lattice energy have been made and compared with experiment both for typically ionic crystals, such as the alkali-halides, and crystals which are only partly ionic, such as the sulphides. We shall therefore give the theory in its simplest form, and

---

† M. Born, *Atomtheorie des festen Zustandes* (Leipzig, 1923).
‡ Cf., for instance, M. Born and M. Göppert-Mayer, *Handb. d. Phys.* 24/2, 623 (1933).

shall then give a critical discussion of what is meant by an ionic crystal and under what conditions the simple theory can be applied.

In the interests of simplicity we shall derive formulae for the sodium-chloride structure only; references are given for other structures. The sodium-chloride structure is shown in Fig. 1.

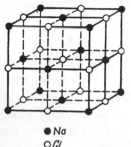

● Na
○ Cl

FIG. 1. The sodium-chloride structure

The theory of the cohesive forces of ionic crystals, worked out mainly by Born, rests on the following assumptions:

1. The crystal is built up of positively and negatively charged ions carrying charges $\pm ze$ respectively, where $z$ is the valency.

2. The ions repel one another with a force which is practically zero until the separation falls below a certain value, when the repulsion increases very rapidly. Following Fowler† we shall call the energy $w(r)$ of a pair of ions due to the repulsive force the 'overlap' energy. In the early work $w(r)$ was assumed to have the form

$$w(r) = \lambda r^{-s}, \qquad (1)$$

where $s \simeq 9$ and $r$ is the inter-ionic distance. The application of quantum mechanics to the problem has suggested that the assumption

$$w(r) = Ae^{-r/\rho} \qquad (2)$$

is preferable, and this has been used in more recent work.

3. The ions are polarizable; in other words, an electric field $E$ produces a dipole $\alpha E$ on any ion. The quantity $\alpha$ is called the polarizability of the ion.

The ions adhere to form a stable crystal because of the electrostatic attraction between unlike ions, which outweighs the repulsion between like ions. They keep apart because, when two ions overlap, the strong repulsive force with energy $w(r)$ comes into play. With the assumptions made above, we may calculate the energy required to separate the crystal into its constituent ions. We require first the electrostatic energy, which may be found as follows:

Let $\phi$ denote the electrostatic potential at any lattice point of the crystal due to all the ions except the one occupying that point. This quantity has been worked out for a number of structures; for the rock-salt structure at a point normally occupied by a positive ion it is

$$\phi = -\frac{ze\alpha_M}{r},$$

† R. H. Fowler, *Statistical Mechanics*, 2nd ed., pp. 295, 320 (Cambridge, 1936).

where $r$ is the shortest distance between ions of unlike sign and $\alpha_M$ a numerical constant known as the Madelung constant. For this structure it has the value†

$$\alpha_M = 1{\cdot}7476\ldots\,.$$

The electrostatic energy per ion is then

$$\tfrac{1}{2}ze\phi = -\frac{\alpha_M}{2}\frac{(ze)^2}{r},$$

the factor $\tfrac{1}{2}$ entering so that each ion pair shall not be counted twice. The electrostatic energy per mol of, for instance, sodium-chloride ($z = 1$) will be
$$-Le^2\alpha_M/r,$$

where $L$ is Avogadro's number.

In calculating the energy due to the overlap forces, the simplest assumption is that the forces fall off so quickly that only ions which are nearest neighbours need be taken into account. Since each ion has six nearest neighbours, the overlap energy per ion is then

$$3w(r)$$

and the total energy, $U(r)$ per ion pair, is given by

$$U(r) = -\frac{e^2\alpha_M}{r} + 6w(r). \qquad (3)$$

With either form for the repulsive potential, (1) or (2), the expression (3) for $U(r)$ contains *two* unknown constants. These may be determined from the condition that the crystal is in equilibrium under zero pressure, viz.
$$\frac{dU(r)}{dr} = 0, \qquad (4)$$

and from the compressibility $\chi$, given by

$$\frac{1}{\chi} = \frac{1}{18r}\frac{d^2U}{dr^2}. \qquad (5)$$

From the observed lattice constant and compressibility the lattice energy $U$ may thus be calculated. This may be compared with the value derived from the observed heat of formation of, for instance, sodium-chloride from sodium metal and chlorine gas, if we know the electron affinity of chlorine, the ionization energy of sodium, and the lattice energy of sodium metal.

† For a table of Madelung constants for other structures cf. J. Sherman, *Chemical Reviews*, **11**, 107 (1932).

We give below the appropriate formulae for the energy:
If $w(r) = \lambda r^{-s}$, then (4) gives

$$\alpha e^2/r^2 = 6\lambda s/r^{s+1},$$

and we have for the lattice energy per ion pair

$$U = -\frac{\alpha_M e^2}{r}\left(1 - \frac{1}{s}\right) \tag{6}$$

and for the compressibility

$$\chi = \frac{18r^4}{\alpha_M e^2(s-1)}. \tag{7}$$

Similar expressions may be obtained with the form (2) of $w(r)$.

Before discussing the agreement between theory and experiment we must describe the refinements which have been introduced into the theory. In the first place it is not usually very accurate to neglect the overlap energy between ions of like sign in calculating the compressibility. If this is taken into account there will enter into the expression for the energy three overlap terms $w_{++}(r)$, $w_{--}(r)$, $w_{+-}(r)$. For the sodium-chloride structure the contribution to the overlap energy is then

$$6w_{+-} + 12(w_{++} + w_{--})$$

per ion pair. The constants in these terms cannot be determined from the compressibility alone; but this fact will not affect the expression (6) for the energy, in which the number of neighbours of any ion does not occur.

In the second place the van der Waals attraction between the ions must be taken into account. This makes a contribution of 2–3 per cent. to the total lattice energy of the alkali-halides and about 10 per cent. for the silver halides.

Finally, the zero-point energy must be subtracted. This is of the order 1 per cent. of the total energy.

*Van der Waals forces.* According to the work of London[†] and of Margenau,[‡] the van der Waals attraction between any two atoms or ions gives rise to an energy

$$V(r) = -C/r^6,$$

where $\quad C = \dfrac{3}{2m^2}(e\hbar)^4 \displaystyle\sum_k \sum_{k'} \dfrac{f_{0k}f_{0k'}}{(E_k - E_0)(E_{k'} - E_0)(E_k + E_{k'} - 2E_0)}.$

Here $E_0$ is the energy of the ground state, $E_k$ of the excited state, and

[†] F. London, *Zeits. f. phys. Chem.* (B), **11**, 222 (1930); *Zeits. f. Physik*, **63**, 245 (1930); *Trans. Faraday Soc.* **33**, 8 (1937).

[‡] H. Margenau, *Phys. Rev.* **38**, 747 (1931).

$f_{0k}$ is the corresponding oscillator strength. For an ion in a crystal the energies $E_k$ and the oscillator strengths $f_{0k}$ are *not* the same as for the ion *in vacuo* (cf. Chap. III, § 7).

Both can in principle be deduced from the optical constants of the crystal (i.e. the absorption coefficient and refractive index), if we can separate that part of the absorption and dispersion due to the negative from that due to the positive ions. For sodium-chloride the absorption bands due to the ions of the two signs lie respectively in quite different parts of the spectrum, namely, 400 and 1,600 A, so it is not difficult to make a rough separation; moreover, the excited states of the positive ion may be taken to be roughly the same as in the free ion.

Once the constants $C$ are determined for the various ion pairs, the contribution to the crystal energy may be found by summing over all ion pairs. The summations may be carried out by using the results of Jones and Ingham.[†] If $C_{++}$, $C_{--}$, $C_{+-}$ are the values of the constants for ions of like and unlike signs, the contribution to the energy is

$$-C/r^6,$$

where
$$C = 6{\cdot}5952C_{+-} + 1{\cdot}8067\frac{C_{++}+C_{--}}{2}.$$

Using these methods Mayer and his co-workers have estimated the van der Waals energy in the alkali-halides,[‡] silver and thallium halides,[||] and for the cuprous halides.[††] Their results will be reviewed below.

*Repulsive energy.* As we have seen, the repulsive forces between ions may be deduced from the compressibility of the crystals. Apart from this, estimates may be made by comparing them with the forces between rare gas atoms having similar structure. These will not be discussed here. A review is given by Fowler.[‡‡]

The most recent work in which the repulsive energy is deduced from the compressibilities of the salts, using formula (5) but including in the crystal energy the van der Waals term, is that of Mayer referred to above for the alkali, silver, thallium, and cuprous halides.[||||] For the alkali-halides the following form is chosen for the overlap energy

$$w(r) = cbe^{-(r-r_1-r_2)/\rho}. \tag{8}$$

† J. E. Jones and A. E. Ingham, *Proc. Roy. Soc.* (A), **107**, 636 (1925).
‡ J. E. Mayer, *J. Chem. Phys.* **1**, 270 (1933).
|| J. E. Mayer, ibid., p. 327.
†† J. E. Mayer and R. B. Levy, ibid., p. 647.
‡‡ R. H. Fowler, *Statistical Mechanics*, 2nd ed., p. 326 et seq. (Cambridge, 1936).
|||| References as above, except for the alkali-halides: M. L. Huggins and J. E. Mayer, *J. Chem. Phys.* **1**, 643 (1933); M. L. Huggins, ibid. **5**, 143 (1937).

Good agreement with experiment is found if $\rho$ is given the value $0.345 \times 10^{-8}$ cm. for *all* the alkali-halides. $b$ is arbitrarily set equal to $10^{-12}$ ergs, and $c$ is a factor calculated by Pauling[†] giving the dependence of the repulsion on the sign of the ions; it is unity for ions of unlike sign, 0.75 for two halogen ions and 1.25 for two alkali ions. The values of $r_1$, $r_2$ obtained are shown in Table 1.

Similar results are obtained for the other halides, $\rho$ being $0.271 \times 10^{-8}$ cm. for AgBr and $0.366 \times 10^{-8}$ cm. for TlBr.

TABLE 1. *Basic Radii $r_1$ and $r_2$ $\times 10^8$ cm.*[‡]

| | | | |
|---|---|---|---|
| $Li^+$ | 0.475 | $F^-$ | 1.110 |
| $Na^+$ | 0.875 | $Cl^-$ | 1.475 |
| $K^+$ | 1.185 | $Br^-$ | 1.600 |
| $Rb^+$ | 1.320 | $I^-$ | 1.785 |
| $Cs^+$ | 1.455 | | |

Sherman[||] has discussed a large number of crystals, including oxides, sulphides, and halides. He used a form $A/r^n$ for the repulsive potential, and found values of $n$ between 6 and 12. Since, however, the van der Waals potential was not included in his treatment, his values are probably not very accurate.

*Zero-point energy.* At the absolute zero of temperature the energy due to the zero-point vibrations is[††]

$$\tfrac{9}{4}h\nu_m$$

per ion pair, where $\nu_m$ is the maximum frequency of the Debye frequency spectrum.

*Lattice energy.* It follows from the considerations above that the work necessary to separate a crystal into the gaseous ions at the absolute zero of temperature is $-W$, given by

$$W = N\left[ -\frac{\alpha_M e^2}{r_0} + 6w_{+-}(r) + 12w_{--}(r) + 12w_{++}(r) - \frac{C}{r^6} + \frac{9}{4}h\nu_m \right], \quad (9)$$

where $N$ is the number of ion pairs in the crystal. The various quantities occurring are tabulated in Table 2 for a few typical crystals having the sodium-chloride structure.

As regards the accuracy of these results, Mayer estimates that the van der Waals energy for the silver salts may be in error by as much as 30 per cent. Moreover, the form assumed for $w(r)$ is entirely arbitrary;

[†] L. Pauling, *Zeits. f. Krist.* **67**, 377 (1928).
[‡] It should be emphasized that these basic radii are considerably smaller than the conventional ionic radii, a table of which is given at the end of this book.
[||] J. Sherman, *Chemical Reviews*, **11**, 153 (1932).
[††] Cf. M. Born and M. Göppert-Mayer, *Handb. d. Phys.* **24**/2, 726 (1933).

TABLE 2

|  | AgBr | RbI | NaCl |
|---|---|---|---|
| Electrostatic energy, $\alpha e^2/r$ . | 13·82 | 10·86 | 14·18 |
| Repulsive energy . . . | 2·20 | 1·07 | 1·63 |
| Van der Waals energy . . | 1·89 | 0·28 | 0·20 |
| Zero-point energy . . . | 0·06 | 0·05 | 0·12 |
| Total . . . . | 13·45 | 10·02 | 12·63 |

Energies in ergs $\times 10^{12}$ per ion pair.

only the values of $w'$ and $w''$ for one $r$ are known. The values of $w(r)$ calculated from (2) differ by from 10 to 30 per cent. from the values calculated from the older assumption[†] (1). Thus an accuracy in the total energy greater than 2 to 3 parts in 100 cannot be claimed.

An important point is the relatively greater importance of the van der Waals energy in salts of the silver-halide type (with high refractive index) compared with that in the alkali-halides. This is due to the greater polarizability of the ions of the noble metals.

## 3. Cohesive forces; comparison with the observed energies

The theory gives the work required to dissociate the crystal into ions; by experiment one measures the heat of formation of the crystal from the metal and the halogen gas. From the experimental data one may obtain the work $W_A$ required to dissociate the crystal into an assembly of neutral atoms; the methods of arriving at this quantity, by means of the Born cycle, will not be discussed here.[‡] $W_A$ is connected with the lattice energy $W$ by means of the equation

$$W_A = W - I + E, \tag{10}$$

where $I$ is the ionization potential of the alkali atom and $E$ the electron affinity of the halogen.

Until recently no experimental determination of the electron affinities had been made. From equation (10), however, using experimental values of $W_A$ and theoretical[‖] values of $W$ from formula (9), $E$ was calculated for each halogen from all the alkali-halides containing the given halogen. The agreement was good, as the following table[††] shows.

† M. Born and M. Göppert-Mayer, loc. cit., p. 726.
‡ Cf. M. Born and M. Göppert-Mayer, loc. cit., p. 727.
‖ From J. E. Mayer and L. Helmholz, *Zeits. f. Physik*, **75**, 19 (1932).
†† From Born and Göppert-Mayer, loc. cit.

TABLE 3. *Electron Affinities of the Halogens in kcals.*

| Metal with which combined | F | Cl | Br | I |
|---|---|---|---|---|
| Li . . . . | 95·0 | 85·7 | 81·2 | 75·8 |
| Na . . . . | 06·5 | 86·5 | 80·9 | 73·9 |
| K . . . . | 95·5 | 87·1 | 81·2 | 73·2 |
| Rb . . . . | 95·8 | 85·7 | 82·0 | 73·8 |
| Cs . . . . | 93·8 | 87·3 | 82·0 | 74·2 |
| [Sutton and Mayer] . | .. | .. | .. | 72·4 |

To obtain experimental lattice energies for the halides of other metals, these values of the electron affinities $E$ were substituted in (10) together with the measured heats of reaction $W_A$.

More recently a direct determination of the electron affinity of iodine has been made;† the result is included in Table 3. As this agreed within 2 per cent. with the value which was already in use (deduced as above), no revision was necessary for experimental lattice energies based upon previous estimates of the electron affinity.

In their work mentioned above both Sherman and Mayer compared their calculated values with experimental lattice energies deduced in this way. Sherman‡ found that the experimental values were in general greater than those calculated by him from the Born theory. He concluded that most of the salts and oxides discussed were not true ionic lattices. This paper, however, was written before the importance of the van der Waals terms in salts of high refractive index had been recognized.

Mayer‖ found that after including an estimate of the van der Waals energy he obtained good agreement for AgCl, CuCl, TlCl, TlBr, and TlI. But the experimental lattice energies of AgBr, CuBr, AgI, and CuI were all higher than the calculated values, which he attributed to the presence of a considerable homopolar binding component.

The CsCl crystal is body-centred at ordinary temperatures, but undergoes a transition at 445° C. to the simple NaCl type of lattice, the heat of transition being 1·34 kcals. Ammonium-chloride, $NH_4Cl$, undergoes a similar transition at 184·3°, the heat of transition being 1·03 kcals. In an attempt to calculate the lattice energies (without introducing homopolar binding) it was found by May†† that, in order to reproduce the observed heats of transition, it was necessary to use van der Waals

† P. P. Sutton and J. E. Mayer, *J. Chem. Phys.* **3**, 20 (1935).
‡ J. Sherman, *Chemical Reviews*, **11**, 153 (1932).
‖ J. E. Mayer, *J. Chem. Phys.* **1**, 372 (1933).
†† A. May, *Phys. Rev.* **52**, 339 (1937).

forces 3·5 times as great as those derived by Mayer. This discrepancy is perhaps due to the presence of homopolar binding.

## 4. Polar and homopolar binding

We must now attempt to give some idea of the conditions under which the theory of the preceeding sections is valid, and to discuss the transition from polar to homopolar binding. We must first remark that

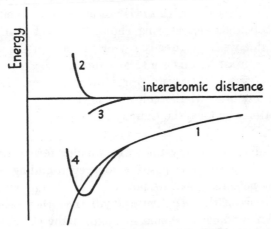

FIG. 2. Energy of a semi-polar crystal. (1) Electrostatic attraction. (2) Overlap repulsion. (3) Homopolar attraction. (4) Total energy

in all polar crystals, even the alkali-halides, the electronic structures of adjacent positive and negative ions will overlap to a considerable extent; the repulsive forces between the ions, which are in equilibrium with the electrostatic attraction, only come into play when one ion penetrates into the other. This overlap will necessarily distort the ions to some extent.

This distortion will be particularly important if the work required to remove an electron from the negative to the *adjacent*† positive ions is small. The electrons in the outermost shell of the negative ion will then be shared with the surrounding positive ions, in just the same sense that the electron in the hydrogen molecular ion is shared between the protons. Such a sharing of electrons always gives rise to an additional cohesive force, and this force may be called homopolar. The type of energy curve that we expect is shown in Fig. 2. The energy of binding is increased by the presence of the homopolar forces.

† This energy must not be confused with the work necessary to bring an electron into the conduction band; cf. Chap. III, § 7.

The values of the first ionization potentials of free atoms of the alkali metals are lower than those of any other metals. In other words, the vacant electronic level in an alkali positive ion is relatively high. When we compare the alkali-halides with the halides of other metals, the absence of homopolar forces in the former is, therefore, to be expected. On the other hand, for a metal like silver, whose first ionization potential is more than 2 eV. greater, there will be a stronger tendency towards electron sharing. Apart from this it is not at present possible to predict for which compounds this sharing should be most marked. On the experimental side we have already reviewed some of the evidence that non-polar forces must be taken into account.

The elastic constants of crystals provide also a sensitive test of the nature of the binding. If the cohesion is due only to central forces between the atoms or ions, the Cauchy relations,

$$c_{12} = c_{44},$$

should be valid for cubic crystals. Homopolar forces are not purely central forces; if one of the positive ions surrounding a negative is moved, it may get more than its fair share of charge, and so decrease the binding between the negative and all the other positives. Thus with homopolar binding we should not expect the Cauchy relations to be satisfied.

A recent determination[†] gives fair agreement with experiment for the Cauchy relations between the elastic constants for NaCl and KCl, but not for MgO. This is shown in the following table.

TABLE 4. *Elastic Constants of Certain Crystals, showing the Breakdown of the Cauchy Relations*

| Crystal | Temperature, degrees K | $c_{12} \times 10^{-11}$, dyne/cm.$^2$ | $c_{44} \times 10^{-11}$, dyne/cm.$^2$ |
|---|---|---|---|
| NaCl . . | 270 | 1·30 | 1·278 |
| KCl . . | 80 | 0·6 | 0·664 |
| MgO . . | 80 | 8·56 | 15·673 |

Further evidence of the existence of homopolar forces is provided by the large dielectric constants of certain crystals (cf. § 5.2 of this chapter).

## 5. The dielectric constant

### 5.1 Polarizability of the ions

The dielectric constant $\kappa$ of the alkali-halides for static fields (or for radio frequencies) is of the order 5. The refractive index $n$ for light of long wave-length ($10^{-4}$ cm.) is of the order 1·5, so that the dielectric

[†] M. A. Durand, *Phys. Rev.* **50**, 449 (1936).

constant $\kappa_0$ ($= n^2$) for these frequencies is about 2·2. A similar difference exists for all ionic crystals. For instance, for the oxides of the alkaline earths $\kappa \sim 10$, $\kappa_0 \sim 3$; for thallium halides $\kappa \sim 30$, $\kappa_0 \sim 5$. The explanation of the discrepancy is as follows. In an applied field there is always a polarization of the medium due to the polarization of the ions, that is to say, a distortion of their electronic structure. For high frequencies the whole of the dielectric constant arises in this way. For

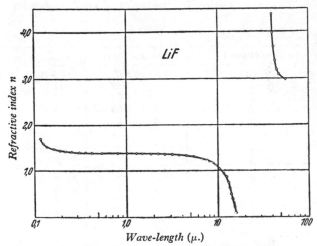

FIG. 3. The refractive index of lithium-fluoride†

static fields or for low frequencies, on the other hand, the positive and negative ions themselves are displaced respectively in opposite directions by the external field. This makes an additional contribution which is of the same order of magnitude. No appreciable movement of the ions in response to the field can take place when the frequency of the radiation exceeds the natural frequency of vibration of the ions, which is of the order $10^{12}$–$10^{13}$ sec.$^{-1}$ On the high-frequency side of this critical region the value of the dielectric constant will consequently fall by a factor of 2 or more. The wave-lengths of the light corresponding to the critical frequencies are of the order $10$–$100\,\mu$.

Fig. 3 shows the refractive index of lithium-fluoride plotted against wave-length. It will be seen that between the regions of anomalous dispersion in the ultra-violet and in the infra-red a region exists in which $n$ is sensibly constant; the quantity defined by

$$\kappa_0 = n^2$$

† From R. W. Pohl, *Proc. Phys. Soc.* 49 (extra part), 4 (1937).

in this region is thus the dielectric constant in the limit of low frequencies, due to the polarizability of the ions alone. From the theoretical point of view it represents the dielectric constant when the mass centres are kept at rest in their equilibrium positions, or when they execute random vibrations about these positions. A table of $\kappa$ and $\kappa_0$ is given below.

TABLE 5. *Dielectric Constants of Ionic Crystals†*

$z$ is the valency of the ion, and $a$ is the lattice constant.

| | Lattice | $z$ | $a \times 10^8$ cm. | $\kappa$ | $\kappa_0$ |
|---|---|---|---|---|---|
| LiF | NaCl | 1 | 2·07 | 9·27 | 1·92 |
| LiCl | ,, | 1 | 2·57 | 11·05 | 2·75 |
| LiBr | ,, | 1 | 2·74 | 12·1 | 3·16 |
| LiI | ,, | 1 | 3·03 | 11·03 | 3·80 |
| NaF | ,, | 1 | 2·31 | 6·0 | 1·74 |
| NaCl | ,, | 1 | 2·81 | 5·62 | 2·25 |
| NaBr | ,, | 1 | 2·97 | 5·99 | 2·62 |
| NaI | ,, | 1 | 3·23 | 6·60 | 2·91 |
| KF | ,, | 1 | 2·66 | 6·05 | 1·85 |
| KCl | ,, | 1 | 3·14 | 4·68 | 2·13 |
| KBr | ,, | 1 | 3·29 | 4·78 | 2·33 |
| KI | ,, | 1 | 3·53 | 4·94 | 2·69 |
| RbF | ,, | 1 | 2·82 | 5·91 | 1·93 |
| RbCl | ,, | 1 | 3·27 | 5·0 | 2·19 |
| RbBr | ,, | 1 | 3·42 | 5·0 | 2·33 |
| RbI | ,, | 1 | 3·66 | 5·0 | 2·63 |
| AgCl | ,, | 1 | 2·77 | 12·3 | 4·01 |
| AgBr | ,, | 1 | 2·88 | 13·1 | 4·62 |
| MgO | ,, | 2 | 2·10 | 9·8 | 2·95 |
| CaO | ,, | 2 | 2·40 | 11·8 | 3·28 |
| SrO | ,, | 2 | 2·57 | 13·3 | 3·31 |
| CsCl | CsCl | 1 | 3·56 | 7·20 | 2·60 |
| CsBr | ,, | 1 | 3·71 | 6·51 | 2·78 |
| CsI | ,, | 1 | 3·95 | 5·65 | 3·03 |
| $NH_4Cl$ | ,, | 1 | 3·34 | 6·96 | 2·62 |
| TlCl | ,, | 1 | 3·33 | 31·9 | 5·10 |
| TlBr | ,, | 1 | 3·44 | 29·8 | 5·41 |
| CuCl | ZnS | 1 | 2·34 | 10·0 | 3·57 |
| CuBr | ,, | 1 | 2·46 | 8·0 | 4·08 |
| ZnS | ,, | 2 | 2·33 | 8·3 | 5·07 |
| BeO | ZnO | 2 | 1·65 | 7·35 | 2·95 |
| $CaF_2$ | $CaF_2$ | 2–1 | 2·36 | 8·43 | 1·99 |
| $SrF_2$ | ,, | 2–1 | 2·50 | 7·69 | 2·08 |
| $BaF_2$ | ,, | 2–1 | 2·69 | 7·33 | 2·09 |

† The values are taken from K. Höjendahl, *K. Danske Vidensk. Selskab*, **16**, no. 2 (1938).

We shall discuss first the quantity $\kappa_0$. The polarizability $\alpha$ of an atom or ion is defined as follows: if the ion is placed in an external field $E$ the dipole $\mu$ induced is given by

$$\mu = \alpha E.$$

On the classical theory the polarizability of the ion depends on its absorption frequencies in the following way: if the ion contains an electron bound to its position of equilibrium by an elastic force equal to $-fx$ for a displacement $x$, the natural frequency $\nu$ is given by

$$4\pi^2\nu^2 = f/m.$$

But in an external field $E$ the displacement of the electron is given by

$$fx = eE,$$

the induced dipole is $ex$, and the polarizability $\alpha$ is therefore given by

$$\alpha = e^2/f = e^2/4\pi^2m\nu^2.$$

The same formula would be true in quantum mechanics for an atom with only one valence electron and one absorption line of frequency $\nu$ much stronger than all the others; the general formula is[†]

$$\alpha = \frac{e^2}{4\pi^2m} \sum_k \frac{f_{0k}}{\nu_{0k}^2}. \tag{11}$$

Here the $\nu_{0k}$ are the absorption frequencies and $f_{0k}$ the corresponding oscillator strengths. The summation must include an integration over the continuous absorption spectrum.

With the help of some special assumptions, making use of the refractivities of the rare gases and of ions in solution, Wasastjerna[‡] and Fajans and Joos[||] have prepared tables of the polarizabilities of free ions. Born and Heisenberg[††] and Pauling,[‡‡] on the other hand, have obtained values from the absorption spectra by means of formula (11) and by similar methods. The various values obtained are shown[||||] in Table 6.

When we come to deduce the refractive index (or dielectric constant $\kappa_0$) of polar crystals, we are faced by the fact that two formulae are in use giving the relation between $\kappa_0$ and $\alpha$. Denoting by $\alpha$ the polarizability

† Cf., for example, *Handb. d. Phys.* **24**/1, 616 (1933).

‡ J. A. Wasastjerna, *Zeits. f. phys. Chem.* **101**, 193 (1922).

|| K. Fajans and G. Joos, *Zeits. f. Physik*, **23**, 1 (1924).

†† M. Born and W. Heisenberg, ibid., p. 388.

‡‡ L. Pauling, *Proc. Roy. Soc.* (A), **114**, 191 (1927).

|||| From *Handb. d. Phys.* **24**/2, 942 (1933).

TABLE 6. *Polarizability of Atomic Ions (in cm.³ × 10⁻²⁴)*

|  |  |  | He | Li⁺ | Be⁺⁺ | B³⁺ | C⁴⁺ |
|---|---|---|---|---|---|---|---|
| Fajans and Joos | . | . | 0·196 | (0·08) | (0·04) | (0·02) | (0·012) |
| Born and Heisenberg | . | . | 0·202 | 0·075 | .. | .. | .. |
| Pauling . | . | . | 0·201 | 0·029 | 0·008 | 0·003 | 0·0013 |
|  | O⁻⁻ | F⁻ | Ne | Na⁺ | Mg⁺⁺ | Al³¹ | Si⁴⁺ |
| F. and J. | 2·75 | (0·98) | 0·392 | 0·196 | (0·12) | (0·067) | (0·04) |
| B. and H. | .. | 0·99 | 0·392 | 0·21 | 0·12 | 0·065 | 0·043 |
| P. | 3·88 | 1·04 | 0·390 | 0·179 | 0·094 | 0·052 | 0·0165 |
|  | S⁻⁻ | Cl⁻ | Ar | K⁺ | Ca⁺⁺ | Sc³⁺ | Ti⁴⁺ |
| F. and J. | 8·6 | 3·53 | 1·65 | 0·88 | 0·51 | (0·35) | (0·236) |
| B. and H. | .. | 3·05 | 1·63 | 0·87 | .. | .. | .. |
| P. | 10·2 | 3·66 | 1·62 | 0·83 | 0·47 | 0·286 | 0·185 |
|  | Se⁻⁻ | Br⁻ | Kr | Rb⁺ | Sr⁺⁺ | Y³⁺ | Zr⁴⁺ |
| F. and J. | 11·2 | 4·97 | 2·50 | 1·56 | 0·86 | .. | .. |
| B. and H. | .. | 4·17 | 2·46 | 1·81 | 1·42 | .. | .. |
| P. | 10·5 | 4·77 | 2·46 | 1·40 | 0·86 | 0·55 | 0·37 |
|  | Te⁻⁻ | I⁻ | X | Cs⁺ | Ba⁺⁺ | La³⁺ | Ce⁴⁺ |
| F. and J. | 15·7 | 7·55 | 4·10 | 2·56 | 1·68 | (1·3) | .. |
| B. and H. | .. | 6·28 | 4·00 | 2·79 | .. | .. | .. |
| P. | 14·0 | 7·10 | 3·99 | 2·42 | 1·55 | 1·04 | 0·73 |

of each molecule (or ion pair), and by $N$ the number of molecules or ion pairs per unit volume, the two formulae are

$$\kappa_0 - 1 = 4\pi N \alpha \tag{12}$$

(the Drude formula), and

$$\frac{\kappa_0 - 1}{\kappa_0 + 2} = \tfrac{4}{3}\pi N \alpha \tag{13}$$

(the Lorentz-Lorenz formula).

These formulae are applicable to non-polar substances and to liquids as well as to polar salts. The most direct tests have been obtained for non-polar liquids (e.g. hydrocarbons) for which the density, and hence $N$, can be varied by changing the temperature. The right-hand sides of both equations (12) and (13) are proportional to the density. There is an extensive literature on this subject. In a recent discussion of the data for a large number of non-polar liquids Kurtz and Ward† find that neither formula is in agreement with experiment; the empirical formula

$$\frac{\kappa_0 - 1}{\sqrt{\kappa_0 + 0·4}} \Big/ \text{density} = \text{constant}$$

gives the best representation of the experimental data.

On the theoretical side the formulae depend, as is well known, on the field that is assumed to be effective in polarizing each molecule or

† S. S. Kurtz and A. L. Ward, *J. Franklin Inst.* **224**, 697 (1937). For some other references see L. Onsager, *J. Am. Chem. Soc.* **58**, 1486 (1936).

ion of the medium. Let us denote by $P$ the polarization of the medium, by $E$ the electric field within the medium, and $E_{\text{eff}}$ the effective field polarizing each atom or molecule. Then the assumption

$$E_{\text{eff}} = E$$

leads to the Drude formula (12), and the assumption

$$E_{\text{eff}} = E + \tfrac{4}{3}\pi P \tag{14}$$

to the Lorentz-Lorenz formula (13).

The factor $4\pi P/3$ is often obtained† in the following way. Consider a molecule at a point in the dielectric where the field strength is $E$. The quantity $E$ represents the averaged field strength in that neighbourhood, including the field due to the dipole on the molecule considered; to obtain the field effective in polarizing the molecule we must subtract the field due to this molecule. But removing the molecule will be roughly equivalent to making a spherical hole in the dielectric; we thus require the field within a spherical hole, as in Fig. 4. This may easily be shown to be

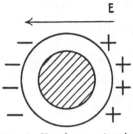

Fig. 4. Showing an atom in a 'hole' in a dielectric

$$E + \tfrac{4}{3}\pi P,$$

which is the required result. The term $\tfrac{4}{3}\pi P$ is due to the charge on the surface of the hole.

This method takes no account of the crystal structure and does not show clearly under what conditions the result is valid. Let us then consider a slab of dielectric of infinite area and finite thickness $l$ placed in an external field $D$. For simplicity we suppose that the crystal structure of the dielectric is simple cubic and that the lattice constant is $a$. If $\mu$ is the dipole induced at each lattice point, the polarization $P$ is given by

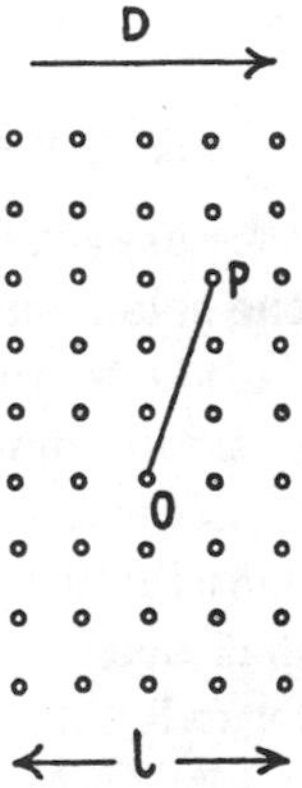

$$P = \mu/a^3.$$

Let us attempt to calculate the field at any one lattice point $O$ due to all the other dipoles. The field due to a dipole at the point $(l_1 a, l_2 a, l_3 a)$ is, resolved in the direction of $E$,

$$E_l = \frac{\mu}{a^3}\frac{l_3^2 + l_2^2 - 2l_1^2}{(l_1^2 + l_2^2 + l_3^2)^{\frac{5}{2}}}. \tag{15}$$

Fig. 5

† Cf., for example, P. Debye, *Polar Molecules* (London, 1929).

The total field at the point $O$ is obtained by summing over all $l_1$, $l_2$, $l_3$, and adding the external field $D$. According to (14) this should be equal to $E + \frac{4}{3}\pi P$, which is equal to $D - \frac{8}{3}\pi P$. Thus the sum of the fields due to all the dipoles should be

$$\sum_l E_l = -\tfrac{8}{3}\pi P = -\tfrac{8}{3}\pi \frac{\mu}{a^3}.$$

A proof that this is the case has been given by Fowler,[†] based on work by Darwin.[‡]

The theorem should be valid for any cubic structure and also for

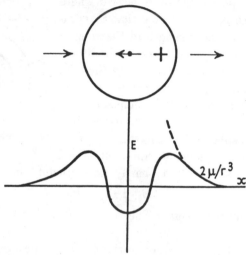

Fig. 6. Field of a polarized atom; the arrows show the direction of the field

the case when the atoms are distributed at random (i.e. that of a gas); the sole assumption made is that the field of a dipole is given by (15). This is, however, only the case if the size of the atom or ion considered is small compared with the distance from it to the point $O$ at which the field is to be calculated. This is by no means the case for the contributions of the atoms which are nearest neighbours to $O$. If the ions overlap to any considerable extent, (15) may be wrong even as regards the order of magnitude.

Fig. 6 shows a polarized atom and, underneath, the field $E$ due to it plotted along a line through its centre parallel to the axis of the dipole; at large distances the field is given by (15), viz. by $2\mu/r^3$, but as we approach the atom the field drops rapidly and, within it, changes sign.

† R. H. Fowler, *Statistical Mechanics*, 2nd ed., p. 441 (Cambridge, 1936).
‡ C. G. Darwin, *Trans. Camb. Phil. Soc.* **23**, 137 (1924).

Fig. 7 shows an atom in a (simple cubic) crystal surrounded by its nearest neighbours. Clearly the deviation from formula (15) will be most important for the atoms $A$ and $B$. Suppose they each make a contribution $2\beta\mu/a^3$ instead of $2\mu/a^3$ to the field polarizing the central atom and that we assume (15) to be valid for all the other ions. $\beta$ is an unknown numerical factor depending on how far the ions penetrate. Thus, since $\mu/a^3 = P$, the total field effective in polarizing the central atom is

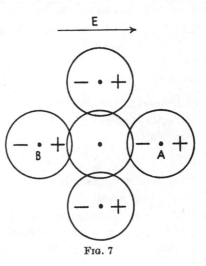

FIG. 7

$$E + \tfrac{4}{3}\pi\gamma P,$$

where $\quad \gamma = 1 - \dfrac{3}{\pi}(1-\beta).$

In § 5.2 we shall see that in certain cases the Drude formula gives a fair account of the observed facts. We may note here that, in these cases, since $\gamma = 0$ the value of $\beta$ must be $-0.05$; penetration will have to be such that the field due to the ions $A$ and $B$ practically vanishes (cf. Fig. 6).

For halide crystals we have seen (§ 4) that there may be a considerable overlap between the negative and adjacent positive ions; but it is probably safe to assume that there is not much overlap between the negative ions themselves, and certainly none between the positives. For these crystals we may then proceed as follows: we denote the polarizabilities of the two ions by $\alpha_1$, $\alpha_2$, and divide the polarization of the medium into $P_1$ due to that of ions of type 1 and $P_2$ due to that of ions of type 2. Then the field effective in polarizing ions of type 1 may be taken to be $\quad E + \tfrac{4}{3}\pi(P_1 + \gamma P_2),$

where $\gamma$ is the numerical factor less than unity already introduced. Similarly, the field polarizing ions of type 2 is

$$E + \tfrac{4}{3}\pi(P_2 + \gamma P_1).$$

For the polarization $P_1$ we thus have

$$P_1 = N\alpha_1[E + \tfrac{4}{3}\pi(P_1 + \gamma P_2)],$$

where $N$ is the number of ion pairs per unit volume; a similar expression is obtained for $P_2$. Since $P = P_1 + P_2$ and $\kappa_0 - 1 = 4\pi P/E$, we may solve the equations and obtain

$$\frac{\kappa_0 - 1}{4\pi} = \frac{\frac{8}{3}\pi N^2 \alpha_1 \alpha_2 (\gamma - 1) + N(\alpha_1 + \alpha_2)}{1 - \frac{4}{3}\pi N(\alpha_1 + \alpha_2) + (\frac{4}{3}\pi)^2 N^2 \alpha_1 \alpha_2 (1 - \gamma^2)}. \tag{16}$$

In § 5.2 we shall give some evidence that $\gamma$ is of the order zero.

In the particular case where $\gamma = 0$, equation (16) reduces to

$$\frac{\kappa_0 - 1}{4\pi} = \frac{N\alpha_1}{1 - \frac{4}{3}\pi N\alpha_1} + \frac{N\alpha_2}{1 - \frac{4}{3}\pi N\alpha_2}. \tag{17}$$

*Numerical values.* Fajans and Joos† have attempted to calculate the refractive indices of the alkali-halides ($\sqrt{\kappa_0}$) from the Lorentz-Lorenz formula ($\gamma = 1$)

$$\frac{\kappa_0 - 1}{4\pi} = \frac{N(\alpha_1 + \alpha_2)}{1 - \frac{4}{3}\pi N(\alpha_1 + \alpha_2)}. \tag{18}$$

They find it impossible to choose a set of polarizabilities $\alpha_1$, $\alpha_2$ for the halide and alkali ions which give agreement with experiment for all these salts. The authors point out that the polarizability of an ion in a crystal lattice is not necessarily the same as that of the free ion; an ion may be distorted by its surroundings. In our opinion the discrepancy may also be partly due to the invalidity of the Lorentz-Lorenz formula (18).

In Table 7 we have calculated $\kappa_0$ from Pauling's values of the polarizabilities of the free ions for the alkali-halides, using both formulae (17) and (18). The formulae do not give very different results for the substances of low refractive index; for the sodium salts there seems to be definite evidence that neither formula gives the correct value of $\kappa_0$.

TABLE 7. *Values of the Dielectric Constant $\kappa_0$*

| | | $\kappa_0$ | | |
|---|---|---|---|---|
| | | From (17) | From (18) | Observed |
| NaF | . . | 1·72 | 1·78 | 1·74 |
| NaCl | . . | 2·62 | 2·71 | 2·25 |
| NaBr | . . | 2·88 | 2·91 | 2·62 |
| NaI | . . | 3·30 | 3·35 | 2·91 |
| KF . | . . | 1·74 | 1·84 | 1·85 |
| KCl | . . | 2·18 | 2·33 | 2·13 |
| KBr | . . | 2·28 | 2·48 | 2·33 |
| KI . | . . | 2·67 | 2·85 | 2·69 |
| RbCl | . . | 2·11 | 2·30 | 2·19 |
| RbBr | . . | 2·21 | 2·39 | 2·33 |
| RbI | . . | 2·49 | 2·70 | 2·63 |

† K. Fajans and G. Joos, *Zeits. f. Physik*, **23**, 1 (1924); cf. also H. G. Grimm and H. Wolff, *Handb. d. Phys.* **24/2**, 943 (1933).

The polarizabilities of ions have already been discussed in § 2 in connexion with the van der Waals forces. To obtain the polarizabilities of the (distorted) ions in the crystal, one can apply formula (11), taking the frequencies $\nu_{0k}$ from the absorption spectrum of the crystal. For this purpose one must decide which parts of the absorption are due to the two kinds of ions. The chief uncertainty in the calculation lies, however, in the estimation of the oscillator strengths; they may be deduced from the dispersion near the absorption bands, but only if one makes some assumption about the value of $\gamma$, i.e. whether to use the Lorentz-Lorenz, Drude, or some intermediate formula such as (16).

Herzfeld and Wolf † have discussed the salts NaCl and KCl on these lines, using the Lorentz-Lorenz formula (18). They take the frequencies from the absorption spectrum of the salt, and find that the oscillator strengths can be chosen to give the correct dispersion according to the formula

$$\frac{n^2-1}{n^2+2} = \tfrac{4}{3}\pi N \frac{e^2}{4\pi^2 m} \sum_k \frac{f_{0k}}{\nu_{0k}^2 - \nu^2} \tag{19}$$

over the whole range of frequencies $\nu$.

### 5.2. The dielectric constant for static fields

Many of the familiar properties of polar crystals depend on the existence of defects in the lattice of the crystal, and a large part of this book must be devoted to the nature of these defects. Any theoretical calculation of the energy of such a defect will depend on the theory which we use for the dielectric constant of the crystal; that is our sole purpose in discussing it here. The theory is by no means simple, and this section may, of course, be omitted by the reader interested in the properties of crystals treated in the following chapters.

The most recent development of the theory is due to Höjendahl,‡ who has developed ideas due to Heckmann‖ and to Born.†† The discussion given here is similar to that of Höjendahl.

As we have already stated, the dielectric constant in static fields is partly due to the displacement of the positive and negative ions relative to each other by the applied field.

Let us consider, then, a crystal in equilibrium in a static field $E$. In equilibrium let the positive and negative ions be displaced distances $\pm x$ from their mean positions, and let the dipoles induced on ions of

† K. F. Herzfeld and K. L. Wolf, *Ann. d. Physik* (4), **78**, 35 and 195 (1925).
‡ K. Höjendahl, *K. Danske Vidensk. Selskab*, **16**, no. 2 (1938).
‖ G. Heckmann, *Zeits. f. Krist.* **61**, 250 (1925).
†† M. Born and M. Göppert-Mayer, *Handb. d. Phys.* 24/2, 759 (1933).

the two kinds be $\mu_1$ on the negative ions and $\mu_2$ on the positive ions. Then the polarization of the medium is given by

$$P = N(\mu_1 + \mu_2 + 2ex),$$

where $N$ is the number of ion pairs per unit volume. We may divide this into three terms

$$P_1 = N\mu_1, \quad P_2 = N\mu_2, \quad P_x = 2Nex.$$

In calculating $x$ we are faced with the same difficulty as before, namely that we do not know the contribution to the force on each ion made by the polarization of the medium.

To fix our ideas, let us consider first a crystal such as NaCl, in which the radius of a positive ion is small compared with that of a negative ion, so that the polarizability of the positive ions is small and will be neglected. When the crystal is polarized, we may imagine that the negative ions remain in their original positions, while the positives are displaced a distance $2x$. Then, since $2x$ is small compared with the inter-atomic distance, it is clear that the displacement of the ions has the effect of introducing a *point* dipole $2ex$ at each positive lattice point; these dipoles make a contribution to the field acting on any one positive ion at one of the other lattice points equal to

$$-\tfrac{8}{3}\pi P_x.$$

On the other hand, the contribution from the dipoles induced on the negative ions will be

$$(-4\pi + \tfrac{4}{3}\pi\gamma)P_1,$$

where $\gamma$ is the numerical factor already introduced to allow for the fact that positive ions penetrate the negatives. Thus the field tending to displace the positive ions is

$$E + \tfrac{4}{3}\pi(P_x + \gamma P_1).$$

In crystals in which the two ions have comparable polarizabilities we shall write

$$P_0 = P_1 + P_2,$$

and take the force tending to displace the positive ions to be

$$E + \tfrac{4}{3}\pi[P_x + \gamma P_0], \tag{20}$$

where the constant $\gamma$ will be assumed to be the same as before. By a similar argument, we may take the field effective in polarizing the negative ions to be

$$E + \tfrac{4}{3}\pi[P_1 + \gamma(P_2 + P_x)], \tag{21}$$

and that effective in polarizing the positive ions

$$E + \tfrac{4}{3}\pi[P_2 + \gamma(P_1 + P_x)]. \tag{22}$$

The dielectric constant may now be calculated, if we know the restoring force on each ion due to the overlap forces when the positive and negative ions are displaced distances $\pm x$. This force, which we denote by $px$, may be calculated as follows.

When the ions are displaced the change in the energy of the crystal per ion pair is, for simple cubic structures,

$$w(a+2x)+w(a-2x)+4w\{\sqrt{(a^2+4x^2)}\}-6w(a),$$

where $w(r)$ is the overlap energy between ions at a distance $r$ (cf. p. 2). This includes contributions of the interaction energy of nearest and next nearest neighbours, the latter being zero. Expanding and differentiating with respect to $x$, we obtain for $p$

$$p = 4[w''(a)+2w'(a)/a].$$

In an exact calculation $w(r)$ should include the van der Waals energy as well as the potential energy due to the overlap forces. For a rough calculation we may, however, neglect the former and set

$$w(r) = A e^{-r/\rho};$$

we then obtain
$$p = 4A\left(\frac{1}{\rho^2}-\frac{2}{a\rho}\right)e^{-a/\rho}. \qquad (23)$$

We may obtain $A$ from the condition that the crystal is in equilibrium, namely

$$\alpha_M \frac{e^2}{a^2} = \frac{6A}{\rho}e^{-a/\rho}.$$

We thus obtain for $p$, 
$$p = \frac{2\alpha_M e^2}{3a^2}\left[\frac{1}{\rho}-\frac{2}{a}\right]. \qquad (24)$$

From equations (20), (21), (22) we now see that the polarization is given by

$$P_x = \frac{2Ne^2}{p}[E+\tfrac{4}{3}\pi(P_x+\gamma P_0)],$$

$$P_1 = N\alpha_1[E+\tfrac{4}{3}\pi(P_1+\gamma P_2+\gamma P_x)],$$

$$P_2 = N\alpha_2[E+\tfrac{4}{3}\pi(P_2+\gamma P_1+\gamma P_x)].$$

Since $P = P_x+P_1+P_2$ and $\kappa-1 = 4\pi P/E$, these equations may be solved for $\kappa$. We shall, however, only give the solutions for the cases $\gamma = 1$ (no overlap between the ions) and $\gamma = 0$. In the former case $(\gamma = 1)$ we obtain

$$\frac{\kappa-1}{\kappa+2} = \frac{\kappa_0-1}{\kappa_0+2}+\tfrac{4}{3}\pi\beta, \qquad (25)$$

where $\beta = Ne^2/p$. In the latter case the polarizations due to displacement and to ionic polarizability do not affect one another. A short calculation shows that

$$\kappa - \kappa_0 = \frac{4\pi\beta}{1 - \frac{4}{3}\pi\beta}. \tag{26}$$

Since the constant $\rho$ occurring in the overlap energy is known from the compressibility, either of these formulae may be used to calculate $\kappa$. We have, however, preferred to use the experimental values of $\kappa$, $\kappa_0$ to calculate $\rho$. The results are given in the following table, and are compared with those deduced from the compressibility.

TABLE 8. *Values of the Constant $\rho$ in the Overlap Energy*

(Those deduced from the dielectric constant use the experimental values of $\kappa$, $\kappa_0$ given in Table 5)

| | $\rho \times 10^8$ cm. | | |
| | | *From dielectric constant* | |
| *Crystal* | *From compressibility* (*Born and Mayer*) | $\gamma = 1$, *formula* (25) | $\gamma = 0$, *formula* (26) |
|---|---|---|---|
| NaF . . | .. | 0·20 | 0·26 |
| NaCl . | 0·326 | 0·20 | 0·32 |
| NaBr . | 0·334 | 0·19 | 0·34 |
| NaI . . | 0·384 | 0·20 | 0·38 |
| KCl . . | 0·316 | 0·21 | 0·32 |
| KBr . | 0·326 | 0·20 | 0·33 |
| KI . . | 0·351 | 0·19 | 0·34 |
| RbCl . | 0·356 | 0·22 | 0·33$_5$ |
| RbBr . | 0·340 | 0·20 | 0·34 |
| RbI . | 0·351 | 0·18 | 0·33 |

It will be seen that rather good agreement is obtained with $\gamma = 0$.

In conclusion, therefore, we may say that even for the alkali-halides no theoretical calculation of the dielectric constant is possible at present, because of the difficulty in estimating the internal field in the crystal, and thus of estimating $\gamma$. The most we can do is to use the experimental results to obtain $\gamma$, and we find the result (rather unexpected *a priori*) that $\gamma \simeq 0$. This result will be of use in our subsequent discussion of the relation between the dielectric constant and the frequency of the infra-red vibrations of a crystal.

Our whole discussion up to the present has been based on the assumption that the crystal is not semipolar in the sense of § 4. If homopolar forces exist between the negative ion and the positive ions which are nearest neighbours to it, then the electrons of the negative ion must be thought of as spending part of their time in the field of the positive ions. Any displacement of the positive ion relative to the negative ions will alter the relative amplitudes of the electronic wave-function in the two ions; the positive ion, by coming nearer to the negative ion, may acquire some negative charge from it.[†] Such an effect will obviously increase the dielectric constant. Eucken and Büchner[‡] have ascribed the high dielectric constant of salts for which $\kappa \sim 30$, such as TlCl, TlBr, or $PbCl_2$, or Rutile ($\kappa \sim 100$), to an effect of this type.

## 6. Lattice vibrations in ionic crystals

In a lattice built from mass-points of two different masses, the frequency spectrum splits into two halves, the acoustic and the optical. For a one-dimensional lattice the two types of vibration are as illustrated in Fig. 8.[||] The character of an optical vibration is that, in every

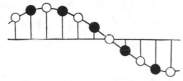 

FIG. 8. (a) Acoustic vibration    (b) Optical vibration

region larger than or comparable with the wave-length, the two species of particles move in opposite directions; in an ionic crystal this gives rise to a polarization, and these vibrations may thus be called polarization waves. For a row of mass-points, according to Born and Kármán,[††] the relation between frequency $\nu$ and wave-length $\lambda$ is that shown in Fig. 9.

For similar curves worked out for a three-dimensional polar lattice, cf. a paper by Lyddane and Herzfeld.[‡‡]

The frequency which gives the strongest absorption of infra-red radiation is the one for which the relation of frequency and wave-length is the same as for light, $$\nu = c/\lambda.$$

Since the frequencies are of the order $10^{13}$ sec.$^{-1}$, this will give a wave-length of the order $10^{-3}$ cm., so that $a/\lambda$ is very small; thus the absorption frequency will be practically the highest of the vibrational spectrum (shown by the point $P$ in Fig. 9). It has been measured directly,[||||]

† It may, however, be mentioned that in an isolated sodium-chloride molecule the opposite effect is obtained; for large distances between the atomic nuclei the molecule becomes non-polar.

‡ A. Eucken and A. Büchner, *Zeits. f. phys. Chem.* (B), **27**, 321 (1934).

|| From M. Born and M. Göppert-Mayer, *Handb. d. Phys.* **24**/2, 639 (1933).

†† M. Born and Th. von Kármán, *Phys. Zeits.* **13**, 297 (1912).

‡‡ R. H. Lyddane and K. F. Herzfeld, *Phys. Rev.* **54**, 846 (1938).

|||| M. Czerny, *Zeits. f. Physik*, **65**, 600 (1930); R. B. Barnes, ibid. **75**, 732 (1932). These workers find subsidiary maxima which, according to M. Born and M. Blackman, ibid. **82**, 551 (1933), M. Blackman, *Phil. Trans. Roy. Soc.* (A), **236**, 103 (1936), are due to the coupling which anharmonic forces allow between different normal vibrations.

using thin films of the halide crystals, and may also be deduced from the maximum in the reflecting power (the *Reststrahlfrequenz*).†

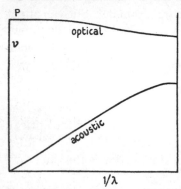

FIG. 9. Vibration spectrum of a solid with ions of unequal mass

We give a short account of the theory of the relation of the optical frequency $\nu$ to the dielectric constant. In a crystal in which the optical vibration is excited let the displacements of the ions of mass $M_1$, $M_2$ be $x_1$ and $x_2$, where

$$x_1 = M_2\xi/(M_1+M_2),$$
$$x_2 = -M_1\xi/(M_1+M_2),$$

so that the centre of gravity is at rest. If the restoring force on each ion is $-q\xi$, the equations of motion are

$$M_1\ddot{x}_1+q\xi = 0, \qquad M_2\ddot{x}_2+q\xi = 0,$$

which give a frequency of vibration

$$\nu = \frac{1}{2\pi}\sqrt{\frac{q}{M}}, \quad \text{where } M = \frac{M_1 M_2}{M_1+M_2}.$$

The restoring force $q$ is made up of two parts: the repulsive overlap forces between the ions, and the force due to the polarization of the medium. We do not, however, have to consider its nature in detail. For suppose infra-red radiation is passing through the crystal, and the field within the crystal is $E$. The *extra* polarization due to the field $E$ is

$$(\kappa_0-1)E/4\pi.$$

Therefore the field acting on any displaced ion is

$$E+\tfrac{1}{3}\gamma(\kappa_0-1)E,$$

where $\gamma$ is the numerical factor already introduced to give the coupling between the displacements and the dipoles induced on the ions. For static fields the ions will be in equilibrium; we have therefore

$$q\xi = eE[1+\tfrac{1}{3}\gamma(\kappa_0-1)],$$

and thus the polarization due to ionic displacement is given by

$$P_x = \frac{e\xi}{a^3} = \frac{Ee^2}{2qa^3}[1+\tfrac{1}{3}\gamma(\kappa_0-1)]. \tag{27}$$

The polarization $P_0$ due to the polarizability of the ions is given by

$$P_0 = \frac{\alpha_1+\alpha_2}{2a^3}[E+\tfrac{4}{3}\pi(P_0+\gamma P_x)]. \tag{28}$$

† Cf., for instance, M. Blackman, loc. cit., p. 130.

Making use of (18) to eliminate $\alpha_1 + \alpha_2$, we obtain

$$P_0 = \frac{\kappa_0 - 1}{4\pi} [E + \tfrac{4}{3}\pi\gamma P_x]. \tag{29}$$

From (27) and (29), and the equation $\kappa - 1 = 4\pi P/E$, we obtain finally

$$\frac{2(\kappa - \kappa_0)}{[1 + \tfrac{1}{3}\gamma(\kappa_0 - 1)]^2} = \frac{4\pi e^2}{qa^3} = \frac{Ne^2}{\pi M\nu^2}. \tag{30}$$

This formula was first given by Heckmann;† the derivation given here is due to Mott and Littleton.‡ In most text-books the same formula is obtained with $\gamma = 0$; i.e. the Lorentz-Lorenz term is entirely neglected in calculating the interaction between the vibrations and induced dipoles on the ions.

In Table 9 we give the values of $\gamma$ deduced from the observed values of $\kappa$, $\kappa_0$, and $\nu$.

TABLE 9

|  | $Ne^2/\pi M\nu^2$ | $\gamma$ |
|---|---|---|
| LiF . . . | 6·20 | 0·29 |
| NaF . . . | 3·10 | 0·04 |
| NaCl . . . | 2·94 | 0·13 |
| NaBr . . . | 1·95 | 0·53 |
| NaI . . . | 2·72 | 0·24 |
| KCl . . . | 2·12 | 0·29 |
| KBr . . . | 2·03 | 0·21 |
| KI . . . | 1·94 | 0·16 |
| RbCl . . . | 1·95 | 0·39 |
| RbBr . . . | 1·65 | 0·44–(0·66) |
| RbI . . . | 1·62 | 0·17 |

It will be seen that $\gamma$ turns out to be of the order 0·25, and thus nearer to zero than to the value unity that we should obtain if there were no overlap between the ions. This is in agreement with our conclusions of § 5.2, where we found from a theoretical calculation of the dielectric constant that $\gamma$ must be nearly zero.

The optical frequency $\nu$ is of course a transverse vibration. As first pointed out by Fröhlich and Mott,‖ the *longitudinal* polarization waves of long wave-length have a different frequency $\nu_l$ given by

$$\nu_l^2 = \nu^2 + \frac{e^2}{2\pi Ma^3}.$$

The longitudinal waves are responsible for the scattering of electrons in polar lattices (cf. Chap. III, § 12).

† G. Heckmann, *Zeits. f. Krist.* **61**, 250 (1925); *Zeits. f. Physik*, **33**, 646 (1925).
‡ N. F. Mott and M. J. Littleton, *Trans. Faraday Soc.* **34**, 485 (1938).
‖ H. Fröhlich and N. F. Mott, *Proc. Roy. Soc.* (A), **171**, 496 (1939). See also Lyddane and Herzfeld, *Phys. Rev.* **54**, 846 (1938).

# LATTICE DEFECTS IN THERMAL EQUILIBRIUM

## 1. The various types of lattice defect

As the temperature of a crystal is raised, the mean amplitude of the thermal vibrations of the atoms about their mean positions increases. Owing to these vibrations there is at any moment a certain departure from periodicity in the positions of the atoms in a crystal lattice. This, however, is not the only way in which the positions of the atoms or ions in a crystal in thermal equilibrium at a high temperature differ from those at the absolute zero. According to the ideas developed mainly by Frenkel,[†] Wagner,[‡] Schottky,[‡] and Jost[||] under the heading of 'Fehlordnungserscheinung', there exist in a crystal in thermodynamical equilibrium a number of vacant lattice points, or, in other words, a number of lattice points from each of which the corresponding atom or ion is missing. Furthermore, according to these authors a number of ions in ionic crystals or atoms in metals will be situated in what they call 'interstitial' positions. An interstitial position is a position in between the normal lattice points, as the point (b) in Fig. 11. One thinks of the atom or ion as being 'squeezed in', the surrounding atoms being displaced slightly to make room for it. Two other representations of an interstitial ion in sodium-chloride are shown in Fig. 10.

There are two ways in which these vacant lattice points and interstitial atoms or ions can arise; we shall call them 'Frenkel defects' and 'Schottky defects'. The difference between the two will be made clear by considering a simple cubic crystal, containing one kind of atom only.

A Frenkel defect is illustrated in Fig. 11. An atom of the crystal can leave its normal position (a) and travel to an interstitial position (b). (a) and (b) are supposed to be so far apart that there is no interaction between the atom at (b) and the atoms round (a). Thus a Frenkel defect consists of an interstitial atom, together with a vacant lattice point, or hole.

The number of Frenkel defects in a crystal may be calculated as follows: let $W$ be the work necessary to take an atom from the point (a) to a distant point (b). Let $N$ be the total number of atoms, and let

---

† J. Frenkel, *Zeits. f. Physik*, **35**, 652 (1926).

‡ C. Wagner and W. Schottky, *Zeits. f. phys. Chem.* (B), **11**, 163 (1930). For references to recent literature cf. C. Wagner, *Trans. Faraday Soc.* **34**, 851 (1938).

|| W. Jost, *J. Chem. Phys.* **1**, 466 (1933); *Trans. Faraday Soc.* **34**, 860 (1938).

the total number of possible interstitial positions be equal to $N'$. In thermal equilibrium let $n$ atoms have left their mean positions; then these atoms can be arranged in the interstitial positions in $P'$ ways, where

$$P' = \frac{N'!}{(N'-n)!\,n!}.$$

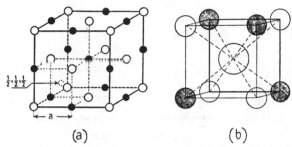

(a)                              (b)

FIG. 10.  An ion in an interstitial position in a sodium-chloride lattice

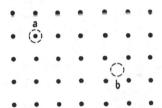

FIG. 11.  A Frenkel defect in a simple cubic crystal

The holes, or vacant lattice points, can be arranged in $P$ ways, where

$$P = \frac{N!}{(N-n)!\,n!}.$$

Therefore the increase in the entropy of the crystal due to putting the atoms into interstitial positions is given by

$$S = k\left[\log\frac{N!}{(N-n)!\,n!} + \log\frac{N'!}{(N'-n)!\,n!}\right], \tag{1}$$

which gives by Stirling's formula

$$S = k[N\log N - (N-n)\log(N-n) - n\log n] + $$
$$+ k[N'\log N' - (N'-n)\log(N'-n) - n\log n]. \tag{2}$$

The increase $E$ in the internal energy due to putting the atoms in interstitial positions is given by

$$E = nW.$$

If at first we neglect any changes in the volume of the crystal, or any change in the vibrational frequencies of the displaced atoms, these are the only terms in the entropy and energy which depend on $n$. The condition for thermal equilibrium is that the free energy,

$$F = E - TS,$$

should be a minimum with respect to changes in $n$. The condition for this is that

$$\left(\frac{\partial F}{\partial n}\right)_T = 0, \tag{3}$$

which gives

$$W = kT \log\frac{(N-n)(N'-n)}{n^2},$$

or

$$\frac{n^2}{(N'-n)(N-n)} = e^{-W/kT}.$$

In practice $n$ is small compared with $N$, $N'$; the assumption of a constant value of $W$ is not otherwise valid; we then have

$$n = \sqrt{(NN')}e^{-\frac{1}{2}W/kT}. \tag{4}$$

Thus, as one would expect, the number of atoms in interstitial positions increases rapidly as the temperature is raised. The factor $\frac{1}{2}$ in the exponential occurs because, by the process of disarranging one atom, two kinds of position of disorder are created simultaneously and in equal concentrations, as in the dissociation of a diatomic gas.

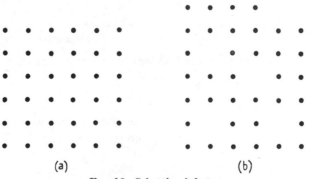

(a)                                   (b)

FIG. 12.  Schottky defects

The second way in which phenomena of this type can occur (Schottky defects) is illustrated in Fig. 12. In Fig. 12 (a) we illustrate a perfect crystal in equilibrium at the absolute zero of temperature; in (b) a certain number of atoms have been removed from their normal lattice points and have been placed on the surface, where they build up new layers of the normal crystal lattice. The formation of Schottky lattice defects will increase the volume of the crystal, though it will not *necessarily* affect the crystal lattice constant. The number of Schottky defects in a monatomic crystal in thermal equilibrium may be calculated as follows. Let $W_H$ represent the work required to remove an atom from the interior of the crystal to a point outside it. Let $W_L$ be the lattice energy of the crystal per atom. Then clearly the work $nW_S$ necessary to form $n$ Schottky holes is given by

$$nW_S = n(W_H - W_L). \tag{5}$$

The change in the free energy if $n$ such holes are formed, neglecting as before any change in the lattice parameter or vibrational frequencies, is given by

$$F = nW_S - kT \log \frac{N!}{n!\,(N-n)!}, \tag{6}$$

where $N$ is the number of atoms of the crystal. From the condition that $F$ must be a minimum for changes of $n$ we obtain as before

$$\frac{n}{N-n} = e^{-W_S/kT}. \tag{7}$$

Note that the factor $\frac{1}{2}$ does not occur in this case.†

We see that a Frenkel defect consists of a vacant lattice point *and* an atom in an interstitial position, a Schottky defect of a vacant lattice point only. In general both types of lattice defect will occur; but, since the energies $W_S$, $W$ are, in practice, of the order of magnitude of 1 eV., in any crystal the type for which the activation energy is the smaller will occur in a very much larger concentration, and in each case we need consider the predominant type only. A derivation of the concentrations when both types are present has been given by Wagner and Schottky.‡

## 2. The degree of disorder; detailed formulae

Formulae (4) and (7) were derived subject to the following two assumptions:

1. The crystal is held at constant volume, so that the energies of activation are independent of temperature.

2. The vibrational frequencies of the solid are unaffected by the presence of holes and interstitial ions.

Neither of these assumptions is valid, and we shall now evaluate the degree of disorder with an improved model. For the vibrational frequencies we shall take an Einstein model of the solid, and shall

---

† A further possibility is the existence of what we may call an 'anti-Schottky defect' —atoms being removed from the surface of a crystal and going into interstitial positions. We do not know any experimental evidence that this occurs.

‡ C. Wagner and W. Schottky, *Zeits. f. phys. Chem.* (B), **11**, 163 (1930); W. Jost, *Diffusion und chemische Reaktion in festen Stoffen*, p. 50 et seq. (Dresden, 1937).

assume that in the perfect crystal each atom can vibrate with frequency $\nu$. Then the free energy of the solid is given† by

$$F = N\left\{E(V) + 3kT\log\frac{h\nu}{kT}\right\},$$

where $N$ is the number of atoms and $E(V)$ is the lattice energy per atom of a crystal with volume $V$. The condition for equilibrium in zero external pressure, $(\partial F/\partial V)_T = 0$, gives

$$(V - V_0)\left(\frac{d^2E}{dV^2}\right)_{V=V_0} + 3kT\frac{d(\log\nu)}{dV} = 0,$$

where $V_0$ is the volume for which $E$ is a minimum. Thus the thermal expansion coefficient $\alpha$ defined by $V - V_0 = \alpha V_0 T$ is given by

$$\alpha = -3k\frac{d(\log\nu)}{V_0\,dV}\bigg/\frac{d^2E}{dV^2}.$$

We now consider a crystal containing $n$ Schottky holes, the energy $W_S(V)$ being itself a function of $V$. We suppose that each atom has $x$ neighbours, and that the vibrational frequencies of the $x$ neighbours of a Schottky hole are $\nu$ as before in the two directions perpendicular to the line joining the neighbour to the hole, but some smaller value $\nu'$ parallel to this line. Then the free energy is

$$NE(V) + nW_S + kT(3N - nx)\log\frac{h\nu}{kT} + nxkT\log\frac{h\nu'}{kT} - kT\log\frac{N!}{n!\,(N-n)!}.$$

The condition that $(\partial F/\partial n)_{V,T}$ should vanish gives

$$W_S(V) + xkT\log\frac{\nu'}{\nu} + kT\log\frac{n}{N-n} = 0,$$

which may be written (for $n \ll N$)

$$\frac{n}{N} = \gamma e^{-W_S(V)/kT}, \tag{8}$$

where $$\gamma = (\nu/\nu')^x. \tag{9}$$

The value of $V$ to be taken in this equation is the volume at the actual temperature considered. Thus $W_s$ itself is a function of the temperature. Assuming that the thermal expansion is linear up to the temperature considered, we may write

$$W_S(V) = W_0 + \alpha V_0 T\frac{dW_S}{dV}. \tag{10}$$

---

† Cf., for example, N. F. Mott and H. Jones, *The Theory of the Properties of Metals and Alloys*, chap. i (Oxford, 1936).

Thus, finally, for the number of Schottky defects we obtain

$$\frac{n}{N} = \gamma B e^{-W_0/kT}, \tag{11}$$

where $W_0$ is the work to form a vacant lattice point at the absolute zero of temperature, and

$$B = \exp\left(-\frac{\alpha V_0}{k}\frac{dW_S}{dV}\right). \tag{12}$$

Since $dW_s/dV$ is negative, $B > 1$, as is also $\gamma$.

In order to make an estimate of $B$, (12) may be written in the form

$$B = \exp\left(-\frac{\alpha W_{SA}}{R}\frac{d(\log W_{SA})}{d(\log V_A)}\right), \tag{13}$$

where the quantities $W_{SA}$, $V_A$ refer to a gramme-molecule. To obtain an idea of the orders of magnitude, we put in values appropriate to rock-salt, $\alpha = 1\cdot2\times10^{-4}$, $W_{SA} \sim 40$ kcals., and, as an estimate,

$$d(\log W_S)/d(\log V) \sim 2.$$

This gives $\qquad\qquad B = e^{4\cdot8} \sim 100.$

Moreover $\nu/\nu'$ may easily be as great as 2, and with, as for the cubic structure, $x = 6$, this gives $\qquad \gamma \sim 64.$

We obtain finally values of the order $10^3$ to $10^4$ for the factor $\gamma B$. In comparing different substances, since $W_{SA}$ occurs in (13), we shall expect a large value of $W_0$ to be accompanied by a large value of $B$, and a small $W_0$ to be accompanied by a smaller value of $B$.

As the number of Schottky defects increases rapidly with the temperature, they will make a contribution to the thermal expansion given by

$$\frac{1}{V}\frac{dV}{dT} = \frac{a^3}{V}\frac{dn}{dT} = \frac{N}{V}\frac{a^3\gamma B W_0}{kT^2}e^{-W_0/kT}.$$

Compared with the main part of the thermal expansion this contribution is small, except perhaps near the melting-point. We do not know of any effect which can be ascribed to it.

For Frenkel defects the energy will depend on volume and temperature in the same way; we shall therefore introduce the same factor $B$, given by (12). In place of (8), however, we have to introduce the following considerations. Let $\nu_i$ be the frequency of an ion in the interstitial position, $\nu_i'$ that of its $y$ neighbours, and $\nu'$, as before, that of the $x$ neighbours of a vacant lattice point; then it may easily be shown that

$$\frac{n}{\sqrt{(NN')}} = \gamma e^{-\frac{1}{2}W/kT}, \tag{14}$$

with $\qquad\qquad \gamma^2 = \nu^{x+y+1}/\nu_i \nu_i'^y \nu'^x. \tag{15}$

Since $\nu_i > \nu$ and $\nu' < \nu$, $\gamma$ may be greater or less than unity. For Frenkel defects, then, we do not expect such large values of $\gamma B$ as for Schottky defects.

The work necessary to form a Frenkel defect depends on the interstitial volume available for the atom or ion. If the crystal is subjected to a high pressure, the atoms are brought closer together and the value of the work $W$ is increased; the number of lattice defects will be diminished, so long as the crystal is at a temperature at which the defects are mobile. The same is true for Schottky defects. An experiment on crystals under high pressures will be mentioned in § 6.

For ionic crystals the actual values of the energy required to form a lattice defect will be discussed in § 7. We may say, however, at this point that for close-packed substances such as metals we should expect the energy of a Frenkel lattice defect to be rather high, because the amount of space in a close-packed structure is small, and to pack an extra atom into an interstitial position one would have to do work against the repulsive forces of the surrounding atoms. For such structures one would therefore expect Schottky disorders to predominate.

Further, for crystals in which the atoms or molecules are held together by van der Waals forces, or by any central force when only one kind of atom is present, we should expect the energy $W_S$ of a Schottky defect to be equal to the lattice energy $W_L$. This may be seen as follows. Let $V(r)$ be the potential energy of interaction of an atom with another atom at a distance $r$ from it. Then the lattice energy per atom is given by

$$W_L = -\tfrac{1}{2} \sum_k V(r_k),$$

where $r_k$ denotes the distance of any other atom from the atom considered, and the summation is over all such atoms. The factor $\tfrac{1}{2}$ enters in order that the interaction between any pair of atoms shall not be counted twice. But the energy $W_H$ required to remove an atom from the interior of the crystal is given by

$$W_H = - \sum_k V(r_k).$$

It follows that

$$W_H = 2W_L \tag{16}$$

and hence from (5) that

$$W_L = W_S.$$

This conclusion does *not*, however, apply either to metals or to polar crystals (§ 7).

The result (16) may also be seen as follows. Consider the sublimation of a solid body; the surface is removed layer by layer. In Fig. 13 the surface layer is half removed. The atom (a) can be removed most easily, and, by removing atoms from positions such as (a), a whole layer can be removed. Thus the work per atom required to remove a whole layer is equal to the work required to remove an atom such as (a). But the interaction energy between (a) and its surroundings is clearly just half of the interaction with its surroundings of an atom in the body of the crystal. If, then, we remove an atom from the interior, we shall receive back exactly half the energy when we place it on the surface.

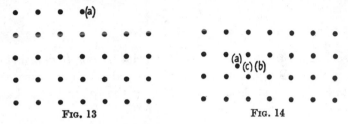

FIG. 13                                    FIG. 14

## 3. The diffusion of lattice defects

Atoms in interstitial positions will be able to move from one interstitial position to another, and will thus have a certain rate of diffusion. An activation energy will, however, be necessary; in Fig. 14, before an atom can move from the point (a) to the point (b) it will have to move through the point (c), where its potential energy will be higher by an amount $U$, say. For only a fraction $e^{-U/kT}$ of the time, then, will the interstitial atom have sufficient energy to carry it over the barrier to a neighbouring interstitial position. If $\nu$ is the frequency with which it can vibrate, the probability $q_i$ per unit time that it moves to a neighbouring position is thus of the order

$$q_i \sim \nu e^{-U/kT}. \tag{17}$$

Consider, then, two parallel planes in the crystal, separated by a distance $a$ equal to the distance between adjacent interstitial positions. Suppose that there is a concentration gradient such that the number of interstitial atoms or ions per cm.³ is on one plane $n$ and on the other $(n+a\,dn/dx)$. The number contained in a slab of thickness $a$ and of unit cross-section is thus $an$ or else $a(n+a\,dn/dx)$. As a result of diffusion the number crossing the slab per second will be

$$q_i a^2 \frac{dn}{dx},$$

and hence the value of the diffusion coefficient of the interstitial ions is given by
$$D_i = q_i a^2. \tag{18}$$

The diffusion coefficient of a vacant lattice point will be given by a formula of exactly the same type, though, of course, with a different value of $U$. For a discussion of the activation energies, cf. § 7.

The motion of interstitial atoms or ions leads to the diffusion of that constituent of the crystal which forms them. In the same way the motion of holes leads to a diffusion of the constituent which is missing from the hole. Thus both the interstitial atoms and the holes make a contribution to the self-diffusion coefficient of the crystal, of amount

$$D = \frac{n}{N} D_i, \tag{19}$$

where $n$ is given by (11) or (14).

In both cases the height of the potential barrier $U$ depends on the distance between adjacent atoms, and its value will decrease with the thermal expansion of the crystal. If $U_0$ is the height of the barrier at the absolute zero, we may write, as in (10),

$$U = U_0 + V_0 \alpha T \frac{dU_0}{dV}. \tag{20}$$

Hence we obtain $\qquad D = \frac{n}{N} \nu a^2 C e^{-U_0/kT}, \tag{21}$

where $C$ is of the same order as $B$ in (11), and is given by

$$C = \exp\left(-\frac{\alpha V_0}{k} \frac{dU_0}{dV}\right). \tag{22}$$

For interstitial atoms or ions, substituting for $n/N$ from (14), we obtain

$$D = (\gamma BC)\nu a^2 \sqrt{\frac{N'}{N}} e^{-(\frac{1}{2}W_0 + U_0)/kT}. \tag{23}$$

The factor $\gamma BC\sqrt{(N'/N)}$ may be of the order 10 to $10^4$, $a \sim 3 \times 10^{-8}$ cm. and $\nu \sim 10^{13}$ sec.$^{-1}$; the diffusion coefficient will thus take the form†

$$D = D_0 e^{-A/T}, \tag{24}$$

with $D_0$ between 0·1 and 100 cm.²/sec. The holes will make a contribution of the same order of magnitude. Observed rates of diffusion will be discussed in § 6.

The existence of Frenkel and Schottky defects in the lattice is not the only mechanism which can give rise to self-diffusion. It is conceivable that two adjacent atoms, or two adjacent ions of the same kind,

---

† Similar equations for the diffusion coefficient, with factors of the same order of magnitude outside the exponential, have been obtained by S. Dushman and I. Langmuir, *Phys. Rev.* **20**, 113 (1922), and by M. Polanyi and E. Wigner, *Zeits. f. phys. Chem.* **139**, 439 (1928).

can change places directly, as illustrated in Fig. 21 on p. 52. Such a process would give rise to a diffusion coefficient of the same type (24), with $D_0$ of the same order of magnitude. For only one substance, $PbI_2$, have we any evidence that this process does not take place.

Bernal[†] has pointed out that the process illustrated in Fig. 15 would also lead to diffusion without the existence of interstitial atoms or of holes. Spontaneous gliding of parts of the crystal over each other,

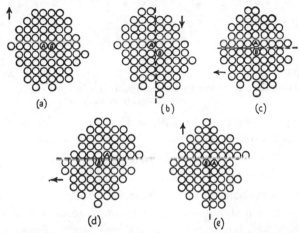

FIG. 15. (a), (b), (c), (d), and (e) represent the manner in which two atoms, A and B, can be considered to interchange their positions in a two-dimensional crystal by means of repeated glides of the whole lattice without at any time leaving gaps. (Bernal)

repeated in different directions, leads to exchange of places between two atoms such as A and B. This mechanism was suggested by Bernal for metals and alloys; as it is unlikely to occur in polar crystals we shall not discuss it.

We shall now consider the mechanism by which lattice defects are formed. It must be emphasized, however, that the conclusion that vacant lattice points and atoms in interstitial positions exist is a result of the application of thermodynamics to a crystal in thermal equilibrium; it does not depend on the mechanism by which they are formed. The mechanism is only important if we want to know how long the crystal takes to get into equilibrium.

Frenkel defects can, of course, be formed anywhere in the crystal; any atom or ion can move away from its proper lattice point. The initial formation of Schottky defects, on the other hand, can take place only at the surface of the crystal, or at the surfaces of internal cracks.

The type of mechanism envisaged is shown in Fig. 16, the hole starting at the surface and moving inwards. It follows that crystals with Schottky disorder will take longer to get into equilibrium than those with Frenkel defects of similar activation energy.

Owing to the existence of the activation energy $U$, at a low enough temperature the lattice defects described here will become practically

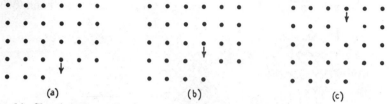

FIG. 16. Showing the mechanism for the formation of a Schottky hole, and its movement into the interior of a crystal

immobile. The condition for this is that the factor $\nu e^{-U/kT}$ should become small compared with 1 sec.$^{-1}$, which gives, since $\nu \sim 10^{13}$

$$kT < U/13 \log_e 10. \tag{25}$$

If $U$ is 1 eV. this will be true already at room temperatures. It follows that if a crystal is cooled from the melt, or from a high temperature at which it is in thermodynamical equilibrium, a certain number of these lattice defects will be 'frozen in'. At low temperatures the crystal will not reach equilibrium in any obtainable time, and will contain *more* defects than the equilibrium number.

The remainder of this chapter will deal with the application of these ideas to polar salts, and in particular to the interpretation of their electrolytic conduction. We may remark that for polar salts there is independent evidence, drawn from their optical properties, of the actual existence of lattice defects of the kinds described.[†]

Whether diffusion in metals is due to the existence of Schottky holes is uncertain.[‡]

Eyring[||] has suggested that holes exist in liquids, and has attempted to connect the viscosity with their properties. Lennard-Jones and Devonshire have applied the model to calculate the properties of liquid rare gases.[††]

## 4. Electrolytic conductivity of polar crystals

Molten polar salts are among the best electrolytic conductors. In the solid state also they show electrolytic conductivity; the conductivity has a value of the order $10^{-4}$ ohm$^{-1}$ cm.$^{-1}$ just below the melting-

† Cf. Chap. IV, § 2.    ‡ C. Wagner, *Zeits. f. phys. Chem.* (B), **38**, 325 (1937).
|| H. Eyring, *J. Chem. Phys.* **4**, 283 (1936).
†† J. E. Lennard-Jones and A. F. Devonshire, *Proc. Roy. Soc.* (A), **169**, 317 (1939).

point and falls rapidly with decreasing temperature. The validity of Faraday's law, and hence the existence of an actual electrolytic transport of matter, has been proved for a number of salts by weighing the metal deposited at the cathode.† We may mention in particular the results of Tubandt and Eggert,‡ who measured the transport of silver in silver iodide. Molten silver iodide was allowed to solidify in a platinum bowl, which acted as cathode, and a silver needle immersed in the iodide acted as anode. With the passage of a current the mass of the silver needle decreased, while on the other side silver separated out as thick crystals over the surface of the platinum bowl. The results of a number of experiments were as follows:

TABLE 10

| Temp. (degrees C.) | Current (amp.) | Silver transported according to Faraday's law (gm.) | Loss of mass of anode (gm.) | Silver deposited at cathode (gm.) |
|---|---|---|---|---|
| 150 | 0·04 | 0·4771 | 0·4776 | 0·4772 |
| 150 | 0·05 | 0·5334 | 0·5338 | 0·5333 |
| 154 | 0·1 | 0·8387 | 0·8396 | 0·8365 |
| 156 | 0·1 | 0·8214 | 0·8183 | 0·8202 |
| 157 | 0·05 | 0·4448 | .. | 0·4444 |
| 200 | 0·09 | 1·4430 | .. | 1·4429 |

The agreement between the figures in the last three columns is good.

For most substances, when a current is passed, the metal released at the cathode is not deposited on the surface of the crystals, but in the form of tree-like threads within the crystals, known as dendrites. When precautions are taken to remove this difficulty, consistent values of the conductivity are always obtained at high temperatures. But for some substances at lower temperatures the values obtained may vary from one specimen to another by factors greater than 100. In common with other well-known properties of crystals, the ionic conductivity in these cases appears to depend in some way on the imperfect structure or lack of purity of the crystal. Such properties are said to be 'structure-sensitive'. Figs. 17 and 18 show some results obtained for NaCl, AgCl, and AgBr. In each case at high temperatures the experimental points for different specimens lie on a single line, but at low temperatures there is considerable divergence. From the sharp kink in the curves it is evident that two separate mechanisms are present.

† Cf. G. von Hevesy, *Handb. d. Phys.* **13**, 264 (1928).
‡ C. Tubandt and S. Eggert, *Zeits. f. anorg. Chem.* **110**, 196 (1920).

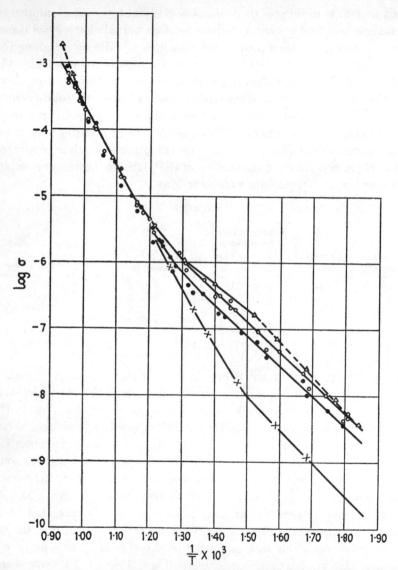

FIG. 17. Conductivity of sodium-chloride (Smekal). $\triangle$, $\bullet$, and $\times$ denote results for single crystals; $\bigcirc$ denotes results for polycrystalline material

Smekal[†] has found that for NaCl the three lower curves reproduced in Fig. 17 may be represented by the formula (in cm.$^{-1}$-ohms$^{-1}$)

$$\sigma_{NaCl} = Ae^{-10,300/T} + 3 \cdot 5 \times 10^6 e^{-23,600/T}, \tag{26}$$

where $A$ has the values $0 \cdot 055$, $0 \cdot 42$, and $0 \cdot 62$ for the three specimens.

† A. Smekal, *Handb. d. Phys.* **24**/2, 881 (1933).

Since the value of the gas constant $R$ is 2·0 cals., the activation energy in the first term is 20,600 and in the second 47,200 cals. per mol. Clearly the first term gives the conductivity due to a small number of ions at special places, which can be released easily, while the second term is that due to a large number (all the ions in the crystal, or all the ions of one sign) which can only be released with greater difficulty. It was suggested

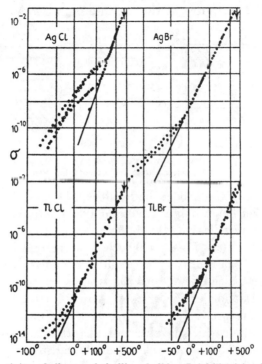

FIG. 18. Conductivity of silver and thallium halides (Lehfeldt),† in ohms⁻¹ cm.⁻¹

many years ago that the former small number of mobile ions were ions moving over the surfaces of internal cracks. In § 6 an alternative explanation will be mentioned. Throughout the rest of this chapter we shall not be concerned with the structure-sensitive part of the conductivity except where stated.

In each case of ionic conductivity one of the first questions to be settled is whether ions of both signs take part, or whether only the positive or only the negative ions move, the others remaining permanently in their proper lattice positions. For this purpose, instead of a single crystal of the substance to be investigated, two or more plates

† W. Lehfeldt, *Zeits. f. Physik*, **85**, 717 (1933).

in contact are used. The principle of the method can be understood from Fig. 19. Fig. 19 (a) represents two plates of the crystal, A and B, held between two electrodes of that metal which is a constituent of the compound. In every case, when a current is passed, the metallic cathode will grow and the anode will lose weight. If in the crystal only the anions are mobile, they will move from A to B, so that the thickness of B will grow at the expense of A as the anions combine

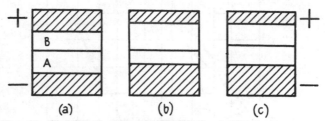

(a)                    (b)                    (c)

FIG. 19. Showing the growth of two slabs of a crystal (unshaded) between metallic electrodes (shaded)

with the metal of the anode; the result will be as shown in Fig. 19 (b). If, on the other hand, only the metallic ions are mobile, they will pass through the crystal leaving the thickness of both plates unchanged, as shown in Fig. 19 (c). Finally, if both positive and negative ions are mobile, the thickness of the plates will be changed by an intermediate amount, from which one obtains the 'transport numbers' of the ions, that is, the fraction of the current carried by the positive and the negative ions respectively. All three types of conduction are found among the crystals which have been investigated. The reasons for these different types of behaviour will be considered in § 5.

Further light on the mechanism of conduction in any substance can be deduced from measurements of the conductivity of the crystal when it contains a small quantity of some other salt in solid solution. It has been found, for example, that the ionic conductivity of AgCl is enormously increased when it contains a few parts in a thousand of $CdCl_2$ or $PbCl_2$. A description of these experimental results will be included in § 6.

## 5. Explanation of ionic conduction in terms of the theory of lattice defects

In § 3 we have seen that Frenkel defects and Schottky holes in a crystal are both mobile, and we have estimated their freedom of movement. That discussion applied equally to neutral atoms and to ions, and we paid no attention to the electrical charges which might be associated with the interstitial particles and the holes. In the absence of an electric field the defects are mobile, and when a field is applied they will drift, each type with its own mobility; and it is natural, therefore, to attempt to account for the observed conductivity of ionic crystals in terms of this drift. Frenkel and Schottky defects are, of course, imperfections of the lattice, but their number per unit volume is a perfectly definite function of the temperature. In a homogeneous and otherwise perfect crystal these lattice defects will give rise to a conductivity which is the same for all specimens, and it is this part of the conductivity which must first be discussed.

In ionic crystals *two* kinds of Frenkel defect are possible; either the cations or the anions may move into interstitial positions. A current may then be carried both by a motion of the interstitial ions and by a motion of the vacant lattice points. If the cation and anion are of different sizes, we should expect the energies required to put either of them into interstitial positions to differ considerably. We expect, therefore, that in a crystal where the current is carried predominantly by Frenkel defects the anions only *or* the cations will be responsible for the electrical conductivity, the others remaining undisturbed.

In ionic crystals which possess Schottky defects there will be vacant anion lattice points and vacant cation lattice points. These are not independent, but must, of course, be equal in number to preserve electrical neutrality in the interior of the crystal. We may say, then, that in an ionic crystal a Schottky defect consists of two separate vacant lattice points, one normally occupied by a positive ion and the other by a negative ion. If $W$ is the work necessary to remove an anion and a cation from two distant points in the interior, and to incorporate them in new layers which are being built up on the surface of the crystal, then the number of (double) Schottky defects is

$$n = N\gamma e^{-\frac{1}{2}W/kT}, \tag{27}$$

where $N$ is the total number of ion pairs and $\gamma$ is the numerical factor already defined by (9), arising from the change in the vibrational frequency of the atoms near to the vacant lattice points (cf. § 2).

A vacant positive-ion lattice point bears an effective negative charge, and a vacant negative-ion lattice point bears an effective positive charge. They therefore attract each other, and tend to form an electrically neutral double hole, in which adjacent ions are missing. These double holes will contribute nothing to the conductivity, but it is of interest to inquire whether they will be numerous. As for a neutral molecule, a certain amount of work will be necessary to dissociate a double hole into two separate holes. We can estimate this dissociation energy $V$; writing for the lattice spacing $a \sim 3 \times 10^{-8}$ cm., and for the dielectric constant $\kappa \sim 5$,

$$V \sim \frac{e^2}{\kappa a} \sim 1 \cdot 0 \text{ electron volt.}$$

This value is quite large—more than twice as large as for molecules which in aqueous solution are only slightly dissociated into ions. In some crystals, then, there may be a dissociative equilibrium between these double holes and the single Schottky holes. Let $x$ be the fraction of double holes dissociated, $n$ the total number of holes, and $N$ the number of lattice points; then the law of mass action gives

$$\frac{x^2}{1-x} = \frac{N}{n} e^{-V/kT}.$$

But from (27), omitting the term $\gamma$,

$$n = N e^{-\frac{1}{2}W/kT},$$

whence

$$\frac{x^2}{1-x} = e^{(\frac{1}{2}W-V)/kT}.$$

If $\frac{1}{2}W > V$ most of the holes will be dissociated. We shall assume this to be the case. If the condition is not satisfied formula (27) is no longer valid.

We may now obtain an expression for the rate of drift of one type of lattice defect in a uniform field. In § 4 we have already discussed the rate of diffusion of lattice defects. Whether we are considering the motion of interstitial ions or the motion of holes, the unit process in

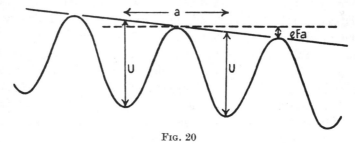

Fig. 20

the absence of a field is the motion of an ion to a neighbouring position of exactly equal energy, passing over a potential barrier of a certain height. Denoting the height of the barrier by $U$, we assumed that the probability that the ion would pass over the barrier was $e^{-U/kT}$ in each vibration, or $\nu e^{-U/kT}$ per second. We must now consider the mechanism which determines the rate of drift in an applied field $F$. In directions perpendicular to the field the height of the potential barriers is unchanged. But in the direction of the field, and against the field, the height, as shown in Fig. 20, is changed by the amounts $\pm \frac{1}{2}eFa$ respectively, where $a$ is the distance between adjacent lattice positions. Fig. 20 and the discussion to follow will apply both to the motion of holes and to the motion of interstitial ions. In both cases the probability per unit time that an ion moves in the direction of the field will now be

$$\nu e^{-(U-\frac{1}{2}eaF)/kT},$$

and in the opposite direction

$$\nu e^{-(U+\frac{1}{2}eaF)/kT}.$$

The mean velocity $u$ of drift is therefore given by

$$u = \nu a e^{-U/kT} 2 \sinh(\tfrac{1}{2}eFa/kT). \tag{28}$$

Since for the fields used in practice $eFa \ll kT$, we may expand the last factor in (28); at the same time, to allow for the dependence of $U$ on temperature, we may make the substitution, as in (22),

$$e^{-U/kT} = C e^{-U_0/kT}, \tag{29}$$

where $U_0$ is the height of the potential barrier at the absolute zero. Thus we obtain for the mobility $v$, defined by $u = vF$,

$$v = v_0 e^{-U_0/kT}, \tag{30}$$

with

$$v_0 = e\nu a^2 C/kT \tag{31}$$

and $C$ a numerical constant greater than unity (cf. §2). The conductivity due to one type of lattice defect is proportional to the number of these defects per cubic centimetre and to their mobility; both of these vary exponentially with the temperature; the conductivity thus takes the form

$$\sigma = \sigma_0 e^{-(\frac{1}{2}W_0+U_0)/kT}, \tag{32}$$

with

$$\sigma_0 = (\gamma BC)Ne^2\nu a^2/kT, \tag{33}$$

where $\nu$ is the vibrational frequency, $a$ the lattice constant, $N$ the number of ion-pairs per cm.³, and $\gamma$, $B$, $C$ are the numerical factors given by (9), (13), and (22). For the conductivity due to an interstitial ion, $N$ in (33) must be replaced by $\sqrt{(NN')}$ as in (14).

We have so far been discussing the contribution from a single type of lattice defect. But lattice defects always occur in pairs. In crystals with Schottky defects the vacant cation lattice points are accompanied by an equal number of vacant anion lattice points. In Frenkel defects the interstitial ions are accompanied by an equal number of holes. It looks, then, at first sight as if the conductivity of every crystal should be given by the sum of two terms, each of the form of (32). But the truth is that the characteristic conductivity of solid salts has been measured over only a small range of temperature. At high temperatures either the crystal melts or measurements have not been made; while at low temperatures the structure-sensitive conductivity intervenes. If within this range the whole of the conductivity is due to the motion of one type of defect only, this cannot be because the value of the coefficient $\sigma_0$ for this type is greater than for the others, but must be because the activation energy $U$ for this type of defect is smaller than for the others; for if one looks at the various factors which compose $\sigma_0$, one sees that there cannot be any large difference in value for various defects in the same crystal. Conversely, if two types of defect make nearly equal contributions to the conductivity, the energies in their exponential terms cannot differ by an amount greater than $kT$. If over the small available range of temperature the observed values of $\log \sigma$ are plotted against $1/T$, a straight line is obtained, irrespective of whether one type or more than one type of defect in the crystal is mobile. When two types of defect make nearly equal contributions, the slope of the straight line corresponds to some mean value between their respective activation energies.

If the values of these two nearly equal activation energies are respectively $(U_0+\beta)$ and $(U_0-\beta)$, then the conductivity takes the form

$$\sigma = 2 \cosh \frac{\beta}{kT} \sigma_0 e^{-(\frac{1}{2}W_0+U_0)/kT}.$$

If in the neighbourhood of a temperature $T^*$ the value of $\beta \sim kT^*$,

$$2 \cosh \frac{\beta}{kT^*} \sim 3. \tag{34}$$

For Schottky defects it will be shown in § 7 that for the vacant cation and anion lattice points we do not expect the activation energies $U^+$ and $U^-$ to differ very much. Thus in crystals in which the Schottky mechanism is the predominant one, we expect both cations and anions to give a measurable contribution to the conductivity at temperatures where $|U^+ - U^-| \gtrsim kT$.

Tubandt[†] and his co-workers have found that in potassium chloride at high temperatures both cations and anions give a measurable contribution to the conductivity. It thus seems that at these temperatures the Schottky mechanism is responsible for the electrolytic conductivity, and probably also in the other alkali-halides. In silver chloride, on the other hand, according to Tubandt and Eggert,[‡] the electrical conductivity is due to the motion of cations only ($Ag^+$). From their results it does not seem certain that this is true for the structure-insensitive

† C. Tubandt, H. Reinhold, and G. Liebold, *Zeits. f. anorg. Chem.* **197**, 225 (1931).

‡ C. Tubandt and S. Eggert, ibid. **110**, 196 (1920); C. Tubandt, ibid. **115**, 105 (1921)

region; if, however, this is established, we may deduce that the Frenkel mechanism is responsible for the conductivity. But there does not seem any experimental method by which one can discover whether the interstitial ions or the accompanying holes are the more mobile, or whether both are equally so. One would guess that the activation energy for motion of a hole would be less than for an interstitial ion.†

Fig. 18 and similar results show that for different specimens of the same crystal the structure-sensitive part of the conductivity may set in at widely different temperatures, spread over a range greater than 200° C. A measurement of the transport numbers of the ions made within this doubtful range of temperatures is of little use, unless it is known whether the specimen on which the experiment was made was showing its characteristic conductivity or not. This information, unfortunately, is seldom recorded. The following list is reproduced from Jost.‡ Details may be found in Landolt and Bornstein's tables under 'Überführungszahlen', but reference should be made in each case to the original papers to see whether there is any indication as to whether the values refer to characteristic or structure-sensitive conductivity.

Negative ions only mobile in

$$BaCl_2, \quad BaBr_2, \quad BaF_2, \quad PbCl_2, \quad PbBr_2.$$

Positive ions only mobile in

$$AgCl, \quad AgBr, \quad AgI, \quad \alpha\text{-CuBr}, \quad \alpha\text{-CuI}$$

(and in most alkali-halides below 500° C.).

Both ions mobile in $PbI_2$ and in alkali-halides at high temperatures.

## 6. The mobilities and activation energies

We have now to consider the absolute magnitude of the conductivity. For the conductivity due to one type of lattice defect we derived the expression

$$\sigma = \sigma_0 e^{-(\frac{1}{2}W_0 + U_0)/kT},$$

with

$$\sigma_0 = (\gamma BC)Ne^2va^2/kT. \tag{35}$$

Substituting $v = 5 \times 10^{12}$, $a = 3 \times 10^{-8}$, $T = 600°$ K., $N \sim 10^{22}$, and converting to practical electrical units (compare (48) below), we find a value

$$\sigma_0 \sim 150(\gamma BC) \text{ cm.}^{-1} \text{ ohm}^{-1}, \tag{36}$$

where $\gamma$ may have larger values for mobile holes than for mobile interstitial atoms.

---

† Calculations by N. F. Mott and M. J. Littleton, *Trans. Faraday Soc.* **34**, 485 (1938), which are referred to in § 7, give for sodium-chloride almost equal values ($\sim 0.5$ eV.).

‡ W. Jost, *Diffusion und chemische Reaktion in festen Stoffen*, p. 80 (Dresden, 1937).

We have seen that at high temperatures the conductivity of rock-salt, for instance, is given by

$$\sigma = 3{\cdot}5 \times 10^6 e^{-23,000/T}. \qquad (37)$$

In order that this should agree with (36), it requires

$$(\gamma BC) \sim 10^4,$$

which seems, from our estimates on p. 34, to be a reasonable value for conduction by Schottky defects.

Silver chloride, according to Koch and Wagner,[†] has a conductivity given by

$$\sigma = 3 \times 10^4 e^{-9,250/T} \qquad (38)$$

and silver bromide by $\quad \sigma = 1{\cdot}8 \times 10^5 e^{-9,100/T}. \qquad (39)$

The constant factor is smaller than for NaCl as we expect for Frenkel defects.

In (30) we derived for the mobility of a lattice defect the expression

$$v = v_0 e^{-U_0/kT},$$

with $\qquad\qquad v_0 = eva^2C/kT. \qquad (40)$

Substituting $\nu \sim 5 \times 10^{12}$, $a \sim 3 \times 10^{-8}$, $T = 600°$, and $C \sim 10$, we obtain

$$v_0 \sim 0{\cdot}5 \text{ cm./sec. per volt/cm.}$$

Estimates of $v_0$ for the defects responsible for the conductivity of AgCl and AgBr were made by Koch and Wagner[†] as a result of some experiments which were referred to at the end of § 4. They measured the conductivity of these crystals when they contained small quantities of $CdCl_2$, $CdBr_2$ (or $PbCl_2$, $PbBr_2$) in solid solution. In these mixed crystals each $Cd^{++}$ ion replaces two $Ag^+$ ions in the lattice; thus the crystal must always contain at least as many vacant $Ag^+$ lattice points as there are cadmium ions. At high temperatures there will be in addition a variable number of (ordinary thermal) vacant lattice points; but at low temperatures the number of these becomes negligible, and we have a constant number of permanent holes. These have the same mobility $v$ as they would have in a pure crystal without cadmium, and they therefore provide a conductivity much greater than that of the pure crystal at these temperatures. For example, at 210° C. the addition of 1 per cent. of $CdCl_2$ increases the conductivity of AgCl more than 100 times. If $N$ is the number of ion pairs of the lattice per cm.³, and $cN$ the number of cadmium ions per cm.³, the conductivity is

$$\sigma = ecNv.$$

By measurements at different temperatures $v$, $v_0$, and $U_0$ are all deter-

† E. Koch and C. Wagner, *Zeits. f. phys. Chem.* (B), **38**, 295 (1937).

mined for the vacant $Ag^+$ lattice points in the mixed crystal. Koch and Wagner then assume that the mobility of an interstitial ion is not very different from that of a hole; setting the mobilities equal, they can estimate the ratio $x$ of interstitial ions and holes to the total number of ion pairs in pure silver halides at any temperature from the formula

$$\sigma = 2eNxv,$$

where $\sigma$ is the observed electrolytic conductivity; the factor 2 arises because the current is assumed to be carried equally by interstitial ions and by holes.

In any pure crystal, when only one type of lattice defect is mobile, the conductivity varies as $e^{-(\frac{1}{2}W_0 + U_0)/kT}$ and it is impossible to separate $\frac{1}{2}W_0$ from $U_0$. But in these mixed crystals at low temperatures the conductivity varies only as $e^{-U_0/kT}$, and hence the separation is effected. At the same time, since the numerical factor $(\gamma B)$ is connected with $W_0$ only, and the factor $C$ is connected by (22) with $U_0$ only, these factors are also separated.

From their experimental results Koch and Wagner deduce values of the mobility in the form $v = v_0 e^{-E/kT}$. We have seen that the quantity $E$ is to be identified with the height $U_0$ of the potential barrier at absolute zero temperature:

$$v = v_0 e^{-U_0/kT}. \tag{41}$$

And similarly for the concentration of holes in the pure crystal

$$x = x_0 e^{-\frac{1}{2}W_0/kT}. \tag{42}$$

The estimates are given in the following table.

|  | AgCl | AgBr |
| --- | --- | --- |
| $x_0$. . . . | 36 | 29 |
| $v_0$ (cm./sec. per volt/cm.). | 0·12 | 0·95 |
| $W_0$ (cal.) . . . | 25,000 | 20,000 |
| $U_0$ „ . . . | 6,000 | 8,200 |

It will be noticed that the order of magnitude of $v_0$ is in agreement with the theoretical value obtained by inserting $C \sim 10$ into (40).

In order that the values of $x_0$ should agree with (14) it is necessary that

$$\gamma B \sqrt{\frac{N'}{N}} \sim 30,$$

which again seems a reasonable value.

Numerical values of the estimated concentration of holes and interstitial ions in pure AgCl and AgBr will be of interest. They are given in Table 11; it should be emphasized, however, that these values have all been obtained on the assumption that the mobility of an interstitial ion is the same as the mobility of a hole. If that of an ion is greater than that of a hole, the numbers are entirely wrong.

TABLE 11. *Concentration $x$ of Interstitial Ions in Silver Halides. The unbracketed values are the results of the actual measurements; the bracketed values are extrapolations using formula* (42)

| Salt | Temperature, °C. | $x$ |
|------|------------------|-----|
| AgCl | 350 | $1.5 \times 10^{-3}$ |
|      | 300 | $5.5 \times 10^{-4}$ |
|      | 250 | $2.2 \times 10^{-4}$ |
|      | 210 | $8.1 \times 10^{-5}$ |
| AgBr | 426 | $(2.0 \times 10^{-2})$ |
|      | 300 | $4.0 \times 10^{-3}$ |
|      | 250 | $1.8 \times 10^{-3}$ |
|      | 210 | $7.6 \times 10^{-4}$ |
|      | 20 | $(8.3 \times 10^{-6})$ |
|      | $-180$ | $(10^{-22})$ |

The very high value 0·02 at the melting-point 426° C. in silver bromide may well be exceptional. If it is correct, it would lead to a large anomaly in the specific heat, since 400 cals. per mol would be required to form this number of interstitial ions. We do not know of any measurements of the specific heat of silver halides near the melting-point.†

As a result of this work Koch and Wagner put forward a new hypothesis about the origin of the 'structure-sensitive', or, as we shall call it, the 'secondary' ionic conductivity, which often predominates at low temperatures. This new suggestion will be discussed below; but first let us consider the effect in relation to diffusion. For, of course, the secondary conductivity must be due to mobile ions or lattice defects, which, in the absence of an applied field, will be moving about at random. Connected with the secondary conductivity there must then be a secondary or structure-sensitive self-diffusion having the same temperature coefficient. This does not seem to have been looked for experimentally. Further, we may remark that, if the mechanisms are quite different, the ions which take part in the secondary conductivity may have the same sign as those which are mobile at high temperatures, or they may be ions of opposite sign.

† The specific heat of mercury has been measured up to the melting-point (234° K.). A slight hump appears in the last 15 degrees, with a heat content of about 1 cal. per gramme-atom (L. G. Carpenter and L. G. Stoodley, *Phil. Mag.* **10**, 249 (1930)).

Koch and Wagner's hypothesis is that the secondary conductivity might be due to a trace of impurity in the crystal, acting in a way similar to the $Cd^{++}$ ions in the silver salts discussed above. The essential feature of the secondary conductivity is that it adds a term of the form $Ae^{-E/kT}$, where $E$ has a value about half of that which determines the conductivity at high temperatures. This is what would result from the presence of a number of permanent vacant lattice points due to an impurity like $Cd^{++}$. For, if the concentration of these is $c$, and that of the thermal vacant lattice points is $Nx$, the conductivity due to all the holes will be given by

$$\sigma/e = (c+Nx)v_0 e^{-U/kT}$$
$$= cv_0 e^{-U/kT} + Nx_0 v_0 e^{-(\frac{1}{2}W+U)/kT}, \tag{43}$$

which is an expression of the observed type. Smekal, on the other hand, had suggested earlier that the additional term arose from a small number of ions which could move along channels where the activation energy was abnormally small, for instance along surfaces of misfit in a mosaic. But, according to the new suggestion, the term arises, not because there exist lower potential barriers than in the lattice, but merely because $U$ is necessarily smaller than $(\frac{1}{2}W+U)$.

The amounts of impurity required to give the observed effects vary from one part in $10^5$ to less than one part in $10^8$. The passage of a current through the crystal will deposit some of the impurity at the electrode; at the same time it may introduce small traces of an impurity from one of the electrodes. Hitherto, we have referred only to positively charged impurities, but the introduction of doubly charged negative ions, such as the sulphur ion $S^{--}$, into a univalent salt will create vacant anion lattice points, which in some substances will be mobile.

The conductivity would vary from one specimen to another according to the impurity content, but would not depend on previous heat treatment, except in so far as this alters the state of dispersion of an impurity through the crystal. If values of $\log \sigma$, obtained when the crystal is in a steady state, are plotted against $1/T$, the slope of the line at low temperatures gives the value of $U_0$, just as the slope at high temperatures gives $(\frac{1}{2}W_0+U_0)$. To what extent this suggestion is capable of accounting for the observed effects must be left for future work to decide.

There is another type of experiment which enables us to estimate the magnitude of the numerical factors $\gamma$, $B$, and $C$; this is the measurement of the conductivity of the crystal when subjected to high pressure.

We have seen already in § 2 that the number of lattice defects in thermal equilibrium will be diminished owing to the increase in $W$; at the same time their mobility will be diminished owing to the increase in $U$. Both effects lead to a change in the conductivity, which has been measured in the case of AgCl and AgBr. The results, as we shall see, enable us to make an estimate of the product $(BC)$ and hence of the factor $\gamma$.

From (32) it follows that

$$\left(\frac{\partial \log \sigma}{\partial p}\right)_T = \frac{\partial \log \sigma_0}{\partial p} - \frac{1}{kT}\frac{\partial}{\partial p}(\tfrac{1}{2}W_0 + U_0).$$

If the temperature is not too high, we may suppose that the first term on the right-hand side is small compared with the second; we may thus write

$$\frac{\partial \log \sigma}{\partial p} = \frac{V_0\chi_0}{kT}\frac{\partial}{\partial V}(\tfrac{1}{2}W_0 + U_0), \tag{44}$$

where $\chi_0$ is the compressibility of the crystal. But we recall from § 2 that it is precisely the quantities $\partial W_0/\partial V$ and $\partial U_0/\partial V$ which led us to introduce the numerical factors $B$ and $C$. In fact, we shall obtain from (12) and (22)

$$\log(BC) = -\frac{\alpha V_0}{k}\frac{\partial}{\partial V}(\tfrac{1}{2}W_0 + U_0) = -\frac{\alpha T}{\chi_0}\frac{\partial \log \sigma}{\partial p}. \tag{45}$$

From measurements of conductivity made under high pressure the quantity $(BC)$ may thus be evaluated by introducing the known values of $\alpha$ and $\chi$, which are included in Table 12.

At 300° C. under a pressure of 290 atmospheres Jost and Nehlep[†] found an increase of 7 per cent. in the resistance of AgCl, and 10 per cent. in the resistance of AgBr. Their results are given in Table 12, together with values of $\alpha$ and $\chi$.

TABLE 12

|  | AgCl | AgBr |
|---|---|---|
| $-\dfrac{\partial \log \sigma}{\partial p}$ (cm.²/kg.) | $2 \cdot 5 \times 10^{-4}$ | $3 \cdot 5 \times 10^{-4}$ |
| $\chi_0$ (cm.²/kg.) | $8 \times 10^{-7}$ | $9 \times 10^{-7}$ |
| $\alpha$ | $3 \cdot 3 \times 10^{-5}$ | $3 \cdot 5 \times 10^{-5}$ |

These authors ascribed their effect to a change only in the mobility of the defects, whereas we ascribe it to a change in the number of defects as well as in their mobility.

† W. Jost and G. Nehlep, *Zeits. f. phys. Chem.* (B), **34**, 350 (1936).

In § 2 we saw, for a crystal with vacant lattice points only, that the value of $\gamma$ might be $\sim 60$; and for NaCl we found that in (37) the value of $\sigma_0$ was consistent with this estimate. For crystals with interstitial ions, on the other hand, the value of $\gamma$ may be less than unity. The results given in Table 12 lead to the conclusion that for the silver salts $\gamma$ is less than unity. For, substituting in (45), we obtain the estimates—for AgCl $(BC) \sim 350$, and for AgBr $(BC) \sim 2,500$. Now we find from (36), (38) and (39) that the values of $\sigma_0$ indicate that for AgCl the product $(\gamma BC) \sim 150$, and for AgBr $(\gamma BC) \sim 900$, values which require that $\gamma \sim \frac{1}{2}$ for AgCl, and $\gamma \sim \frac{1}{3}$ for AgBr.

In the remainder of this section we shall discuss the connexion between diffusion and conductivity. In § 3 we estimated the freedom of movement of interstitial ions. If we were to consider the whole of the rest of the crystal as a medium through which the interstitial ions are diffusing, the interstitial ions would have a diffusion coefficient $D_i = ND/n$, where $D$ is given by (21). On comparing (40) with (21), we see that $D_i$ and the electrical mobility $v$ satisfy the Einstein relation†

$$v/D_i = e/kT. \tag{46}$$

If $v$ is expressed in cm./sec. per volt/cm., the right-hand side of (46) is numerically equal to the value of $kT$ in electron-volts, i.e. $1/40$ at room temperature.

On the other hand, if we are concerned with one constituent of a crystal, and wish to compare the electrical conductivity due to it with the diffusion coefficient of that constituent, both quantities depend on the number of lattice defects; from (35) and (21) we obtain the relation

$$\sigma/D = Ne^2/kT. \tag{47}$$

If $\sigma$ is expressed in ohm$^{-1}$ cm.$^{-1}$, the factor $10^9$ must be introduced to convert from electromagnetic units. Thus we have

$$\sigma/D = \frac{10^9 \times 2 \cdot 5 \times 10^{-40}}{1 \cdot 37 \times 10^{-16}} \frac{N}{T}$$

$$= 1 \cdot 8 \times 10^{-15} N/T. \tag{48}$$

For $N$, the number of ion pairs per cm.$^3$, the value is of the order $10^{22}$, and in these experiments $T \sim 600° \text{K}$. Hence for all substances we expect the ratio to be given approximately by

$$\sigma/D \sim 3 \times 10^4. \tag{49}$$

We obtain this unambiguous value for the ratio $\sigma/D$, because the same exponential term and the same product $(\gamma BC)$ occur in the

† A general proof of this is given in the appendix to this chapter.

expressions both for $\sigma$ and for $D$. We cannot predict the absolute value of $D_0$ for any type of lattice defect until we know more about these numerical factors. But with values of $\sigma_0$ like those given in (37) and (38) we expect to find values of $D_0$ greater than unity, whenever the diffusion is due to the presence of mobile lattice defects in thermal equilibrium, or is due to any mechanism characteristic of the ions of the lattice (i.e. is not due to the presence of an impurity nor to motion along cracks).

The question arises whether there are processes which contribute to

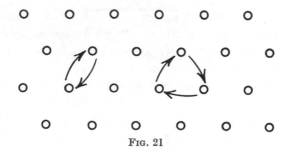

Fig. 21

the diffusion without contributing to an electric current. There are two obvious possibilities. In the first place, we saw in §5 that double holes may be present in which adjacent ions are missing. If these are mobile they will contribute to diffusion without adding anything to an electric current. In the second place, there is a question which is important in all solid substances—in various types of crystal can adjacent atoms or ions exchange places directly, without the temporary formation of a lattice defect, in, for instance, either of the ways illustrated in Fig. 21. The result of such interchanges, if they occur, could be detected by the use of atoms or ions with radioactive nuclei. If the interchanges take place with an activation energy *as low as* that which governs diffusion by lattice defects, they will contribute to the measured diffusion of the radioactive material through the crystal. If the activation energy is *lower*, the rate of diffusion will be determined by this process and not by the motion of lattice defects. In an ionic crystal the mobility deduced from the diffusion will in this case disagree with the mobility deduced from electrical conductivity; for when a pair of positive ions exchange places, or a pair of negative ions, this makes no contribution to an electric current.

For one polar substance, lead iodide, direct experimental evidence on this point has been obtained. The rate of diffusion of radioactive

$Pb^{++}$ ions through $PbI_2$ was measured[†] at temperatures between 100° and 300° C., and it was found that the diffusion coefficient could be represented by

$$D = 10 \cdot 6 \, e^{-E/kT},\tag{50}$$

with $\qquad\qquad E = 30,000$ cals./mol $= 1 \cdot 3$ eV.

This radioactive method measures the movement of the positive ions $Pb^{++}$, irrespective of whether the negative ions are mobile or not. According to Tubandt,[‡] lead-iodide at high temperatures is one of those substances where both positive and negative ions are nearly equally mobile, as mentioned in the list in § 5. The electrical conductivity of $PbI_2$ can be expressed by a formula of the common type which has been discussed on p. 38:

$$\sigma = 9 \cdot 78 \times 10^{-4} \, e^{-9,360/RT} + 1 \cdot 15 \times 10^5 \, e^{-30,000/RT},\tag{51}$$

where the second term is predominant at high temperatures above 275° C., and the first term, with its very small coefficient, is predominant at low temperatures, as in (26). It will be seen that the activation energy in the second term agrees with the value found for the $Pb^{++}$ by radioactive diffusion measurements in (50) above. Before accepting this agreement, however, one must inquire whether the coefficients in front of the exponential term in (50) and (51) are in the required ratio. The observed ratio is

$$\frac{1 \cdot 15 \times 10^5}{10 \cdot 6} \sim 10^4.\tag{52}$$

In $PbI_2$ the number of Pb ions per cm.³ is $7 \times 10^{21}$; hence from (49), p. 51, at 700° K. we expect a ratio $\sim 1 \cdot 8 \times 10^4$. The agreement is sufficiently satisfactory. But the first term in (51), with its very small coefficient, cannot be identified with the contribution from the iodine ions, as stated by Jost.[||] It cannot be a contribution from ions of the lattice, but must be due either to the presence of an impurity in the specimen or to movement of ions along cracks.

With regard to the other term, however, it appears that the good agreement found for the activation energy may be significant. In this case the mechanism of diffusion and conductivity will be the same; and we can presumably say that the direct exchange of places between adjacent $Pb^{++}$ ions is certainly not an important factor in determining their diffusion in $PbI_2$. It should be noted, however, that very few of

---

[†] G. von Hevesy and W. Seith, *Zeits. f. Physik*, **56**, 790 (1929), and **57**, 869 (1929).

[‡] C. Tubandt, H. Reinhold, and W. Jost, *Zeits. f. anorg. Chem.* **177**, 253 (1928); W. Seith, *Zeits. f. Physik*, **57**, 869 (1929).

[||] W. Jost, *Diffusion und chemische Reaktion in festen Stoffen*, chap. iii (Dresden, 1937).

the measurements on diffusion were made above 275° C. In the specimen on which the measurements of conductivity were made the second term in (51) was swamped by the first term at all temperatures below 275° C., so the result is not quite conclusive.

In passing, mention should be made here of the similar experiment which has been made on the diffusion of radioactive $Pb^{++}$ ions in the chloride. In this case a direct comparison of mobilities is impossible, as $PbCl_2$ is one of those substances where the electric current is said to be carried entirely by the negative ions. Nevertheless, the positive ions are to some extent mobile, and (in the absence of a field) their diffusion coefficient was measured by the radioactive method; it could be represented by

$$D = 7 \cdot 8\, e^{-E/kT} \text{ cm.}^2/\text{sec.,}$$

with $\qquad\qquad E = 35,800 \text{ cals./mol} = 1 \cdot 55 \text{ eV.}$

The coefficient has a reasonable value and the activation energy is more than three times larger than the value found by Seith† for the electrical conductivity over the same range of temperatures. He found

$$\sigma = 6 \cdot 55\, e^{-E/kT},$$

with $\qquad\qquad E = 10,960 \text{ cals./mol} = 0 \cdot 48 \text{ eV.}$

With their much larger activation energy the $Pb^{++}$ ions would not be expected to carry an appreciable part of the current, and the comparison is at first sight satisfactory. The value $\sigma_0 = 6 \cdot 55$ shows, however, that the conductivity measured by Seith cannot have been characteristic of the lattice at all; and if his measurements had been carried to higher temperatures a conductivity with a larger activation energy and a larger $\sigma_0$ would doubtless have been found. In fact, in his diagram there appears to be an indication of such a trend at the highest temperatures recorded.

In polar crystals which are found to be ionic conductors it is always possible that at the same time electrons are contributing to the current. In this case mobilities deduced for the ions from the conductivity will be incorrect. It is desirable, then, to have an independent method of investigating the freedom with which the ions themselves can move. The only direct method—that of radioactive indicators, just described —is of limited application, and has given a check in the case of lead-iodide only. For several other substances an indirect method has been attempted. Unfortunately, from the discussion of these results which

† W. Seith, *Zeits. f. Physik*, **56**, 804 (1929).

will be given below it appears that they cannot by any means bear the simple interpretation that has been put upon them.

In connexion with Fig. 19 it was pointed out that, when two crystals of the same substance are pressed together, the mobile ions are able to pass freely from one crystal into the other. In the same way, if two crystals of two different substances, having a mobile ion in common, e.g. AgCl and AgI, are pressed together, and a voltage is applied, the mobile ions pass across the boundary in spite of the disparity in the lattice spacing. The same doubtless happens in the absence of an electric field; for similar behaviour is found for foreign ions which a crystal is able to take into solid solution. When, for example, a crystal of $Ag_2S$ containing 1 per cent. of $Cu_2S$ in solution is put into contact with a crystal of pure $Ag_2S$, and the whole is raised to a temperature between 200° and 300° C., it is found after a few hours that the amount of copper in the second crystal is comparable with that in the first.† Several pairs of crystals have been investigated in this way, and the diffusion coefficients deduced can in most cases be put in the form

$$D = D_0 e^{-E/kT}.$$

The values of $E$ and of $D_0$ are given in Table 13, where the values for $Pb^{++}$ ions, obtained by the radioactive method, have been included for comparison.

TABLE 13

| Diffusing ion | Crystal in which diffusion takes place | $D_0$ cm.²/sec. | $E$ cals. |
|---|---|---|---|
| $Ag^+$ | $\alpha$-$Cu_2S$ | $38 \times 10^{-5}$ | 4,570 |
| $Cu^+$ | $\alpha$-$Ag_2S$ | $12 \times 10^{-5}$ | 3,180 |
| $Ag^+$ | $\alpha$-$Cu_2Te$ | $2 \cdot 4$ | 20,860 |
| $Cu^+$ | $\alpha$-$AgI$ | $16 \times 10^{-5}$ | 2,250 |
| $Li^+$ | $\alpha$-$AgI$ | $50 \times 10^{-5}$ | 4,570 |
| $Se^{--}$ | $\alpha$-$Ag_2S$ | $17 \times 10^{-5}$ | 20,040 |
| $Pb^{++}$ | $PbCl_2$ | $7 \cdot 8$ | 35,800 |
| $Pb^{++}$ | $PbI_2$ | $10 \cdot 6$ | 30,000 |

It will be seen that among the foreign ions in one case only is the coefficient $D_0$ greater than unity. The others are all some $10^5$ times smaller than the coefficient for the self-diffusion of $Pb^{++}$ in the lead salts. If we compare and contrast the properties of different substances, it is true that the freedom of movement of the ions varies by factors much larger than $10^5$. But if we ask to what these large variations are due, we find that they are due entirely to differences in the energies

† W. Jost and H. Rüter, *Zeits. f. phys. Chem.* (B), **21**, 48 (1933).

$W$ and $U$ which occur in the exponential term. The whole of the discussion of this chapter has brought out the important fact that between one lattice and another no difference as large as $10^5$ can occur in the values of $D_0$, $\sigma_0$, $v_0$, and $x_0$, although smaller differences will result from different values of the factors $\gamma$, $B$, and $C$. Very small values of $D_0$, like those included in Table 13, would be found if the mixed crystal contains a trace of a suitable impurity, present to about one part in 100,000; or, alternatively, such values might perhaps arise from diffusion along cracks.

As mentioned above, attempts have been made to deduce coefficients of self-diffusion from these rates of diffusion of foreign ions.† The conclusions drawn would be valid if in both cases the diffusion were uninfluenced by the presence of impurities or cracks in the crystal.

Some results using metallic electrodes may be mentioned. When a crystal of NaCl or KCl at a temperature of 600° C. is electrolysed, using a gold foil as anode, ions of gold enter the crystal. On cooling, the depth to which the gold has penetrated may be seen as a coloration due to the presence of colloidal gold. From the dependence on field strength and temperature, the mobility was estimated‡ and found to take the usual form

$$v = v_0 e^{-E/kT}, \tag{53}$$

with values of $E$ between 24,000 and 30,000 cals. per mol.

Attempts were made by rapid cooling of the crystal to obtain the gold in the form of ions or atoms dispersed through the lattice; but it invariably took the colloidal form.

Crystals of rock-salt were electrolysed at temperatures above 640° C. using an anode of metallic nickel.‖ Under subsequent illumination with ultra-violet light the depth of penetration of the nickel is seen by the intense luminescence which it emits. The mobility of the nickel ions was given by (53) with $v_0 = 2.72$ and $E = 25,400$ cals. per mol. In the absence of an electric field a slow diffusion of the nickel into the crystal was observed. Attempts were made to observe the penetration of nickel into NaCl by electrolysing the crystal, using as anode a crystal of $NiSO_4$, $NiCl_2$, $Ni(NO_3)_2$, or NiO; but the results were negative.

## 7. Theoretical calculation of the activation energies

In § 1 we showed that in solids built up of molecules bound together by van der Waals forces the work necessary to remove a molecule or atom from the interior of the crystal to a distant point outside the

† W. Jost, *Diffusion und chemische Reaktion in festen Stoffen*, p. 117 (Dresden, 1937).
‡ M. G. Bogomolowa, *Acta Physicochimica*, **5**, 161 (1936).
‖ I. A. Parfianowitsch and S. A. Schipizyn, ibid., **6**, 263 (1937).

crystal is $2W_L$, where $W_L$ is the lattice energy per molecule. Hence we showed that the work $W_H$ necessary to form a hole was equal to $W_L$. This is not the case for the removal of an ion from a polar crystal.† In this section we shall show why, and shall discuss the attempts that have been made to calculate $W_H$.

The first attempt to estimate $W_H$ is due to Jost.‡ In order to explain his ideas we shall consider a crystal having the alkali-halide structure.

The lattice energy $W_L$ *per ion pair* may be written

$$W_L = \frac{\alpha_M e^2}{a} - xw(a). \tag{54}$$

Here $\alpha_M$ is the Madelung constant, $a$ the interionic distance, $w(a)$ the repulsive 'exchange' interaction between a pair of ions of opposite sign, and $x$ the number of nearest neighbours which each ion has. If only the electrostatic and repulsive forces had to be taken into account, and the polarizability of the ions could be neglected, the work required to remove to infinity a negative or positive ion would be $W_L$, and hence the work required to form a pair of vacant lattice points (a Schottky defect) would be $W_L$. The numerical value of $W_L$ is about 6 to 8 eV., or, say, 140 kcals. As Jost points out, however, this is a serious over-estimate. When an ion is removed, the medium surrounding the vacant lattice point will find itself in an electric field. It therefore becomes polarized, and in calculating $W_H$ the energy of this polarization must be taken into account. This can be done most simply in the following way. The polarization of the surrounding medium will set up at the vacant lattice point an electrostatic potential, which we denote by $\phi$. Then the work necessary to remove an ion will be, instead of $W_L$,

$$W_H = W_L - \tfrac{1}{2}e\phi. \tag{55}$$

Our problem, then, is to calculate $\phi$. Jost (loc. cit.) has assumed that the hole from which the ion is missing may be treated as a spherical cavity in a continuous medium of dielectric constant $\kappa$. In the medium surrounding the hole is an electric field, since a charge $e$ has been removed from the hole. If $r$ is the distance from the centre of the hole, we thus have for the dielectric displacement $D$ and the field $E$

$$D = e/r^2, \qquad E = e/\kappa r^2,$$

and hence for the polarization $P$

$$P = \frac{D - E}{4\pi} = \frac{1}{4\pi}\left(1 - \frac{1}{\kappa}\right)\frac{e}{r^2}. \tag{56}$$

† It is probably not the case for metals either.
‡ W. Jost, *J. Chem. Phys.* **1**, 466 (1933).

The potential $\phi$ at the centre of the cavity due to the polarization is given by

$$\phi = \int\limits_{R}^{\infty} \frac{P}{r^2} 4\pi r^2 \, dr = \left(1 - \frac{1}{\kappa}\right)\frac{e}{R}. \tag{57}$$

The difficulty with this method is to know what value to take for $R$. It should clearly be of the order of the interatomic distance. More exact calculations for the alkali-halides to be reviewed below show that for these crystals $R \sim 0.9a$

$$\sim 0.6a$$

according as the missing ion is negative or positive. For alkali-halides, with $\kappa \sim 5$, we see from (57) that

$$\tfrac{1}{2}e\phi \sim e^2/2a \sim 2.5 \text{ eV.}$$

Formula (57) shows that $\phi$ will be the greater, and hence $W_H$ the less, the greater is the dielectric constant of the material.

A more detailed method of calculating $\phi$ has ·been given by Mott and Littleton.[†] The problem at issue is to calculate the polarization in a crystal due to a point-charge at any one of the lattice points, and hence the potential $\phi$ at that lattice point, which will be referred to as the point $Q$. We may divide our problem into two halves:

1. To calculate $\phi$ if all the ions of the crystal are held at rest in their mean positions, so that only the dielectric constant $\kappa_0$ has to be considered; and

2. To calculate $\phi$ if the ions are allowed to move into their new positions of equilibrium.

In order to obtain the energy of a 'hole' we require, of course, the value of $\phi$ calculated in the latter conditions; for other problems (Chap. III, § 7) we shall, however, require the former value, and it will be convenient to treat them together here.

We suppose at first that the ions are held at rest in their equilibrium positions. Then at large distances from the hole $Q$, where the atomic structure of the medium may be neglected, the polarization of the medium will be, from (56),

$$P = \frac{e}{r^2} \frac{1}{4\pi}\left(1 - \frac{1}{\kappa_0}\right).$$

From this we may deduce the dipoles induced on the ions. We again assume that the crystal has the rock-salt structure, and that the ions

† N. F. Mott and M. J. Littleton, *Trans. Faraday Soc.* **34**, 485 (1938).

have polarizabilities $\alpha_1$, $\alpha_2$ (cf. Chap. I, § 5). Then the dipoles on the ions of either type are respectively

$$M_1 a^3 e/r^2, \qquad M_2 a^3 e/r^2, \tag{58}$$

where
$$M_1 = \frac{2\alpha_1}{\alpha_1 + \alpha_2} \frac{1}{4\pi}\left(1 - \frac{1}{\kappa_0}\right),$$

with a similar expression for ions of type 2.

As our approximation of zero order we may consider that (58) is valid for *all* the ions of the lattice. Then, since a dipole $\mu$ at a given lattice point gives a potential $\mu/r^2$ at the hole, we can obtain the potential $\phi$ by summation:

$$\phi = -ea^3\left[M_1 \sum_1 \frac{1}{r^4} + M_2 \sum_2 \frac{1}{r^4}\right].$$

The summations 1 and 2 are over the lattice points of the two types of ion.

Summations of these types have been carried out by Jones and Ingham.† If the vacant lattice point is of type 2, they obtain

$$a^4 \sum_1 \frac{1}{r^4} = 10 \cdot 1977, \qquad a^4 \sum_2 \frac{1}{r^4} = 6 \cdot 3346.$$

As our approximation of first order, we take as unknown the dipoles $\mu$ on the six nearest neighbours to $Q$, viz. those at the (100) lattice points. We assume (58) to be valid for all the other ions. The field at a (100) lattice point due to the dipoles on all the ions outside it we found by direct summation‡ to be

$$E_1 = -\frac{e}{a^2}(0 \cdot 388 M_1 + 1 \cdot 965 M_2) \tag{59}$$

and that due to the other five (100) ions is

$$E_2 = -2 \cdot 371 \mu/a^3,$$

the minus sign denoting that the field is in the opposite direction to that due to $e$. The equation for $\mu$ is then

$$\mu = \alpha_1\left(\frac{e}{a^2} + E_1 + E_2\right),$$

giving, if we write $\mu = eam$, $\beta_1 = \alpha_1/a^3$, $\beta_2 = \alpha_2/a^3$,

$$m = \frac{\beta_1(1 - 0 \cdot 388 M_1 - 1 \cdot 965 M_2)}{1 + 2 \cdot 371\beta_1}. \tag{60}$$

† J. E. Jones and A. E. Ingham, *Proc. Roy. Soc.* (A), **107**, 636 (1925).

‡ In the summation the potentials due to 23 rings of lattice points were included. The contribution of each ring after the fourteenth was less than $0 \cdot 001 M/a^2$.

The potential at the centre is then, to the *first* order,

$$\phi = -\frac{e}{a}(\ 4 \cdot 1977 M_1 + 6 \cdot 3346 M_2) - \frac{6\mu}{a^2}. \tag{61}$$

The process could be carried out to any desired degree of approximation; in the paper cited it was carried out to the fourth, the dipoles at the points (100), (110), (111), (200) being taken as unknowns.

In Table 14 we show the results obtained for an ideal crystal with $\alpha_1 = \alpha_2$ and $\kappa_0 = 4$, and for three of the alkali-chlorides. The vacant lattice point for the halides is taken to be that normally occupied by a positive ion. The results are expressed as the ratio of $\phi$ to $\phi_0$, where

$$\phi_0 = \frac{e}{4\pi a}\left(1 - \frac{1}{\kappa_0}\right).$$

TABLE 14. *Potential at a Positive Lattice Point due to Dipoles induced by a Charge Q placed at that Point, when Ions are held at Rest in their Equilibrium Positions*

| Crystal | | | NaCl | KCl | RbCl |
|---|---|---|---|---|---|
| Dielectric constant $\kappa_0$ . | 4 | | 2·33 | 2·17 | 2·18 |
| $\alpha_1/\alpha_2$ . . . . | 1 | | 20·3 | 4·4 | 2·6 |
| | *Order of approx.* | | | | |
| | 0 | 16·53 | 20·03 | 18·96 | 18·25 |
| | 1 | 18·57 | 21·88 | 20·60$_5$ | 19·82 |
| $-\phi/\phi_0$ . . | 2 | 18·15 | 21·83 | 20·44 | 19·59$_4$ |
| | 3 | 18·03 | 21·62 | 20·27 | 19·46 |
| | 4 | 18·5 | 21·69 | .. | .. |

It will be seen that the first approximation gives fairly satisfactory results.

In Table 15 we give similar results for the case where a negative lattice point is vacant, worked out to the first approximation only.

TABLE 15

| | NaCl | KCl | KBr |
|---|---|---|---|
| $-\phi/\phi_0$ | 13·21 | 14·69 | 14·35 |

As stated above, in Jost's calculations the 'hole' was treated as a spherical hole of radius $R$ in a medium of uniform dielectric constant. Comparing formula (57) with the results obtained here, we obtain the following values for $R$.

TABLE 16. *Effective Radius R of a Vacant Lattice Point*

| Crystal | R/a | |
|---|---|---|
| $\alpha_1 = \alpha_2$, $\kappa_0 - 1 \ll 1$ | 0·76 | |
| $\alpha_1 = \alpha_2$, $\kappa_0 = 4$ | 0·68 | |
| | Positive ion | Negative ion |
| NaCl . . . . | 0·58 | 0·95 |
| KCl . . . . | 0·61 | 0·85$_5$ |
| RbCl . . . . | 0·635 | .. |
| KBr . . . . | .. | 0·88 |

We include a value for the limiting case $(\kappa_0 - 1) \ll 1$, in which case our approximation of zero order is valid.

We may note that the values of $\phi$ given here are the potentials induced by any charge $e$ at a vacant lattice point, whether the charge is due to addition or removal of an electron or an ion.

We now turn to the calculation of $\phi$, and of the total energy, in the case where the ions are allowed to move, which, of course, is the case which occurs in nature. The calculation is complicated, and involves a consideration of the forces acting on the displaced ions next to the vacant lattice point. Furthermore, one has to make some allowance for the Lorentz-Lorenz force and the overlap of the ions considered in Chap. I, § 5. The details need not be considered here. We give only some results.

For sodium-chloride the ions adjacent to the hole are displaced a distance $\sim 0\cdot07a$ *outwards*. $\phi$ is of the order $1\cdot3e/a$. The energies for crystals for which they have been calculated are given in Table 17.

These theoretical estimates of $\frac{1}{2}W_0$ are of the same order as the values expected from the ionic conductivity and rates of diffusion. From measurements on the silver salts we estimated on p. 47 that $U_0$ and $\frac{1}{2}W_0$ were of the same order; for the alkali-halides the observed values of $(\frac{1}{2}W_0 + U_0)$ are of the order 2 eV.

TABLE 17

Energies in eV.

| | NaCl | KCl | KBr |
|---|---|---|---|
| Work $W_H^+$ to remove positive ion | 4·62 | 4·47 | 4·23 |
| Work $W_H^-$ to remove negative ion | 5·18 | 4·79 | 4·60 |
| Lattice energy per ion pair $W_L$ . | 7·94 | 7·18 | 6·91 |
| $\frac{1}{2}W_0 = \frac{1}{2}W_H^+ + \frac{1}{2}W_H^- - \frac{1}{2}W_L$ . . | 0·93 | 1·04 | 0·96 |

Attempts have also been made to calculate the activation energies $U$ for the motion of holes, and also the energies to form interstitial ions. The results are probably less reliable than those for the energies of holes, because they depend sensitively on the repulsive exchange energy between ions. For details the reader is referred to the original papers (Jost, loc. cit., and Mott and Littleton, loc. cit.).

## 8. Crystals with abnormally high ionic conductivity

Among the phenomena described and discussed above is included the behaviour of nearly every ionic crystal up to its melting-point. At least two or three substances are, however, known to show quite different behaviour. Silver iodide, for example, at room temperature is hexagonal, but above 140° C. exists in a high-temperature modification, known as α-AgI, which possesses an abnormally high ionic conductivity with a very low activation energy.† The lattice of this α-AgI has a very open structure; the silver ions appear to have no special positions but move through the whole available space. Such a crystal would be expected to have an unusually high ionic conductivity. The substance $Ag_2HgI_4$ likewise has a high-temperature modification, stable above 50°, with similar properties, so that between 50° and 140° it has an ionic conductivity about 1,000 times greater than any known ionic conductor.‡ In this α-$Ag_2HgI_4$ the three metal ions are distributed at random among the four points of a face-centred lattice; on the average every fourth lattice point will be unoccupied.

In normal crystals the ionic conductivity is due to the motion of lattice defects; but in these crystals any one of the metal ions is evidently able to jump to a position of equal energy. The distinction between interstitial ions and lattice ions is lost. Furthermore, the number of mobile ions is independent of temperature. We therefore expect the conductivity to be of the form

$$\sigma = \sigma_0 e^{-U_0/kT},$$

where the energy in the exponential term is the height of the potential barrier only, instead of the usual ($\frac{1}{2}W_0 + U_0$). We expect the coefficient $\sigma_0$ to be unusually small, because the factors $\gamma$ and $B$ will be absent, and because a small value of the factor $C$ will accompany the small value of $U_0$. It is satisfactory, then, that for $Ag_2HgI_4$ the value is found to be as low as $\sigma_0 = 400$, while $U_0 = 4,300$ cals. or 0·19 eV.; for α-AgI, α-CuI, and β-CuBr even lower values are recorded.||

For $Ag_2HgI_4$ the transition from the low- to the high-temperature

---

† L. W. Strock, *Zeits. f. phys. Chem.* (B), **25**, 441 (1934), and **31**, 132 (1936); J. A. A. Ketelaar, *Trans. Faraday Soc.* **34**, 880 (1938).

‡ J. A. A. Ketelaar, *Zeits. f. phys. Chem.* (B), **26**, 327 (1934).

|| J. A. A. Ketelaar, loc. cit., p. 333.

modification has been investigated in detail by Ketelaar. The transition is gradual and is accompanied by the phenomena characteristic of order-disorder transformations in alloys, including the abnormal specific heat.[†] Below 35° C. the work $W$ to form an interstitial ion is 7,400 cals., but as the temperature rises towards 50° C., the value decreases towards zero, like the activation energy in a disordered alloy.

**9. Appendix.** *Theoretical derivation of the Einstein relation between the mobility $v$ and the diffusion coefficient $D$ of a charged particle*

Suppose the particles are in equilibrium in a field $F$, of which the potential is $\phi$. For simplicity let us assume that $F$ varies only in the $x$ direction, so that

$$F = -\frac{\partial \phi}{\partial x}.$$

Then the number of particles $n(x)$ per unit volume for any value of $x$ is, by Boltzmann's law,

$$n(x) = \text{const. } e^{-e\phi/kT}. \tag{62}$$

But one can also obtain $n(x)$ from the condition that no current is flowing, namely,

$$vneF - eD\frac{dn}{dx} = 0,$$

which, on integration, gives

$$n = \text{const. } e^{-v\phi/D}. \tag{63}$$

On comparison with (62) we obtain

$$\frac{v}{D} = \frac{e}{kT}.$$

[†] Cf, for example, F. C. Nix and W. Shockley, *Rev. Mod. Phys.* **10**, 1 (1938).

# III

## ELECTRONS IN POLAR CRYSTALS

### 1. Electrons in a periodic field

IT is a well-known deduction from quantum mechanics that in any *periodic* electrostatic field, such as would exist in an ideal crystal with its atoms at rest, an electron can move freely without being deflected. This theorem is used to explain the high conductivities of metals at low temperatures. An account of the behaviour of electrons in periodic fields is given in any text-book on the theory of metals;† here we shall summarize certain results.

Fig. 22 (a) shows the potential energy of an electron in an atom; in the field of the atom the electron may have any positive energy, but only certain discrete negative energies, which are shown by horizontal lines. In the field formed by arranging such atoms in a periodic array, the possible energies fall into a series of allowed bands, separated by bands of forbidden energy (Fig. 22 (b)). In certain cases two allowed bands may overlap. For cubic crystal structures, a band of allowed energy states will correspond to each level of the individual atom. In this case the number of allowed electronic levels in the band is $N\omega$, where $N$ is equal to the number of atoms in the lattice and $\omega$ to the statistical weight of the state considered (for an $s$-state $\omega = 2$).

In a given band the state of an electron is specified by a wave number $\mathbf{k}$, which gives the direction of motion of the electron through the lattice. The wave function of the electron is of the form

$$\psi = e^{i(\mathbf{k}\mathbf{r})}u(x, y, z), \tag{1}$$

where $u$ is a function having the periodicity of the lattice. The function $\psi$ thus consists of a plane wave modified by the periodicity of the lattice. Wave functions of this type are shown in Fig. 24 on p. 72.

In an external field $F$ an electron in a lattice moves according to the equation

$$m_{\text{eff}}\ddot{x} = eF, \tag{2}$$

where $m_{\text{eff}}$ is termed the 'effective mass' of an electron in the lattice. The narrower is the band of allowed energies in which the energy of the electron, the greater is the effective mass $m_{\text{eff}}$. This is because, if the band is narrow, the atoms are far apart and the electron will take

† Cf., for example, N. F. Mott and H. Jones, *The Theory of the Properties of Metals and Alloys*, chap. ii (Oxford, 1936); A. H. Wilson, *Theory of Metals* (Cambridge, 1936).

a comparatively long time to jump from atom to atom. $m_{\text{eff}}$ is independent of energy only near the bottom of a band; for higher values it varies with energy and may even change sign.

For electrons in the conduction bands of alkali-halides $m_{\text{eff}}$ is probably of the order of magnitude of the mass of a free electron;† for positive holes in alkali-halides it may well be greater; for positive holes in oxides there is some evidence that it is about five times less.‡

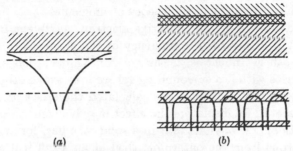

(a)            (b)

Fɪɢ. 22. Energy levels of an electron: (a) in an atom, and (b) in a periodic field. The shaded areas show allowed energy levels, the curved lines the potential energy. Discrete energy levels are dotted

## 2. Methods used in discussing cohesion in solids; the atomic model (Heitler-London) and the collective electron model (Bloch)

Two different models have been used in theoretical investigations of the properties of solids. In the first the solid is pictured as being made up of separate atoms or ions which interact with each other. Solid rare gases‖ and alkali-halides†† have been treated quantitatively by this method. Its application to metals is possible in principle, provided that some of the interacting metal atoms are taken to be ionized, but mathematical difficulties have prevented any useful results from being derived in this way for the conduction electrons, though Heisenberg and Bloch have used it to describe the inner $d$ electrons in ferro-magnetic materials.‡‡ The method is analogous to that of Heitler and London‖‖ in the theory of molecules.

The second method is due originally to Bloch, and will be called the collective electron††† treatment. In this model the electrons in the

† Cf. Chap. V, § 13.                          ‡ Cf. Chap. V, § 5.
‖ Cf. R. H. Fowler, *Statistical Mechanics*, 2nd ed., p. 319 (Cambridge, 1936).
†† Cf. Chap. I.            ‡‡ Cf. N. F. Mott and H. Jones, loc. cit., chaps. iv and vi.
‖‖ W. Heitler and F. London, *Zeits. f. Physik*, **44**, 455 (1927).
††† Following E. Stoner, *Magnetism and Matter* (London, 1934).
3595.32

outermost shell of the atoms concerned are not supposed to be bound
to their individual atoms, but are assumed to be free to move through
the lattice as described in § 1. The field in which the electrons are supposed
to move is that of the atomic cores and the *average* field of all the other
electrons. This field is periodic with the period of the lattice. The
most successful application of the method has been to metals, notably
by Wigner and Seitz,[†] but it has also been applied to insulators—e.g.
diamond[‡] and the hydrogen- and alkali-halides.[||] It is analogous to
the method of orbitals[††] in the theory of molecules.

The disadvantage of the collective electron treatment in its crude
form is that it disregards the tendency of the electrons to keep away
from one another. In metals, as the work of Wigner[‡‡] has shown, each
electron carries with it a surrounding sphere into which other electrons
are unlikely to come. Wigner has calculated the effect of this on the
energy of a metal. In insulators the effect may be even more important
than in metals; it is obvious that in a solid rare gas, for example, one
of the electrons from the outermost shell of an atom will not be able
to move far into the next atom unless an electron from the next atom
gets out of the way to make room for it. In discussing optical absorption by insulators we shall find that the results of the collective electron
treatment are qualitatively incorrect (§ 6).

An important advantage of the collective electron picture is that it
enables a simple explanation to be given of the difference between a
conductor and an insulator.[||||] As we saw in § 1, the possible energies
of an electron moving in a periodic field are divided into bands separated
by bands of forbidden energy. The number of electronic states in each
allowed band is limited, and by the Pauli exclusion principle not more
than one electron can occupy each state. If all the states of a given
band are occupied, the electrons in that band can make no contribution
to the electric current. An insulator is therefore a crystal in which each
band is either fully occupied or completely empty.[†††] A current is
only possible if electrons are brought into the empty band, either from
outside, or by raising them from lower levels.

† Cf. N. F. Mott and H. Jones, loc. cit., chap. iv.
‡ G. E. Kimball, *J. Chem. Phys.* **3**, 560 (1935).
|| W. Shockley, *Phys. Rev.* **50**, 754 (1936); D. H. Ewing and F. Seitz, ibid. **50**, 760 (1936).
†† J. E. Lennard-Jones, *Trans. Faraday Soc.* **25**, 668 (1929).
‡‡ E. Wigner, *Phys. Rev.* **46**, 1002 (1934).
|||| First given by A. H. Wilson, *Proc. Roy. Soc.* (A), **134**, 277 (1932).
††† The discussion (Chap. V, § 4) of the properties of certain semi-conductors such as NiO suggests that the picture is too simple.

Solid argon may be cited as an example. In the argon atom the $3p$-levels are fully occupied with six electrons and the $4s$-level is empty. In a crystal of $N$ atoms we have to consider a band of $6N$ energy states corresponding to the $3p$-states of the atom, and a higher band corresponding to the $4s$-level. In the unexcited crystal at low temperatures all the levels in the $3p$-band are occupied and all those in the $4s$-band empty. No current can flow, therefore, when a voltage is applied to the crystal. If, however, an electron is introduced into the $4s$-band, either from outside or by raising it from the $3p$-band, the electron can move and a current is possible (cf. § 11).

For quantitative investigations of non-metallic crystals from the point of view of the collective electron picture, it is important to realize that in the above example an excited electron in the $4s$-band does not move in the same field as one of the $3p$-electrons; in the $4s$-band an electron moves through a lattice of neutral atoms. A $3p$-electron, on the other hand, can only come into an atom if another $3p$-electron moves away to make room for it; therefore the field in which the $3p$-electron moves near any one lattice point is that of the positively charged *ion*.

In the calculations of this book we shall not find the collective electron treatment useful for the *unexcited* electrons of insulating crystals. For quantitative work it is better to regard the crystal as built of separate atoms or ions as in Chapter I, though possibly the ions may be much distorted by their neighbours. Of course if an *extra* electron is introduced into the crystal (i.e. into the $4s$-band in argon), the wave function of *that* electron must be taken to be of the type described in § 1, extending through the whole crystal. The electron will be perfectly free to move, and the possible values of its energy will form a band, which we shall call the 'conduction band'. Our deduction from theory that a (normally empty) conduction band exists does *not* depend on the use of any special model, such as the collective electron treatment.

Probably in most insulators the first band of *empty* levels overlaps the higher empty bands, so that we have in fact a continuum of allowed energies, with a lowest allowed energy. In measuring these energies we take for our zero of energy that of an electron at rest in free space far from the crystal. The energy of the lowest allowed state is the minimum energy required to bring an extra electron from outside into the crystal; it will be denoted in this book by $-\chi$. $\chi$ may be called the electron affinity of the crystal. Electrons in energy states near the bottom of a band will be accelerated by an applied field according to

(2), like a free electron. For high energies (several electron volts) the effective mass is no longer constant; for most problems of this book this does not concern us, since in semi-conductors and photo-conducting materials the energies of the electrons are of the order $kT$ (cf. Chap. V, §§ 2 and 10).

### 2.1. Positive holes

If an electron is removed from a full band of energy levels of an insulator, the remaining electrons with energies in this band can make a contribution to any electric current flowing. From the point of view of the collective electron model this is obvious. A full band cannot carry a current because, by Pauli's exclusion principle, for every electron moving in one direction there must be another electron moving with the same velocity in the opposite direction. If the band is not full this is no longer the case.

The conclusion that an insulator can carry a current if an electron is removed from it does *not*, however, depend on the collective electron treatment, any more than our conclusion about the behaviour of an extra electron depends on it. Consider for instance the example, solid argon, cited above. Suppose that an electron is removed from the outermost shell of one of the atoms. Then clearly an electron can move over from the next atom without receiving any energy; the thin 'potential barrier' separating two atoms will be completely transparent to an electron. The process can be repeated, and so the place where the electron is missing can wander freely through the crystal.

A place from which an electron is missing will be called in this book a 'positive hole'. Positive holes behave like positive carriers of electricity, and in many crystals their motion is as important as that of electrons (e.g. in $Cu_2O$, Chap. V, § 4).

A discussion of the behaviour of positive holes based on the Heitler-London model may be of interest. Let the suffix $n$ denote the lattice points of the crystal. Let $\psi_n(x)$ denote the wave function of an atom at the point $\mathbf{r}_n$, $x$ denoting the coordinates, including spin, of all the $Z$ electrons. Let $\phi_n(x')$ be the wave function of a positive ion at the point $\mathbf{r}_n$, $x'$ denoting the coordinates of the $Z-1$ electrons. A wave function describing a crystal in which the atom $n$ has lost an electron is

$$\psi_1(x_1)\psi_2(x_2)...\psi_{n-1}(x_{n-1})\phi_n(x'_n)\psi_{n+1}(x_{n+1})....$$

This wave function is not antisymmetrical in the coordinates of the electrons; an antisymmetrical determinant can, however, be formed in the usual way; we denote this by $\Psi_n(X)$, where $X$ stands for the coordinates of all the electrons.

$\Psi_n(X)$ does not, however, represent a stationary state of the electron, since the positive hole will not remain in a given atom but will travel through the crystal. It may be shown that the wave functions which do correspond to stationary states are of the form

$$\sum_n e^{i(\mathbf{k}\mathbf{r_n})}\Psi_n^{\circ}(X).$$

This wave function represents a state of affairs in which the positive hole is travelling through the crystal with wave number $\mathbf{k}$. The energy of the whole crystal depends on $\mathbf{k}$; for a simple cubic crystal this energy will have the form

$$E(\mathbf{k}) = -A(\cos k_x a + \cos k_y a + \cos k_z a). \tag{3}$$

The parameter $A$ is small if the overlap between the atoms is small.

## 3. Electrons in polar crystals

The discussion given in the foregoing sections is applicable to simple insulators, such as diamond, as well as to compounds. In all the following chapters of this book we shall be concerned with electrons in polar crystals. We shall confine our attention almost entirely to compounds containing one metallic and one non-metallic constituent—i.e. to halides, oxides, sulphides, etc. In a crystal such as diamond or a rare gas, in which every atom in the interior is similar to every other atom, the electronic density is evenly distributed, and this makes every atom electrically neutral. In a crystal containing two species of atom there is no reason why the electronic density should be equally distributed; and it usually is not. The atoms of the two constituents may differ from neutrality to any extent. A truly *ionic* crystal is one where the ions bear integral charges $\pm e$, $\pm 2e$, etc., as they would in a vacuum. In a semi-polar crystal the charge on the metal atoms may be less than $+e$ for univalent ions, or it may lie between $e$ and $2e$ for divalent ions, and so on.

An important class of ionic crystals contains those compounds in which the metal ions have the closed electronic shells of the rare-gas structure. The most loosely bound electrons which remain in the metal ions will in this case be in such deep energy levels that they will play no part in any phenomena other than X-ray processes. Thus in these crystals the only electrons to which we shall pay attention in this book are the electrons from the negative ions or else from impurities in the crystal. It is the electrons in the negative ions which fill the levels of the full band with which we shall be concerned. When a positive hole travels through this band, it does so by the repeated jumping of an electron from a negative ion to an adjacent neutral atom,[†] the positive ions offering no obstacle. On the other hand, when an electron travels through the conduction band it may be regarded as moving rapidly from one positive ion to the next, the negative ions offering very little obstacle, as will be seen from the wave functions illustrated in Fig. 24.

We may at this stage emphasize that an electron in the conduction band with small (e.g. thermal) energies can move equally easily in any direction. Its effective mass $m_{eff}$ cannot, for cubic structures and for small values of $\mathbf{k}$, depend on the direction. Thus a slow electron has no particular tendency to move in the (110) direction (cf. Chap. V, § 13).

We shall begin by considering the field within a polar crystal. We discuss first the electrostatic field due to an array of point-charges $\pm e$ arranged in a simple cubic lattice. It is convenient to discuss, instead of the electrostatic potential $\phi$, the potential energy of an electron, $V = -e\phi$. We saw (Chap. I, § 2) that the potential energy of an electron at any lattice point due to all the charges except the one at that point is $\pm \alpha e^2/r_0$, where $\alpha = 1.74$ and $r_0$ is the interatomic distance. Thus in the neighbourhood of any lattice point the potential energy takes the form

$$\pm \frac{\alpha e^2}{r_0} \mp \frac{e^2}{r}.$$

Further, it is clear that the potential is zero in the plane lying midway between two (100) planes. Thus the potential drawn along the line (100) passing through the lattice points will be as in Fig. 23.

The field at the boundary of the crystal has been calculated by Lennard-Jones and Dent.[‡] The potential at a plane boundary is plotted also in Fig. 23, which shows the rapidity with which the field falls away outside the crystal.

It is convenient to introduce the quantity $\alpha'$, defined so that $\pm \alpha' e^2/r_0$ is the potential energy at a lattice point on the surface of a crystal. For the rock-salt structure[||] $\alpha' = 1.681$.

We turn now to the consideration of the energy of an electron in the conduction band. To fix our ideas we consider a crystal, for instance an alkali-halide, and consider an extra electron brought from infinity and introduced into the crystal. Its energy will then lie in the con-

---

[†] Or from a doubly charged negative ion to an adjacent singly charged negative ion.
[‡] J. E. Lennard-Jones and B. M. Dent, *Trans. Faraday Soc.* **24**, 92 (1928).
[||] K. F. Herzfeld, *Zeits. f. phys. Chem.* **105**, 329 (1923).

duction band of energy levels. Suppose that its energy has its lowest possible value. Then, as in § 2, we shall denote by $-\chi$ the work done to bring the electron from infinity and place it in this state. Our aim will be to calculate $\chi$. $\chi$ may be called the 'electron affinity' of the crystal.

We might imagine our extra electron placed on one of the metal ions to form a metal atom. It would not, of course, remain on any

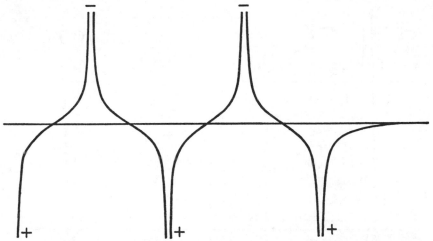

FIG. 23. Potential energy of an electron in a lattice of point charges, showing also the effect at the edges

one atom, but would be free to move from atom to atom. However, this picture gives us a suggestion for estimating $\chi$. If the interatomic distance were large compared with the normal radius of the alkali *atom*, the work $\chi$ could be calculated by means of the following cycle:

1. Remove an alkali ion from the crystal; the work done is $\alpha e^2/r_0$.
2. Bring an electron from infinity to the normal state in this ion to form an alkali atom; the work done is $-I$, where $I$ is the ionization potential of the alkali atom.
3. Bring the alkali atom back to the place vacated by the alkali ion. The total work required to introduce an electron is thus

$$-\chi = \frac{\alpha e^2}{r_0} - I. \qquad (4)$$

This always gives negative values of $\chi$; for sodium-chloride, in electron-volts, $\alpha e^2/r_0 = 8 \cdot 8$, $I = 5 \cdot 12$, and so $\chi = -3 \cdot 7$.

Actually, however, the radius of the alkali atom is by no means small compared with the interatomic distance. Therefore we must take into account the fact that the potential in the region occupied by the alkali atom is not constant as assumed in deriving (4). Actually the electron's orbit will overlap the surrounding ions. Further, we must add the energy due to the quantum-mechanical 'exchange' effect, i.e. the possibility of the electron jumping from ion to ion and thus moving through the crystal. This is too large to be considered as a mere correction to (4), and our best course will be to calculate *ab initio* the

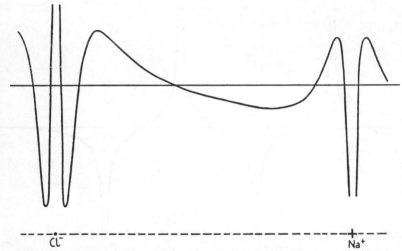

FIG. 24. Wave function of an 'additional' electron introduced into the conduction band of sodium-chloride; the wave function is for the state of lowest energy

energy of an electronic state of the type described in §1 of this chapter, where the wave function is spread out through the whole crystal.

To do this accurately would be somewhat difficult, but an attempt has been made by Tibbs,† whose wave function is shown in Fig. 24 plotted along the (100) direction in the crystal. It will be noticed that the amplitudes of the wave functions are of the same order of magnitude in the two atoms; this means that the electron can pass without difficulty from one sodium ion to the next through a chlorine ion. It follows that the effective mass of an electron in the conduction band should be of the same order as that of a free electron.

An estimate of the energy suggested that the work $-\chi$ necessary to bring an electron from outside the crystal into the lowest state in the conduction band should be about zero; the calculation was not sufficiently accurate to show whether the value is positive or negative. In the calculations quoted above a considerable (negative) term in

† S. R. Tibbs, *Trans. Faraday Soc.* **35**, 1471 (1939).

the energy of an electron in the conduction band was due to the polarization of the surrounding ions.

For crystals other than the alkali-halides, e.g. the silver halides, similar calculations have not been made. We expect the conduction band to be lower (and hence $\chi$ to be greater) because

1. The ionization potential of an atom of a metal such as silver is greater than those of the alkalis.
2. The dielectric constants are greater, and hence the polarization term will be more important.

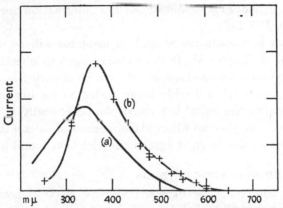

FIG. 25. (a) Photoelectric emission from a clean sodium surface.†
(b) Photoconductive current in (blue) rock-salt containing colloidal metal (Gyulai, loc. cit.)

We see, then, that these theoretical calculations of the energy $\chi$ required to remove an electron to infinity from the lowest state in the conduction band are unlikely to have achieved great accuracy. An experimental estimate of $\chi$ may be deduced,‡ however, from measurements of the photoelectric current in crystals of alkali-halide coloured by the presence of particles of colloidal metal. Fig. 25 shows the results of Gyulai‖ using blue rock-salt, i.e. rock-salt containing colloidal particles of metallic sodium. The curve shows current plotted against wavelength. At the long-wave limit the curve is similar to that obtained for the current emitted by a clean sodium surface (Fig. 25, curve a), but is displaced by 0·5 eV. in the direction of lower energy. Thus the energy that a quantum of radiation must have in order to eject an

† A. L. Hughes and L. A. DuBridge, *Photoelectric Phenomena*, p. 161 (New York, 1932).

‡ N. F. Mott, *Trans. Faraday Soc.* **34**, 500 (1938).

‖ Z. Gyulai, *Zeits. f. Physik*, **35**, 411 (1926).

electron from metallic sodium into the conduction levels of sodium-chloride is 0·5 eV. less than the work $\phi$ required to eject it into a vacuum.

These experiments may be interpreted in terms of Fig. 67 (Chap. V, p. 169), which represents the energy levels of a metal in contact with an insulator. Assuming that the contact is so close that the barrier between the metal and salt is of negligible thickness, so that electrons can penetrate it quite easily, it is clear that the work necessary to eject electrons from the metal into the conduction band is $\phi-\chi$. Thus for sodium-chloride

$$\chi \sim 0·5 \text{ eV.}$$

In Chapters V and VII we obtain similar information for $Cu_2O$ and for AgBr (pp. 185, 245).

The contact between a metal and an insulator will be discussed in greater detail in Chapter V. It is of course open to question whether the surface layers of the metal and salt will be distorted in such a way as to set up an electrical double layer, owing to the intimate contact which exists when the metal is formed photochemically from the salt. In § 7, however, we give an alternative method of calculating $\chi$ which for NaCl gives a value in good agreement with that found here.

## 4. Positive holes in ionic crystals

From the point of view of the collective electron treatment the highest full band in alkali-halide crystals corresponds to the outermost $p$ electrons of the halide ions. Similarly, in oxides the full band corresponds to the $p$ electrons of the oxide ion, $O^{--}$. The question arises as to the width and form of such a band of occupied levels.

These quantities can, as in the case of metals,[†] be deduced from measurements of the wave-length range of the X-rays emitted when the substance is bombarded with electrons of suitable energy. Under the bombardment, electrons are ejected from one (or more) of the inner X-ray levels of the ions of the crystal, and the vacancies are then filled by electrons falling down from any level in the upper full band with the emission of an X-ray quantum. That a range of emitted quantum energies is to be expected in transitions where the outermost electrons fall into an inner X-ray level should be clear from Fig. 26; the electron may come from any one of the broad band of states. It is found that this band can be determined most accurately by investigations in the region of *soft* X-rays, from about 10 A upwards.

After the emission process, a positive hole remains in the full band;

† H. W. B. Skinner, *Reports on Progress in Physics*, **5**, 257 (1938).

the breadth of the band actually gives the energy spectrum of a positive
hole (cf. §§ 2.1). This interpretation does not depend on the validity
or otherwise of the collective electron treatment. The band-width is
of particular interest as giving an indication of the 'effective mass'
(§ 1) of a positive hole. If the band-
width is large ($\sim 10$ eV.) we expect the
effective mass to be of the order of that
of a free electron, or even, as we shall see
(p. 76), considerably less; if, on the other
hand, it is narrow ($\sim 1$ eV. or less) the
effective mass should be considerably
higher than that of an electron.

In Fig. 27 we show some emission
bands obtained by O'Bryan and
Skinner† for oxides and for boron
nitride and silicon carbide. The bombardment of the crystal removes electrons from an X-ray level of both the
oxygen and metal ions, and emission
bands are obtained corresponding to
both types of transition, as indicated

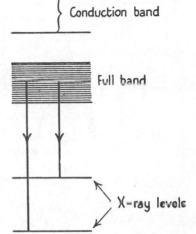

FIG. 26. Showing emission of X-ray
bands in an insulator

in Fig. 26. In all these bands the electrons come from the energy levels
corresponding to the oxygen ions; the X-ray levels may be considered
sharp. In Fig. 27, for each of the five oxides the isolated peak at the
right is the oxygen $K$-spectrum, which consists of a single band with a
breadth of about 10 eV. It has a well-defined structure, and in the
examples of Fig. 27 it will be seen that, in spite of differences in detail,
there is a marked resemblance of form for these oxides, which all have
hexagonal crystal structures. The cubic oxides, as O'Bryan and Skinner
have shown, give bands of quite a different characteristic form. It is
reasonable to suppose that all these bands represent closely the level
structure of the six $2p$-electrons of the oxygen ion since the transition
probabilities for the two $2s$-electrons to the $K$ level will be very small.
Band-widths for some cubic oxides are shown below:

|  | $Li_2O$ | CaO | SrO | BaO |
|---|---|---|---|---|
| Band width (eV.) . | 12·8 | 10·8 | 9·2 | 8·4 |

The $K$ and $L_3$ emission spectra of the *metallic* ions of the oxides are
shown on the same diagram. They are very complex, and therefore

† H. M. O'Bryan and H. W. B. Skinner, *Proc. Roy. Soc.* (A) (to be published). We
are indebted to Dr. Skinner for giving us much detailed information about his results
prior to publication.

are much more difficult to interpret. For covalent compounds such as SiC, the characteristics appear to be similar to those found for lattices composed of only one element. We may consider BeO and MgO as the most ionic of these compounds; the remaining cases are intermediate.

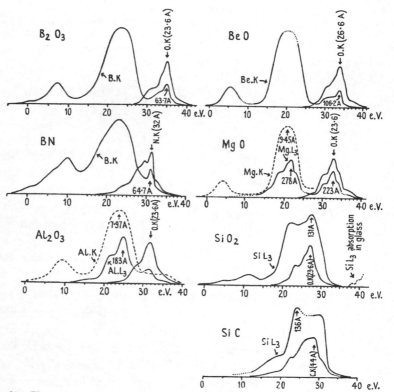

FIG. 27. X-ray emission bands for some oxides and for boron nitride and silicon carbide. The bands marked C.K, O.K, and N.K are the K-emission bands of the carbon, oxygen, and nitrogen ions respectively. The wave-lengths in Angstrom units of characteristic points of the bands are shown in each case.

For the boron and beryllium compounds the K-emission band of the metal ion is shown and for MgO and $Al_2O_3$ the K† and $L_{III}$ bands. These positive-ion bands are fitted on the energy scale to the negative-ion bands in such a way that the part of the former band which we believe to be due to the 2p-electrons of oxygen comes underneath the oxygen K-band

In the cases of the most ionic oxides, two characteristics of the metal-ion spectra seem to stand out.

1. There appears to be an identity in the case of the $L_3$ spectrum of Mg in MgO, and a more or less close parallelism in other cases, especially $B_2O_3$, BeO, between the high-energy part of the metal-ion spectrum

† H. Karlsson and M. Siegbahn, *Zeits. f. Physik*, 88, 76 (1934).

and the oxygen $K$-spectrum obtained from the oxide in question; for this reason the metallic ion's spectra have been placed on the diagram so that these bands come under the oxygen $K$-band.

2. There is a general tendency for parts of the observed spectrum to be duplicated at least approximately; e.g. in the case of MgO the detailed structure of the Mg $L_3$-spectrum and the smooth shape of the Mg $K$-spectrum both appear as double with an energy interval of 10 to 15 eV.

O'Bryan and Skinner consider that the broad smooth bands, for instance the central band in the case of BeO, represent the $2s$-electrons of the oxygen ion, which cannot make a transition into an oxygen $K$-level, but can make one into the $K$-shell of a positive ion, since for this the usual selection rules do not apply. The energy interval between this and the band of highest energy, which fairly certainly represents transitions of the oxygen $2p$-electrons into the inner shell of a metal ion, is about 10 volts, and this is nearly the value of the $2p$–$2s$ separation that one would estimate for the *free* oxygen ion. The $2s$ levels are supposed, apart from the effect of the lattice, to be broadened by a mechanism which we have no space to discuss here. It is, perhaps, surprising that the intensity of the $2s$-band in the $K$-spectra is so great. This probably means that the $2s$ wave functions overlap the positive ions considerably more than the $2p$ wave functions, in spite of the fact that the former lie lower in energy, and the behaviour must presumably be ascribed to a kind of resonance effect. The $2s$-levels, on the other hand, seem at most to show themselves weakly in the $L_3$ metal-ion spectra.

Thus we form the picture that the two parts of the band of highest energy, in the case of BeO for example, represent in a distorted form the $2p$- and $2s$-bands of the negative ions, the former of which is fairly accurately represented by the oxygen $K$-spectrum. There remains the problem of the duplication of the characteristic features of the bands. O'Bryan and Skinner suggest that this may be due to the following mechanism, analogous to one found to exist for soft X-ray emission from metals.

After the emission of the quantum, the lattice (apart from the hole in its band of valence levels) may not always be left in its lowest state: it may be left in a *discrete* excited state in which an electron is transferred, by a secondary transition, from an oxygen ion on to a neighbouring positive ion. Thus the repetition of observed characteristics of a band at a lower energy in the spectrum is accounted for if the

energy of the excited state of the crystal is 10 to 15 eV. above the
ground state. Such an excited state of the lattice is, as we shall see,
one which is used to explain the first ultra-violet absorption band of
a crystal. If the above explanation is correct, it shows that this
absorption band should occur, for the oxides, at an energy of 10 to
15 eV., and thus for a wave-length of the order of 1,000 A.

In $Al_2O_3$ and SiC, which are probably progressively less polar in
character, the metal emission bands suggest that the oxygen bands
have broadened in such a way that the $2s$- and $2p$-bands overlap and
the similarity of form with the negative-ion spectrum becomes lost.

Whatever may be the final interpretation of the complexities of the
positive-ion spectra, there can be little doubt that the oxygen $K$-
spectrum represents the $2p$-level system of the negative ions. The high-
energy tail of the oxygen band will be noticed. A band form of this
type implies that the effective mass of a positive hole near the top of
the band, and thus in its state of lowest energy, will be small, considerably less than that of a free electron.† Some evidence that this is
in fact the case is given in Chap. V, § 5.

Fig. 28 shows similar $2p$-bands of levels for the crystalline metallic
halides deduced from the emission bands. A part of the radiation
observed to be emitted from the negative ion has been ascribed by
O'Bryan and Skinner to the effect of double ionization, and has therefore been omitted in the diagram. The bands for the fluorides are from
the $K$-emission spectra, and those for the bromides are deduced from
transitions in which the final state is a $d$-level; the bands, therefore,
are due to the six $p$-electrons in the halide ion. For the chlorides the
bands are deduced from the $L_{2,3}$ emission spectrum, and are thus due
to the two $3s$-electrons.

It will be noticed that the bands are much narrower than the corresponding bands for oxides. This shows, as might have been expected,
that the negative ions overlap each other much less in the halides than
in the oxides. Also the figure shows that as the atomic number of the
*metal* ion increases the band-width narrows. This must be because the
radii of the heavier metal ions are greater (p. 6) and so, as the atomic
number of the metal ion increases, the halide ions are pushed farther
apart and overlap less with each other. A similar interpretation applies
to the oxide band-widths, given on p. 75. It will be seen that the
fluoride $2p$-bands show similar characteristics of form to those of
the oxide bands. The alkali bromides show a doublet structure; this

† This follows since near the top of the band the density of states is proportional to $m^{\frac{3}{2}}$

corresponds to the doublet structure of the bromine atom (p. 95). Thus for RbBr, at any rate, the interaction between the bromine ions is not sufficient to break down the spin-orbital interaction.

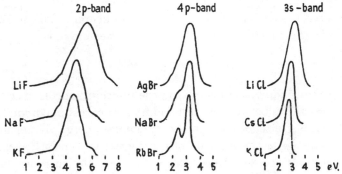

FIG. 28. Energy bands for the occupied states in metallic halides, deduced from X-ray emission bands (O'Bryan and Skinner, loc. cit.)

Table 18 gives the observed band-width for the fluorides and bromides and CsI. In contrast to the figures given for the oxides, these values represent 'half-widths', treating the band as a line. In the case of doublet bands, they refer only to one component.

TABLE 18. *Width of p-bands (eV.)*

| LiF | NaF | KF | LiBr | NaBr | KBr | RbBr | AgBr | CsI |
|-----|-----|-----|------|------|-----|------|------|-----|
| 2·1 | 1·7 | 1·5 | 1·2 | 0·75 | 0·55 | 0·45 | 1·1 | 0·7 |

Turning now to theoretical calculations, for sodium-chloride Slater[†] and his co-workers have obtained wave functions for the electrons in the full band (the 3p-band of Cl⁻). They find a breadth of about 4·5 eV.[‡] In this calculation each electron is treated as moving in an electrostatic field; it must, however, be recognized that to treat an electron in the full or partially filled band of a solid as moving in an electrostatic field involves a certain approximation, as the interaction with the other electrons is not equivalent to an electrostatic field (cf. p. 67). In view of O'Bryan and Skinner's results quoted above, we think this estimate for the breadth is too great. For lithium-fluoride Ewing and Seitz[||] have carried out similar calculations on the breadth for the 2p-band of the fluoride ion and find 2·3 eV., in good agreement with experiment.

† J. C. Slater and W. Shockley, *Phys. Rev.* **50**, 705 (1936); W. Shockley, ibid., p. 754.
‡ W. Shockley, loc. cit., Fig. 2.
|| D. H. Ewing and F. Seitz, ibid., p. 760.

If the band is narrow, as experiment suggests for the alkali-halides, one can calculate the position of its centre by means of a cycle, neglecting the interaction between the negative ions altogether. The steps in the cycle are as follows:

1. Remove a negative ion from the crystal, keeping the surrounding ions fixed in their mean positions. The work necessary is

$$\frac{\alpha e^2}{r_0} - 6w(r_0) - \tfrac{1}{2}e\phi.$$

Here $\alpha$ is the Madelung constant, $r_0$ the interionic distance, $w(r_0)$ the energy of repulsion between an ion and its six nearest neighbours. The first two terms are together equal to the lattice energy $W_L$ per ion pair of the crystal. $\phi$ is the electrostatic potential at the lattice point of the displaced ion due to the dipoles induced on the surrounding ions. This has been calculated by Mott and Littleton,† as explained in Chapter II, § 7.

2. Remove an electron from the negative ion forming a halogen atom, the necessary work is $E$, the electron affinity.

3. Replace the halogen atom; the necessary work may be assumed to be zero.

Adding up these energies, we obtain the work,

$$\psi = W_L - \tfrac{1}{2}e\phi + E, \tag{5}$$

which is necessary to remove an electron from the centre of the highest full band to a point outside the crystal. The values obtained are shown in Table 19.

If the band-width may be neglected, $\psi/h$ is the low-frequency limit for photoelectric emission from the crystal surface.

TABLE 19. *Energy $\psi$ required to remove an Electron from the Full Band to a Point outside the Crystal (Energies in eV.)*

| Crystal | $W_L$ | $\tfrac{1}{2}e\phi$ | $E$ | $\psi$ |
|---------|-------|---------------------|------|--------|
| NaCl .  . | 7·94 | 1·52₅ | 3·75 | 10·17 |
| KCl .  . | 7·18 | 1·44 | 3·75 | 9·49 |
| KBr .  . | 6·91 | 1·43 | 3·52 | 9·00 |

## 5. Trapping of electrons at irregularities in the crystal lattice

### 5.1. Trapping at lattice defects

We have hitherto been discussing crystals in which there is no electrostatic field other than the periodic field due to the ions of the

† N. F. Mott and M. J. Littleton, *Trans. Faraday Soc.* **34**, 485 (1938).

lattice. For an electron in the conduction band the free motion through-out the whole crystal depends upon the fact that every positive ion offers a position of exactly equal energy; and likewise for a positive hole every negative ion offers a position of exactly equal energy.

Any irregularity in a crystal, such as a foreign atom in solid solution, or a vacant lattice point, or a surface or crack, will lead to a modification of this crystal field  For many of the discussions of this book, it is important to know whether an electron can be 'trapped' by one of these irregularities; in other words, whether the modification in the field leads to the existence of one or more discrete energy levels *below* the lowest state of the conduction band.

We shall first discuss the number of discrete stationary states for electrons in 'potential holes', treating the crystal as a continuous medium in which the field tends to zero outside the 'hole'. The exten-sion to the case of an electron in an actual crystal lattice will be con-sidered later. If $V(r)$ is the potential energy of the electron in the 'hole', we have then to investigate under what conditions the Schrödinger equation

$$\nabla^2\psi + \frac{2m}{\hbar^2}(E-V)\psi = 0 \tag{6}$$

has solutions with discrete energy values, corresponding to a bound electron.

The following theorems may easily be verified:

I. If $V(r)$ tends to zero more rapidly than $1/r$, the number of states will be finite, *and may be zero*. For instance, if

$$V(r) = -\frac{e^2}{r}\exp(-qr), \tag{7}$$

or if

$$V(r) = -D \quad (r < a)$$
$$= 0 \quad (r >' a),$$

then the number of states is finite and will become zero if $q$ is large or $a$ small.

The field of an electron in a negative ion is of the form (7); for un-stable ions (e.g. A$^-$) no stationary states exist.

II. In the one-dimensional problem

$$V(x) = -D \quad (-a < x < a)$$
$$= 0 \quad (\text{otherwise})$$

there is always at least one stationary state however small $D$ and $a$ may be.

3595.32

III. If, for large $r$, $V(r) \sim -e^2/\kappa r$, where $\kappa$ is any positive constant, then there will be an infinite number of stationary states (as in an atom), *whatever the behaviour of $V(r)$ for small $r$*. For large azimuthal quantum number the energy will be given by the modified Bohr formula $E = -e^4 m/2\hbar^2 n^2 \kappa^2$.

Theorems I and II are elementary and may be proved very easily. We shall give a proof of III, which is of great importance in certain problems treated in this book. We shall limit ourselves to the case of spherical symmetry. Then the Schrödinger equation (6) becomes

$$\frac{d^2}{dr^2}(r\psi) + \frac{2m}{\hbar^2}(E-V)r\psi = 0, \tag{8}$$

and we require a solution such that $r\psi$ vanishes at the origin and at infinity.

Consider a negative value of $E$, and the corresponding solution $r\psi$ which vanishes at the origin. For sufficiently large $r$, $V(r)$ may be replaced by $-e^2/\kappa r$. Let us choose $|E|$ so small that $E-V$ is positive for a range of $r$ where this substitution may be made. Let $r_0$ be the radius such that
$$V(r_0) = -E.$$
Consider two radii $\alpha r_0$, $\beta r_0$ such that

$$\alpha < \beta < 1. \tag{9}$$

Then in the range $\alpha r_0 < r < \beta r_0$

$$E - V > \frac{e^2}{\kappa \beta r_0} + E.$$

Therefore the distance between successive zeros of the function $r\psi$ is less than

$$\frac{1}{2}\left\{\frac{2m}{\hbar^2}\left(\frac{e^2}{\kappa \beta r_0} + E\right)\right\}^{-\frac{1}{2}}.$$

Therefore at least $n$ zeros of the function will occur for $\alpha r_0 < r < \beta r_0$ if

$$\frac{1}{2}\left\{\frac{2m}{\hbar^2}\left(\frac{e^2}{\kappa \beta r_0} + E\right)\right\}^{-\frac{1}{2}} < \frac{(\beta-\alpha)r_0}{n}$$

or, substituting for $E$,

$$\sqrt{\left\{\frac{\hbar^2 \kappa}{2me^2}\middle/\left(\frac{1}{\beta}-1\right)\right\}} < \frac{\beta-\alpha}{n} r_0^{\frac{1}{2}}. \tag{10}$$

We may take arbitrary values of $\alpha$, $\beta$, subject to (9). Then, for given $n$, (10) can always be satisfied by taking $r_0$ large enough, i.e. by taking $|E|$ small enough.

Thus, however great $n$ may be, we can find a solution $\psi$ of (8) bounded at the origin and having $n$ zeros. Consider now the solution with $n$ zeros; as the energy is increased, a solution bounded at infinity must occur before the $(n+1)$th zero appears. It follows that an infinite series of solutions exist, which are bounded at the origin and at infinity.

This theorem can be extended to the case of electrons moving in a crystal lattice, if $V(r)$ is the *difference* between the actual potential and the periodic potential of the perfect lattice. Thus let $U(r)$ be the potential energy of an electron in the perfect lattice, and let

$$V(r) \sim -e^2/\kappa r$$

as before. We have then to show that the equation

$$\nabla^2 \psi + \frac{2m}{\hbar^2}(E - V - U)\psi = 0$$

has an infinite series of solutions, corresponding to bound states of the electron, with energies below each allowed band of levels of the perfect lattice.

Let $E_0$ be the lowest energy level in any one of the bands of allowed energy levels. The corresponding solution $u_0(x, y, z)$ is periodic with the period of the crystal lattice. The solution $\psi$ for any other energy $E$ lying in the band is of the form

$$\psi = A e^{i(\mathbf{kr})} u_k(x, y, z) + B e^{-i(\mathbf{kr})} u_k^*(x, y, z),$$

where $u_k$ also is periodic. If $E - E_0$ is small compared with the width of the band, the relation between $k$ and $E$ is

$$E - E_0 = \hbar^2 k^2 / 2m^*,$$

where $m^*$ is the 'effective mass' of an electron with energy in the band considered. The theorem is also valid if $E - E_0$ is small and negative; $k$ is then imaginary.

In view of these properties of the wave function, one can prove in just the same way as before that, by taking $E - E_0$ negative but $|E - E_0|$ small, solutions of (8) may be found having any number of zeros in addition to those of the functions $u_k$, and tending to zero exponentially for large distances. Thus a series of bound levels must exist below the conduction band. *For large distances, in fact, where $V(r)$ is small, the electron will behave exactly like a free electron with mass $m^*$.*

For levels of high quantum number (especially those of high azimuthal quantum number) the state of affairs for small $r$ should be unimportant, and we should have $E - E_0$ given by the hydrogen-like formula

$$E - E_0 = -\frac{e^4 m^*}{2\hbar^2} \frac{1}{n^2 \kappa^2} = -\frac{1}{n^2 \kappa^2} \frac{m^*}{m} \times 13 \cdot 53 \text{ eV.},$$

where $n$ is an integral quantum number. For the conduction band of polar crystals, $m^*/m$ is probably of the order unity.

These formulae bring out a point about electrons in crystal 'lattices which is important for many of the discussions of this book; namely, that in considering the behaviour of an electron in the field of some extraneous charge, we can treat it like an electron in a vacuum, but with the appropriate effective mass. The lattice field will impose periodic fluctuations on the wave function of the electron; but it will not prevent the electron, trapped in a field of the type described, from having a quite definite wave function, similar to that of an electron in an atom *in vacuo*; and this wave function may well spread over many atomic 'distances of the crystal.

The physical examples to which this theorem is applied in this book are:

1. The field round an interstitial positive ion.

2. The field round a lattice point from which a negative ion is missing.

3. The field round a 'positive hole'.†

According to our theorem, an electron can be trapped in the field of any of these, there being an infinite series of stationary states leading up to a series limit. We may mention that a 'positive hole' can be trapped, similarly, in the field of an interstitial negative ion or a missing positive ion; but a separate discussion of these will not be necessary.

In all these cases the electron may, to a fair approximation, be treated as moving simply in a field $e/\kappa r^2$; $\kappa$ is a suitable value of the dielectric constant which will be discussed below.

We have seen that the excited states of the trapped electron form a system similar to that of an isolated atom in a vacuum. We can, however, predict that in two important respects they will be different. Consider, for example, an isolated potassium atom; its ionization potential is 4·3 eV., while the energy of its first excited state is only 1·6 eV.; that is to say, its set of excited states are spread over a range of 2·7 eV. In a crystal we must expect the excited states to occupy a much narrower range of energy owing to the term $\kappa^2$ in the above formula for $E-E_0$.

In a crystal, then, we must get used to the idea that, when an electron has been raised to its *lowest* excited state, it requires only a small additional energy before it becomes free; and this small energy can often be supplied by the thermal vibrations of the lattice (Chap. IV, § 6).

† In a perfect crystal the combination of electron and positive hole trapped in one another's field is able to move as a whole through the crystal. It is called an 'exciton'. Excitons are discussed in § 6.

The other respect in which the excited states will differ from those in a vacuum is that the orbits of the electron may be much larger. Owing to the weak binding forces, the wave functions will be spread out over a larger volume (cf. Chap. V, § 4).

Another point which must be emphasized is that the field $V(r)$ depends on the wave function of the electron. To see this, let us consider a singly charged interstitial positive ion, or else a vacant lattice point from which a singly charged negative ion has been removed. In either case there exists round it a field of intensity

$$e/\kappa r^2,$$

where $\kappa$ is the dielectric constant for static fields. If now an electron is trapped in this field, the centre as a whole is neutral and there is no field at large distances. If an electron were removed instantaneously from the centre to a more distant point at a distance $r$, the field in which it would move there would be $e/\kappa_0 r^2$, where $\kappa_0$ is the dielectric constant when the ions are held in their normal positions. To find the field at smaller distances one would have to know the wave function of the electron. At large distances from the centre the medium is unpolarized, and the field is $e/\kappa_0 r^2$; at small distances it is $e/\kappa r^2$. At intermediate distances, let $p(r)$ be the fraction of the electron's charge normally within a radius $r$. Then the field is

$$\frac{e}{\kappa r^2}[1-p(r)]+\frac{e}{\kappa_0 r^2}p(r)$$

and our potential $V(r)$ is the potential of this. Since, if $\psi$ is the wave function of the electron,

$$p(r) = \int\limits_0^r |\psi|^2\, 4\pi r^2\, dr,$$

and since $\psi$ and $V$ are related by Schrödinger's equation, they could only be calculated by a self-consistent method. Calculations of this type have not been carried out.

We see from these considerations that if an electron makes an optical transition from one state to another, the wave function of the final state will be determined by the potential function $V(r)$ appropriate to the initial state. The ions surrounding the centre will move into new positions of equilibrium *after* the absorption act. Thus after the absorption act the positions of the levels will change. This is discussed further in Chap. V, § 3.

### 5.2. Surface levels

It was first pointed out by Tamm,[†] that if a perfectly periodic field is broken off along some surface, there will exist at that surface *bound* levels, in which an electron can exist without being free to move through the crystal. In our case we see that, if the quantum-mechanical exchange effect be neglected, the work required to bring an electron from infinity to a metal ion on the surface is

$$\frac{\alpha' e^2}{r_0} - I \quad (\alpha' = 1 \cdot 681), \tag{11}$$

which is *less* than that required to bring an electron into the body of the crystal. Similarly, the work required to remove an electron from a halogen ion on the surface will be

$$\frac{\alpha' e^2}{r_0} + E.$$

Both positive hole and electron will be free to migrate from atom to atom along the surface, but will have to receive energy $(\alpha - \alpha') e^2 / r_0$ before they can migrate into the interior of the crystal. Actually the surface levels may well be much lower than formula (11) suggests. Formula (11) gives the value that the energy would have if the electron were localized at the lattice point considered; actually its wave function extends towards the outside of the crystal, where, as Fig. 23 shows, the potential energy drops below the value that it would have if the ion were in the body of the crystal.

We do not know of any very definite experimental evidence about the existence of Tamm levels; see, however, Chap. VI, § 2, p. 215.

### 5.3. Landau's trapped electrons in a perfect lattice

We have seen that an electron introduced from outside into a polar lattice is perfectly free to move from ion to ion, and behaves very like a free electron so long as the ions of the lattice remain at rest in their positions of equilibrium. When, however, we take into account the fact that the ions can be displaced by an electric field, the position is somewhat different.

Let us imagine that by some supernatural agency an electron could be held at rest in one of the metal ions for a time long compared with the vibrational period, say $10^{-12}$ sec. Then the crystal would become polarized round this electron; at distances from the electron so large

---

† I. Tamm, *Zeits. f. Physik*, **76**, 849 (1932); *Phys. Zeits. d. Sowjetunion*, **1**, 733 (1932). See also E. T. Goodwin, *Proc. Cambridge Phil. Soc.* **35**, 205 (1939), and W. Shockley, *Phys. Rev.* **56**, 317 (1939).

that the atomic structure of the crystal could be neglected the force (on an electron) would be $e^2/\kappa r^2$

outwards, where $\kappa$ is the dielectric constant. We have seen (Chap. I, § 5) that the polarization of a polar medium is partly due to the displacement of the ions themselves. If the ions did not move, the field would be $e^2/\kappa_0 r^2$.

The force on an electron in the crystal, therefore, due to the actual displacement of the ions is

$$- \frac{e^2}{r^2}\left(\frac{1}{\kappa_0} - \frac{1}{\kappa}\right).$$

The displacement of the ions, therefore, creates a field which tends to prevent the electron from escaping from its place.

Now let us imagine that the ions, again by some supernatural agency, are held in their displaced positions, while the electron is removed from the crystal. There will then exist in the crystal, superimposed on the periodic field of the unperturbed crystal, a field in which the potential energy of a negative charge can be described as a 'potential hole' of the type considered in § 5.1. Moreover, since this potential behaves at infinity as $-1/r$, it follows that an electron can be captured in this potential hole and that in fact a whole series of energy levels exist in which the electron is bound in its neighbourhood.

Now if an electron is introduced into this potential hole and its energy assumes one of the quantized values, the displaced positions of the neighbouring ions become stable. We have thus a stable configuration; an electron surrounded by a polarized medium. We shall call such an electron 'an electron trapped by digging its own hole'. The conception was first introduced by Landau,[†] and has been discussed by von Hippel,[‡] Gurney and Mott,[||] and others. If the electron migrates through the crystal, moving from atom to atom, *at the same time* the surrounding ions must move into new displaced positions as required. Owing to the large mass of the ions the required configurations will occur very seldom at low temperatures. It follows that the mobility of one of these electrons is very much less than that of an electron in the conduction band.

It must be emphasized that if an electron is introduced into the conduction band it will move about for some time before it polarizes

† L. Landau, *Phys. Zeits. d. Sowjetunion*, **3**, 664 (1933).

‡ A. von Hippel, *Zeits. f. Physik*, **101**, 680 (1936).

|| R. W. Gurney and N. F. Mott, *Proc. Phys. Soc.* **49**, extra part, 32 (1937); N. F. Mott, *Nature*, **139**, 951 (1937).

the medium round itself and becomes trapped, because in general an electron moves from atom to atom in a time much less than the $10^{-12}$ sec. required for the ions to move to new positions of equilibrium.

A point of interest is that this trapping must be possible in all polar crystals, because the potential of the field due to the displaced ions falls off as $1/r$. For monatomic substances, on the other hand, this is not the case. A point-charge distant $r$ from a neutral atom will exert on it a force proportional to $1/r^4$, so that the displacement of the atoms from their mean positions is also proportional to $1/r^4$. The atoms being neutral, the change in the potential due to the displacement of the atoms is also proportional to $1/r^4$; it follows from the considerations of § 5.1 that the number of stationary states in the hole is at most finite, and there may be none at all.

In the literature† it has often been assumed that the 'F-centres' investigated by Pohl and others are electrons trapped in this way. In Chapter IV we shall show, however, that this hypothesis cannot be maintained and that F-centres are probably electrons trapped at points where a negative ion is missing.

We do not know of any definite evidence that trapping of the kind described here ever takes place. Experiments on photoconductivity in alkali-halides seem to show that an electron which has been raised into the conduction levels by the absorption of a quantum of light is captured at a point where an F-centre already exists (cf. Chap. IV, § 5). If this is the case, we must assume that the probability of trapping at any of the relatively few points where a negative ion is missing is much greater than at any of the ordinary lattice points.

Nevertheless, we feel convinced that the theoretical arguments for the existence of electrons trapped in this way are correct; it is surprising that there is no experimental evidence that trapping of this type takes place.

Naturally, positive holes can be trapped in a similar manner. In alkali and silver halides, owing to the high effective mass of a positive hole, this trapping may take place more easily.

## 6. Absorption of light by non-metals

The absorption spectrum of a solid insulator differs in important respects from that of a free molecule on the one hand and that of a metal on the other. We must treat our crystal as a single giant molecule, and calculate the energies of its excited states and the transition

† A. von Hippel, loc. cit.; R. W. Gurney and N. F. Mott, loc. cit.

probabilities between them. As in the analogous case of molecules, the calculation falls into two halves: we calculate first the energy that the electrons would have if the nuclei were at rest in their mean positions, and then take into account the vibration of the nuclei. In our case we consider first the excited states that the crystal would have if the nuclei were at rest in their positions of equilibrium in the unexcited crystal.

In this section we confine ourselves also to the absorption spectrum characteristic of the pure solid; for the wave-lengths for which the absorption reaches its greatest value the absorption coefficient is very large, of the order $10^5$ cm.$^{-1}$ The absorption coefficients discussed are thus obtained for thin films.

Peierls[†] showed first that the optical absorption spectrum of an ideal insulating crystal in which the atoms are supposed fixed in their mean positions would be similar to that of a vapour of free atoms. It consists of a series of sharp lines leading up to a series limit, beyond which there will be a continuous absorption band. In this respect the absorption spectrum of a non-metal is in sharp contrast to that of a metal, which consists of continuous bands only.

The reason why one obtains absorption lines may be understood as follows. In order that a quantum of light shall be absorbed it is necessary that an electron should be removed from the full band of levels to the empty conduction band of levels. If the quantum of light has sufficient energy, a free positive hole and a free electron will be produced, both of which can move independently through the lattice. It is not, however, necessary that the light quantum should have enough energy to separate the electron and positive hole. As we have seen, in the field of any positive charge there will always exist a series of bound stationary states for an electron, leading up to a series limit. A series of states of this type must exist in the field of a positive hole. Or, more exactly, since electron and positive hole both have effective masses of the same order of magnitude, there will exist for the pair of them a series of stationary states in which they both revolve round their centre of mass. The electron and positive hole may move as a whole through the crystal, or may be at rest. For given velocity of their centre of mass, then, we have a series of stationary states leading up to a series limit.

An electron and positive hole coupled together in this way have

† R. Peierls, *Ann. d. Physik*, **13**, 905 (1932). Cf. also for the development of these ideas: J. Frenkel, *Phys. Rev.* **37**, 17 (1931); *Phys. Zeits. d. Sowjetunion*, **8**, 185 (1935), **9**, 158 (1936); J. C. Slater and W. Shockley, *Phys. Rev.* **50**, 705 (1936); G. H. Wannier, ibid. **52**, 191 (1937).

been called by Frenkel an 'exciton'. An exciton in a given excited state may, as we have seen, be at rest, or may move as a whole through the crystal. In the latter case its momentum will be described by a wave vector **k** which can have all values between $-\pi/a$ and $+\pi/a$, where $a$ is the lattice parameter of the crystal. Thus each state of excitation of the exciton gives rise to a band of energy levels for the crystal as a whole. The unexcited crystal can, however, only make transitions to *one* of the states of each band, namely that with wave vector **k** equal to the wave vector **q** of the absorbed quantum. The proof will be given below.

We see then that the absorption spectrum of a non-metal should consist of a series of sharp lines leading up to a series limit beyond which there will be true continuous absorption. The continuous absorption in a crystal, unlike that of a vapour, may be expected to show a structure, for the same reason that a structure is observed to the short-wave-length side of the X-ray absorption edge in metals,[†] namely, the existence of overlapping energy bands for an electron in a crystal lattice (cf. Fig. 29 b).

The effect of lattice vibrations will be to broaden the absorption lines into bands. Even at the absolute zero of temperature some broadening is to be expected, owing to the zero-point vibrations. As the temperature is raised, the broadening will increase.

Fig. 29 a shows the absorption spectrum of a (metallic) vapour.[‡] Fig. 29 b shows the type of absorption spectrum that we expect for a non-metallic crystal, and Fig. 31 on p. 96 some absorption spectra for the alkali-halides.

In the discussion given above we have approached the problem from

---

[†] Cf. N. F. Mott and H. Jones, *The Theory of the Properties of Metals and Alloys*, p. 128 (Oxford, 1936), and H. Jones and N. F. Mott, *Proc. Roy. Soc.* (A), **162**, 49 (1937).

[‡] The fact calls for comment that, both for free atoms and for insulators the absorption is finite at the series limit, although the density of electronic states varies as $\sqrt{E}$, where $E$ is the energy of the electron after the absorption. The transition probability is given by the square of an integral of the type

$$\int \psi_0 x \psi_f \, d\tau,$$

where $\psi_0$ is the wave function of the initial state, $\psi_f$ that of the final state. $\psi_f$, normalized to represent a plane wave $e^{ikz}$ at infinity, is equal at the origin to $e^{\frac{1}{2}\pi\alpha}\Gamma(1-i\alpha)$ (cf. N. F. Mott and H. S. W. Massey, *The Theory of Atomic Collisions*, p. 35 (Oxford, 1933)). Here $\alpha$ denotes $e^2/\hbar v$, where $\frac{1}{2}mv^2 = E$. Thus

$$\psi^2 = 2\pi\alpha/(1 - e^{-2\pi\alpha})$$

$$\sim 2\pi\alpha \quad \text{as } \alpha \to \infty.$$

Thus, although the density of states tends to zero as $E^{\frac{1}{2}}$, the transition probability tends to infinity as $1/E^{\frac{1}{2}}$, and so the absorption coefficient remains finite.

the point of view of the collective electron treatment. We may also approach it from the alternative point of view, which regards the crystal as made up of a number of atoms which interact only slightly with their neighbours.†

Let us denote by $\psi_n(x)$ the wave function of an unexcited atom

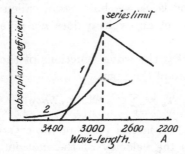

FIG. 29 a. Absorption coefficient of a metallic vapour (potassium): (1) calculated (Oppenheimer);‡ (2) observed (Ditchburn)||

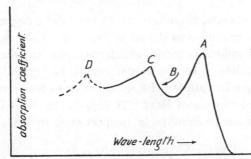

FIG. 29 b. Theoretical absorption spectrum of an insulating crystal. (A) One (or more) absorption lines broadened by the lattice vibrations. (B) Unresolved lines leading up to the series limit. (C) The series limit. To the left of C: continuous absorption showing structure (as at D) depending on the lattice field

located at the lattice point $n$, and let $\psi'_n(x)$ be the wave function of the excited atom. Then we may form a crystal by bringing together $N-1$ unexcited atoms and one excited one. If the excited atom is placed at the lattice point $n$, the wave function will be††

$$\Psi_n(x_1,...,x_N) = \psi_1(x_1)...\psi'_n(x_n)...\psi_N(x_N).$$

† This discussion is due originally to R. Peierls, *Ann. d. Physik*, **13**, 905 (1932).

‡ J. R. Oppenheimer, *Zeits. f. Physik*, **41**, 268 (1927).

|| R. W. Ditchburn, *Proc. Roy. Soc.* (A), **117**, 486 (1928); *Zeits. f. Physik*, **107**, 719 (1937).

†† Strictly speaking, a wave function antisymmetrical in the coordinates of the electrons should be written down, but this is not relevant to our discussion.

This is the wave function of a crystal with the atom $n$ excited. However, the excited atom $n$ can exchange its energy with its neighbour, so that, for example, the atom $n+1$ becomes excited and the atom $n$ unexcited. The region of excitation can wander round the crystal, without, of course, any of the atoms themselves moving. A wandering region of excitation of this kind is, as we have seen, called an 'exciton'. It is clear that the motion of an exciton does *not* give rise to an electric current.

It may be shown that the wave functions of these excitons moving through the crystal are of the form

$$\Psi_k^c = \sum_n e^{i(\mathbf{k}\mathbf{r}_n)}\Psi_n^c(x_1,...,x_N),$$

where $\mathbf{r}_n$ denotes the $n$th lattice point of the crystal and $\mathbf{k}$ the 'wave number' which gives the velocity of the motion. The energy $W(\mathbf{k})$ of the exciton depends on $\mathbf{k}$, and ranges from a maximum to a minimum value. The dependence on $\mathbf{k}$ will be the same as that given by formula (3) on p. 69.

The energy spectrum, therefore, of an insulating crystal in which a single electron is excited is as shown in Fig. 30 a. There will be a series of bands of non-conducting levels (which may overlap), and above them a band corresponding to conducting states of the crystal.

We have now to investigate the selection rules for electronic transitions under the influence of light. If $2\pi/q$ is the wave-length of the light, the transition probability is proportional to the square of the integral

$$\int \Psi_0^c(x) \sum_n e^{i(\mathbf{q}\cdot\mathbf{x}_n)} \frac{\partial}{\partial x_n} \Psi_k^c(x)\, dx,$$

where $\Psi_0^c$ is the wave function of the unexcited crystal and $x$ is written for all the coordinates. It is clear that this integral vanishes unless

$$\mathbf{k}+\mathbf{q} = 0,$$

which is the required selection rule. Since, if $a$ is the interatomic distance, $q$ is small compared with $1/a$, this gives approximately

$$\mathbf{k} \sim 0.$$

Thus optical transitions are only possible to one particular state in each of the non-conducting bands. It follows that (neglecting nuclear vibrations) the absorption spectrum of an insulating solid consists of a series of sharp lines leading up to a continuous band. This analysis also, then, shows that the absorption spectrum is similar to that of a free atom and markedly different from that of a metal, which seems to consist of bands only (see below). The experiments on absorption in insulators are discussed in §§ 7, 8.

The series limit will not in general have the energy of the lowest conducting state, because the transition from the ground state is forbidden. This should be clear from Fig. 30 (b) which shows the Brillouin zones in k-space for an insulator with the simple cubic

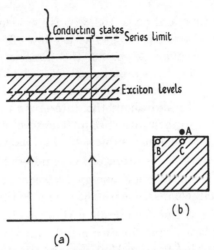

(a)

Fig. 30.  Energy levels of crystal as a whole; the vertical
lines show allowed transitions

structure.† The first zone is normally occupied by electrons, and the other zones empty. If the crystal is in the lowest conducting state, there will be a positive hole at the point $B$ in the first zone and an electron at the point $A$ in the second zone. To produce these two through the absorption of a single quantum would obviously correspond to a forbidden transition; the series limit will correspond to the formation of an electron at $A$ and a hole at $C$.

In the same way the exciton of lowest energy will correspond to the coupling together of a hole and electron at $B$ and $A$, while the first absorption line will correspond to the formation of a hole at $C$ coupled to an electron at $A$.

If the energy spectrum of the positive holes is a band of several electron-volts in width (as in oxides, cf. p. 76), then there may be a wide band of exciton levels and even of conducting levels below the first optically allowed exciton level. Probably, owing to lattice imperfections

† Cf. N. F. Mott and H. Jones, *The Theory of the Properties of Metals and Alloys*, Fig. 24, p. 65 (Oxford, 1936).

and thermal and zero-point vibrations, these transitions are not absolutely forbidden, but allowed with a small transition probability. We make the tentative suggestion that the long-wave-length tail of the absorption band observed in many insulators is due to these transitions (cf. Fig. 33). This explanation accounts for the absence of such a tail in NaCl (Fig. 33d), because the full band is narrow in the alkali-halides (cf. p. 79).

In § 4 of this chapter and on p. 168, we give evidence that a positive hole near the top of a full band has a very low effective mass. Thus, according to the formulae of p. 83, the dissociation energy $E - E_0$ should be rather small. This may account for the absence of any line spectra in the long-wave-length tail (cf. also Chap. IV, § 6.2).

A few words may be said about the differences between metals and insulators in respect to their absorption. The results of the calculation given above are quite rigorous, subject to the following assumptions:

1. The ground state of the atom or ion is non-degenerate.

2. The 'exchange' interaction energy between neighbouring atoms or ions is small compared with the excitation potential.

Condition (1) is not true for metals with an odd number of valence electrons, and (2) is not true for any metal. As we have stated (§ 2), for metals the use of the London-Heitler approximation is very difficult and the collective electron treatment has proved more fruitful.

Let us then consider the absorption of light by a metal from the point of view of the latter model. Suppose that an electron is ejected into one of the empty states of the conduction band. Then a 'positive hole' is left behind, just as in an insulator. The difference between the metal and the insulator is that, whereas in the latter the potential energy of the electron in the field of the 'hole' is of the form $-e^2/\kappa r$, in a metal it is of the form† $-e^2/r \exp(-qr)$, where $q$ is a screening constant. Without detailed calculation, one cannot say whether the latter field will give rise to any stationary states at all.

From the optical absorption of metals it is difficult to deduce with certainty that no line absorption is present because total reflection rather than absorption is mainly responsible for their optical properties. The most direct evidence comes from the fine structure of the X-ray absorption edge of metals such as lithium; no trace of line absorption is found.‡

† N. F. Mott, *Proc. Cambridge Phil. Soc.* **32**, 281 (1936); N. F. Mott and H. Jones, *The Theory of the Properties of Metals and Alloys*, p. 86 (Oxford, 1936).

‡ H. W. B. Skinner and J. E. Johnston, *Proc. Roy. Soc.* (A), **161**, 420 (1937).

## 7. The ultra-violet absorption spectrum of alkali-halide crystals

It is to be emphasized that in the region of true characteristic absorption, where every atom of the crystal absorbs, the absorption coefficient is very large, of the order $10^5$ to $10^6$ cm.$^{-1}$ Absorption measurements in the region of true characteristic absorption must therefore be carried out with very thin films.

The ultra-violet absorption spectra of the alkali-halides have been investigated by Hilsch and Pohl[†] and their colleagues, and by Schneider and O'Bryan.[‡] Schneider and O'Bryan's results are shown in Fig. 31, and some of those obtained by the Göttingen school in Fig. 32.

We discuss first the absorption spectra of the fluorides and chlorides. In view of the considerations of the last section, the form of the absorption strongly suggests that in Fig. 31 for the chlorides the second peak (the third in caesium-chloride) represents the series limit.[||]

In order to understand the absorption spectra of the bromides and iodides we have to consider rather more closely the mechanism of absorption. An electron is ejected from a halogen negative ion; a neutral halogen atom is left behind. The ground state of a halogen atom is, however, a doublet, the separations being

| F | Cl | Br | I |
|------|------|------|------|
| 0·03 | 0·11 | 0·44 | 0·94 eV. |

For fluorine and chlorine these are below the limits of resolution in the absorption experiments; for the bromides and iodides they cause splitting of each line into a doublet, as the curves for the bromides show clearly.[††]

In all of these the first peak appears as a doublet; and the second, also, for rubidium- and caesium-bromide. For the sodium- and potassium-bromides the latter doublet does not seem to be resolved; since the quantum number $j$ has the value $\frac{3}{2}$ for the lowest state of the doublet and $\frac{1}{2}$ for the upper state, the first line of the doublet has twice the intensity of the second, and thus the series limit should be $\frac{1}{3} \times 0.44$ eV. below the observed peak.

The assumption that the second peak in the absorption spectrum

† R. Hilsch and R. W. Pohl, *Zeits. f. Physik,* **59,** 812 (1930); H. Fesefeldt, ibid. **64,** 623 (1930) (measurements at the temperatures of liquid hydrogen).

‡ E. G. Schneider and H. M. O'Bryan, *Phys. Rev.* **51,** 293 (1937).

|| N. F. Mott, *Trans. Faraday Soc.* **34,** 500 (1938).

†† Similar doublets are observed in the absorption spectra of iodide ions in solution in water, and were interpreted in this way by J. Franck and G. Scheibe, *Zeits. f. phys. Chem.* **139,** 22 (1928).

is the series limit has been used† to obtain an estimate of $-\chi$, the lowest energy of the conduction band (cf. p. 71). The calculation is

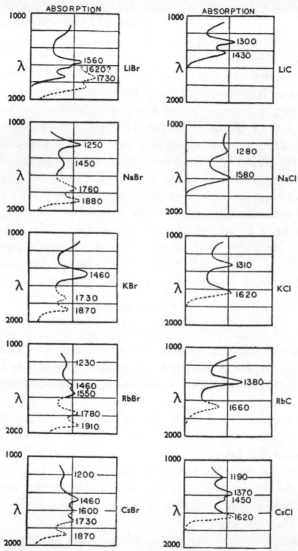

Fig. 31. Absorption spectra of alkali-halides, observed by Schneider and O'Bryan, at room temperatures. The dotted lines show results due to Hilsch and Pohl

based on the assumption that the breadth of the full band (Fig. 28) is negligible. The cycle is as follows:

† N. F. Mott, loc. cit.

1. Remove an electron from the full band to a point outside the crystal, keeping all the ions in their normal positions. We have shown on p. 80 that the necessary work is

$$W_L - \tfrac{1}{2}e\phi + E.$$

2. Bring the electron back into the conduction band, but to a point in space distant from the 'positive hole'. The necessary work is $-\chi$.

Thus if $\nu$ is the frequency of the series limit we have

$$h\nu = W_L - \tfrac{1}{2}e\phi + E - \chi. \tag{12}$$

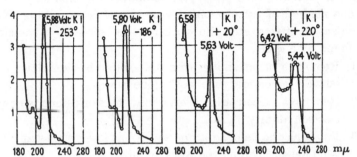

Fig. 32. Absorption spectra of KI; dependence of the first absorption band on temperature (Fesefeldt, loc. cit.)

Only for sodium-chloride have we independent experimental evidence of the value of $\chi$; we shall thus take the frequencies of the series limit shown in Fig. 31 and shall calculate $\chi$ from them. This is done in the following table. For sodium-chloride the agreement with the value of $\chi$ given on p. 74, namely 0·5 eV., is good.

TABLE 20

| Crystal | Position of second maximum in absorption spectrum | | Electron affinity‡ | Lattice energy‖ | $\tfrac{1}{2}\lvert e\phi \rvert$ | $-\chi$ |
|---|---|---|---|---|---|---|
| | A | eV. | eV. | eV. | eV. | eV. |
| RbF | 1,150 | 10·7 | 4·15 | 7·85 | .. | .. |
| NaCl | 1,280 | 9·6₄ | 3·75 | 7·94 | 1·52₅ | −0·5₃ |
| KCl | 1,310 | 9·4₂ | .. | 7·18 | 1·44 | −0·0₇ |
| RbCl | 1,380 | 8·9₄ | .. | 6·97 | 1·38 | −0·4₉ |
| NaBr | 1,450 | 8·5₁(8·3₄)† | 3·52 | 7·56 | .. | .. |
| KBr | 1,460 | 8·4₅(8·3₀)† | .. | 6·91 | 1·43 | −0·7₀ |
| RbBr | 1,550 | 7·9₅ | .. | 6·66 | .. | .. |

† These values give the positions of the series limit, obtained as in the text.
‡ M. Born and M. Göppert-Mayer, *Handb. d. Phys.* 24/2, 728 (1933).
‖ Ibid., p. 726.

We consider now the position of the first absorption band. Von Hippel† and others have calculated the position of the first absorption band in the alkali-halides on the assumption that an electron is removed from a halogen ion to a *neighbouring* metal ion. They obtain good agreement with experiment. This seems to us to show that the wave function of an electron ejected to the first excited state spreads over the six nearest metal ions, but does not reach very much farther. This would not necessarily be the case, however, for other polar crystals, and we do not believe that agreement would in general be found between experimental and theoretical results obtained in this way.

The method of calculation of von Hippel is as follows: Neglecting polarization effects, etc., the work required for such a transition may be found by a cycle.

1. Remove a negative ion from its position in the lattice to infinity outside the crystal; the work done is $\alpha e^2/r_0$.

2. Remove an electron from this ion; the work done is equal to the electron affinity $E$.

3. Put back the halogen atom which has lost its electron; since this is no longer charged the work required is zero.

4. Remove an adjacent positive ion; the work required is $(\alpha-1)e^2/r_0$.

5. Add the electron to the positive ion; the work done is $-I$, where $I$ is the ionization potential.

6. Replace the alkali atom in the crystal.

The total work required is

$$\frac{(2\alpha-1)e^2}{r_0} + E - I. \tag{13}$$

This is somewhat greater than the quantum energy $h\nu$ of the first absorption band. This has been ascribed to the interaction between the doublet formed when an electron is transferred from the halogen to the adjacent alkali ion and the dipoles induced by it in the surrounding ions. Attempts to calculate this energy of interaction $\psi_{pol}$ have been made by Klemm‡ and by de Boer.‖ Their values are shown in Table 21.

The further discrepancy of about 2 eV. must be ascribed to the interaction between the alkali *atom* and its surroundings. It is not surprising that this is considerable, since the radius of the wave function of the alkali atom is by no means small compared with the interionic distance.

† A. von Hippel, *Zeits. f. Physik*, **101**, 680 (1936); J. H. de Boer, *Electron and Emission Phenomena* (Cambridge, 1935); W. Klemm, *Zeits. f. Physik*, **82**, 529 (1933).

‡ W. Klemm, loc. cit.                    ‖ J. H. de Boer, loc. cit., p. 135.

## TABLE 21

Energies in electron-volts.

| Salt | $\dfrac{(2\alpha-1)e^2}{r_0}+E-I$ | $\psi_{\text{pol}}$ | $h\nu_{\text{calc}}$ | $h\nu_{\text{obs}}$ |
|------|------|------|------|------|
| NaCl . . . | 11·3 | 1·6 | 9·7 | 7·7 |
| KCl . . . | 10·9 | 1·3 | 9·6 | 7·6 |
| RbCl . . . | 10·5 | 1·2 | 9·3 | 7·4 |
| LiBr . . . | 11·1 | 2·2 | 8·9 | 6·67 |
| NaBr . . . | 10·4 | 1·7 | 8·7 | 6·50 |
| KBr . . . | 10·1 | 1·4 | 8·7 | 6·58 |
| RbBr . . . | 9·8 | 1·4 | 8·4 | 6·43 |
| LiI . . . | 0·6 | 2·2 | 7·4 | 5·59 |
| NaI . . . | 9·2 | 1·8 | 7·4 | 5·39 |
| KI . . . | 9·0 | 1·4 | 7·6 | 5·63 |
| RbI . . . | 8·8 | 1·4 | 7·4 | 5·55 |

$$h\nu_{\text{calc}} = \frac{(2\alpha-1)e^2}{r_0} + E - I - \psi_{\text{pol}}.$$

$h\nu_{\text{obs}}$ is the maximum (in eV.) of the first absorption band.

Since there are six positive ions adjacent to any one negative ion, and since an electron ejected from a negative ion would have the same energy whichever of these six it found itself in, it is clear that the electron would not stay localized on any particular ion of these six. In a proper quantum-mechanical treatment of the problem one would have to consider transitions of the electron from its normal state in the halogen ion to a state in which it is shared between the six positive ions. There will be *six* such states; and owing to the interaction between the atoms they will not, of course, all have the same energy. The ground state may easily be shown to be non-degenerate. Its wave function should spread over the six metal ions adjacent to the halogen atom. The wave function will have the symmetry associated with an *s*-state in the neighbourhood of the halogen atom.

Passing on now to the absorption bands of shorter wave-length, shown in Fig. 31, attempts have been made to assign these to a process in which an electron is transferred from a halogen ion to one of the next-nearest metal ions. We do not believe that the absorption spectrum can be accounted for in quite such a simple way as this, because there is no reason why the electron should stay on a particular one of these more distant ions.

For these excited states of higher quantum number it is instructive to think of the electron and positive hole as moving together in a medium of dielectric constant $\kappa_0$, thereby neglecting the atomic structure of the crystal. Owing to the comparatively long time that a hole will take to move from ion to ion through the crystal, it will have a much larger effective mass than the electron, and may be considered practically at rest. The separations between the energies of the higher states should thus be similar to those for the hydrogen atom, decreased by a factor $\kappa_0^2$ because the force between electron and positive hole is $e^2/\kappa_0 r^2$ instead of $e^2/r^2$.

It must be emphasized that in considerations of this type we must take the dielectric constant $\kappa_0$ deduced for radiations of frequency greater than that of the residual rays, and *not* the larger dielectric constant for static fields, partly due to a displacement of the ions. This follows from the Franck-Condon principle; during an absorption act (say $10^{-16}$ sec.) the ions have not time to move. *After* the absorption act the ions may move into new positions of equilibrium; but this does not affect the frequency of the absorbed radiation.†

## 8. Absorption spectra of other polar crystals

Fig. 33 (a), (b), and (c) shows the absorption spectra of thin films of some silver, cadmium, and thallous halides‡ measured at liquid air and at room temperatures. The absorption spectra differ from those of the alkali-halides in several ways:

1. The peaks are not so distinct as for the alkali-halides.
2. In the thallium salts they are closer together.
3. The absorption spectrum has a much more pronounced tail on the long-wave-length side, extending into the visible. For comparison, the long-wave edge of the ultra-violet absorption spectrum of sodium-chloride is shown for a number of specimens in Fig. 33 (d).

As regards (2), these crystals have a higher refractive index than that of the alkali-halides, and therefore higher values of $\kappa_0$. It follows from the arguments of the last section that the excited states should be more crowded towards the series limit.

The nature of the long-wave-length tail has often been discussed.‖ It is responsible for the active absorption in, for instance, photographic emulsions and phosphorescent materials. It seems very little dependent on temperature, and so can hardly be due to thermal vibrations. It may be due to atoms situated on the surfaces of cracks (cf. § 5.2) or

† Cf. a recent paper by R. Landshoff, *Phys. Rev.* **55**, 631 (1939), for a further discussion of this.

‡ H. Fesefeldt, *Zeits. f. Physik*, **64**, 741 (1930). Fesefeldt's paper contains absorption spectra for Ag, Pb, Tl, Cd, Zn, Ni, and Co halides.

‖ Cf. Discussion on Luminescence, F. Seitz, *Trans. Faraday Soc.* **35**, 98 (1939).

to impurity atoms; an alternative explanation is given on p. 94, which ascribes at least part of it to optically forbidden transitions, and explains its absence in alkali-halides. Further discussion of the long-wavelength tail is given in Chapter IV, § 6.2.

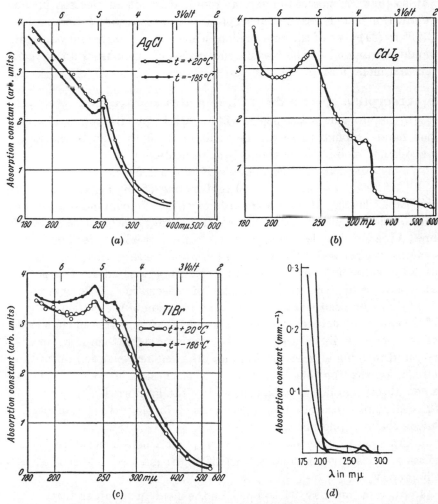

FIG. 33. Absorption spectra of polar crystals (from Fesefeldt, loc. cit.): (a) AgCl; (b) CdI₂; (c) TlBr; (d) absorption edge of NaCl

Little is known about the absorption spectra of oxides. In § 4 we have given some indirect evidence that the first peak of the ultraviolet absorption spectrum in transparent oxides lies at a wave-length of the order of 1,000 A, or an energy $h\nu$ of 10 to 15 eV. In cuprous oxide, on the other hand, according to the arguments of Chapter VII, § 11, absorption by the perfect lattice sets in in the visible or near ultra-violet. This difference may be explained by the assumption that the copper $3d$-band of cuprous oxide lies above the oxygen $2p$-band (cf. Chap. V, § 4), so that the smallest energy $h\nu$ required to lift an electron into a conduction band is less. The absorption will correspond to the transition $(3d)^{10}$ to $(3d)^9(4s)^1$ of the cuprous ion, while in the transparent oxides it would correspond to the transference of an electron from an oxygen ion to a metal ion.

## 9. Absorption spectra due to impurities and trapped electrons

Any impurity or lattice defect will in general give rise to new absorption bands, though these will be visible only if they lie to the long-wave-length side of the characteristic absorption.

We may distinguish various kinds of lattice defect:

1. A foreign negative ion may replace one of the negative ions of the perfect lattice. If the electron affinity of the foreign ion is less than that of the ions of the perfect lattice, this should give rise to a series of lines (broadened by lattice vibrations) leading up to a series limit. An example is discussed in Chapter IV, § 9, where the absorption spectrum of KBr containing small quantities of KH is discussed. The series limit may be hidden by the characteristic absorption of the crystal.

2. A foreign positive ion replaces a positive ion of the perfect lattice. If the ionization potential of the foreign metal atom is greater than that of the metal atoms whose ions make up the crystal, then less work is required to bring an electron from an adjacent negative ion on to the foreign ion than on to an ion of the perfect crystal (cf. eq. (13)). Thus a new absorption line is to be expected to the long-wave-length side of the continuous absorption (cf. the discussion in Chap. VI, § 4, of alkali-halide thallium phosphors).

3. An electron may be trapped at a point where a negative ion is missing. This gives a similar kind of spectrum, and is discussed in Chapter IV, § 3.

4. An electron may be trapped in the field of an interstitial ion. This again should give rise to a line spectrum leading to a series limit.

5. A positive hole may be trapped at a point where a positive ion is missing. The negative ions adjacent to the vacant lattice point have one less than their full complement of electrons. Absorption of light throws an electron up from the full band into this vacant level, again giving rise to a line spectrum as well as a continuous absorption (see Chap. V, § 4)

We may, however, note that the series limit may always lie in the region of characteristic absorption.

6. *Absorption due to cracks.* We have seen that, to a rough approximation, the first absorption band of alkali-halide crystals may be ascribed to transitions of an electron from a halide ion to an adjacent metal ion, and that the work required for the transition (cf. eq. (13)) is given by

$$hv = \frac{(2\alpha - 1)e^2}{r_0} + E - I. \tag{14}$$

To the same degree of approximation, it follows from the considerations of p. 70 that if both ions lie on the surface of a crystal the work required, $hv$, is

$$\frac{(2\alpha' - 1)e^2}{r_0} + E - I, \tag{15}$$

which is less than (14) by

$$\frac{2(\alpha - \alpha')e^2}{r_0} \simeq 0.68 \text{ eV. for NaCl.}$$

The same should be true of ions lying at the surfaces of internal cracks. It is possible that the long-wave-length tail of the characteristic absorption is due to absorption by such ions.[†]

## 10. Absolute magnitude of the absorption coefficient

An estimate of the absolute value of the absorption coefficient due to a given concentration of impurity will be of interest. Let us suppose that a given impurity centre gives rise to an absorption line with $B$-coefficient equal to $B$, and that lattice vibrations broaden the line, giving it a breadth $\Delta v$. Then if the intensity of (monochromatic) radiation is $I$ ergs cm.$^{-3}$, the probability per unit time that a quantum is absorbed is $IB/\Delta v$. Suppose now that there are $N$ absorbing centres per cm.$^3$, and that $n$ quanta are incident per cm.$^2$ per sec. Then $I = hvn/c$, and $IBN/\Delta v$ quanta are absorbed per cm.$^3$ per sec. The absorption coefficient $\kappa$ is thus

$$\kappa = hvNB/c\,\Delta v \text{ cm.}^{-1}$$

For $B$ we set[‡]
$$B = \pi e^2 f/(hvm),$$

where $f$ is the oscillator strength of the line; hence

$$\kappa = \pi N e^2 f/mc\,\Delta v \text{ cm.}^{-1}$$

Taking numerical values, set $f = \frac{1}{2}$ and $h\,\Delta v = 0.5$ eV., thus

$$\kappa \simeq N \times 1.0 \times 10^{-16} \text{ cm.}^{-1}$$

---

[†] K. F. Herzfeld, *Zeits. f. phys. Chem.* **105**, 329 (1923).
[‡] Cf., for example, *Handb. d. Phys.* **24/1**, 430 (1933).

Comparing this with experiment, we may note that Pohl records that a crystal of KCl with $10^{15}$ colour centres per cm.$^3$ has an absorption coefficient of 0·22 cm.$^{-1}$

## 11. Photoconductivity

The absorption by a crystal of a quantum of radiation of frequency greater than that of the series limit will give rise to a free electron and a free positive hole. If a voltage is applied to the crystal, these should drift in opposite directions, contributing to an electric current. We therefore expect that a crystal illuminated with radiation of these frequencies should show photoconductivity. Experiments on photoconductivity will be described in Chapter IV. In no case does the observed conductivity seem to be due to the simple mechanism under discussion. For these wave-lengths in the extreme ultra-violet the absorption coefficient is very high, of the order $10^5$ to $10^6$ cm.$^{-1}$ The radiation therefore enters only the surface film of the material, and only this surface film could be made conducting. The high rate of absorption would compensate only partly for the thinness of the conducting film, because a high rate of absorption leads to a high rate of recombination. Therefore the current to be expected is much smaller than for frequencies where the absorption coefficient is smaller, say of the order 1 mm.$^{-1}$

For frequencies below the series limit, the electron and positive hole are not separated directly by the light. Therefore we do not expect any photoconductivity, at any rate at low temperatures. As we shall see in Chapter IV, § 6, in certain cases it is possible for the thermal agitation of the surrounding atoms to separate the electron and positive hole before they recombine.

Smakula† illuminated alkali-halide crystals in the long-wave-length tail of the absorption band; as we expect, he did not observe any photoconductivity. A certain coloration of the crystal is however observed, which we shall discuss in Chapter IV. On the other hand, crystals of high refractive index such as AgBr and ZnS do show photoconductivity when illuminated in the long-wave tail of the absorption band; the reason for this is discussed in Chapter IV, § 6.

## 12. The mean free path of an electron in an insulator

In this section we have to consider the interaction between an electron in the conduction band of a non-metallic crystal and the thermal vibrations of the lattice. Unless otherwise stated our results may be applied also to a positive hole in a normally full band.

† A. Smakula, *Zeits. f. Physik*, **63**, 762 (1930).

We have two problems to consider: the probability that an electron moving in a given direction will suffer a deflexion, and the probability that it will gain or lose energy from or to the lattice. Consider an electron in the conduction band of an insulating crystal with energy $E$, measured from the bottom of the band, and velocity[†] $u(E)$. Then we define the mean distance that an electron will travel through the crystal before suffering a deflexion as $l(E)$, the mean free path. If $1/\tau(E)$ is the probability per unit time that an electron suffers a deflexion, $\tau(E)$ may be called the time of relaxation. $\tau$ and $l$ are connected by the relation

$$\tau = l/u.$$

From a knowledge of $\tau$ and $l$ we may deduce the mobility $v(E)$ of an electron in the conduction band,[‡]

$$v(E) = \frac{e}{m}\cdot\tau(E).$$

If we are dealing with electrons having a Maxwell distribution, as in a semi-conductor or a photoconductor in which the time spent in the conduction band is long enough for the electrons to get into equilibrium, then the mean mobility will be required,

$$\bar{v} = \int_0^\infty v(E)C\sqrt{E}\,e^{-E/kT}\,dE,$$

where

$$\int C\sqrt{E}\,e^{-E/kT}\,dE = 1.$$

As regards the rate of loss of energy, each time that it is deflected an electron will either gain or lose from the lattice vibrations a quantum of energy $h\nu$, where $\nu$ is the frequency of the lattice vibrations. This is of the order of $\frac{1}{20}$ to $\frac{1}{40}$ eV. If $p_1$, $p_2$ denote the probabilities that, on each collision, a quantum is gained or lost,

$$h\nu\tau(E)\{p_1-p_2\}$$

denotes the rate of loss of energy. We may thus estimate the rate at which an electron ejected into the conduction band with energy large compared with $\frac{3}{2}kT$ will lose energy.

A theory of the mean free path in polar crystals has been given by Fröhlich.[||] According to Fröhlich the scattering of electrons in a polar

---

† This is, of course, the group velocity; near the bottom of the band $E = \frac{1}{2}m^*u^2$, where $m^*$ is the effective mass.
‡ Cf. § 1.
|| H. Fröhlich, *Proc. Roy. Soc.* (A), **160**, 230 (1937); H. Fröhlich and N. F. Mott, ibid. **171**, 496 (1939).

crystal is mainly due to the polarization waves (Chap. I, § 6), i.e. to those vibrations in which positive and negative ions move in opposite directions, producing thereby a polarization field within the crystal. This field leads to electron scattering. Since the polarization field depends on the vibration spectrum of the crystal, the latter is all that is required for the calculation of the mean free path. One does not, as for metals, have to know the field within the ions.

No analogous calculations have been made for non-polar substances. Methods similar to those used in the theory of metals[†] would have to be used.

We give below Fröhlich's results for a crystal having a single vibrational frequency $\nu$. For the time of relaxation

$$\frac{1}{\tau} = \frac{1}{CE^{\frac{1}{2}}}\begin{cases} 1+2q & (E > h\nu), \\ q & (E < h\nu), \end{cases}$$

where

$$q = \frac{1}{e^{h\nu/kT}-1}$$

and

$$\frac{1}{C} = \frac{e^4 m^{\frac{1}{2}}}{2^{\frac{1}{2}}\hbar M\nu a^3}, \qquad \frac{1}{M} = \frac{1}{M_+}+\frac{1}{M_-}.$$

Here $M_+$, $M_-$ are the masses of the ions, and $a$ the interionic distance. For the mean free path we have therefore

$$\frac{1}{l} = \frac{e^4 m}{2E\hbar Ma^3\nu}\begin{cases} 1+2q \\ q. \end{cases}$$

The rate of loss of energy is

$$h\nu/(C\sqrt{E}). \tag{16}$$

We may note several things about these formulae:

1. For given energy $E$ greater than $h\nu$ the mean free path does *not* tend to infinity as $T$ tends to zero. This is on account of the zero-point vibrations; an electron can always be scattered, with the loss of a quantum of energy, even at the lowest temperatures.[‡]

2. For energies $E$ of the order of several electron volts the mean free path is of the order $10^{-5}$ to $10^{-6}$ cm. as in metals; as, however, the energy is decreased the mean free path decreases, and, if $T$ is not small compared with $h\nu/k$, reaches values of the order of the interatomic distance. For such short free paths the methods of approximation used in obtaining the formulae are not valid. However, if $T \ll h\nu/k$ the factor $q$

---

[†] Cf. N. F. Mott and H. Jones, *Theory of the Properties of Metals and Alloys*, p. 253 (Oxford, 1936).

[‡] In metals at the absolute zero the electrons are in their lowest quantum states; the scattering of an electron with loss of energy is thus impossible.

becomes very small, so that if $E \ll h\nu$ the mean free path becomes large again.

Thus for the mobility of electrons in thermal equilibrium we can at present only deduce values when $T \ll h\nu/k$.

For energies less than $h\nu$ and temperatures less than $h\nu/k$ Fröhlich and Mott† find the following formulae for the mean free path,

$$l = \frac{3(\kappa - \kappa_0 + 1)}{\kappa - \kappa_0} \left(\frac{E}{h\nu}\right)^{\frac{1}{2}} a_0 (e^{h\nu/kT} - 1). \tag{17}$$

Here $\kappa$ and $\kappa_0$ are the dielectric constants for static and high-frequency fields respectively defined in Chapter I, § 5, and

$$a_0 = \hbar^2/m^*e^2,$$

where $m^*$ is the effective mass of the electron. If $m^* \sim m$,

$$a_0 \sim 0.5 \times 10^{-8} \text{ cm.}$$

For the mean value of $l$ for electrons in thermal equilibrium we have

$$\bar{l} = \frac{6}{\sqrt{\pi}} \frac{\kappa - \kappa_0 + 1}{\kappa - \kappa_0} a_0 \left(\frac{T}{\Theta}\right)^{\frac{1}{2}} (e^{\Theta/T} - 1), \tag{18}$$

$(\Theta = h\nu/k)$, and for the mobility

$$\bar{v} = 2 \Big/ \sqrt{\left(\frac{3}{\pi m k \Theta}\right)} \frac{\kappa - \kappa_0 + 1}{\kappa - \kappa_0} e a_0 (e^{\Theta/T} - 1). \tag{19}$$

For the frequency $\nu$ one should *not* take the frequency of the optical vibrations $\nu_t$ but the frequency of the longitudinal vibrations, given (cf. Chap. I, § 6) by $\nu^2 = \nu_t^2 + e^2/\pi M\Omega$,

where $\Omega$ is the volume of the unit cell. $\Theta$ for salts and oxides may be between 300° and 800°.

For $T = \Theta$ we see that $\bar{l} \sim 3 \times 10^{-8}$ cm., but the formula is not valid in this range, except perhaps as regards the order of magnitude. As $T$ decreases, $\bar{l}$ and $\bar{v}$ rise rapidly as $e^{\Theta/T}$. Fig. 66, on p. 168, shows the type of variation to be expected. We do not know how to calculate $\bar{l}$ for $T$ greater than $\Theta$.

These formulae are compared with experiment in Chapter V, § 5 (cf. also Chap. IV, § 5).

As in metals, the presence of foreign ions in solid solution decreases the mean free path; this is discussed further in Chapter V, § 13.

Finally, we must give some discussion of the processes by which an electron in the conduction band with thermal energy can be captured by one of the traps or impurity centres mentioned in §§ 5.1, 5.2.

† Loc. cit.

First of all, we may remark that a direct *radiative* transition from the conduction band to *any* state in the impurity centres has a low probability; in cases where luminescence occurs, it is much more likely that the electron is first trapped in an excited state, and then emits radiation in falling to the ground state. In the initial trapping into an excited state the energy would be communicated to the lattice in the form of heat.

As the discussion of Chapter VI, § 3, will show, the theory of the transfer of energy between electrons and lattice vibrations is not in a very satisfactory state. We are, however, fairly safe in assuming that it will be much easier for an electron to lose energy of the order of $h\nu$ ($\sim \frac{1}{30}$ eV.), thus exciting one quantum of vibrational energy, than energies of larger amounts. Thus, whether radiation is emitted or not, the normal process of capture will be for an electron to fall into an excited state, and then to drop to the ground state of the impurity centre.

We shall denote by $\sigma$ the effective area for capture of an electron into an excited state. Then let $B$ be the probability per unit time that it escapes again and $A$ the probability per unit time that it drops to the ground state. If $B \gg A$, the electron must on the average be captured $B/A$ times before it finally comes to rest in the ground state.

In Chapter IV, p. 131, we give evidence that $\sigma$ is of the order of $10^{-15}$ cm.², that is to say of the cross-section of an atom. In Chapter IV, § 6.1, we give a discussion of $B$ and its variation with temperature for a certain special case. $A$ should be of the order of $10^8$ sec.⁻¹ for allowed transitions, less for forbidden transitions (Chap. VI, § 3).

It seems unlikely that $\sigma$ varies rapidly with temperature.

We may deduce a relation between $B$ and $\sigma$ from the law of detailed balancing. For this purpose we may consider centres with one state only. If there are $N$ impurity centres and $N$ electrons, of which $n$ are in the conduction band and $N-n$ in the centres, then for a steady state

$$n^2 \ \sigma = (N-n)uB,$$

where $u$ is the mean velocity of the electrons. But (Chap. V, eq. (7))

$$\frac{n^2}{N-n} = \left\{\frac{2\pi mkT}{h^2}\right\}^{\frac{3}{2}} e^{-E/kT},$$

where $E$ is the energy required to remove an electron from the centre into the conduction band. Thus, writing $\frac{1}{2}mu^2 = \frac{3}{2}kT$,

$$\frac{B}{\sigma} = \frac{2\pi m(kT)^2}{h^3} \sqrt{(6\pi)} e^{-E/kT}. \tag{20}$$

Use will be made of this formula in Chapter IV, § 6.1. With $\sigma \sim 10^{-15}$ cm., $B$ is equal to $1{\cdot}5 \times 10^{11} e^{-E/kT}$ sec.⁻¹

## COLOUR CENTRES IN ALKALI-HALIDES, AND ALLIED PHENOMENA

### 1. Crystals with non-stoichiometric composition

MANY polar salts, when heated in the vapour of one of their constituent elements, acquire a stoichiometric excess of that constituent. A well-known example is the effect of heating an alkali-halide crystal in alkali vapour; the crystal acquires a stoichiometric excess of alkali metal and at the same time takes on a deep colour. We have then to consider in what ways it is geometrically possible for excess metal, for instance, to be included in a polar crystal. We confine ourselves in this section to cases where the second constituent is dispersed in an atomic state; the discussion of a few of the properties of colloidal particles of metal embedded in the crystal is given in Chapter VII.

The first possibility is that *atoms* of the metal are present in interstitial positions. At first sight one might object to this conception, on the grounds that an *atom* is in general too big to be pushed into an interstitial position. If, however, a positive ion is placed in an interstitial position, then, as we have seen in Chapter III, § 5, an electron can be trapped in its field. The absorption spectrum of such an electron, and the energy required to remove it from the field of the ion into the conduction band of the crystal, will bear no relation to the absorption spectrum and ionization potential of the free atom. Moreover, we shall see in Chapter V, § 4, that the 'orbit' of such a trapped electron may well extend over many atomic diameters. Nevertheless, it is convenient to speak of the interstitial ion with its trapped electron (or electrons) as an interstitial atom.

The second way in which excess metal may be taken up by an ionic crystal is the following: We have seen that a crystal of stoichiometric composition in thermal equilibrium at temperature $T$ contains a number of vacant lattice points (Schottky defects). The numbers of these of either sign are necessarily equal to each other. A crystal will contain an excess of metal, however, if the number of vacant lattice points from which a negative ion has been taken is in excess of the number from which a positive ion has been taken. Since the crystal would then be positively charged, a sufficient number of electrons must be added to the lattice points whence a negative ion is missing. We have already seen (Chap. III, § 5) that in fact an electron can be trapped in the neighbourhood of such a point. Actually its 'orbit' may embrace (for the rock-salt structure) the six surrounding metal ions (Fig. 34 $b$). For certain purposes, however, it is convenient to think of the electron as located on a metal ion next to a vacant lattice point (Fig. 34 $a$). Thus the excess metal is taken up by replacing metal ions by atoms at one of the lattice points adjacent to that from which each negative ion is missing.

(a)                                    (b)

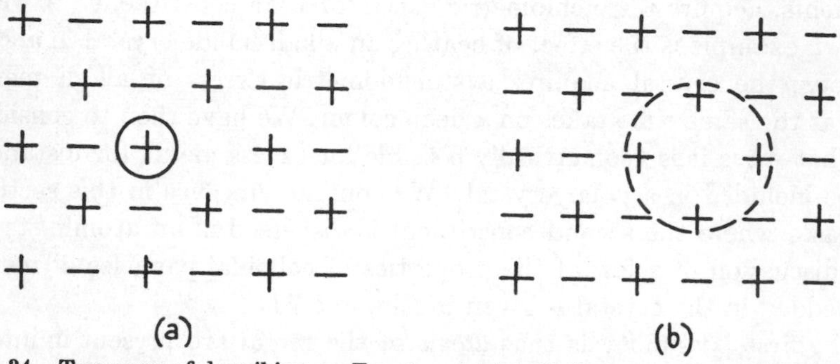

FIG. 34. Two ways of describing an $F$-centre: (a) An alkali atom at the point adjacent to that from which a negative ion is missing. (b) An electron shared between the six neighbours of a vacant lattice point

We do not know of any name usual in the literature for singularities of this type. We shall call them $F$-centres, or singularities of $F$-centre type, anticipating our hypothesis (§ 2) that they are to be identified with the $F$-centres investigated by Pohl and his school.

We shall leave until § 8 the discussion of how they are formed when the salt is heated in the vapour of the metal.

We may remark here that, in a similar way, a salt may carry an excess of the electro-negative constituent by having lattice points whence the *positive* ion is missing, and an electron missing from one of the adjacent negative ions.†

There are thus two possible ways in which excess metal, or excess of the electro-negative constituent, can be taken up. The entropy of a crystal containing $n$ excess atoms is practically the same in either case. If the atoms are absorbed interstitially, then it is

$$k \log \frac{N!}{n!\,(N-n)!},$$

where $N$ is the number of interstitial positions. In the second case it is

$$k \log \frac{(N+n)!}{n!\,N!},$$

† An example is provided by cuprous oxide with excess of oxygen, cf. Chap. V, § 4.

where $N$ is the number of ion pairs. Since in practice $n \ll N$, this gives in either case for the entropy

$$-Nkc \log c \quad (c = n/N).$$

## 2. A model for the colour centres

As mentioned above, when an alkali-halide crystal is heated in the vapour of the corresponding alkali metal, it acquires a deep colour; yellow for rock-salt, blue for potassium-chloride, and so on. This coloration is due to the presence of a characteristic absorption band

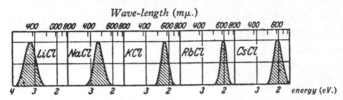

Fig. 35. Absorption bands of the colour centres at 20° C.

whose maximum lies in or very near the visible region of the spectrum (Fig. 35). Chemical methods† have shown that these crystals contain also a stoichiometric excess of alkali metal, present in proportions up to about one part in ten thousand.

The properties of these coloured crystals have been studied in great detail by R. W. Pohl‡ and his co-workers, and the results that they have achieved enable a fairly complete theoretical picture to be given of these phenomena in alkali-halides. It therefore seems worth while to discuss them in detail, partly for their intrinsic interest, partly for the light they may shed on the more complicated materials of technical importance (luminescent powders, semi-conductors, etc.).

Pohl has called the absorption band shown in Fig. 35 the $F$-band, and the absorbing centres $F$-centres (German *Farbzentren*, or colour centres).

The $F$-band is due to an electronic transition, to be correlated in some way with the stoichiometric excess of metal. We have seen that there are two possible ways in which this excess may be present in the crystal. The electron responsible for the $F$-band must then be either the valence electron of an interstitial neutral atom or else an electron replacing a negative ion at a (vacant) lattice point. We believe that the second explanation is the correct one. One piece of evidence for this is that

† F. G. Kleinschrod, *Ann. d. Physik*, **27**, 97 (1936).
‡ Cf., for example, R. W. Pohl, *Proc. Phys. Soc.* **49** (extra part), 3 (1937).

the same $F$-band can also be produced in alkali-halide crystals of normal stoichiometric composition when the cold crystal is irradiated with X-rays. The $F$-band formed by this method has exactly the same shape as that which accompanies a stoichiometric excess of metal, but the maximum intensity obtainable is very much smaller. Electrons ejected from ions of the lattice by the X-rays will travel through the conduction levels, and be trapped at the Schottky vacant negative-ion lattice points, of which there are a certain number 'frozen in' (Chap. II, § 5). The maximum intensity that can be obtained is greater in crystals that have been deformed; since the gliding of a crystal along slip planes is believed to cause intense local heating followed by rapid cooling, it is natural that the process will lead to an increase in the number of frozen-in holes.

In this connexion it is of interest that crystals coloured by X-rays can be bleached by illumination with light absorbed in the $F$-band; and illumination in any part of the band bleaches the *whole* band. This proves that in any crystal all the $F$-centres are similar; the breadth of the $F$-band is not due to overlapping bands arising from different kinds of centres in the crystal. As we shall see, when a quantum of light is absorbed by an $F$-centre, its electron is usually set free and can travel through the conduction levels. In a crystal which has been coloured by X-rays, this will give the electron a chance to return to one of the neutral halogen atoms in the lattice from which an electron had been ejected by the X-rays. Negative halide ions will be re-formed, and the crystal will revert to its original transparent state. Such bleaching, of course, cannot occur in crystals where the coloration is due only to the presence of excess metal; in these crystals the coloration is stable.

The same $F$-band can be obtained in other ways: by illumination with ultra-violet light, or by bombardment of the crystal with cathode rays. The coloration of crystals by ultra-violet illumination will be discussed in § 9. The $F$-band produced by cathode rays was found to be more stable than that formed by X-rays or light. The reason appears to be that, under the bombardment, some halogen escapes from the crystal, leaving a stoichiometric excess of metal.

In recent years attention has been mainly confined to crystals with stable coloration obtained by heating the crystal in alkali vapour. In this chapter, whenever the $F$-band is mentioned, this will refer to a crystal containing excess alkali metal, unless otherwise stated.

In the alkali-halides both the positive and negative ions have closed electronic shells of the rare-gas type, with paired electrons; the salts are therefore diamagnetic.† Consider, however, a crystal containing $F$-centres and a stoichiometric excess of metal. The excess metal is in the form of additional positive ions, but at each $F$-centre is an unpaired electron in an $s$-state. With a sufficient concentration of $F$-centres it should be possible to detect a change in the magnetic susceptibility of the crystal. This has been measured by Jensen.‡

Various authors‖ suggested earlier that the $F$-centres were electrons 'trapped by digging their own holes'—i.e. by the mechanism discussed in Chapter III, § 5.3. The most direct proof that this mechanism is incorrect seems to us the following: when $F$-centres are formed by heating an alkali-halide in alkali vapour, the concentration of $F$-centres is proportional to the pressure of the vapour. If, however, $F$-centres were electrons trapped in the perfect lattice, this would mean that the alkali atom had dissociated into an electron and an additional ion; the latter would have to be absorbed at an interstitial position of the crystal, since there are with this model no negative ions available with which it can build up new layers of the perfect crystal. Thus, for each alkali atom absorbed, there would be formed a trapped electron and an interstitial ion; it would follow that the concentration of $F$-centres should be proportional to the square root of the pressure of alkali vapour. Besides, there are other properties of $F$-centres which we cannot explain with this model, e.g. the formation of $F'$-centres from $U$-centres, and the trapping of electrons by $F$-centres to form $F'$-centres (§§ 5 and 9).

## 3. Absorption spectrum of an electron trapped at a vacant lattice point

The field in the neighbourhood of a vacant lattice point is illustrated in Fig. 36. Some of its properties have been discussed in Chapter III, §§ 5 and 10. At large distances, as explained there, we have to superimpose on the potential energy of an electron in the perfect lattice a term $-e^2/\kappa r$ or $-e^2/\kappa_0 r$, according as the 'hole' is empty or contains an electron.

The wave functions for a trapped electron may conveniently be written in the form
$$\psi = u_0(\mathbf{r})f(\mathbf{r}),$$
where $u_0(\mathbf{r})$ is the wave function for the lowest state in the undistorted lattice. The function $f(\mathbf{r})$ may be expected to have the symmetry of a $1s$, $2p$, $2s$, etc., wave function for the successive excited states.

Calculations of the wave function of the ground state have been carried out for sodium-chloride by Tibbs,†† using an approximation

---

† G. W. Brindley and F. E. Hoare, *Proc. Roy. Soc.* (A), **152**, 342 (1935).
‡ P. Jensen, *Ann. d. Physik*, **34**, 161 (1939).
‖ A. von Hippel, *Zeits. f. Physik*, **101**, 680 (1936); R. W. Gurney and N. F. Mott, *Proc. Phys. Soc.* **49** (extra part), 32 (1937); N. F. Mott, *Nature*, **139**, 951 (1937).
†† S. R. Tibbs, *Trans. Faraday Soc.* **35**, 1471 (1939).

which need not be discussed here. He finds that the lowest state lies
about 3 eV. below the level of the conduction band, and the first excited
state 0·6 eV. below. His wave function $f(\mathbf{r})$ is shown also in Fig. 36
for the normal $1s$ and $2p$ states. It will be seen that the electron is

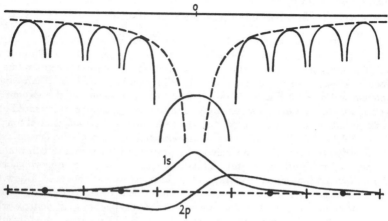

FIG. 36. *Above*: Potential energy of an electron in the field of a vacant lattice point
(full line). The broken line represents $-e^2/\kappa_0 r$. *Below*: The wave functions $f(\mathbf{r})$ of an
electron in an $F$-centre; the fluctuations given by $u_0(\mathbf{r})$ are not shown

shared between the six metal ions which are neighbours of the vacant
lattice point, two of which are shown in the figure.

As regards the absorption spectrum of a trapped electron, from the
theoretical point of view it should consist of a series of lines, broadened
by the lattice vibrations, leading to a series limit (cf. Chap. III, § 8),
beyond which is a continuous absorption band in which the absorption
of light throws the trapped electron into the conduction levels. Fig. 37
shows the most accurate measurements[†] that have been made of the
absorption spectrum on the short-wave side. The curves are for KCl
with different concentrations of $F$-centres. The main bell-shaped band
is certainly due to a transition from the ground $s$-state to the first
excited $p$-state. The slight hump between 4,000 and 4,500 A may
represent the other lines and the series limit. It is not clear at present,
however, why the continuous absorption is so much weaker than the
band absorption; in the characteristic ultra-violet absorption of pure
alkali-halide crystals they appear to have equal intensities.

In the alkali-halides with the absorption spectra shown in Fig. 37
the concentration of excess alkali metal, and hence the number of

† F. G. Kleinschrod, *Ann. d. Physik*, **27**, 97 (1936).

*F*-centres, was found by chemical means. Assuming the optical oscillator strength of the main band to be unity, the number of *F*-centres could be deduced from the absorption coefficient and half-band-width; this is done frequently in Pohl's work.† The number of atoms determined chemically was 1·24 times that determined optically. We may deduce that the oscillator strength of the main band is actually

$$1/1{\cdot}24 = 0{\cdot}81.$$

As emphasized in Chapter III, § 5, the excited states, especially those of high azimuthal quantum number, should have energies given by the hydrogen-like formula

$$E = -h\,R c/n^2\kappa_{\text{eff}}^2,$$

where $\kappa_{\text{eff}}$ is an 'effective' dielectric constant. When an *F*-centre is in the ground state, the surrounding medium is not acted on by an electric field; therefore in calculating the energies of the excited states into which an electron can make a transition, we must take the field at large distances to be $e/\kappa_0 r^2$, and thus

$$\kappa_{\text{eff}} = \kappa_0.$$

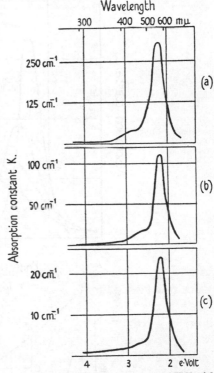

Fig. 37. Absorption constant of KCl with *F*-centres: (a) $1{\cdot}15\times10^{18}$ centres per cm.³; (b) $4{\cdot}25\times10^{17}$ centres per cm.³; (c) $9{\cdot}3\times10^{16}$ centres per cm.³

For sodium-chloride, applying this formula to the 2*p*-state of an *F*-centre, with $\kappa_0 = 2{\cdot}33$ and $n = 2$, we obtain
$$E \sim -0{\cdot}6 \text{ eV.}$$

*After* the absorption process, the ions move into new positions of equilibrium, and the value of $\kappa_{\text{eff}}$ will increase. The energy of the electron is thus raised. We shall give evidence in § 6 that the work required to eject an electron from the 2*p*-state of an *F*-centre into the conduction band after the absorption process is in fact of the order 0·1 eV.

† Cf. Chap. III, § 10.

The breadth of the $F$-band is very sensitive to temperature, as Fig. 38 shows. From the theoretical point of view we expect a broadening $\Delta\nu$ given by

$$h\,\Delta\nu = \sqrt{(h\nu_0\,kT)},$$

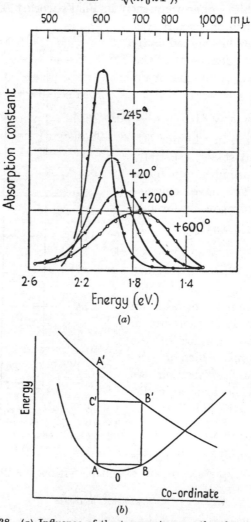

FIG. 38. (a) Influence of the temperature on the absorption spectra of KBr with colour centres.† (b) Energies of ground and excited states

where $\nu_0$ is of the same order as the absorption frequency itself. The reason is the following: In the excited state the ions surrounding the $F$-centre will no longer be in equilibrium positions. If then we

† From R. W. Pohl, *Proc. Phys. Soc.* **49** (extra part), 3 (1937).

plot the energies of the normal and excited states of the $F$-centre against some configurational coordinate expressing the positions of the surrounding ions, we shall obtain curves as in Fig. 38 ($b$). At a temperature $T$ the energy associated with each configurational co-ordinate will be $kT$; thus in Fig. 38 ($b$), if we draw a horizontal line $AB$ at a height $kT$ above the minimum $O$, the value of the configurational coordinate will range over all values between $A$ and $B$. Thus the energy of the quantum of light absorbed may have any value between $AA'$ and $BB'$. The breadth of the absorption band will be given by

$$h \Delta \nu = C'A';$$

this is clearly proportional to the square root of $kT$.

In the chlorides and fluorides the main $F$-band was found by Ottmer† to be accompanied by a subsidiary maximum, lying in every case on the long-wave side of the main band. In the fluorides the intensity of this second band was comparable with that of the main band; but, as the crystals had only been coloured by means of X-rays, this does not imply a high intensity. The subsidiary band arises either from some impurity or from some other type of centre.‡

## 4. Photoconductivity in insulating crystals

It has already been mentioned in Chapter III, § 11, that for alkali-halide crystals the absorption of ultra-violet light is not accompanied by any conductivity. When, however, $F$-centres have been formed in a crystal either by excess of metal or by X-rays, or by other methods, the crystal shows photoconductivity when illuminated with light of any wave-length lying within its $F$-band.‖ In the case of other sub-stances, such as the silver halides, zinc sulphide, diamond, etc., the pure crystal (or rather the crystal of normal purity) shows conductivity immediately on illumination with ultra-violet light. A complete descrip-tion of this phenomenon must include an account of the absorption of the quantum of light which releases the electron. The details of this process will vary greatly from one type of crystal to another. On the other hand, the electrical behaviour of the photocurrent takes very similar forms in widely different types of crystal, even when the under-lying mechanisms differ. It is convenient, then, to begin by discussing the electrical effects, leaving until later a discussion of the optical absorption which releases the electrons; for alkali-halides with $F$-centres the absorption process will be discussed in § 6.1, for other crystals in § 6.2.

---

† R. Ottmer, *Zeits. f. Physik*, **46**, 798 (1928).
‡ H. Pick, *Ann. d. Physik*, **35**, 73 (1939); A. Smakula, *Zeits. f. Physik*, **63**, 762 (1930).
‖ It has been suggested in the last section that the $F$-band corresponds to a transition to an excited state of the $F$-centre. It will be shown in § 6 how such transitions produce free electrons.

In this section we shall confine our attention to crystals which are *insulators* at the temperature at which the experiment is carried out (for a consideration of semi-conductors, cf. Chap. V, § 10). The crystal is mounted between electrodes, and illuminated, either throughout its volume or in a small slice only. The current passing through the circuit is measured by a galvanometer, or, for an illumination of short duration, by an electrometer, as in Fig. 39.

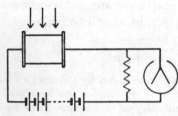

Fɪɢ. 39. Experimental set-up for the measurement of primary photoelectric current

Pohl distinguishes between the *primary* and *secondary* currents. The primary part is a direct photoelectric current. In an insulating crystal we know (Chap. III, § 3) that any electrons put into the conduction levels will be able to move. But, when an insulator is placed between metal electrodes, in the dark no current flows because the conduction levels are empty, and because the electrons in the cathode have not sufficient energy to pass into the conduction levels of the insulator.† When such a crystal (or part of it) is illuminated with light of suitable wave-length, electrons in the crystal are raised to the conduction levels, and are drawn towards the anode. The positive holes which are produced at the same time *may* be mobile, in which case they will be drawn towards the cathode. The motion of the photoelectrons, together with any motion of the positive holes, constitutes the primary photoelectric current. So long as only this primary current is flowing, no electrons enter the crystal from the cathode, except to neutralize any positive holes which may be drawn to the cathode by the field.

In some crystals, however, the continued passage of the primary current appears to break down the resistance of the crystal, so that electrons can enter the crystal from the cathode and pass through it, as in a semi-conductor. The resulting current is known as the secondary photoelectric current. Its origin will be discussed in Chapter V, § 9. In this chapter we shall deal with the *primary* current only.

In alkali-halides at room temperature and silver halides at low temperatures the positive charges released by the light do not move.‡ Thus in these experiments no electrons enter the crystal to replace those

---

† For a more detailed discussion of the contact between a metal and an insulator, cf. Chap. V, § 6.

‡ This is to be expected in cases where electrons are released from impurity centres.

pulled away by the field. A space-charge will thus be set up in the crystal, which changes the distribution of the field within the crystal. As a result it is found in many cases that as the illumination is prolonged the field drops to a small fraction of its original value. Pohl's experiments were carried out with illuminations short enough to avoid the setting up of a space-charge (flash illumination). Between each experiment the crystal must be brought back to its original state; this is usually done either by warming or by illumination with intense infrared light.

When a slice of the crystal is illuminated, the electrons released by a flash of light will be drawn by the field into the unilluminated portion, and one might suppose that all the electrons would eventually reach the anode, irrespective of the voltage. In no type of crystal, however, does the photocurrent behave in this way. For weak fields the current is not independent of the voltage, but is always roughly proportional to it. It is evident that in every case the electrons get stuck in the crystal by some means after drifting a certain distance. In zero applied field each electron will execute a kind of Brownian motion before getting trapped.† Though the point where each electron is trapped may, for example, lie about $10^{-3}$ cm. from the point where it was released, the total length of the Brownian path that has been covered by each electron may be more than a centimetre. When a weak field is applied to the crystal we have to consider both the electrons which are trapped at points lying *towards the anode* from the point where they were released, and those which are trapped at points lying *towards the cathode* from the point where they were released. In any field the number of the former is greater than the number of the latter, and consequently an effect is observed on the galvanometer. The deflexion of the galvanometer has the same value as it would have if *all* the photoelectrons had drifted down the field a certain small distance $w$, the same for all. This distance $w$ is known as the mean range, or *Schubweg*, of the photoelectrons in this field.

In § 5 we shall discuss in detail the factors determining the mean range $w$ and the mechanisms of trapping in different types of crystal. First, however, we have to consider the charge that will pass through the circuit illustrated in Fig. 39 if an electron is released by the light and travels a certain distance before it is trapped, or before it reaches the anode. If an electron travelled right across the crystal, the charge

---

† If in any crystal the positive holes are mobile, these also must be trapped after executing a Brownian movement.

measured by the galvanometer or by the electrometer would clearly be equal to the electronic charge $e$. Thus if the electron travels a distance $x$ only, the charge measured will be

$$ex/l, \tag{1}$$

where $l$ is the distance between the electrodes. It must be emphasized that the galvanometer will measure a current, even if no charge flows from the crystal to the electrode, i.e. if all the electrons are trapped in the crystal. It should not even be necessary for the electrodes to be in contact with the crystal.

Now the mean range $w$ is, as we shall see below, proportional to the field. Suppose then that a crystal is illuminated in a section at a distance $x_0$ from the anode. For weak fields the mean distance $x$ travelled by the electron is equal to $w$, and the current measured will be proportional to the field $F$. When, however, $w$ becomes comparable with $x_0$, we shall expect the current measured to show a saturation value, as in Fig. 40. The maximum charge to be obtained during a given illumination by increasing the field indefinitely should, according to (1), be given by

$$Q_{max} = nex_0/l, \tag{2}$$

where $n$ is the number of electrons released. If the crystal is illuminated uniformly between the two electrodes, then we shall have

$$Q_{max} = \tfrac{1}{2}ne.$$

If the positive holes as well as the electrons are free to move, then we have in either case

$$Q_{max} = ne.$$

Fig. 40 shows a curve giving the primary photoelectric current observed in AgBr at $-185°$ C. illuminated in a narrow band at a distance $x_0$ say, from the anode.[†] The total charge passing during a flash is plotted. It will be seen that with increasing voltage this rises to a maximum value $Q_{max}$. From (2), dividing $Q_{max}$ by $ex_0/l$, the number of electrons released was obtained, and compared with the number of quanta absorbed by the AgBr. For a number of wave-lengths it was found that the ratio $\eta$, defined by

$$\eta = \frac{\text{number of electrons released}}{\text{number of quanta absorbed}},$$

had the following values:[‡]

| Wave-length (A) . | . | . | 4,360 | 4,050 | 3,650 | 3,340 | 3,130 | 2,800 | 2,540 |
|---|---|---|---|---|---|---|---|---|---|
| Absorption coefficient (mm.$^{-1}$) | | 50 | 170 | 580 increasing to 10,000 | | | | | |
| $\eta$ . | . | . | . | 0·61 | 0·61 | 0·60 | 0·50 | 0·38 | 0·22 | 0·17 |

[†] W. Lehfeldt, *Göttinger Nachrichten*, Fachgruppe II, **1**, 171 (1935).
[‡] See also p. 140.

Thus for fairly long wave-lengths $\eta$ was of the order unity; the drop for shorter wave-lengths will be discussed in § 6.2.

Curves of the type shown in Fig. 40 showing saturation have been obtained also for zinc blende[†] and diamond.[‡] The intensity of the electric field required for saturation of the current takes widely different values for different substances; evidently the mean distance travelled by a photoelectron before being trapped also takes widely different values. In diamond, saturation was obtained with a field of 15,000 volts/cm. In the alkali-halides, saturation could only be obtained with very thin crystals, in which the light absorption could not be measured.[‖] There is, however, indirect evidence that here too $\eta$ is of

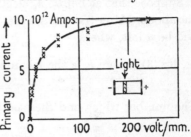

FIG. 40. Current-voltage curve for AgBr at $-185°$ C. illuminated with $6\cdot5 \times 10^{10}$ quanta per second of wave-length 5,460 A in a narrow band as shown (from Lehfeldt, loc. cit.)

the order unity at not too low a temperature (see § 5).

A theoretical expression for the mean range $w$ may be obtained as follows: Suppose we assume that an electron remains in the free state for a time $T$ before it is captured, and that $T$ is independent of the field $F$. Then the range $w$ is given by

$$w = vFT, \tag{3}$$

where $v$ is the mobility (velocity of drift in unit field) of an electron in the free state in the crystal.

The mobility is the product of $e/m$ and $\tau$, the time of relaxation or time between collisions, so that

$$v = e\tau/m.$$

For numerical values of the mean free path, cf. § 5.

In strong fields, the actual track travelled by an electron is no longer than usual; it is merely less coiled back on itself. In a crystal containing $10^{15}$ $F$-centres per cm.$^3$ the length of the actual track before capture is of the order of a centimetre, irrespective of the field.

By generalizing the assumptions given above we may obtain a theoretical form[††] for the current-field curve shown in Fig. 40. We assume

† B. Gudden and R. W. Pohl, *Zeits. f. Physik*, **17**, 334 (1923).
‡ Ibid., p. 338.
‖ W. Flechsig, *Zeits. f. Physik*, **46**, 788 (1928).
†† R. Hilsch and R. W. Pohl, *Zeits. f. Physik*, **108**, 55 (1937).

that, if an electron is in the free state, the probability per time $dt$ that it is captured is $dt/T$. If then, at a given instant of time, $n_0$ electrons are freed, there will remain after a time $t$ a number

$$n = n_0 e^{-t/T}.$$

Suppose that as before $n_0$ electrons are released at a distance $x_0$ from the anode. After travelling a distance $x$ in the direction of the field there will be $n$ left, where

$$n = n_0 e^{-x/vFT},$$

or, by (3), where $w$ is the mean range,

$$n = n_0 e^{-x/w}.$$

The number which end their path in the range $dx$ is

$$-\frac{dn}{dx}dx = \frac{n_0}{w}e^{-x/w}dx.$$

The total distance drifted by the $n_0$ particles is made up of two terms; the first is the distance drifted by particles which do not reach the anode; this is

$$\int_0^{x_0} x\frac{dn}{dx}dx = \frac{n_0}{w}\int_0^{x_0} xe^{-x/w}\,dx,$$

which reduces to    $n_0\{w(1-e^{-x_0/w})-x_0 e^{-x_0/w}\}.$

The second is the distance drifted by the $n_0 e^{-x_0/w}$ particles which do reach the anode, which is equal to

$$n_0 x_0 e^{-x_0/w}.$$

Taking the sum, and dividing by $n_0$, we find for the mean distance drifted by an electron    $\bar{x} = w(1-e^{-x_0/w}).$

If $l$ is the breadth of the crystal, we obtain for the ratio $\psi$ between the charge $n_0 e$ released and the charge $n_0 \bar{x}e/l$ passing through the galvanometer

$$\psi = \frac{w}{l}(1-e^{-x_0/w}), \tag{4}$$

a formula due to Hecht.[†]

If the crystal is illuminated throughout, we obtain, averaging over all $x_0$ from 0 to $l$,

$$\psi = \frac{w}{l}\left[1-\frac{w}{l}(1-e^{-l/w})\right]. \tag{5}$$

The function (5) is plotted against $w/l$ (and hence against applied field) in Fig. 41.

† K. Hecht, *Zeits. f. Physik*, **77**, 235 (1932).

We shall discuss later the mechanisms by which the electrons end their paths in different substances. We may note here that there are, *a priori*, two possibilities:

1. The electron may be captured at some crystal imperfection, or in some other way, into a bound state of higher energy than its original state before it was freed by the light. If this is the case the crystal is

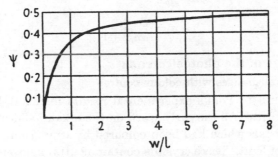

FIG. 41. Current-voltage curve according to formula (5). $\psi$ is the charge recorded per absorbed quantum; $w/l$ is proportional to the field

left in a metastable condition; it is not the same after illumination as before. The mean range $w$ in this case is independent of the intensity of the light, so that the total current passing through the galvanometer is directly proportional to the light absorbed by the crystal.

2. If the crystal is uniformly illuminated, or illuminated in a slab thick compared with the mean range $w$, the electrons may recombine with centres from which they have been ejected by the light. In this case, in the absence of an applied field the crystal will return to its original state. Let then $n$ be the number of free electrons at any moment. The probability $1/T$ per unit time that an electron will be captured will be proportional to the number of vacant places, which is equal to $n$. Denoting this probability by $\alpha n$, we see that $\alpha n^2$ electrons are captured per second.

We now have to distinguish two cases. In the first case $(2a)$ let $T$ be small compared with the period of illumination. Then the current will reach its maximum value soon after the illumination begins, and die away rapidly after the illumination ends. If $I$ is the intensity of illumination, and $AI$ electrons are released per second, we have during illumination

$$AI = \alpha n^2.$$

$n$ is thus proportional to $I^{\frac{1}{2}}$.

Since the current is proportional to $n$, we see that the total current passing through the galvanometer is proportional to $I^{\frac{1}{2}}$. The time $T$ and hence the mean range $w$ are proportional to $I^{-\frac{1}{2}}$.

The other case $(2b)$ that we have to consider is when the period of the flash is small compared with $T$. In this case let the flash produce $n_0$ free electrons. The number will decay according to the law

$$\frac{dn}{dt} = -\alpha n^2,$$

giving $\qquad\qquad n = \dfrac{n_0}{\alpha n_0\, t + 1}.$ \hfill (6)

## 5. The range of the photoelectrons

### 5.1. In alkali-halides with colour centres

We now turn to Pohl's experimental results for alkali-halides containing $F$-centres. All the early work on the alkali-halides was carried out upon crystals which had been coloured by irradiation with X-rays or ultra-violet light. These crystals contain neutral halogen atoms, and are therefore subject to bleaching, as already mentioned above. Consequently in recent years attention has been concentrated on photoconductivity in crystals coloured by excess of alkali metal, and it is these results which will be discussed here.

The conductivity obtained by illumination of an alkali-halide crystal in its $F$-band is of an exceptionally simple kind, since every wavelength shows equal quantum efficiency. This is to say, under monochromatic illumination the value of the current follows the value of the absorption coefficient. This is true, whether the $F$-band is due to stoichiometric excess of metal or to irradiation by X-rays.

Fig. 42 shows some results for sodium-chloride containing stoichiometric excess of metal. The current is plotted against time for various temperatures. The crystal was first illuminated for 5 seconds with a wave-length (4,700 A) lying in the $F$-band, and 12 seconds later by infra-red light.

At 30° C., illumination in the $F$-band gave a current which stopped and started instantaneously with the light. The total current was found to be proportional to the intensity of the light. It follows that the mean range $w$ is independent of the number of electrons ejected. Therefore electrons must be captured into metastable positions, which exist before the crystal is illuminated. We are thus dealing with case (1) of the last section. At higher temperatures, however, the current continues after illumination. It follows that the trapped electrons are not stable at these temperatures, and eventually escape. As the figure shows, infra-red radiation can also free the electrons. In these two cases the simplest assumption is that the current continues until every electron has either reached the anode or has found a vacant lattice point (either a 'frozen in' Schottky hole or an $F$-centre which lost its electron by absorption of a quantum of the light); before reaching a

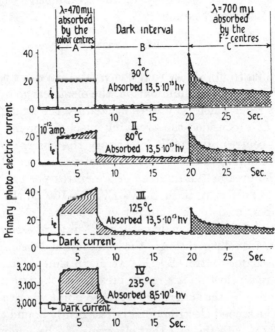

FIG. 42. Photoelectric current in a sodium-chloride crystal as a function of time. The electrodes were 4·2 mm. apart, and the field was $1·07 \times 10^5$ volt/cm.† The crystal was illuminated first with blue and subsequently with red light, the red light being absorbed by $F'$ centres as explained on p. 128

vacant lattice point an electron may visit several metastable centres. When the current has ceased to flow the number of $F$-centres is in every case the same as the initial number minus the number of electrons that have reached the anode.‡

Similar phenomena occur in zinc-sulphide phosphors at room temperature and in silver bromide at $-180°$ C.; in both cases the primary photoelectric current is proportional to the intensity of the light, which

† From R. W. Pohl, *Proc. Phys. Soc.* **49** (extra part), 16 (1937).

‡ In early work the current which flows under the influence of subsequent illumination with infra-red or of heating was called the replacement current, since it was believed to be due to the motion of the positive charge. For alkali-halides, at any rate, this has been shown not to be the case.

shows that the electrons are trapped in metastable centres of some kind. As before, when the crystal is warmed up the electrons become free; this is shown by the fact that a crystal which has been illuminated at low temperatures without an applied field, and is then warmed up in the dark, shows electronic conductivity like a semi-conductor. For zinc sulphide, the rate of decay of this conductivity ($\sigma$) has been measured by Reimann;[†] he found

$$\frac{1}{\sigma} = A(t+\text{const.}),$$  (7)

which, according to (6), shows that the crystal is returning to the condition that it had prior to illumination, the electrons going back to the atoms or ions from which they were ejected by the light.[‡]

We must now consider the trapping mechanism in alkali-halides containing $F$-centres. In Pohl's laboratory the current was measured in crystals containing different amounts of excess metal, and it was found that the greater the number of $F$-centres per cm.³ the smaller the range of the electron; in fact, in KCl at −100° C. the range $w$ was inversely proportional to the number of $F$-centres per cm.³ (Fig. 43). To account for this proportionality, the most natural assumption is that each electron, travelling through the conduction levels, is eventually trapped by a colour centre. By this we mean that it is trapped by an $F$-centre where an electron is already present, so that we now have two electrons trapped by the field round a lattice point where a negative ion is missing. The second electron must be less firmly bound than the first; this is consistent with the fact that electrons can be removed from the metastable levels by infra-red light, or by a small rise of temperature.

We know (Chap. III, § 5) that the field round a vacant lattice point can trap *one* electron. Let us then consider the field in which a second electron will move. We have first, of course, the field of the undistorted lattice; what interests us, however, is the additional field due to the $F$-centre. The potential energy $V$ of our second electron in this field will decay exponentially with distance at large distances, since the $F$-centre (electron replacing a negative ion) is neutral. But since the wave function of the electron in the $F$-centre extends over a greater volume than that of the negative ion which it replaces, $V$ will show a small 'potential hole' in this volume. For an undistorted crystal one could not say without detailed calculation whether there would exist any stationary states in this hole; just as, without calculation, one

† A. L. Reimann, *Nature*, **140**, 501 (1937).     ‡ Cf. also Chap. VI, § 2.

cannot say whether any neutral atom will have a positive electron affinity. Actually, however, we do not have to deal with an undistorted crystal; for, if two electrons are held at the vacant lattice point, the negative charge of the second electron will polarize the surrounding medium, the adjacent ions moving into new positions of equilibrium.

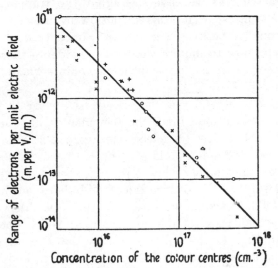

FIG. 43. Range of electrons in KCl at −100° C. (R. W. Pohl, loc. cit.)

As in the considerations of Chapter III, § 5.3, the spherical field due to this polarization is

$$\frac{e}{r^2}\left(\frac{1}{\kappa_0}-\frac{1}{\kappa}\right)$$

and its direction such as to push the electron back towards the centre. As we have seen, in a Coulomb field of this type there must exist a set of stationary states, in which the second electron can be trapped; this series of stationary states will be lower than those of an electron which has 'dug its own hole' as described on p. 87. We thus conclude that two electrons *can* be trapped at a vacant lattice point.

To describe the mechanism of the photoelectric current, then, consider first a crystal containing a certain number of $F$-centres, but with no applied field. An electron released by the light will execute a Brownian path, as described above, until it is captured by an $F$-centre. The length of this Brownian path is naturally inversely proportional to the number of $F$-centres per cm.[3] When a field is applied to the crystal, the mean distance that an electron drifts down the field before being trapped is directly proportional to the total length of the Brownian path, and is consequently inversely proportional to the number of $F$-centres per cm.³ This proportionality has been found over the range of concentrations between $2 \times 10^{15}$ and $10^{17}$ $F$-centres per cm.³ as is shown by the results illustrated in Fig. 13.

It appears then, as we have seen, that the trapping centres are themselves $F$-centres. So far, this conclusion has been drawn only from the proportionality between $1/w$ and the concentration of $F$-centres. We may go on now to inquire what other evidence there is that the metastable centres are really vacant lattice points where two electrons are trapped.

In all types of crystal the photoelectrons appear to get stuck at metastable centres of some kind. Since incident light of suitable wavelength will be able to free these electrons again, a sufficient concentration of trapped electrons should give rise to a new absorption band. As the traps are presumably shallow, the new absorption will lie towards longer wave-lengths. Not only in the alkali-halides, but in other types of crystal as well,† such an increased absorption is observed for longer wave-lengths than those of the incident light which liberates photoelectrons. In Fig. 44 the curve $A$ shows the $F$-band in KCl with stoichiometric excess of metal before illumination, and the curve $B$ gives the appearance of the absorption spectrum after prolonged illumination with a wave-length lying in the $F$-band;‡ the illumination was carried out at $-100°$ and the absorption was measured at $-235°$ C. The new band lying in the red and infra-red, and shaded in the figure, is known as the $F'$-band. It was not possible to destroy more than two-thirds of the original $F$-band (presumably owing to the overlapping of the two bands). In crystals which have been coloured by X-rays, illumination in the $F$-band causes simultaneously a partial bleaching of the crystal and a partial development of the $F'$-band, the relative amounts of these two processes depending very much upon the state of perfection of the crystal. In crystals with stoichiometric excess of metal we are concerned only with conversion of the $F$-band into the $F'$-band, and its converse;‖ for at any temperature illumination with wave-lengths lying in the $F'$-band restores the $F$-band in its original form. When a voltage has been applied to the crystal, illumination in

† B. Gudden and R. W. Pohl, *Zeits. f. Physik*, **37**, 881 (1926).

‡ H. Pick, *Ann. d. Physik*, **31**, 365 (1938); R. W. Pohl, *Proc. Phys. Soc.* **49** (extra part), 11 (1937).

‖ The efficiencies of these two processes at different temperatures will be discussed in § 6.1.

the $F'$-band is accompanied by electrical conductivity with efficiency similar to that of the $F$-band; and it is evident that in all these illuminations we are chasing electrons through the conduction levels from one type of centre to another. Under monochromatic illumination in the $F'$-band the sensitivity is independent of wave-length, indicating that the $F'$-band is a single band, arising from centres of one type; these are known as $F'$-centres.

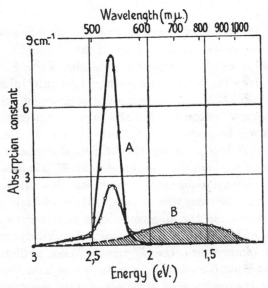

Fig. 44. $F$ and $F'$ bands in KCl at $-235°$ C.

The quantum efficiency of light in converting the $F$-band into the $F'$-band was measured by Pick.† He found that, between $-80°$ and $-100°$ C., when a crystal is illuminated with wave-lengths lying in the $F$-band one quantum of light absorbed destroys two $F$-centres. This supports the view that the trapping centres are themselves $F$-centres. When a quantum of light is absorbed, an electron is ejected from one $F$-centre, leaving behind a vacant lattice point, and the electron is captured by another $F$-centre, which it converts into an $F'$-centre.‡ Conversely, when an $F'$-centre absorbs a quantum of red or infra-red light, one of the electrons is removed from it. This electron may

† H. Pick, loc. cit.
‡ It was mentioned on p. 121 that the quantum efficiency in these crystals is not directly known from measurements of the photoelectric current, owing to the difficulty in saturating the current. The evidence from conversion of $F$-centres indicates that, in an applied field, each quantum can liberate one electron at these temperatures.

3595.32

combine with another $F$-centre, or it may find a vacant lattice point; in the latter case two $F$-centres are re-formed.

Another point that may be raised with regard to the $F'$-centres is the question of their thermal stability. At what temperatures will the thermal energy be sufficient to eject the trapped electrons from the metastable levels? The condition that such a metastable centre has a half-lifetime $\tau$ is that

$$\nu e^{-U/kT} \sim \frac{1}{\tau}, \tag{5}$$

where $\nu$ is of the order of frequency of the atomic vibrations, say $10^{12}$ sec.$^{-1}$, and $U$ is the thermal depth of the trap.

From Fig. 44 it will be seen that the middle of the $F'$-band in KCl lies near $h\nu = 1\cdot 7$ eV. If we were to introduce this value for $U$ into (5), we should find that the centres were completely stable, even at $100°$ C. But here we encounter for the first time a property of ionic crystals which will be discussed in Chapter V, §3. It will be shown in detail there that in any polar crystal the optical depth of any electron trap is very different from the thermal depth. This is to say, the value of the thermal energy required to remove an electron from any kind of trap is *less* than the energy $h\nu$ of the quantum which is just sufficient to eject the electron; in the alkali-halides it is rather more than half. When crystals of KCl and NaCl containing $F'$-centres are kept in the dark at room temperature, the $F'$-centres have a lifetime of some hours, indicating that $U \sim 1\cdot 0$ eV., a value, as we have stated, less than that given by the position of their absorption spectrum. The lifetime decreases rapidly with rise of temperature; and for this reason, in photoconductivity experiments, warming the crystal may be used to bring it back to its original state. The short lifetime is also responsible for the fact that, with flash illumination, the photocurrent at these temperatures does not stop when the light is cut off, as shown in Fig. 42 above.

The evidence given here shows that in these crystals the capture by an $F$-centre is the most important mechanism of trapping. This rules out the mechanism described in Chapter III, §5.3, as 'trapping by digging its own hole' as an important agency in crystals containing high concentrations of $F$-centres.

Some quantitative values for the probability of trapping will be of interest. Suppose that each $F$-centre has a cross-sectional area for trapping which we may denote by $\sigma$. $\sigma$ is thus the actual area multiplied by the probability of capture. Then, if $u$ is the mean velocity of an electron in the conduction band, the mean time $t$ that an electron can exist in the free state before it is trapped will be given by

$$t = 1/N\sigma u,$$

where $N$ is the number of $F$-centres per unit volume. Thus for the range we have

$$w = vF/N\sigma u,$$

where $v$ is the mobility. Setting

$$v = \frac{e}{m} \frac{l}{2u},$$

where $l$ is the mean free path, we have

$$\frac{w}{F} = \frac{e}{2mu^2} \frac{l}{N\sigma}.$$

Putting $\frac{1}{2}mu^2 = \frac{3}{2}kT$, this gives

$$\frac{w}{F} = \frac{e}{6kT} \frac{l}{N\sigma}.$$

In this equation all the quantities are known except $l$ and $\sigma$. We may, however, estimate $l$ from the discussion on p. 107 to be of the order $10^{-7}$ to $10^{-8}$ cm.

As an example, let us consider KCl at $-100°$ C. with $10^{17}$ $F$-centres per cm.³ From Fig. 43 we see that $w/F$ is $3 \times 10^{-9}$ cm. per volt/cm. We obtain

$$\sigma = l \times 5 \times 10^{-8} \text{ cm.}^2,$$

which is of the order $10^{-14}$ to $10^{-15}$ cm.², so that an electron is likely to be captured by the first $F$-centre with which it collides.

These large cross-sections show that we are not dealing with radiative capture; probably the energy of the electron is given up to the lattice vibrations in the form of heat, as discussed in Chapter III, § 12.

### 5.2. Photoelectrons in crystals other than the alkali-halides

In the crystals that we have been discussing the proportionality between $1/w$ and the number of $F$-centres was found to hold over the range investigated, namely, from $2 \times 10^{15}$ to $10^{17}$ $F$-centres per cm.³ In alkali-halides containing fewer $F$-centres the proportionality between concentration and $1/w$ must break down at some point where another type of trapping centre becomes active. For the capacity to trap photo-electrons is a property common to all crystals that are photoconducting. We may expect the range in other types of crystal to be much longer than in crystals containing a large number of $F$-centres. For the trapping centres there are various possibilities; singularities of the

$F$-centre type, interstitial atoms or ions, or Tamm levels (Chap. III, § 5) at internal surfaces or cracks. The range of an electron in a given field is in general a structure-sensitive property.

Measurements of the range in single crystals of silver and thallium halides at $-170°$ C. have been made in Pohl's laboratory,[†] and have already been mentioned in connexion with saturation. The values found (for an applied field $F$) were of the order

$$w/F \sim 2 \text{ to } 4 \times 10^{-4} \text{ cm. per volt/cm.}$$

This is about $10^4$ larger than for a KCl crystal with $2 \cdot 7 \times 10^{16}$ $F$-centres per cubic cm. If one assumes that the mean free path is about the same in silver halides as in alkali-halides, it follows that the number of trapping centres in the silver halides is of the order $10^{12}$ per cubic cm. We shall, however, give evidence that in the silver halide grains of photographic emulsions the number of trapping centres is somewhat greater than this (Chap. VII, § 7).

The range in pure silver halide crystals (at $-170°$ C.) can be enormously *decreased* by previous illumination with blue light at room temperatures, by which the crystal is partially decomposed with the formation of specks of colloidal metal in the crystal. Lehfeldt[‡] found that in pure silver bromide at $-170°$ C. the current-voltage curve under illumination gave saturation in the sense shown in Fig. 41 for a field of 3,000 volt/cm.; but after a previous illumination at room temperature in which $\sim 5 \times 10^{17}$ quanta had been absorbed per cm.$^3$, saturation of the photocurrent could not be obtained at 20,000 volt/cm.

It follows from these results that specks of colloidal metal act as efficient electron traps, and in fact that in the crystal investigated the normal fate of an electron (in not too strong an applied field) was to be trapped by a colloidal particle of metal. In alkali-halide crystals containing specks of colloidal metal a similar trapping of electrons is found.[||]

In order to understand how a particle of metal acts as an electron trap, the reader is referred to Fig. 67 on p. 169; the highest unoccupied level in the metal will be *below* the lowest level of the conduction band of the salt.

On the other hand, long irradiation of a silver halide at a *low* temperature (where colloid formation is impossible) *increases* the range. This is illustrated by Fig. 73 on p. 187, in which some further results

† W. Lehfeldt, *Göttinger Nachrichten*, Fachgruppe II, **1**, 171 (1935).
‡ Loc. cit., p. 185.
|| G. Glaser and W. Lehfeldt, ibid. **2**, 91 (1936).

of Lehfeldt are shown. The figure shows the normal current-voltage curve at $-170°$ C. for a specimen of AgBr which had been cooled slowly in the dark (cf. Fig. 41 above); also the curves for the same crystal after it had been irradiated at the same temperature with $10^{13}$ quanta and with $10^{14}$ quanta. Saturation is more easily obtained after pre-illumination, indicating a longer range.

The most natural explanation is that electrons released from halogen ions by the light are trapped in the ordinary way, until eventually all the shallow traps become occupied, and thus put out of action; an equal number of neutral halogen atoms are left instead. When subsequently a voltage is applied to the crystal to measure a photoelectric current, the electrons will be able to travel much longer distances, if the probability of being permanently captured by a halogen atom is less than for one of the usual traps. According to the interpretation given below, this will be so. When an electron encounters a neutral halogen atom it will be captured into an excited state, and will fall to the ground state if it stays long enough to radiate. But we shall ascribe the observed photoconductivity to the fact that, at the temperature of experiment, the thermal vibrations are sufficient to liberate an electron from an excited state before it is likely to have fallen back to the ground state (p. 138).

The number of quanta required to fill all the shallow traps with electrons is in fair agreement with the estimate ($10^{12}$ per cm.$^3$) which we made above of the number of shallow traps in the silver halides. An effect of the same kind occurs in luminescent materials; this will be discussed in Chapter VI, § 2.

## 6. Dependence of photocurrent on temperature

### 6.1. Alkali-halides

We have hitherto been discussing the behaviour of photoelectrons after they have been thrown into the empty conduction levels of the crystal. We must now consider experimental data which throw some light on the initial process whereby the absorption of a quantum releases an electron. We begin with coloured alkali-halide crystals illuminated in the $F$-band.

Figs. 45 and 46 show, for NaCl and KCl, the charge passing through the electrometer in Fig. 39 divided by the number of quanta absorbed by the crystal.† This is expressed as the product of the range

---

† From R. W. Pohl, *Proc. Phys. Soc.* **49** (extra part), 13 (1937); see also H. Pick, *Ann. d. Physik*, **31**, 373 (1938).

$w$ and the number $\eta$ of electrons released per absorbed quantum ($\eta \leqslant 1$).

The sharp drop in $\eta w$ which occurs at $-150°$ C. for both salts is

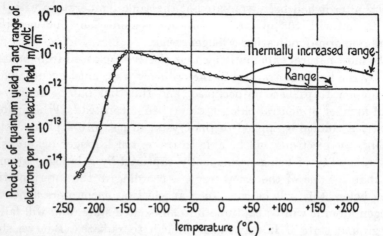

FIG. 45. Current-temperature curve for NaCl with $10^{16}$ colour centres per cm.³ irradiated with $\lambda = 4,700$ A. The 'range' gives the current during exposure, the thermally increased range includes the current after exposure (cf. Fig. 42)

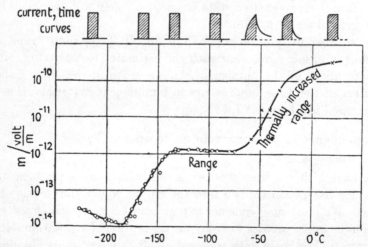

FIG. 46. Current-temperature curve for KCl with $2.7 \times 10^{16}$ colour centres per cm.³ irradiated with $\lambda = 5,550$ A

almost certainly due to a drop in $\eta$. A similar drop occurs in the quantum efficiency of the transformation of $F$-centres into $F'$-centres in the absence of an electric field (Fig. 47). We see, then, that the probability $\eta$ that an absorbed quantum frees an electron decreases rapidly as the temperature is lowered below $-150°$ C.

The new rise in $\eta w/F$ below $-180°$ C. in KCl is certainly due to electrons which are liberated not from $F$-centres but from traces of colloidal metal. The efficiency of liberation of electrons from colloidal particles, then, does not show a similar drop.

A theoretical interpretation of this temperature drop in the photo-current was given by the present authors.[†] As we have seen, the absorption of a quantum of radiation in the $F$-band moves the electron

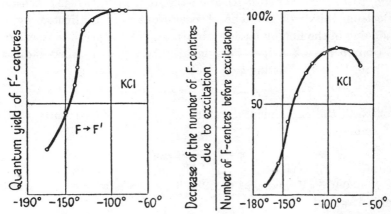

FIG. 47.  Quantum yield of $F'$-centres when a crystal is irradiated in the $F$-band[‡]

into an excited state in the potential hole around the vacant lattice point; it does not eject it into the conduction band. The electron can, then, only make a contribution to the current if the thermal agitation of the surrounding ions is sufficient to eject the electron into the conduction band before it drops back into its normal state in the $F$-centre. In this way a qualitative explanation is given of the drop in the photo-conductivity.

To attempt a quantitative explanation, we denote by $A\,dt$ the probability per time interval $dt$ that the electron drops back to the normal state, and by $B\,dt$ the probability that the thermal agitation frees the electron. Then the number $\eta$ of electrons released per absorbed quantum will be given by

$$\eta = \frac{B}{B+A} = \frac{1}{1+A/B}. \tag{6}$$

We may assume that $B$ will be of the form (cf. formula (20) on p. 108)

$$B = B_0\,e^{-E/kT},$$

† R. W. Gurney and N. F. Mott, *Trans. Faraday Soc.* **34**, 506 (1938); N. F. Mott, *Proc. Phys. Soc.* **50**, 196 (1938).                    ‡ From R. W. Pohl, loc. cit.

where $E$ is the energy required to remove an electron from the excited state of an $F$-centre into the conduction band, and $B_0$ is a constant. If $A$ corresponds to a radiative transition, we shall have, from the ordinary formula for the Einstein $A$ coefficient,

$$A = 8 \times 10^9 f \left( \frac{h\nu}{13 \cdot 54} \right)^2,$$

where $f$ is the oscillator strength and $\nu$ the frequency, $h\nu$ being measured in electron volts. (N.B.—The $A$ coefficient is not affected by the broadening of the line by lattice vibrations.) We expect the re-emitted radiation to have a longer wave-length than the absorbed radiation (cf. Chap. VI, § 3). Putting $h\nu = 1$ eV. and $f = 1$, this gives

$$A \sim 0 \cdot 5 \times 10^8 \text{ sec.}^{-1}$$

For NaCl the experimental values of $\eta$ can be fitted fairly well to the formula

$$\eta = \frac{1}{1 + p e^{E/kT}}, \tag{7}$$

with $E \sim 0 \cdot 075$ eV. and $p = 0 \cdot 0033$. This agrees with our theoretical formula if we set

$$B_0 = \frac{0 \cdot 5 \times 10^8}{0 \cdot 0033} = 1 \cdot 5 \times 10^{10} \text{ sec.}^{-1}$$

As regards the rather small value of $E$, a discussion has already been given (§ 2). The value of $B_0$ seems to us quite reasonable (cf. p. 108). We expect $B_0$ to be considerably less than the frequency of the lattice vibrations ($10^{13}$ sec.$^{-1}$) for the following reason: if one plots (Fig. 48) against any parameter ($d$) specifying the displacements of surrounding ions, the energies of the (excited) bound state and the state when the electron is removed from the $F$-centre into its lowest state in the conduction band, the two curves can never cross; for one always has to do work to remove an electron from a positive charge. Thus our transition probability $B$ would be the product of the probability ($10^{13} e^{-E/kT}$) per unit time that the excited system is raised from $A$ to $B$ and the probability of a transition such as that from $B$ to $C$; the latter may be quite a small quantity.

It is not certain, however, that the transition probability $A$ is that for an optical transition; the transition may take place with the emission of heat. Against this hypothesis we have two arguments:

1. *One* mechanism (to be discussed later, see Chap. VI, § 3, p. 222) for the conversion of energy into heat is impossible for $F$-centres.

2. It is difficult to understand the small value of $p$, or in other words the sharp drop of $\eta$, on this hypothesis.

It would be of interest to see if *at low temperatures* (where $\eta$ is small) there is any fluorescence in the near infra-red for alkali-halides illuminated in the $F$-band.

One would expect that crystals illuminated to the short-wave side of the $F$-band, and hence in the region of true continuous absorption

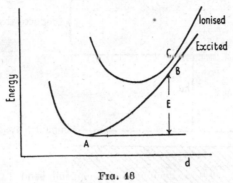

Fig. 18

(Fig. 37), would not show this drop in the photocurrent, since free electrons would be produced even at low temperatures. Experiments to test this have not been made.

The quantum efficiency for the transition $F'-F$ (measured in the absence of an. electric field) does not show any decrease as the temperature is lowered. As the $F'$-centre is negatively charged, this is to be expected; the absorption process will be similar to that in a free negative ion; i.e. the $F'$-band is due to the removal of an electron directly into the conduction band.

### 6.2. Other insulating crystals

The $F$-band in a coloured alkali-halide crystal is a well-defined absorption band, and it is certain that, for illumination in this band, the photoelectrons come from the $F$-centres. It will be recalled that absorption of ultra-violet light is not accompanied by any photoconductivity, and that other crystals are in marked contrast to the alkali-halides in this respect. The experiments on the silver and thallous halides, zinc sulphide, and so on, make use of light absorbed in the long-wave-length tail of the characteristic ultra-violet absorption band (cf. Chap. III, § 8). For wave-lengths near the tail of the absorption band, where the light can penetrate a reasonable distance into the crystal, it is not at present certain whether the absorption is due to atoms and ions of the perfect lattice or to ions situated on the surface of cracks (Herzfeld absorption, Chap. III, §9). Evidence for the latter point of view is afforded by the behaviour of the positive holes left behind by the electron. In the photoconduction of silver halides at low temperatures the positives do not move, a positive space-charge being left behind in the crystal when the photoelectrons are removed

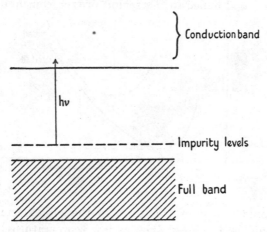

Fig. 49. Showing absorption of light by an impurity centre

by the field. On the other hand, in zinc-sulphide phosphors activated by α-particles, and probably also by light, there is very definite evidence that positive holes do move (cf. Chap. VI, §1).

If the absorption is at impurity centres or by atoms at cracks, we should expect the holes to be trapped at low temperatures, though they might become mobile at higher temperatures; as illustrated in Fig. 49, the electron is released from an impurity centre just above the full band.

As regards temperature dependence, the evidence is contradictory. In thallium and silver halides the primary current has only been investigated down to −180° C., at which temperature there is very direct evidence that about one electron is produced per quantum absorbed (p. 120). A drop is observed,† however, in the *secondary* photocurrent at very low temperatures (20° K. for AgBr); this may be due to a drop in the primary current at these temperatures. On the other hand, the sensitivity of AgBr photographic emulsions does not show any striking drop at these temperatures (cf. Chap. VII, §8).

We suggest the following mechanism, proposed in the first place by

† W. Lehfeldt, *Göttinger Nachrichten*, Fachgruppe II, **1**, 171 (1935).

von Hippel† in another connexion, and since developed by Seitz:‡ In
the primary absorption act an electron is ejected from a halogen ion
to an unstable position on a neighbouring metal ion. The halogen atom
left behind is then too small for its place; energy will be gained if it is
displaced sideways. The energy of the resultant state may cross that
of the original ground state, as shown in Fig. 50. In this case the
excited state will be metastable.

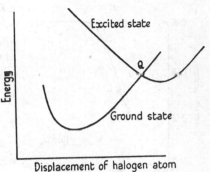

Consider now the work required to
remove the electron from its new
position into the conduction band.
If this energy is less than the energy
required to bring the electron to
the state $Q$, then except at high
temperature an electron will nearly
always become free before it can
pass over the hill at $Q$ and return to
the ground state. The drop in the
photocurrent at low temperatures

Displacement of halogen atom
FIG. 50

may be due to the very long time required to free an electron. If $w$ is
the necessary activation energy, and‖ $10^{10}e^{-w/kT}$ is the probability per
second that an electron is freed, and if this drops to, say, $10^{-3}$ sec.$^{-1}$
at $20°$ K., then

$$w = 15\log_e 10 \times 20k \sim \tfrac{1}{20} \text{ eV.,}$$

which is reasonable.†† The failure of photographic sensitivity to show
any drop at low temperatures can also be understood in the light of
this model; the trapped electrons would be released when the emulsion
was warmed up.

The spectral sensitivity for the photoelectric current in AgBr and
AgCl has been investigated by Lehfeldt,‡‡ whose results were discussed
on p. 120 and are plotted in Fig. 51. At a wave-length of 3,650 A the
absorption coefficient has already risen to a value 580 mm.$^{-1}$, and rises
above $10^4$ mm.$^{-1}$ Yet the quantum efficiency only falls from 0·6 to 0·17
at a wave-length of 2,540 A. The results for AgCl at a temperature of
$-170°$ C. were very similar.

This behaviour must be contrasted with that of ZnS‖‖ and diamond,

† A. von Hippel, *Zeits. f. Physik*, **101**, 680 (1936).
‡ F. Seitz, *Trans. Faraday Soc.* **35**, 74 (1939).
‖ Cf. § 6.1, where this expression is obtained for $F$-centres.
†† Cf. Chap. III, § 5.
‡‡ W. Lehfeldt, loc. cit., p. 177.
‖‖ B. Gudden and R. W. Pohl, *Zeits. f. Physik*, **17**, 340 (1923); F. Hlučka, ibid. **113**,
56 (1939).

where the photoelectric current becomes effectively zero as soon as the absorption coefficient rises above 1 mm.$^{-1}$

The reason for the drop in quantum efficiency as the absorption coefficient rises is not understood. It may perhaps be explained if we assume, as suggested in Chapter III, § 8, that the long-wave-length tail is due to forbidden transitions. As shown there, the exciton due to a forbidden transition would dissociate more easily than that due to an optically allowed transition. Thus, in the region of high absorption, a higher temperature would be needed to cause the excitons to dissociate.

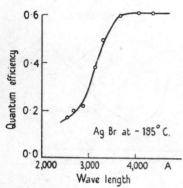

FIG. 51. Quantum efficiency of production of electrons in AgBr at −185° C.

### 7. The migration of $F$-centres

One of the best-known experiments with $F$-centres is that illustrated in Fig. 52. A crystal containing stoichiometric excess of metal (and hence $F$-centres) is mounted between two electrodes. At temperatures above two or three hundred degrees centigrade, in a field of a few hundred volts/cm., the colour is observed to migrate towards the anode, the migration taking place with a definite sharp edge and with a uniform velocity, the value of which increases rapidly with the temperature.

A volume including an $F$-centre is electrically neutral; no energy would be gained if an $F$-centre were to move in the direction of the field by changing places with a neighbouring negative ion. Thus an applied field does not exert any pull on an $F$-centre as a whole. The migration takes place because at the temperatures considered a small fraction of the $F$-centres are dissociated into free electrons and vacant lattice points. The electrons will migrate towards the anode, the vacant lattice points towards the cathode; but at these temperatures the crystal is an electrolytic conductor, and contains a large number of vacant lattice points of both signs (Chap. II, § 5). Thus electrons, drifting into previously uncoloured regions, will always find new holes which they can occupy, thus forming new colour centres there.

If the conductivity due to the $F$-centres is small compared with the electrolytic conductivity (small concentration of $F$-centres), the motion of the coloured region will not be hindered by the setting up of space-charges. Under these conditions we may write:

Velocity of drift of the coloured region = velocity of drift of free electrons multiplied by the proportion of the $F$-centres dissociated.

The velocity of drift in different alkali-halides was measured in Pohl's laboratory; and it was found that it varies with the temperature $T$ and the field $F$ according to the formula

$$\text{velocity} = vF, \qquad v = v_0 e^{-w/kT}. \tag{7}$$

Pohl has called $v$ the 'mobility' of a colour centre. The values of $w$ for several halides are given in Table 22 on p. 143; $v_0$ is of the order 100 cm./sec. per volt/cm.

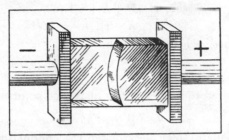

Fig. 52. Migration of $F$-centres in KCl at 580° C.

In order to give a theory of the significance of the experimental quantity $w$ above, we must calculate the degree of dissociation of the $F$-centres in a crystal, taking into account the influence of the vacant lattice points, which give rise to the electrolytic conduction. We shall consider, then, a crystal of $N$ ion pairs, containing in addition $n$ excess metal atoms, and thus $n$ colour centres. Of these let $x$ be dissociated; also let $E_F$ be the dissociation energy of an $F$-centre, i.e. the energy required to take an electron from its lowest state in the field of a vacant lattice point to the lowest state in the conduction band of the crystal. Let the energy required to form a pair of separate vacant lattice points be $W$, and at the temperature considered let $X$ such pairs exist.

Our purpose is to calculate the free energy $F$ as a function of $x$ and $X$; their equilibrium values will then be given by

$$\frac{\partial F}{\partial x} = \frac{\partial F}{\partial X} = 0.$$

The crystal contains $N + X + n$ pairs of lattice points. Of these, $X$ lattice points normally occupied by positive ions and $X + x$ normally occupied by negative ions are vacant. There are $n - x$ undissociated $F$-centres and $x$ free electrons in the conduction band.

Consider first the lattice points normally occupied by positive ions. $X$ of these are vacant; their positions can be chosen in

$$P_1 = \frac{(N+X+n)!}{(N+n)!\,X!}$$

ways. Their random distribution makes a contribution to the entropy of $k \log P_1$ and hence to the free energy of

$$-kT \log P_1. \tag{8}$$

Among the lattice points normally occupied by negative ions, $X+x$ are vacant and $n-x$ occupied by $F$-centres. Their positions can be chosen in

$$P_2 = \frac{(N+X+n)!}{(X+x)!\,(n-x)!\,N!} \tag{9}$$

ways, giving a further contribution

$$-kT \log P_2 \tag{10}$$

to the free energy.

The work required to form the vacant lattice points and to dissociate the $F$-centres is

$$XW+xE_F. \tag{11}$$

Finally, the free energy of $x$ electrons in the conduction band is†

$$-xkT\left[\log\left(\frac{2\pi mkT}{h^2}\right)^{\frac{3}{2}}+\log\frac{V}{x}+1\right], \tag{12}$$

where $V$ is the volume considered.

The total free energy is the sum of (8), (10), (11), and (12). In applying the conditions for equilibrium, we use the approximation

$$d \log z! \sim \log z\, dz.$$

Then, since $F$ is a minimum with respect to variation of $X$, we obtain for a crystal containing $x$ dissociated $F$-centres

$$-kT \log \frac{(N+X+x)^2}{X(X+x)}+W = 0.$$

Since $N$ is in practice large compared with $X$ and $n$, this may be written

$$\frac{X(X+x)}{N^2} = e^{-W/kT}, \tag{13}$$

a formula which corresponds to equation (7) of Chapter II for a crystal with no $F$-centres. From the condition that $F$ is a minimum with respect to variations of $x$ we have

$$kT\left[\log\frac{X+x}{n-x}-\log\left(\frac{2\pi mkT}{h^2}\right)^{\frac{3}{2}}-\log\frac{V}{x}\right]+E_F = 0,$$

† Cf. Chap. V, § 1.

or
$$\frac{x(X+x)}{n-x} = \left(\frac{2\pi mkT}{h^2}\right)^{\frac{3}{2}} V e^{-E_F/kT}. \tag{14}$$

Equations (13) and (14) give the required values of $x$ and $X$ for a crystal in equilibrium. Of particular interest is the case where the concentration of $F$-centres is small, so that $x$ (the number of free electrons) is small compared with $X$ (number of vacant lattice points). This means in practice that the concentration of $F$-centres is not sufficient to affect appreciably the conductivity of the crystal. Then (13) becomes, as for a crystal without $F$-centres,

$$X = N e^{-\frac{1}{2}W/kT},$$

and (14) becomes (assuming $x \ll n$)

$$x = \frac{n}{N} V \left(\frac{2\pi mkT}{h^2}\right)^{\frac{3}{2}} e^{-(E_F - \frac{1}{2}W)/kT}. \tag{15}$$

The correctness of the factor occurring outside the exponential in (15) is very uncertain; in deriving it we have, for instance, neglected the change in the vibrational frequency of the atoms next to holes (Chap. II, § 5). From the exponential factor, however, we see that the interpretation of $w$ is
$$w = E_F - \frac{1}{2}W. \tag{16}$$

From formula (16) we may at once evaluate the dissociation energy $E_F$ of an $F$-centre, using Pohl's values of $w$ obtained from the mobility of $F$-centres when the concentration is low. For $W$ we take the calculated values (Chap. II, § 7). The results are as follows:

TABLE 22. *Dissociation Energy $E_F$ of an $F$-centre (in eV.)*

| Crystal | NaCl | KCl | KBr |
|---|---|---|---|
| $w$ (observed)   .     .     . | 0·94 | 1·00 | 0·84 |
| $\frac{1}{2}W$ (calculated in Chap. II) | 0·95 | 0·95 | 0·94 |
| $E_F$ (formula (16))   .     . | 1·89 | 1·95 | 1·78 |
| $h\nu$ (observed)   .     .     . | 2·7 | 2·3 | 2·05 |

We give also the observed optical excitation energy $h\nu$ of an $F$-centre; $\nu$ is the frequency at the maximum of the $F$-band at the temperature of liquid hydrogen. It will be seen that the thermal dissociation energy $E_F$ is less than the optical excitation energy, and *a fortiori* less than the optical dissociation energy. This is a general property of trapped electrons in solids, which has already been mentioned with reference to $F'$-centres, and will be discussed in Chapter V, § 3.

## 8. A crystal in thermal equilibrium with a vapour

The foregoing sections have dealt mainly with crystals into which a stoichiometric excess of metal had been introduced by heating the crystal in the vapour of the metal. This is a process of a very general type, which is not confined to the metallic constituent. Cuprous oxide, for example, heated in an atmosphere of oxygen, acquires an excess of oxygen.† It is of interest, therefore, to discuss the factors which determine the composition of crystals under such treatment.

We have to calculate the concentration of $F$-centres in a crystal in thermal equilibrium with a vapour of alkali metal. Let us suppose that the vapour is monatomic, and contains $n_v$ atoms per unit volume. Its free energy is then

$$-n_v kT\left[\log\left(\frac{2\pi mkT}{h^2}\right)^{\frac{3}{2}}+\log\frac{1}{n_v}+1\right]$$

and the increase in the free energy, if one atom is removed from the vapour, is

$$kT\left[\log\left(\frac{2\pi mkT}{h^2}\right)^{\frac{3}{2}}+\log\frac{1}{n_v}\right]. \tag{17}$$

Let us now put this atom into the solid as a positive ion plus an $F$-centre. When the solid is in equilibrium with the vapour, the change in the free energy of the solid must be equal to the change in the free energy of the vapour. To calculate the former, let $W_F$ be the work required to add an atom to the crystal and to form an $F$-centre. We require also the entropy change. Let the solid contain $N$ ion pairs, and $n_F$ $F$-centres and thus $n_F$ excess positive ions. Then the entropy, assuming that the number of dissociated centres is negligible, is

$$k\log\frac{(N+n_F)!}{n_F!\,N!},$$

and the change in the entropy when $n_F$ is increased by unity is

$$k\log\frac{N+n_F}{n_F}.$$

Thus the increase in the free energy is

$$W_F-kT\log\frac{N+n_F}{n_F}.$$

The condition for equilibrium is thus

$$W_F-kT\log\frac{N+n_F}{n_F}+kT\log\left(\frac{2\pi mkT}{h^2}\right)^{\frac{3}{2}}+kT\log\frac{1}{n_v}=0,$$

which gives

$$\frac{n_F}{N+n_F}=n_v\left(\frac{2\pi mkT}{h^2}\right)^{\frac{3}{2}}e^{-W_F/kT} \tag{18}$$

† For a discussion of this, cf. Chap. V.

This formula is calculated neglecting the free energy due to the vibrations of atoms of the crystal; the factor outside the exponential is therefore unreliable. It also assumes that most of the $F$-centres have not lost their electrons at the temperature $T$.

For KBr in potassium vapour Pohl and his colleagues have determined the ratio $n_F/n_v$ of colour centres per unit volume of crystal to

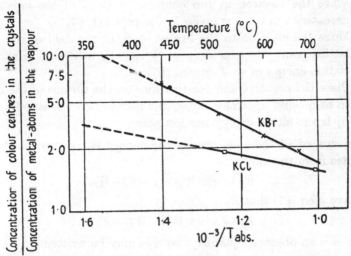

Fig. 53. Concentration of colour centres in alkali-halides in equilibrium with alkali vapour†

atoms per unit volume of vapour; their results are shown in Fig. 53. Plotting $\log(n_F/n_v)$ against $1/T$ they obtain a straight line, from which they deduce $W_F$. From measurements at two temperatures they have also deduced a value for KCl. The values are

|  | KCl | KBr |
|---|---|---|
| $W_F$ (eV.) | $-0.10$ | $-0.25$ |

Thus energy is *gained* if an atom is dissolved forming an $F$-centre.

Owing, however, to the neglect of a possible temperature factor outside the exponential, these values must be considered as approximate only.

If a crystal containing a high concentration of $F$-centres is cooled slowly, colloidal particles of metal form; by rapid quenching, however, the centres can be frozen in.‡

As regards the energy $W_F$ required to form an $F$-centre, a theoretical

---

† R. W. Pohl, *Proc. Phys. Soc.* **49** (extra part), 3 (1937).
‡ R. W. Pohl, loc. cit., p. 8.

calculation has been given by Gurney and Mott.† An $F$-centre can be added to a crystal by means of the following cycle:

1. Remove a negative ion from the body of the crystal; the work $W_{\bar{H}}$ was calculated in Chapter II, § 7.
2. Ionize an atom of the vapour; the necessary work is $I$, the ionization potential.
3. Place the electron in the conduction band of the crystal; the necessary work $-\chi$ is given in Chapter III, § 7.
4. Move the electron to the lowest state in the field of the vacant lattice point; the necessary work is $-E_F$, where $E_F$ is the dissociation energy of an $F$-centre (§ 7).
5. Place the negative and positive ions on the surface of the crystal, to help build up a new layer; the necessary work is $-W_L$, where $W_L$ is the lattice energy per ion pair.

The sum of all these energies is the energy $W_F$ required to form an $F$-centre from the vapour:

$$W_F = I + W_{\bar{H}} - \chi - E_F - W_L.$$

We have seen (§ 7) that $E_F$ is given by

$$E_F = w + \tfrac{1}{2}(W_{\bar{H}}^+ + W_{\bar{H}} - W_L),$$

where $w$ is an observed quantity, so this may be written

$$W_F = I + \tfrac{1}{2}(W_{\bar{H}} - W_{\bar{H}}^+) - \tfrac{1}{2}W_L - \chi - w.$$

The only quantity which has to be calculated theoretically in this is the small difference $W_{\bar{H}} - W_{\bar{H}}^+$. The agreement with experiment is shown below.

### TABLE 23

Energies in eV.

|  | NaCl | KCl | KBr |
|---|---|---|---|
| Ionization energy ($I$) of alkali atom (observed) | 5·11 | 4·32 | 4·32 |
| Energy $-\chi$ of conduction band . . | −0·53 | −0·07 | −0·70 |
| $-w$ ($w$ is observed activation energy for mobility of $F$-centres) . . . . | −0·94 | −1·00 | −0·84 |
| $\tfrac{1}{2}(W_{\bar{H}} - W_{\bar{H}}^+)$ . . . . | +0·28 | +0·16 | 0·19 |
| Lattice energy per ion $-\tfrac{1}{2}W_L$ . . . | −3·97 | −3·59 | −3·45 |
| Total energy $W_F$ . . . . . | 0·05 | −0·18 | −0·48 |
| Energy $W_F$ observed . . . . | .. | −0·10 | −0·25 |

Finally, it may be of some interest to discuss the mechanism by which $F$-centres are formed when a crystal is heated in the vapour. We must imagine that first of all an atom is adsorbed on the surface

† R. W. Gurney and N. F. Mott, *Trans. Faraday Soc.* **34**, 506 (1938).

at a point such as that shown in Fig. 54 (a). After a certain time the atom loses its electron, which becomes an electron in the conduction band; also a negative ion will move up from the layer beneath and take its place by the side of the adsorbed positive ion; this will be the

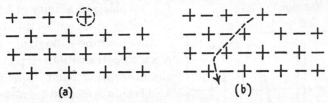

(a)                                    (b)

FIG. 54. Illustrating the formation of an $F$-centre

way in which new layers of the crystal are built up. At the high temperatures used the vacant lattice point can migrate to the interior of the crystal, and eventually trap the electron and form an $F$-centre.

## 9. Formation of $F$-centres from $U$-centres

Pohl and his collaborators have carried out experiments with KBr containing about 10⁻⁴ parts of KH. The hydride can be shown to go into solid solution in KBr, since by means of X-rays a linear decrease

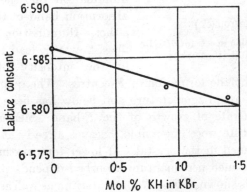

FIG. 55. Lattice constants of KBr+KH†

of lattice constant can be observed up to about 1·5 mols per cent. of KH (cf. Fig. 55). It is thus almost certain that hydrogen negative ions H⁻ replace bromide ions in the lattice.

The presence of the hydride gives rise to a new absorption band (the $U$-band) in the ultra-violet, lying on the long-wave-length side of the characteristic absorption, Fig. 56. The maximum is at 5·4 eV., while

† R. Hilsch and R. W. Pohl, *Trans. Faraday Soc.* **34**, 883 (1938).

the first maximum of the characteristic absorption of pure KBr is at 6·7 eV. The difference 1·3 eV. may perhaps be ascribed to the difference between the electron affinities of Br and H; the electron affinity of Br

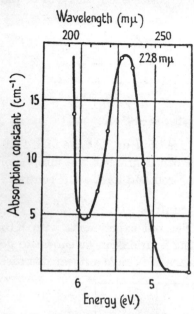

FIG. 56. Absorption spectrum of KBr containing KH (*U*-centres)†

*in vacuo* is 3·52, which would give 2·2 for the electron affinity of hydrogen, according to formula (13) on p. 98.

There can be little doubt that the electronic transition responsible for the absorption band is one in which an electron is ejected from the hydrogen ion into a state extending over the neighbouring metal ions and similar to the excited state of a halogen ion in the pure crystal.

When a voltage is applied, absorption of light in the *U*-band does not give rise to any measurable photoelectric current. This is as we should expect; no current is observed for illumination in the characteristic absorption band of the pure crystal either. Illumination in the *U*-band does, however, lead to a diminution in the intensity of the *U*-band accompanied by the formation of *F*-centres. The quantum yield $\eta$ of the process at room temperature and below has been determined by measuring the rate of growth of the *F*-band. Measurements above room temperature were impossible, because already at 40° C. colloidal metal was formed in the crystal. At lower temperatures the number of *F*-centres formed per quantum absorbed depends strongly on temperature, and is shown in Fig. 57 for deuterium as well as for hydrogen.‡ The results for low temperatures are expressed by

$$\eta_H = 6·6 \exp\left(-\frac{0·08 \text{ eV.}}{kT}\right),$$

$$\eta_D = 6·6 \exp\left(-\frac{0·092 \text{ eV.}}{kT}\right).$$

† From R. W. Pohl, *Proc. Phys. Soc.* **49** (extra part), 3 (1937).

‡ F. G. Kleinschrod, *Göttinger Nachrichten*, Fachgruppe II, **3**, 143 (1939); R. Hilsch and R. W. Pohl, loc. cit.

The fact that the quantum efficiencies for hydrogen and for deuterium are different suggests that a motion of atoms, and not only of electrons, is concerned. The most straightforward explanation of the process seems to us to be the following: The absorption of a quantum of radiation lifts an electron into an excited state, in which it stays on the neighbouring metal ions. A hydrogen atom is left behind. If the tem-

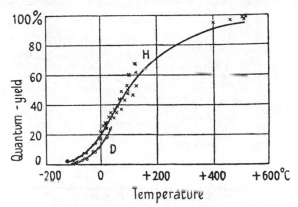

FIG. 57. Influence of the temperature on the quantum yield of the photochemical decomposition of KH and KD molecules which are formed in KBr with the production of a solid solution

× Measurements of Hilsch and Pohl.
● and ○ Measurements of Kleinschrod.

perature is sufficiently high for the hydrogen atom to diffuse away before the electron returns to its original position, the electron will fall back into the hole left at the vacant lattice point, and an $F$-centre will be formed. In an applied field no photoconductivity will be observed.

To make a quantitative theory we proceed as in § 6. We denote by $A\,dt$ the probability per time $dt$ that the excited electron returns to its ground state, and by $B\,dt$ the probability per time $dt$ that the hydrogen atom escapes. Then the probability $\eta$ that an $F$-centre is formed is

$$\eta = \frac{1}{1+A/B}.$$

Fair agreement with experiment is found if we take

$$\frac{A}{B} = \tfrac{1}{7}e^{W/kT}$$

with $W \simeq 0.083$ eV.

The most simple assumption is the one that we have made for $F$-

centres, namely, that $A$ is the probability for an optical transition. Then by the formulae of Chapter IV, § 6, we have

$$A \sim 10^9 \text{ sec.}^{-1},$$

and hence $$B \sim (10^8 \text{ sec.}^{-1})e^{-W/kT}.$$

There are, however, three difficulties in the way of this interpretation: (1) no fluorescent radiation is observed;[†] (2) it is difficult to understand

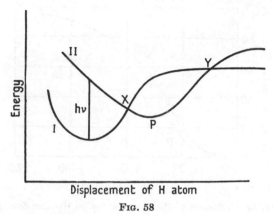

FIG. 58

so small a constant term in the expression for $B$; and (3) if the activation energy for the escape of a hydrogen atom is as small as 0·083 eV., one would not expect so large a difference in the activation energies for $H$ and $D$.[‡]

We suggest tentatively that KBr containing KH is a non-fluorescent system of the type described in Chapter VI, §3. In this case, then, the energies of the system, plotted against the displacement of the hydrogen atom, should be as shown in Fig. 58. Curve I represents the energy of the system in its lowest state. If the hydrogen atom were pushed right out of its lattice position into an interstitial position, the state of lowest energy for the second electron would probably be near the vacant lattice point rather than in the field of the hydrogen atom; thus curve I represents the energy of the system as one pushes away the hydrogen atom leaving the electron behind. The flat part represents the energy in the interstitial positions, where the atom is free to migrate.

† It has been stated (E. Hirschlaff, *Fluorescence and Phosphorescence*, p. 114 (London, 1938)) that in coloured NaCl the $F$-band is re-emitted as phosphorescence. This idea seems, however, to have arisen through some misunderstanding; nothing is known of this effect at Göttingen (private communication from Dr. Hilsch).

‡ For the proof of this, see N. F. Mott, *Trans. Faraday Soc.* **34**, 888 (1938).

Curve II represents the energy of the excited state. We assume that, as the hydrogen atom is displaced, the energy of the excited state first descends and crosses curve I. Then when a quantum of energy $h\nu$ is absorbed, the system moves into the state $P$, which is metastable. Heat motion may cause the system to return to its original state, but for this an activation energy $E_1$ is necessary to lift it over the point $X$. We may thus write

$$A = ae^{-E_1/kT}.$$

Similarly, the probability $B$ per unit time that the hydrogen atom will move right away from its original centre may be written

$$B = be^{-E_2/kT},$$

where $E_2$ is the activation energy to lift the system from $P$ to $Y$. As we see from the figure, $E_2 > E_1$. Thus the equation for the quantum efficiency,

$$\eta = 1 \Big/ \left( \frac{a}{b} e^{-(E_1 - E_2)/kT} \right),$$

is of the form required by experiment.

In pure alkali-halide crystals $F$-centres may also be produced by irradiation in the long-wave-length tail of the ultra-violet absorption band. This effect has been studied at intervals since 1896. For the initial rate of coloration Smakula found that the quantum efficiency was of order of magnitude unity.[†] In some respects the process is sensitive to temperature. In an applied field the formation of $F$-centres is not accompanied by any conductivity; in this respect the process resembles the formation of $F$-centres from $U$-centres. But, whereas the $U$-band is used up by conversion to $F$-centres, it is found that the intensity of absorption in the tail of the ultra-violet band increases.[‡] The nature of the process is not yet understood.

† A. Smakula, *Zeits. f. Physik*, **63**, 762 (1930).
‡ E. Rexer, ibid. **106**, 70 (1937).

# V

## SEMI-CONDUCTORS AND INSULATORS

## 1. Types of semi-conductor

IN Chapter IV we have dealt with the motion of electrons in coloured alkali-halides; in this chapter we deal with a more general class of electronic conductors, namely, semi-conductors. In this book we shall use the term semi-conductor to denote a solid which shows electronic conductivity at sufficiently high temperatures, but whose conductivity tends to zero as the temperature is lowered.

The accepted theory of semi-conductors is due to A. H. Wilson.† We know that the possible energy levels of an electron in a crystal may be divided into bands, separated by bands of forbidden energy. Wilson supposes that in a semi-conductor, as in an insulator, at the absolute zero of temperature all the allowed bands are either completely full or completely empty, so that the crystal cannot carry any current. In a semi-conductor, however, as the temperature is increased, some electrons are raised into the lowest empty band of allowed levels (the conduction band). These electrons give to the crystal its conductivity.

Wilson distinguishes between intrinsic and extrinsic semi-conductors. An intrinsic semi-conductor is one which conducts in the pure state; electrons are raised into the conduction levels from the normally full band. Most semi-conductors, however, owe their conductivity to the presence of impurities in solid solution, and the actual value of the conductivity is very sensitive to the amount of these impurities present. The theory assumes that the energy required to bring an electron from an impurity centre into the conduction band is considerably less than that required to bring it from the full band of the pure substance, so that the conduction is mainly due to electrons removed from the impurities.

Although intrinsic semi-conductors are theoretically possible, it is doubtful whether any are known, though it has been claimed that cuprous oxide is an intrinsic semi-conductor at high temperatures (cf. p. 164). It seems that in the whole class of substances that lie inter-mediate between metals and insulators the conductivity is due to the impurities which they contain. In some cases the conductivity is due to the presence of atoms of a foreign species; but recent work has brought

---

† A. H. Wilson, *Proc. Roy. Soc.* (A), **133**, 458 (1931), and **134**, 277 (1932); *Theory of Metals*, p. 65 (Cambridge, 1936); *Semi-Conductors and Metals* (Cambridge, 1939). See also R. H. Fowler, *Statistical Mechanics*, 2nd ed., p. 397 (Cambridge, 1936).

out the important fact that in most compounds the impurities in the crystal are not atoms of a foreign element, but are a stoichiometric excess of one constituent—e.g. in the metallic oxides, either an excess of oxygen or an excess of metal.

Semi-conductors in which the current is carried by electrons raised from normally occupied impurity levels into the conduction band may

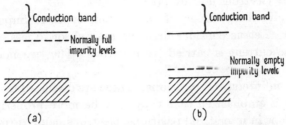

Fig. 59. Energy levels in semi-conductors: (a) a normal, or excess, conductor; (b) an abnormal, or deficit, conductor. The shaded band in both cases represents the full band

be called 'excess' conductors. In the literature they have been called also 'normal' semi-conductors. In the case of materials whose conductivity is due to stoichiometric excess of metal they are also called 'reduction' conductors, for reasons which will become clear below.

In another type of semi-conductor the conductivity is due to the presence of empty impurity levels lying above a full band. If electrons are raised from the full band into the impurity levels, a current may be carried by the positive holes in the full band. Substances in which the current is carried in this way may be called 'deficit' or 'abnormal' conductors, or, as we shall see below, 'oxidation' conductors. The energy levels of the two types are illustrated in Fig. 59.

The conductivity $\sigma$ of either type of conductor will be given by

$$\sigma = env,$$

where $n$ is the number of electrons per unit volume in the conduction band, or holes in the full band, and $v$ is their mobility. If $v$ depends on the energy of the electron within the range, of order $kT$, in which the energies are distributed, it will be necessary to take an average value.

Valuable information may be obtained from measurements of the Hall coefficient. The theoretical value of the Hall coefficient $R$ is (in e.s.u.)

$$R = -3\pi c/8n|e| \quad \text{(electronic conduction)},$$
$$R = 3\pi c/8n|e| \quad \text{(hole conduction)},$$

if the density of electrons in the conduction band is not so great that the Maxwell distribution law becomes inapplicable and Fermi-Dirac statistics have to be applied.† Determinations of the Hall coefficient thus enable direct estimates of $n$ to be made, and also provide a test of whether the conduction is due to electrons or holes.

We may note that in an intrinsic semi-conductor the current will be carried by electrons *and* by positive holes.

We now give a discussion of the various types of impurity centre which occur. Let us consider first the normal, or excess, conductors, in which the current is carried by electrons. The two main types of centre are

1. Atoms in interstitial positions. These are discussed in Chapter IV, § 1, where it is emphasized that they may be more properly described as positive ions in interstitial positions, electrons being trapped in their fields. The radius of the orbit of the electron, i.e. the radial extent of its wave function, may be several interatomic distances. The interstitial atoms may be either foreign atoms (e.g. Cu atoms in copper-activated zinc-sulphide phosphors, Chap. VI, § 4) or excess atoms of the metallic constituent of the crystal (e.g. Zn atoms in ZnO containing a stoichiometric excess of Zn). The properties of the semi-conductor in either case will be similar.

2. Singularities of the $F$-centre type, where an electron is trapped at a point where a negative ion is missing. We do not know of any substance in which these give rise to electronic conductivity at temperatures at which the electrolytic conductivity is negligible (cf. Chap. IV, § 7).

It will be noticed that in both cases the crystal must contain an excess of metal.

In the case of abnormal, or deficit, conductors, the most important kind of centre is similar to the type (2) discussed above; at points in the crystal from which a *positive* ion is missing there will be an electrostatic field attracting positive holes. The centre thus consists of a lattice point from which a positive ion is missing, with an electron missing from one of the adjacent negative ions. The 'positive hole' or place from which the electron is missing will be shared between the surrounding negative ions. The conductivity of these crystals at room temperature arises from the fact that the thermal energy detaches a certain number of positive holes from the attracting centres, just as in

---

† Cf. N. F. Mott and H. Jones, *Theory of the Properties of Metals and Alloys*, p. 281 (Oxford, 1936).

a normal conductor the thermal energy detaches electrons from some of the impurity centres.

In principle, centres of type (1) also could exist for positive holes; an electro-negative atom (e.g. oxygen or a halogen) in an interstitial position could receive an electron from the full band of levels. We do not however know of any examples of this type of semi-conductor. The work necessary to bring an electro-negative atom into an interstitial position will in general be rather large, and this may account for the rarity of this type of conductor.

It will be noticed that both types of abnormal conductor contain a deficit of metal.

There are thus four possible types of semi-conducting crystals of non-stoichiometric composition; but only two of these are important, namely normal conductors with interstitial metal, and deficit conductors with vacant positive-ion lattice points.

Other properties of such crystals, into which impurities or a stoichiometric excess of one constituent have been deliberately introduced, are discussed elsewhere in this book, for example in the chapters on coloured alkali-halides and on luminescent materials (Chaps. IV and VI).

The oxide semi-conductors ($Cu_2O$, $ZnO$, $U_2O$, etc.), whose properties have been investigated in detail, show very great variations in conductivity according to their previous heat treatment. This is because the heat treatment determines the stoichiometric excess of either constituent which the crystal shall contain. In principle any oxide or other polar substance could exist as a normal semi-conductor with excess of metal, or as an abnormal conductor with excess of oxygen or other electro-negative constituent. In practice it seems to be possible, for a given substance, to obtain only one type of conductivity.

For one class of oxide, on heating in a vacuum so that oxygen is driven off, the conductivity increases. These are known as 'reduction' semi-conductors; they are, as we have seen, semi-conductors of the normal, or excess, type showing a negative Hall coefficient. Zinc oxide is an example of this class.

The other class of oxide shows an increase of conductivity on heating under pressure in oxygen, so that an excess of oxygen is absorbed. These substances, of which cuprous oxide is an example, are called 'oxidation semi-conductors'. The conductivity is of the abnormal, or deficit, type.

The properties of these semi-conductors do not depend exclusively on the concentration of excess metal or oxygen. Let us consider the case of a normal conductor in which the impurity centres are interstitial metal atoms of the same element as the metallic constituent of the crystal. We have seen that each of these excess metal atoms consists of an ion wedged into an interstitial position, with an electron trapped in its field. We are considering in this section semi-conductors at temperatures at which the ionic conduction is negligible. However, as we saw in Chapter II, in any crystal at a sufficiently high temperature, whether of stoichiometric composition or not, a certain number of ions will leave their normal positions and go into interstitial positions. There will certainly be a fairly high concentration of these ions at the temperatures at which the semi-conductors are prepared. Thus, further, when they are cooled and the diffusion coefficient of these ions drops practically to zero, a certain number will be frozen in, accompanied by an equal number of holes; but the latter play no part in the conductivity. Thus, in any real crystal we shall expect to find, besides the $n_1$ interstitial *atoms*, a certain number $n_2$ of frozen-in interstitial *ions* with an equal number $n_2$ of vacant positive lattice points. In other words, we have $n_1+n_2$ centres where electrons can be trapped, but only $n_1$ electrons available.

The number $n_2$ depends on the rate of cooling from the high temperature at which the crystal has been prepared. We shall see in § 2 that the value of $n_2$ has an effect on the rate of variation of conductivity with temperature.

Similar conclusions apply for defect conductors, if vacant cation lattice points are formed at high temperatures and become frozen-in on cooling. There will then be more vacant cation lattice points than there are positive holes in the conduction band.

## 2. Variation of the conductivity with temperature

In this section we shall consider the variation with temperature of the conductivity $\sigma$ and the Hall coefficient $R$. For both purposes we require the variation of $n$, the number of carriers of electricity which are free to move † These may either be electrons in the conduction band or positive holes in the full band. The analysis which we shall

† In §§ 4 and 5 of Chap. IV we saw that in every crystal the value of the photo-conductivity is governed by the number of traps in the crystal at which a free electron may be caught. In normal semi-conductors too the electrons in the conduction band will be caught in this way. Nevertheless, the value of the conductivity will be independent of the presence of these traps. If, on the one hand, they are deeper than the impurity centres, they will be permanently filled by electrons which have come from these. If, on the other hand, they are shallower, electrons caught in them will escape even more easily than they do from the impurity centres. In neither case can they affect the conductivity, since they are much smaller in number than the impurity centres.

give refers to either; we shall, however, discuss explicitly the case of electrons.

We denote by $E$ the work required to remove an electron from an impurity centre and bring it into the conduction band. We first consider the case where the number of centres and the number of electrons are equal. Then $n$ may be calculated as follows.

We make the assumption that the crystal is in thermodynamical equilibrium at a temperature $T$. Consider a volume $V$ of the crystal, containing $N$ impurity centres. We have to calculate the free energy $F$ of the crystal when $n$ electrons have been raised into the conduction band, the equilibrium value of $n$ will then be given by the condition

$$\left(\frac{\partial F}{\partial n}\right)_T = 0. \tag{1}$$

The free energy is made up of three terms:

1. The energy $\qquad\qquad nE \qquad\qquad\qquad$ (2)

required to raise the electrons to the lowest state in the conduction band.

2. The free energy of the electron gas; the density will be so small that classical statistics may be used.† The free energy is thus

$$-nkT\left[\log\left(\frac{2\pi mkT}{h^2}\right)^{\frac{3}{2}} + 1 + \log\frac{V}{n} + \log_e 2\right]. \tag{3}$$

The term $\log_e 2$ comes from the spins of the electrons.

3. The free energy of the vacant places from which the electrons have been removed. The electrons may be removed in $P$ ways, where

$$P = \frac{N!}{n!\,(N-n)!},$$

giving a contribution to the entropy equal to $k \log P$ and to the free energy $\qquad\qquad -kT \log P. \qquad\qquad$ (4)

The contribution from the spins to the free energy is

$$-kT(N-n)\log_e 2 \tag{5}$$

if the impurity levels contain unpaired electrons (as do, for instance, $F$-centres); if they contain paired electrons (as do, for instance, ions with inert-gas configuration), the contribution is

$$-kTn \log_e 2. \tag{6}$$

† For a derivation of the formulae using Fermi-Dirac statistics, cf., for example, R. H. Fowler, *Statistical Mechanics*, 2nd ed., p. 397 (Cambridge, 1936).

Adding together the terms (2), (3), (4), and (5) or (6), we obtain the free energy. From equation (1), making use of Stirling's formula in the form

$$\frac{d}{dn}\log n! \sim \log n,$$

we obtain

$$\frac{n}{\sqrt{(N-n)}} = (2)V^{\frac{1}{2}}\left\{\frac{2\pi mkT}{h^2}\right\}^{\frac{3}{4}} e^{-\frac{1}{2}E/kT}. \tag{7}$$

The factor (2) occurs only if the impurity levels contain paired electrons.

If $n \ll N$, we obtain from (7) for the number $n$ of conduction electrons

$$\frac{n}{V} = (2)\frac{N^{\frac{1}{2}}}{V^{\frac{1}{2}}}\left\{\frac{2\pi mkT}{h^2}\right\}^{\frac{3}{4}} e^{-\frac{1}{2}E/kT}. \tag{8}$$

At 300° K. we have

$$\left\{\frac{2\pi mkT}{h^2}\right\}^{\frac{3}{4}} \simeq 3 \times 10^9 \text{ cm.}^{-\frac{3}{2}}$$

Thus

$$n = n_0 e^{-\frac{1}{2}E/kT},$$

with

$$\frac{n_0}{V} \sim 3 \times 10^9 \left(\frac{N}{V}\right)^{\frac{1}{2}}.$$

According to the considerations of Chap. III, § 12, the mobility $v$ of an electron does not vary rapidly with temperature above the characteristic temperature; for lower temperatures it varies as $e^{\Theta/T}$, but $k\Theta$ will usually be small compared with $\frac{1}{2}E$. Thus the conductivity, $evn$, for temperatures where $T \ll \frac{1}{2}E/k$, varies with $T$ according to the law

$$\sigma = \sigma_0 e^{-\epsilon/kT}, \tag{9}$$

where $\epsilon = \frac{1}{2}E$ and $\sigma_0$ varies slowly with $T$. The mobility of a free electron or hole for $T \geqslant \Theta$ probably lies between 1 and 100 cm./sec. per volt/cm. Thus, if $N$ refers to unit volume, the order of magnitude of $\sigma_0$ is given by

$$\sigma_0/\sqrt{N} \sim 3 \times 10^{-8} \text{ to } 3 \times 10^{-10} \text{ cm.}^{-1} \text{ ohm}^{-1}.$$

For intrinsic semi-conductors where for unit volume $N \sim 10^{22}$, this gives

$$\sigma_0 \sim 30 \text{ to } 3{,}000 \text{ cm.}^{-1} \text{ ohm}^{-1}.$$

The expression (8) and these values derived from it are equally true for conduction by positive holes.

For any intrinsic semi-conductor which contains impurity centres as well, the conductivity will behave in precisely the same way as that described in Chapter II for the analogous ionic conductors containing an impurity. That is to say, the conductivity will be given by the sum of two terms,

$$\sigma = A_1 e^{-\epsilon_1/kT} + A_2 e^{-\epsilon_2/kT}, \tag{10}$$

of which one term has a large activation energy and a large coefficient, while the term due to the impurity has a smaller activation energy and a much smaller coefficient. When $\log \sigma$ is plotted against $1/T$ in the usual way, the curve will show a kink separating two straight lines, as in Fig. 60 (a), like those already given in Fig. 18 for ionic conductors. Somewhat similar behaviour will be shown by a crystal which is not an intrinsic semi-conductor, but contains two kinds of impurity centre with different activation energies.

In the derivation of formula (7) for the number of electrons in the conduction band it was assumed that all the $N$ impurity levels are, at low temperatures, occupied by an electron. In many semi-conductors, in which the impurities consist of excess atoms of one or other constituent of the crystal, we have seen in § 1 that this is not necessarily the case. It is thus necessary to investigate the case where the number of impurity levels is greater than the number of electrons available.[†] In a volume $V$, then, let there be $N$ impurity levels and $N_e$ electrons, of which, at temperature $T$, $n$ are excited. Let $E$, as before, be the energy required to remove an electron from an impurity level into the conduction band. Then the free energy, as before, consists of the terms (2) and (3); but the term (4) is changed; among $N$ impurity levels we have $n+N-N_e$ vacant places, which can be distributed in $P$ ways, where

$$P = \frac{N!}{(n+N-N_e)!\,(N_e-n)!},$$

giving as before a contribution $-kT \log P$ to the free energy. Making $F$ a minimum with respect to $n$, we obtain in place of (7)

$$\frac{n(N-N_e+n)}{N_e-n} = V \left\{ \frac{2\pi mkT}{h^2} \right\}^{\frac{3}{2}} e^{-E/kT}. \tag{11}$$

This reduces to (7) if $N = N_e$.

In order to simplify formula (11) let us assume that only a small number of electrons are excited, so that $n \ll N_e$. Then two limiting cases present themselves; if $n \ll N-N_e$, we have approximately

$$n = \frac{N_e}{N-N_e} V \left\{ \frac{2\pi mkT}{h^2} \right\}^{\frac{3}{2}} e^{-E/kT}, \tag{12}$$

while, if $n \gg N-N_e$,

$$n = N_e^{\frac{1}{2}} V^{\frac{1}{2}} \left\{ \frac{2\pi mkT}{h^2} \right\}^{\frac{3}{4}} e^{-\frac{1}{2}E/kT}. \tag{13}$$

† J. H. de Boer and W. C. van Geel, *Physica*, **2**, 286 (1935); B. R. A. Nijboer, *Proc. Phys. Soc.* **51**, 575 (1939).

The critical temperature, $T_c$, in the neighbourhood of which the formula changes over from one form to the other, may be obtained by putting $n = N - N_e$ in (11). We obtain

$$\frac{2(N - N_e)^2}{V(2N_e - N)} = \left\{\frac{2\pi mkT_c}{h^2}\right\}^{\frac{3}{2}} e^{-E/kT_c}. \tag{14}$$

It will be seen, therefore, that from a portion of the $(\log \sigma, 1/T)$ curve one cannot deduce with any certainty the activation energy $E$; the slope may give $E$ or $\frac{1}{2}E$. The slope will change over at the critical temperature, as shown in Fig. 60 (b).

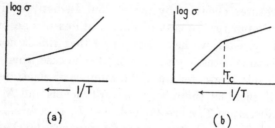

(a)                              (b)

Fig. 60. Types of conductivity-temperature curve for semi-conductors: (a) an intrinsic semi-conductor with impurity centres; (b) a semi-conductor with more centres than electrons, as explained in text

## 3. Relation between thermal and optical activation energies

In Chapter III, § 9, we have discussed the optical absorption spectrum of an impurity centre; whether the centre is an interstitial atom or a centre of the $F$-centre type, its absorption spectrum should in principle consist of a series of sharp lines leading up to a series limit, though the lines may be so broadened by lattice vibrations as to be indistinguishable. If $\nu$ is the frequency of the series limit, we may call $E_0$, where

$$E_0 = h\nu,$$

the optical activation energy.

Now when an electron is removed from an impurity centre by the absorption of a quantum of light, then, by the Franck-Condon principle, the surrounding ions do not move during the process. Thus the energy $h\nu$ necessary to remove the electron optically is the energy required to remove it with the ions stationary. After the absorption process, however, when the electron has been removed to a distant point of the lattice, its energy being that of the lowest state in the conduction band, the ions surrounding the impurity centre will no longer be in equilibrium, but will move into new positions of equilibrium. In the process they will give out energy, which we denote by $U$. This is illustrated in Fig. 61. Here we plot the energy of the crystal against a coordinate $x$ representing the position of any one of the ions or atoms in the neighbourhood of the impurity centre. Curve I represents the energy when the electron is in its lowest state in the impurity centre, curve II the energy when the electron is raised into the conduction band and removed to a distant point of the crystal.

Both energy curves will show minima for some value of $x$, but not in general for the same value. In the figure, $AB$ represents the onorgy required to free an electron optically, $BB'$ the energy $U$ given out after the absorption process.

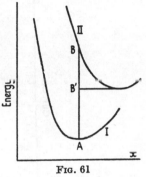

Fig. 61

The thermal activation energy $E$ which occurs in equations (7) and (11) is the energy difference between two states of the crystal, in one of which the electron is in the impurity level, and in the other it is removed to a distant point in the conduction band; but in both states the atoms or ions surrounding the impurity centre are supposed to be in equilibrium. Thus $E$ is given by the height $AB'$ in Fig. 61, or, in other words,

$$E = h\nu - U.$$

Thus the thermal activation energy is always less than the optical activation energy.[†]

We see then that it is not possible to make direct comparisons between the absorption spectra of semi-conductors and the activation energies. An example of the former is provided by the work on $Cu_2O$ by Schönwald,[‡] who measured the photoelectric response in the infra-red, and found evidence for a broad band. His curves showing current against frequency of the incident radiation are given in Fig. 62.

Engelhard[||] has attempted to associate the minimum energy of this band with the activation energy $E$; the conductivity varies as $e^{-\epsilon/kT}$ with $\epsilon \sim 0.3$ eV. As we have seen, however, there is no theoretical justification for doing this, since $h\nu$ is not equal to $E$. There is also doubt, as we have seen, as to whether $\epsilon$ is equal to $E$ or $\frac{1}{2}E$.

A rough estimate may be made of the energy $U$. If $\kappa_0$ and $\kappa$ are the

† This was first pointed out by J. H. de Boer and W. Ch. van Geel, *Physica*, **2**, 286 (1935).

‡ B. Schönwald, *Ann. d. Physik*, **15**, 395 (1932).

|| E. Engelhard, ibid. **17**, 501 (1933).

dielectric constants for high-frequency and static fields respectively (Chap. I, § 5), the displacement of the ions after the electron is removed will cause the field at large distances from the centre to drop from $e/\kappa_0 r^2$ to $e/\kappa r^2$. Since the energy of the medium per unit volume is

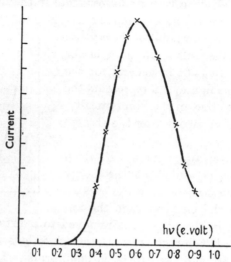

Fig. 62. Photoelectric current in cuprous oxide†

$(\mathbf{E}\mathbf{D})/8\pi$, we see that the energy given out when the ions move into their new positions is, per unit volume,

$$\left(\frac{1}{\kappa_0}-\frac{1}{\kappa}\right)\frac{e^2}{8\pi r^4}. \tag{15}$$

If we suppose that the impurity centre has a definite 'radius' $R$, and that (15) is valid for $r > R$, we see that the total energy given out, $U$, is

$$\int_R^\infty \left(\frac{1}{\kappa_0}-\frac{1}{\kappa}\right)\frac{e^2}{8\pi r^4}\, 4\pi r^2\, dr,$$

which gives

$$U = \frac{e^2}{2R}\left(\frac{1}{\kappa_0}-\frac{1}{\kappa}\right). \tag{16}$$

Since the depth of the potential hole with this model is $e^2/\kappa_0 R$, we shall have

$$h\nu \sim e^2/2\kappa_0 R$$

and hence

$$E \sim e^2/2\kappa R.$$

For crystals with, say, $\kappa_0 \sim 4$, $\kappa \sim 10$, we see that $E$ is of the order $\frac{1}{2}h\nu$.

† B. Schönwald, loc. cit.

## 4. A discussion of some experimental results for semi-conductors

Within the limits of a book of this kind it is not possible to give any general review of experimental results; we confine ourselves to certain recent investigations which exhibit the more important properties of these substances, and enable a comparison with theory to be made.

Cuprous oxide ($Cu_2O$) has been investigated by Jusé and Kurtschatow† and by Engelhard.‡ The conductivity is found to increase with increasing oxygen content, and Engelhard's measurements of the Hall effect show that the substance is a defect conductor, the current being carried by 'positive holes'. The nature of the impurity centres has already been outlined (§ 1). The oxygen atom is probably too big to fit 'interstitially' into the lattice of $Cu_2O$, and it is more likely that in the oxygen-rich lattice there are vacant lattice points normally occupied by copper ions. Since the crystal as a whole is electrically neutral, an equal number of ions must have an electron missing. In other words, there will exist positive holes in one of the full bands. These holes will be either in the band of full levels corresponding to the $O^{--}$ ions or to the $Cu^+$ ions, whichever has the higher energy.||

When the crystal is in its state of lowest energy the holes will be trapped in the neighbourhood of a point where a copper ion is missing. In other words, at the points where copper ions are missing there exist empty states for an electron above the lowest level in the full band (Fig. 59). The crystal becomes a semi-conductor when, owing to the thermal energy, some of these empty states are filled, and an equal number of mobile positive holes left empty (see § 1).

Jusé and Kurtschatow found that the conductivity of cuprous oxide can be represented by a formula of the type (10), where $\epsilon_1 = 0.7$ eV., $A_1 \sim 100$ cm.$^{-1}$ ohm$^{-1}$, both being independent of the oxygen content, and $\epsilon_2$ varies between 0·129 and 0·134 eV., while $A_2$ depends strongly

---

† W. P. Jusé and B. W. Kurtschatow, *Phys. Zeits. d. Sowjetunion*, **2**, 453 (1933).

‡ E. Engelhard, *Ann. d. Physik*, **17**, 501 (1933).

|| In Chap. III, § 8, some evidence is given that the copper $(3d)^{10}$ band is higher. This hypothesis is, however, rather difficult to reconcile with the deduction from experiment made in § 4, that the effective mass of a positive hole is rather low.

Various authors have found that pure $Cu_2O$ is diamagnetic with a susceptibility $-0.188 \times 10^{-6}$ (W. Klemm and W. Schüth, *Zeits. f. anorgan. Chem.* **203**, 104 (1931); S. S. Bhatnagar and N. G. Mitra, *Current Science*, **1**, 343 (1933)). The last-named authors have found that copper-oxide films removed from the surfaces of copper foil heated in nitric oxide were paramagnetic. This may be due to the presence of CuO; if not, it may be due equally well to holes in the copper or oxygen bands.

on the oxygen content. For specimens with about 0·1 per cent. by weight of excess oxygen

$$A_2 \sim 0.3 \text{ cm.}^{-1} \text{ ohm}^{-1}.$$

These authors suggested that the first term represents the conductivity of *pure* cuprous oxide—the electrons being excited from levels of the

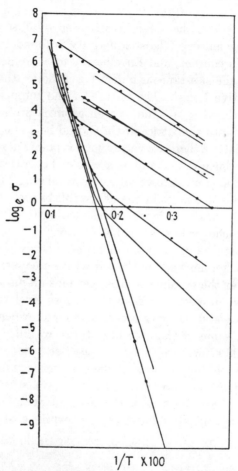

FIG. 63. Logarithm of the conductivity of various specimens of cuprous oxide (Jusé and Kurtschatow)

perfect lattice—and that the second term represents the conductivity due to excess oxygen. The experimental results are shown in Fig. 63. The value 100 cm.$^{-1}$ ohm$^{-1}$ for the coefficient $A_1$ is consistent with the estimate which we made above for an intrinsic semi-conductor. Further, in these crystals the ratio of the two coefficients $A_2/A_1$ should be equal to the square root of the relative concentration of excess oxygen.

Engelhard's results both on the Hall constant and on the conductivity show certain kinks when $\log \sigma$ is plotted against $1/T$. He found that his conductivities and Hall coefficients could be represented by formulae of type (10), with $\epsilon_1 = 0\cdot35$ eV. and $\epsilon_2 = 0\cdot18$ eV.

Some experiments of Hartmann† on $Al_2O_3$ illustrate a common

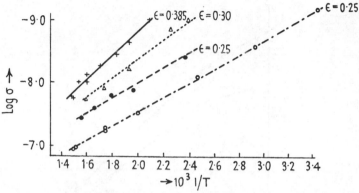

FIG. 64. Conductivity of $Al_2O_3$ as a function of temperature for differently treated specimens, according to the experiments of Hartmann

phenomenon with semi-conductors, the variation of the activation energy with increasing concentration of impurity (Fig. 64). Nijboer‡ has attempted to explain this variation by means of the mechanism of 'frozen-in' vacant lattice points, which, as we have seen, may lead to a variation in the slope.

Some experiments on zinc oxide at high temperatures by Jander and Stamm‖ and by Baumbach and Wagner†† may perhaps be explained by a similar mechanism. They give a curve of the type shown in Fig. 65.

In the slope of the $(\log \sigma, 1/T)$ curve, variations much greater than these occur in very many cases. Obviously the theory given above cannot explain any variation greater than a factor 2. The detailed investigations of Fritsch‡‡ on ZnO containing excess zinc are an example of this. The activation energy decreased with increasing concentration of metal from a maximum value, in eV., of about $0\cdot6$ down to a minimum of about $0\cdot01$. $\log \sigma$ at a given temperature was in fact found to be

† W. Hartmann, *Zeits. f. Physik*, **102**, 709 (1936).
‡ B. R. A. Nijboer, *Proc. Phys. Soc.* **51**, 575 (1939).
‖ W. Jander and W. Stamm, *Zeits. f. anorgan. Chem.* **199**, 165 (1931).
†† H. H. von Baumbach and C. Wagner, *Zeits. f. phys. Chem.* (B), **22**, 199 (1933).
‡‡ O. Fritsch, *Ann. d. Physik*, **22**, 375 (1935).

roughly proportional to $E$, the variation of $A$ with concentration being unimportant.

Fritsch found that the mobility (product of Hall coefficient and conductivity) was also sensitive to the concentration of metal, decreasing with increasing concentration. Similar results have been obtained by Meyer and Neldel[†] for $TiO_2$ and for a number of other compounds. It seems to us that results such as these can only be explained if it is

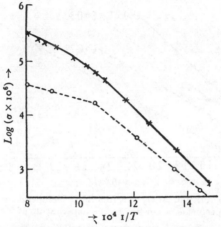

FIG. 65. Conductivity of ZnO as a function of temperature. —— according to von Baumbach and Wagner. ---- according to Jander and Stamm

assumed that the impurity centres interact with each other. Since the concentration of impurity appears to be of the order of 0·1 per cent., this would imply that the impurity centres have a radius of the order of five times the distance between the atoms of the crystal. We have to consider whether this is at all probable.

Let us consider, for instance, the case of zinc oxide. Here we have zinc ions in interstitial positions, and electrons trapped in the field of these ions. If the electron moves in a rather large orbit, the field acting on it, due to the ion, may be taken to be[‡] $e/\kappa_{\text{eff}} r^2$, where $\kappa_{\text{eff}}$ is an 'effective' dielectric constant, somewhere between the dielectric constants $\kappa$ and $\kappa_0$ for static and high-frequency ($> 10^{12}$ sec.$^{-1}$) fields. In a field of this type the energy values are proportional to $1/\kappa_{\text{eff}}^2$ and the radii of the orbits to $\kappa_{\text{eff}}$. Since for low impurity content the energy required to remove an electron is of the order 0·5 eV. instead of $\sim 10$ eV., as for the isolated atom, we may suppose that $\kappa_{\text{eff}} \sim \sqrt{20}$.

[†] W. Meyer and H. Neldel, *Phys. Zeits.* **38**, 1014 (1937).
[‡] Cf. Chap. III, § 4.

It thus appears possible that the radii of the centres are of the order of four to five times that of the free zinc atom.

If this is the case, the dissolved zinc atoms in ZnO may, for sufficiently high concentration, behave like a divalent metal. In a divalent metal we have two bands of allowed energy and enough electrons exactly to fill the first band:† for large interatomic distance these two bands would not overlap; but, as the atoms are brought nearer together, the energy gap between the two bands diminishes and finally disappears. We suggest that, if $\epsilon$ is the observed activation energy, $2\epsilon$ is the width of this gap.

A type of semi-conductor which is at present difficult to discuss from the theoretical point of view is presented by NiO; here the nickel ion is in the $(3d)^8$ state; thus the band of levels corresponding to this state is incomplete, and we should expect metallic conduction, which is not observed.‡

## 5. Mobility of the electrons in semi-conductors

Our formula for the conductivity,

$$\sigma = env,$$

where $n$ is the number of excited electrons (or holes) and $v$ the mobility, assumes that all excited electrons have the same mobility. Subject to this assumption we may deduce the mobility from the conductivity $\sigma$ and the Hall coefficient $R$, using the formulae for $R$ on p. 153.

Thus                    $v = 8R\sigma/3\pi c.$

This has been done for $Cu_2O$ by Engelhard.‖ The mobilities are of the order of magnitude of 100 cm./sec. per volt/cm., and are shown in Fig. 66 (a).

For $UO_2$, another deficit conductor, similar results have been obtained by Hartmann,†† $R\sigma c$ dropping from 40 at $-60°$ C. to 10 at $+20°$. For CuO Hartmann obtained smaller values ($\sim 0.5$ at $-50°$). For ZnO Fritsch‡‡ found values between 5 and 40.

By writing                $v = \dfrac{e}{m}\dfrac{l}{u},$

where $l$ is the mean free path and $u$ the mean velocity, and by assuming

$$\tfrac{1}{2}mu^2 = \tfrac{3}{2}kT,$$

† Cf. N. F. Mott and H. Jones, *Theory of the Properties of Metals and Alloys*, chap. iii (Oxford, 1936).
‡ Cf. J. H. de Boer and E. J. W. Verwey, *Proc. Phys. Soc.* **49** (extra part), 59 (1937).
‖ E. Engelhard, *Ann. d. Physik*, **17**, 501 (1933).
†† W. Hartmann, *Zeits. f. Physik*, **102**, 709 (1936).
‡‡ O. Fritsch, *Ann. d. Physik*, **22**, 375 (1935).

one can obtain values of $l$, the mean free path. These depend, of course, on the assumption that the effective mass of an electron or hole in the crystal lattice is equal to the electronic mass. Engelhard's results for the mean free path are shown in Fig. 66 (b).

Fröhlich and Mott† have attempted to fit the curves of Fig. 66 (a) and (b) to the theoretical formulae (18) and (19) of Chapter III. The formulae contain two unknown parameters: the effective mass $m^*$ and

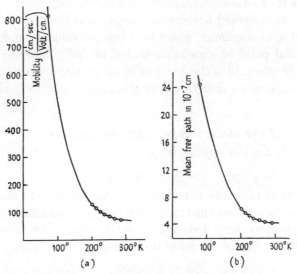

FIG. 66. (a) Mobility, and (b) mean free path in $Cu_2O$

$\Theta$ the characteristic temperature ($k\Theta/h$ is the frequency of longitudinal polarization waves of long wave-length). A value of 280° for $\Theta$ gives the right dependence on temperature; to get sufficiently large absolute values of the mobility we have to take $m^*/m \sim 0\cdot25$. (The mobility is proportional to $m^{*-\frac{5}{2}}$.) A low value of $m^*$ is not improbable for a positive hole near the top of a broad band (cf. p. 76). If these values of $m^*$ be accepted, the values of $l$ shown in Fig. 66 (b) must be reduced by a factor 8, giving $l \sim 5$ A at room temperature.

## 6. The contact between a metal and an insulator

An insulator (such as sodium-chloride at low temperatures) can carry a current only if electrons are raised into a band of energy levels (the conduction band) which is normally empty. As we have seen, this can take place in certain cases through the absorption of light, or through

† H. Fröhlich and N. F. Mott, *Proc. Roy. Soc.* (A), **171**, 496 (1939).

heat agitation. In this section we have to consider whether it is possible, if neither of these agencies is available, for electrons to flow from a metal electrode into the conduction band of an insulator.

The reason why this does not happen in general is probably that the highest occupied state of the electrons in the metal at low temperatures is below the lowest conduction level of the insulator. Electrons can

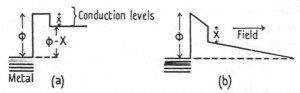

FIG. 67. Insulator in contact with a metal. $\phi$ is the work function of the metal, $\chi$ the electron affinity of the insulator (Chap. III, § 3). (a) In the absence of a field; (b) with a field

thus only leave the metal and pass into the insulator under the same conditions as from a metal into a vacuum—i.e. in such strong fields that electrons can pass through the potential barrier in Fig. 67 (b) (cold emission), or at such high temperatures that an appreciable fraction of the electrons have energies more than $\phi - \chi$ above the surface of the Fermi distribution (thermionic emission).

There is, however, rather definite evidence (Chap. VII, § 10) that in some cases $\phi - \chi$ is very much less than the work function of a clean metal surface *in vacuo*, perhaps less than 1 eV., so that even at room temperature some thermionic emission from the metal into the insulator ought to be possible. It is even possible that in certain special cases $\phi$ may be less than $\chi$; the evidence for this will be reviewed below. We must, then, consider what will happen at a surface where $\phi - \chi$ is not too large compared with

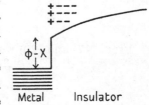

FIG. 68. Showing the shift in the energy levels of an insulator due to a space-charge

$kT$. In the first place, suppose no external field is acting. Then a vapour of electrons will form in the insulator, the electrons having energies lying in the conduction band. An equal positive charge will be formed on the surface of the metal. This will give rise to a local field in the insulator, which will raise the conduction levels as we go farther from the metal, as shown in Fig. 68. The problem of calculating the field and the electron density is exactly that of calculating the density of an electron gas round a thermionic emitter; this has been treated by a number of authors.† We consider here only the case of a plane surface.

Let $F$ be the field in the insulator, then

$$\frac{dF}{dx} = \frac{4\pi Ne}{\kappa}, \tag{17}$$

where $N$ is the number of electrons per unit volume at a distance $x$ from the metal electrode, and $\kappa$ is the dielectric constant. If $v$, $D$ are the mobility and diffusion coefficient of the electrons, we have, since no current is flowing

$$NveF - eD\frac{dN}{dx} = 0. \tag{18}$$

Integrating this, we obtain

$$\log\frac{N}{N_0} = \frac{v}{D}\int_0^x F\, dx, \tag{19}$$

where $N_0$ is the density of electrons in the insulator immediately at the metal boundary. Since $v/D = e/kT$ (cf. Chap. II, § 9) and the potential energy $V(x)$ of an electron measured from the boundary $x = 0$ is given by

$$V(x) = -e\int_0^x F\, dx,$$

equation (19) gives Boltzmann's law

$$\frac{N}{N_0} = e^{-V/kT}. \tag{20}$$

From (17) and (20) we obtain

$$\frac{d^2V}{dx^2} = -\frac{4\pi N_0 e^2}{\kappa}\exp(-V/kT).$$

We integrate, subject to the condition that the field tends to zero as $x \to \infty$; actually $V$ increases logarithmically. We obtain

$$\frac{1}{2}\left(\frac{dV}{dx}\right)^2 = \frac{4\pi N_0 e^2 kT}{\kappa}e^{-V/kT},$$

and hence

$$V = 2kT\log\left(\frac{x}{x_0}+1\right), \tag{21}$$

where

$$x_0 = (2\pi N_0 e^2/\kappa kT)^{-\frac{1}{2}}.$$

Hence

$$\frac{N}{N_0} = \left(\frac{x_0}{x_0+x}\right)^2. \tag{22}$$

† Cf. R. H. Fowler, *Statistical Mechanics*, 2nd ed., p. 364 (Cambridge, 1936).

The density $N_0$ of electrons in the insulator at the boundary will be determined by the same Fermi distribution function as for the electrons in the metal, and is thus

$$N_0 = \int_0^\infty \frac{N(E)\,dE}{e^{(E-\phi+\chi)/kT}+1},$$

where $N(E)$ is the density of states in the insulator, which may be taken to be $4\pi(2m/h^2)^{\frac{3}{2}}\sqrt{E}$. Since $\phi-\chi \gg kT$, the integration gives approximately

$$N_0 \simeq 2\left(\frac{2\pi mkT}{h^2}\right)^{\frac{3}{2}} e^{-(\phi-\chi)/kT}.$$

Thus we may write $\qquad N_0 \sim 10^{19} e^{-(\phi-\chi)/kT}.$

We give some values of $x_0$ and $N_0$ at 300° K. with $\kappa \sim 10$.

TABLE 24

| $\phi-\chi$ (eV.) | . | . | 0·1 | 0·5 | 1·0 |
|---|---|---|---|---|---|
| $N_0$ (cm.$^{-3}$) | . | . | $10^{17}$ | $10^{10}$ | $10^2$ |
| $x_0$ (cm.) . | . | . | $10^{-6}$ | $10^{-2}$ | $10^2$ |

From formula (21) we learn that if the density of electrons at the boundary layer is great, $V$ may rise rapidly by a few multiples of $kT$; but in any case one will have to go a very long distance to obtain a large rise of potential.

Formula (21) is, of course, no longer valid at distances where the density of electrons thrown up from the *full* bands becomes comparable with $N$. Since, however, these densities are of the order $< 10^{20}$ per cm.$^3$ for insulators, the distances required will be of astronomical order of magnitude. Semi-conductors are discussed in § 7.

We must now discuss whether it will be possible to get a current to flow from the cathode through an insulating crystal, if $\phi-\chi$ is small. If $L$ is the thickness of the crystal and $V$ the applied voltage, one will get a current $j$,

$$j = eN_0 vV/L, \tag{23}$$

if $V$ is so big that space-charges are unimportant. If $N_0 = 10^{10}$, $v = 100$ cm./sec./volt/cm. (cf. § 5) and $V/L = 1,000$ volt/cm., this gives a current of $10^{-4}$ amp./cm.$^2$ Moreover, the order of the magnitude of the field necessary for the effect of the space-charge to be negligible, so that $j$ should be proportional to $V$, is clearly given by

$$V \gtrsim eN_0 L^2; \tag{24}$$

with $L = 1$ mm., we obtain $V/L \gtrsim 100$ volt/cm. Currents should thus be observable with quite weak fields.

The dependence of current on voltage for smaller fields, for which the space-charge is important, is of some interest. Consider a crystal of thickness $L$ carrying a current $j$. Let $F(x)$ be the field at a distance $x$ from the surface, and $N(x)$ the number of electrons per unit volume. Then the current is given by

$$j = NevF - De\frac{dN}{dx},$$

where $v$ is the mobility and $D$ the diffusion coefficient. Laplace's equation gives for the field

$$\frac{dF}{dx} = 4\pi Ne.$$

Hence, eliminating $N$, we have

$$4\pi j = vF\frac{dF}{dx} - D\frac{d^2F}{dx^2}.$$

On integrating, we obtain

$$4\pi jx + \text{const.} = \tfrac{1}{2}vF^2 - D\frac{dF}{dx}. \tag{25}$$

Since $D = kTv/e$ and $dF/dx \sim F/L$, we may neglect the last term if $kT\dfrac{dF}{dx} \ll eF^2$. This will certainly be the case if $kT \ll eFL$, and thus if the potential across the crystal is large compared with 0·025 volt. We may assume this to be the case. Equation (25) then becomes

$$F = \sqrt{\left\{\frac{8\pi j}{v}(x+x_0)\right\}},$$

where $x_0$ is a constant. Since, at $x = 0$, $N = N_0$, we have

$$x_0 = j/8\pi vN_0^2 e^2. \tag{26}$$

It follows that the potential drop across the crystal is

$$V = \frac{2}{3}\sqrt{\left(\frac{8\pi j}{v}\right)}[(L+x_0)^{\frac{3}{2}} - x_0^{\frac{3}{2}}]. \tag{27}$$

Equations (26) and (27) give us $j$ in terms of $V$. For small $V$, $j$ is small and $x_0 \ll L$, so that

$$j = \frac{9}{32\pi}\frac{vV^2}{L^3}.$$

Thus the current increases as the square of $V$. For large $V$, $x_0 \gg L$ and we obtain

$$j = evN_0 V/L,$$

and the order of magnitude of the critical field is easily seen to be given by (24).

Finally, we must discuss the actual values of $\phi-\chi$ for contacts between metals and insulators, and see whether they are likely to be small enough for any current to pass.

In Chapter III, § 7, we deduced the energy $\chi$ of the lowest state in the conduction band in the alkali-halides from the positions of the ultra-violet absorption bands. For sodium-chloride we found that $\chi = 0\cdot5$ eV. Since the work function of clean sodium is $2\cdot2$ eV., this gives $\phi-\chi = 1\cdot7$ eV. We also saw (Chap. III, § 3) that the long-wave limit of the internal photoelectric effect in rock-salt crystals containing colloidal particles of metal was at a wave-length 7,200 A, corresponding to $1\cdot7$ eV. Now the surface between the metal particles and the salt is certainly uncontaminated by gas. Thus we have experimental evidence that for clean metal in contact with a salt no appreciable double layer is set up at the interface, which would alter the work required to take an electron from the metal into the crystal.

In Chapter VII, § 10, we shall see that the energy necessary to take an electron from colloidal silver particles into the conduction levels of AgBr is of the order 1 eV.; this fixes $\chi$ for the lowest conduction level at $3\cdot5$ eV., which is considerably greater than the work function of many metals (e.g. Cs, $\phi = 1\cdot8$ eV.). Thus if a caesium layer could be evaporated on to a *clean* crystal of AgBr (no adsorbed gas layer!), there would appear to be no potential step to prevent electrons from flowing from the metal into the salt.

In any real crystal of, for instance, silver bromide, there exist electron traps where, at sufficiently low temperatures, an electron finds a lower energy level than in the conduction band and can be held in a stable position. If electrons flowed out from our metal electrode into the non-metal, these traps would acquire electrons and the resulting space-charge would prevent the passage of any further electrons into the crystal. Even if the number of traps is as low as $10^{12}$ per cm.$^3$ (cf. Chap. IV, § 5.1), then, if all the traps in a layer $10^{-5}$ cm. thick were charged, this would produce a potential difference of 1 volt between the interior of the crystal and the surface. Space charges of this type would probably prevent the passage of any current at low temperatures.

Probably, when a crystal is bombarded by cathode rays, the electrons entering the crystal get trapped in a similar way.

At moderately high temperatures, however, a trapped electron is not stable but is released again after a short interval of time; and under these conditions it seems that a small current should flow.

## 7. The contact between a metal and a semi-conductor

In this section we confine ourselves to a discussion of the behaviour in the absence of an external field. We shall consider an electronic semi-conductor in which the current is carried by electrons released from impurity centres. Let us suppose that before the metal and semi-conductor are brought into contact the impurity levels are above the highest occupied level in the metal (Fig. 69 (a)). Then, when the semi-

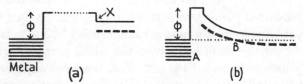

Fig. 69. Contact between a metal and a semi-conductor.
- - - - denotes position of impurity levels

conductor and metal are brought into contact, the impurity centres in the layer of the semi-conductor near to the metal will lose electrons to the metal. A positive space-charge will therefore be set up in the semi-conductor, and an induced negative charge on the surface of the metal. A field will therefore exist in the surface layers of the semi-conductor, in such a direction that the force on an electron is away from the metal. The potential energy of an electron in the lowest state in the conduction band will thus be pushed down, as shown in Fig. 69 (b), until the impurity levels are below the level of the Fermi distribution.

The breadth $AB$ of the potential barrier may be estimated as follows: Let there be in the semi-conductor $N$ impurity centres per unit volume. Then if all these have lost an electron there will be in the surface layer a space-charge $Ne$ per unit volume. The potential energy $V$ of an electron thus satisfies

$$\frac{d^2V}{dx^2} = 4\pi Ne^2/\kappa$$

Measuring $x$ from the point $B$ (Fig. 69) the value of $V$ in the boundary layer is thus

$$V = 2\pi Ne^2x^2/\kappa$$

so that the breadth $AB$ is given by

$$AB = \{(\phi-\chi)/2\pi Ne^2\}^{\frac{1}{2}}/\kappa$$

If we take reasonable values, such as $\phi-\chi = 1$ eV. and $N = 10^{19}$ per cm.³, we obtain

$$AB \sim 10^{-6} \text{ cm.}$$

Thus, only in a layer some 20 atoms thick will all the impurity centres lose their electrons.

At large distances from the metal the distribution of electrons in the semi-conductor cannot be affected by the presence of the metal. We can make use of this fact to obtain the exact positions of the energy levels in the semi-conductor relative to those of the metal. For equilibrium the density of electrons in any energy state on both sides of the barrier must be identical. Thus we may equate the density of electrons in the conduction band of the semi-conductor to the density of electrons with the same energies in the metal.

Let, then, the lowest state in the conduction band have energy an amount $U$ above the surface of the Fermi distribution in the metal. If $N(E)$ as before is the density of states in the conduction band of the semi-conductor, the total number of electrons in the conduction band is

$$\int_0^\infty \frac{N(E)\,dE}{e^{(E-U)/kT}+1}.$$

As in our calculation on p. 171, this may be replaced by

$$2\left(\frac{2\pi mkT}{h^2}\right)^{\frac{3}{2}} e^{-U/kT}.$$

If we equate this, for instance, to formula (8) on p. 158 for the density of electrons in the conduction band, we obtain, with $E$ equal to the energy interval between the impurity levels and the conduction band,

$$U = \tfrac{1}{2}E - kT \log \frac{N^{\frac{1}{2}}}{(2)\{2\pi mkT/h^2\}^{\frac{3}{4}}}. \tag{28}$$

Approximately, at low temperatures, we may write

$$U \sim \tfrac{1}{2}E.$$

Thus the surface of the Fermi distribution will lie half-way between the conduction band and the impurity levels, as in Fig. 69 (b).

The form of the field within the semi-conductor in the neighbourhood of the point $B$ and to the right of it may be investigated as follows:[†] Denote by $n_0$ the number of electrons in the conduction band at a large distance from the contact; denote by $V(x)$ the potential energy gained by an electron in the semi-conductor in bringing it from a large distance to the point $x$. Then the density of electrons $n(x)$ is given at any point $x$ by

$$n(x) = n_0 e^{-V/kT}$$

† N. F. Mott, *Proc. Cambridge Phil. Soc.* **34**, 568 (1938).

and the density of positive charges, i.e. vacant impurity levels, by

$$n'(x) = n_0 e^{V/kT}.$$

Laplace's equation then gives

$$\frac{d^2V}{dx^2} = 4\pi n_0 e^2 [e^{V/kT} - e^{-V/kT}]. \tag{29}$$

This equation may be compared with (20), for the case where there are no impurity centres. A solution valid at large distances will be sufficient for our purposes; $V$ is thus small, and (29) may be replaced by

$$\frac{d^2V}{dx^2} = \frac{8\pi n_0 e^2}{kT} V,$$

of which the solution is

$$V = \text{const.}\ e^{-2x/x_0},$$

where

$$x_0 = (kT/2\pi n_0 e^2)^{\frac{1}{2}}.$$

Values of $x_0$ are given in Table 24 on p. 171; for cuprous oxide, for instance, $n_0 \sim 10^{14}$ at room temperature and $x_0 \sim 10^{-5}$ cm.

## 8. The rectifying properties of a contact between a metal and a semi-conductor

The contact between a metal and semi-conductor has a resistance which varies, in many cases considerably, with the direction of the current. In this section it is our purpose to consider the theories of this effect which have been put forward. A well-known example of such a contact occurs in the copper-cuprous oxide rectifier, which consists of a copper plate on which a layer of cuprous oxide has been formed by heating, the surface of the cuprous oxide being pressed into contact with a lead plate. The type of resistance-voltage curves obtained with these oxide rectifiers is shown in Fig. 70.

From the point of view of the theories which we shall consider, it appears that any contact between a metal and a semi-conductor should begin to rectify when the potential difference *across the contact* exceeds $kT/e$, that is to say, at about 0·025 volts at room temperature. A circuit, then, will not have rectifying properties unless at least one of the contacts has a high resistance, equal to a considerable fraction of the resistance of the whole rectifier. We have then to consider the behaviour of bad contacts; we wish to emphasize that a high-resistance contact is *necessary* only in order that the main part of the drop in potential shall take place at the contact. We shall see, however, that the form of the current-voltage curve, and even the direction of rectification, depend on the nature of the contact.

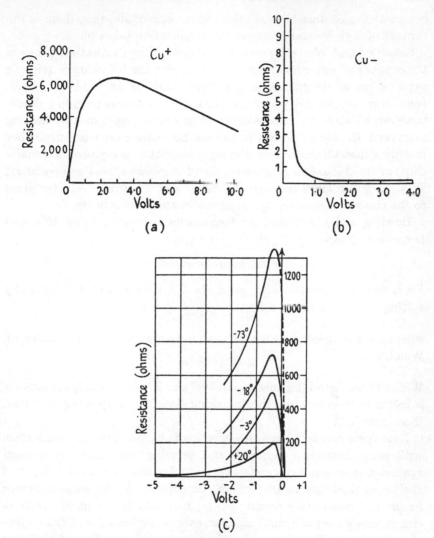

Fig. 70. Observed resistance of a copper-cuprous oxide rectifier:† (a) and (c) in the direction of high resistance, (b) in the direction of low resistance. (c) shows the effect of temperature

In the case of the copper-oxide rectifier Schottky‡ and his collaborators have shown, using a probe and a vacuum-tube voltmeter, that in the direction of high resistance practically all the potential difference

† (a) and (b) from L. O. Grondahl, *Rev. Modern Physics*, 5, 141 (1933), (c) from W. Schottky and W. Deutschmann, *Phys. Zeits.* 30, 839 (1929).

‡ W. Schottky, R. Störmer, and F. Waibel, *Zeits. f. Hochfrequenztechn.* 37, 162 and 175 (1931).

occurs at the contact between the copper and oxide; this, then, is the contact of high resistance where the rectification takes place.

Schottky and Waibel[†] postulate a layer of high resistance between the copper and the conducting oxide, and give the following convincing explanation of its existence. Cuprous oxide is an oxidation semi-conductor, the impurity centres being due to excess oxygen. When, however, a slab of cuprous oxide is formed on a copper disk by heating in oxygen, the layers nearest to the mother copper are naturally richer in copper than the remainder; the layer nearest to the copper is actually $Cu_2O$ of stoichiometric composition, and therefore almost an *insulator*.[‡] This insulating layer between the metal and the semi-conductor gives to the rectifier a considerable capacity in alternating fields.

Dowling and Place[||] find for frequencies between 60 and $10^6$ cycles per second a capacity, $C$, of

$$0.006 \text{ microfarad/cm.}^2$$

From the capacity one may estimate the thickness of the layer, by setting

$$C = \kappa/4\pi d,$$

where $\kappa$ is the dielectric constant, which we may take to be of order 10. We obtain

$$d \sim 10^{-4} \text{ cm.}$$

Waibel[††] has found thickness up to $10^{-3}$ cm. The layer of high resistance is called in the literature the 'blocking layer' or 'stop layer' (German 'Sperrschicht').

Rectifying contacts have also been made by painting a metal surface with some insulating material, and pressing the surface so formed against a semi-conductor. Hartmann,[‡‡] for instance, used a layer of shellac, of thickness about $10^{-4}$ cm., on copper. As the semi-conductor he used cuprous oxide or zinc oxide; he found that cuprous oxide (a deficit conductor) and zinc oxide (an excess conductor) rectify in opposite directions. For zinc oxide the direction of easy flow of electrons is from the oxide to the metal. For cuprous oxide it was in the same direction as for the normal copper-oxide rectifier, from metal to oxide.

Both for excess and deficit conductors, then, the direction of easy

† W. Schottky and F. Waibel, *Naturwiss.* **20**, 297 (1932).

‡ The very small conductivity of the pure oxide (p. 164) does not affect the argument.

|| Quoted by L. O. Grondahl, *Rev. Modern Physics*, **5**, 141 (1933).

†† F. Waibel, *Wiss. Veröff. a. d. Siemens-Werken*, **15**, 75 (1938).

‡‡ W. Hartmann, *Phys. Zeits.* **37**, 862 (1936).

flow corresponds to a flow of the carriers (electrons or holes) from semi-conductor to metal.†

Since positive holes in a full band behave in most ways just like electrons with a positive charge, in our theoretical discussion we need consider excess conductors only.

We shall discuss then a rectifier of the zinc-oxide type: in the oxide a layer of thickness $d$ ($\sim 10^{-4}$ cm.) at one surface is supposed to

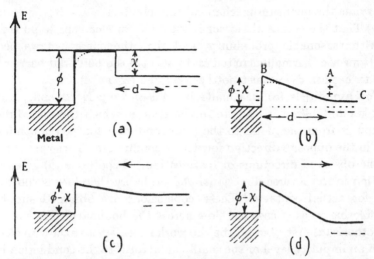

FIG. 71. Energy levels in an impurity semi-conductor separated from a metal by a layer of pure material of thickness $d$. (a) See text. (b) In equilibrium. (c) With a field in the direction of easy flow. (d) With a field in the direction of high resistance. The dotted line in (a) and (b) represents the effect of the image force. The arrows in (c) and (d) mark the direction of flow of electrons in an excess conductor, or holes in a defect conductor

be free of impurity centres. If there were a wide gap between the semi-conductor and the metal, the presence of the rather small concentration of impurity centres would make very little difference to the energies of the conduction levels; the energy levels would then be as in Fig. 71 (a).

Since, however, the crystal is actually in contact with the metal (as in Fig. 71 (b)), the electrons in the impurity centres nearest to the metal will escape to it. Thus to the right of the insulating layer, at $A$ in Fig. 71 (b), there will be a positive space-charge. An equal negative charge will be induced on the surface of the metal. There is thus an electric field in the insulating layer, which brings the impurity levels down below the surface of the Fermi distribution of the metal. To the

† This was first pointed out by W. Schottky and W. Hartmann, *Zeits. f. techn. Physik*, **16**, 512 (1935); *Naturwiss.* **24**, 558 (1936).

right of $A$ the field dies away slowly, as explained at the end of the last section.

We see, then, that there is a potential barrier between the metal and the semi-conductor; we have to make some assumption about how the electrons get across this barrier. Two assumptions are possible; they are

(a) That electrons near the bottom of the conduction band of the semi-conductor can go *through* the potential barrier, by the process known as the quantum-mechanical tunnel-effect.

(b) That the potential barrier is too wide for electrons to go through it with reasonable probability, and that the current flows because electrons are thermally excited and pass *over* the potential barrier. For this to happen $\phi - \chi$ must not be too large ($< 1$ eV.).

The hypothesis (a) was made by Wilson,[†] by Nordheim,[‡] and by Frenkel and Joffé;[||] it leads to rectification in which the easy direction of flow is from the metal to the semi-conductor for excess conductors and in the opposite direction for deficit conductors. These are contrary to the observed directions of rectification. Hypothesis (b) gives rectification in the reverse directions, and probably therefore is the correct one for actual contacts. These conclusions are obtained simply by considering in each case the flow across the boundary. We shall take hypothesis (a) first. Let $2E_0$ be the work necessary to excite an electron from an impurity level of the semi-conductor into the conduction band. It is clear from Fig. 71 that in the absence of an external field all electrons in the metal with energy greater than $E_0$ above the surface of the Fermi distribution are in a position to penetrate the potential barrier into the conduction levels of the semi-conductor; these must just be balanced by the number coming in the opposite direction. Now suppose that a potential difference $V$ is applied across the contact. As before, all the electrons in the conduction band of the semi-conductor can flow into the metal, but now electrons in the metal with energies greater than $E_0 + eV$ can flow in the reverse direction, $eV$ being the drop in potential energy from metal to semi-conductor. The number of such electrons available will vary as $\exp[-(E_0 + eV)/kT]$ and, for $V \gg kT/e$ ($\sim 0.025$ volt), will vary rapidly with $V$. The direction of easy flow of electrons is clearly from the metal to the semi-conductor, since the number of electrons available can be increased almost without limit.

The number of electrons incident per square centimetre on the wall

† A. H. Wilson, *Proc. Roy. Soc.* (A), **136**, 487 (1932).

‡ L. Nordheim, *Zeits. f. Physik*, **75**, 434 (1932).

|| J. Frenkel and A. Joffé, *Phys. Zeits. d. Sowjetunion*, **1**, 60 (1932).

of the metal with energies between $E$, $E+dE$ above the surface of the Fermi distribution is[†]

$$\frac{4\pi mkT}{h^3} e^{-E/kT} dE.$$

Assuming a probability $p$ of penetrating the potential barrier, and neglecting the variation of $p$ with energy over the small range $kT$, we see that the current from metal to semi-conductor is

$$\frac{4\pi mek^2 T^2}{h^3} p \exp[-(E_0-eV)/kT]$$

and in the reverse direction

$$\frac{4\pi mek^2 T^2}{h^3} p \exp[-E_0/kT].$$

The current is thus

$$\frac{4\pi mek^2 T^2}{h^3} pe^{-E_0/kT}[\exp(eV/kT)-1].$$

Actually $p$ will itself vary with $V$ because the shape of the potential barrier changes; the variation will not however depend on the temperature, and so cannot alter the direction of the rectification for low temperatures. For square potential barriers Wilson finds that $p$ varies as $p_0 e^{-\alpha V}$. The variation with $V$ has not been worked out for the fields shown in Fig. 71.

The resistance for low fields is given by

$$\frac{1}{\rho} = \frac{4\pi me^2 kT}{h^3} pe^{-E_0/kT} \text{ e.s.u./cm.}^2$$

To obtain an idea of the order of magnitude we set $T = 300°$ K., $e^{-E_0/kT} = 10^{-3}$; we obtain

$$\rho \sim \frac{1}{p} \times 10^{-5} \text{ ohm/cm.}^2$$

To obtain reasonable values of the resistance, say 100 ohms/cm.[2], $p$ must be of the order $10^{-7}$. Now if $W$ is the mean height of the barrier and $d$ its width,

$$p \sim e^{-2\sqrt{(2mW)}\,d/\hbar},$$

so we must have

$$2\sqrt{(2mW)}\,d/\hbar \sim 16.$$

Putting $W = 1$ eV., this gives

$$d \sim 1·5 \times 10^{-7} \text{ cm.}$$

This is a reasonable order of magnitude, though much less than the thickness of the insulating layer found by experiment ($\sim 10^{-4}$ cm.).

[†] Cf. R. H. Fowler, *Statistical Mechanics*, 2nd ed., p. 348 (Cambridge, 1936).

On the other hand, $p$, and hence the resistance of the insulating layer, is extremely sensitive to $W$ and $d$. If one doubles the thickness $d$ the resistance rises by a factor $10^7$; if one halves it the resistance drops by $10^3$. For this reason, since rectifying contacts are easy to make and their properties do not depend so violently on the method of preparation, it seems to us unlikely that the resistance of rectifying contacts is actually due to potential barriers through which the electrons penetrate.

A more fatal objection to that mechanism is, as we have seen, that it gives rectification in the wrong direction; it gives low resistance when electrons flow from metal to semi-conductor for an excess conductor and in the opposite direction for a deficit conductor, e.g. $Cu_2O$.

We discuss now the alternative hypothesis, that the potential barrier is too big for appreciable penetration, so that electrons have to receive thermal energy and go *over* the potential barrier. We can see at once that rectification will be in the opposite direction to that given by the penetration theory. For it is clear from Fig. 71 that in order to flow from the metal to the semi-conductor electrons must receive thermal energy $\phi - \chi$; therefore in the layer of the insulator immediately in contact with the metal there is a rather low density of electrons, which is independent of the field. Thus if we apply a potential in the direction to pull electrons from metal to semi-conductor, we do not obtain any *rapid* increase in the flow of electrons from the metal. If, however, a field is applied in the opposite direction (Fig. 71), the slope of the hill up which the electrons must flow is decreased and the hill may be wiped out; so the current in this direction will increase very rapidly.

We shall work out the current on the following assumptions:

1. That $\phi - \chi$ is large compared with $E_0$, so that only the straight part of the curve $BAC$ need be taken into account.

2. That space-charges due to currents through the blocking layer may be neglected, so that a constant field $F$ may be assumed in the blocking layer. For a thickness of $10^{-4}$ cm. the considerations of § 6, equation (24), show that this is valid unless the density of electrons is of the order $10^{15}$ cm.$^{-3}$ in the semi-conductor, giving a conductivity of the order $0 \cdot 1$ cm.$^{-1}$ ohm$^{-1}$.

3. The mean free path, $l$, is small compared with the thickness, $d$, of the blocking layer. For cuprous oxide at room temperature $l = 5 \times 10^{-7}$ cm. or less; cf. § 5.

4. That practically the whole potential drop in the rectifier takes place in the blocking layer.

Let $v$ be the mobility and $D$ the diffusion coefficient of an electron in the conduction band of the insulator or semi-conductor. Let $x$ denote distance measured from the metal face into the blocking layer, and let $n(x)$ be the density of electrons at any point. Then the current $j$ per square centimetre in the blocking layer will be given (cf. eq. (18)) by

$$j = nevF - De\frac{dn}{dx}. \tag{30}$$

Integrating this equation for $n$, and making use of the Einstein equation, $v/e = D/kT$ (Chap. II, § 9), we obtain

$$n(x) - \frac{j}{evF} + C \exp\left(\frac{eFx}{kT}\right),$$

where $C$ is a constant.

$n(x)$ satisfies the following boundary conditions: at $x = 0$, adjoining the metal, $n(x)$ will be determined by the same distribution function as the density of electrons in the metal. Thus, as on p. 175, $n(x) = n_0$, where

$$n_0 = \int\limits_0^\infty \frac{N(E)\,dE}{\exp[(eV_0 + E)/kT] + 1},$$

where $eV_0$ is written for $\phi - \chi$ and $N(E)$ is the density of states in the semi-conductor, the zero of energy being taken as the lowest state in the conduction band. Writing†

$$N(E) = 4\pi\left(\frac{2m}{h^2}\right)^{\frac{3}{2}} \sqrt{E},$$

and remembering that $eV_0 \gg kT$, this reduces to

$$n_0 = A \exp(-eV_0/kT),$$

where

$$A = 2\left(\frac{2\pi mkT}{h^2}\right)^{\frac{3}{2}} \sim 3 \times 10^{19} \text{ cm.}^{-3}$$

At $x = d$, on the other hand, $n(x)$ will be equal to the density of electrons in the conduction band of the semi-conductor, which we may denote by $n_1$; $n_1$ is large compared with $n_0$, since $n_1 \sim 10^{19} e^{-\frac{1}{2} E_0/kT}$.

Putting in these boundary conditions we obtain

$$j = evF \frac{n_0 \exp(eFd/kT) - n_1}{\exp(eFd/kT) - 1}. \tag{31}$$

If, however, the applied voltage in the direction of easy flow exceeds $V_0$, so that $F$ becomes negative, the potential barrier disappears altogether.

† Cf., for instance, N. F. Mott and H. Jones, *The Theory of the Properties of Metals and Alloys*, p. 84 (Oxford, 1936).

The blocking layer has then a resistivity comparable with the semi-conductor, so formula (31) is no longer valid. Thus we have only to consider positive values of $F$, and indeed values for which

$$eFd/kT \gg 1.$$

Equation (31) then reduces to

$$j = evF[n_0 - n_1 \exp(-eFd/kT)].$$

In the absence of an external field the term in the bracket vanishes, since no current flows. If a potential difference $V$ is applied across the contact, the current is thus

$$j = evn_0 F[1 - \exp(eV/kT)].$$

Since $Fd = V_0 - V$, this may be written

$$j = \frac{V_0 - V}{\rho_\infty}[1 - \exp(eV/kT)], \tag{32}$$

where

$$\rho_\infty = d/evn_0. \tag{33}$$

This formula is valid for all negative $V$ (direction of high resistance) and all positive $V$ less than $V_0$; as $V$ approaches $V_0$ the resistance of the rectifier as a whole should, as already stated, tend to a constant value.

According to the theory developed here, in the direction of high resistance the resistance $V/j$ should tend to the constant value $\rho_\infty$ given by (33). Actually the resistance is observed to rise to a maximum and then drop (cf. Fig. 70). This has been ascribed by Mott[†] and by Schottky[‡] to the image force between the electron and the metal, and thus to the same cause as the increase of thermionic emission in strong fields.[||] According to Mott the resistance for negative values of $V$ is then given by

$$\frac{1}{\rho} = \frac{1}{\rho_\infty}\left(1 + \frac{V_0}{|V|}\right)\exp\left[-e^{\frac{3}{2}}\frac{\sqrt{(V_0 - V)} - \sqrt{V_0}}{kT\sqrt{(\kappa d)}}\right], \tag{34}$$

where $\kappa$ is the dielectric constant.

With suitable values of the parameters, formulae (32) and (34) give curves closely resembling the experimental results, as is shown in Fig. 72.

From the observed values of $\rho_\infty$ one can obtain an estimate of $V_0$. The observed maxima for oxide rectifiers are of the order $10^4$ ohms/cm.$^{-2}$; $v$ is 80 cm./sec. per ohm/cm. (cf. § 5), $d$ is of the order $10^{-4}$ cm., and hence $n_0 \sim 10^{10}$ cm.$^{-3}$, whence $\exp(-eV_0/kT)$ must be $3 \times 10^{-9}$ and $V_0 \sim 0.55$ volts. The resistance in the direction of high resistance should vary

† N. F. Mott, Proc. Roy. Soc. (A), 171, 27 (1939).
‡ W. Schottky, Zeits. f. Physik, 113, 367 (1939).
|| Cf. R. H. Fowler, Statistical Mechanics, 2nd ed., p. 355 (Cambridge, 1936).

rapidly with temperature, as $\exp(eV_0/kT)$. A rapid variation is shown by the results of Fig. 70.

Finally, we must state that these are not the only recent theories of rectification. We may mention one due to Davydov[†] which ascribes the rectification to a contact between copper-rich and oxygen-rich cuprous oxide.

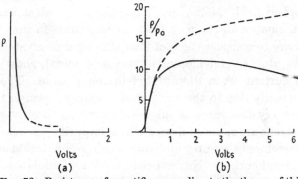

Volts         Volts
(a)            (b)

FIG. 72. Resistance of a rectifier according to the theory of this section. (a) In direction of low resistance; the resistance drops as $\exp(-eV/kT)$, and flattens out at about $\frac{1}{2}$ volt, as shown by the broken line. (b) In the direction of high resistance (in arbitrary units), calculated from formula (34) with $V_0 = 0.5$ volt, $kT/e = 1/40$ volt, $d = 10^{-4}$ cm., $\kappa = 10$. The broken line is calculated from (32), thus neglecting the image force

## 9. Secondary photoelectric currents in insulators

In our discussion of the primary photoelectric current in insulators (Chap. IV, § 4) it was emphasized that the current is due to the motion towards the anode of the electrons released by the light, and possibly also to the motion towards the cathode of 'positive holes'. The maximum charge that can pass through the circuit in Fig. 39 on p. 118 is $Ne$, where $N$ is the number of quanta absorbed. Thus, so far as the primary photoelectric current is concerned, there is no question of any passage of electrons from the cathode into the crystal (except to neutralize any positive holes). There is, however, considerable evidence that the passage of the primary current after it has been flowing for a certain time will increase the conductivity of a crystal which was originally practically an insulator in the dark; in other words, it alters the crystal in such a way as to allow the entrance of electrons from the cathode.

There is first of all the early work of Gudden and Pohl[‡] on zinc

[†] B. Davydov, *Techn. Phys., U.S.S.R.* **5**, 87 (1938).

[‡] B. Gudden and R. W. Pohl, *Zeits. f. Physik*, **6**, 248 (1921); A. L. Hughes and L. A. Du Bridge, *Photoelectric Phenomena*, p. 316 (New York, 1932).

blende. These authors find that for prolonged illumination the charge passing may be represented by

$$Q = At + Bt^2.$$

The second term, increasing as the square of the time, they call the secondary photoelectric current and ascribe to a progressive lowering of the resistance of the crystal. The secondary current increases rapidly with the applied field. Moreover, it reaches its greatest value if the crystal is illuminated all the way from one electrode to the other.

Then we have to consider the fact that alkali-halide crystals containing $F$-centres, due to stoichiometric excess of metal, show a certain small *steady* current when illuminated in the $F$-band. The primary current is certainly due to the motion of electrons towards the anode only; in these crystals there is no question of the positives moving, since the electrons are released from shallow impurity centres. A space-charge will therefore be set up which, one would think, would eventually inhibit the current entirely. Nevertheless, a certain small steady current is observed, but only if the whole crystal is illuminated.[†]

Finally, we may cite some more recent experiments from Pohl's laboratory[‡] on silver-chloride at $-170°$ C. The crystal was first heated to $400°$ C. and cooled slowly in the dark. It showed no conductivity in the dark up to 5,000 volt/cm. and under illumination showed the usual type of saturation curve (Fig. 73). After illumination with about $2 \times 10^{13}$ quanta of a wave-length 4,050 A in the absence of a field, the crystal showed a certain conductivity in the dark, and the primary current reached saturation more quickly. After an illumination with about $10^{17}$ quanta, the current obtainable in the dark was larger by many powers of ten than the primary current.

In order to explain these experiments let us consider a crystal (such as AgCl at $-170°$ C., or an alkali-halide with $F$-centres) in which the electrons but not the positive holes released by the light are free to move. The crystal having been placed between two metal electrodes, consider first what will happen if it is illuminated near each electrode without any potential difference being applied. Some of the electrons ejected into the conduction band will find their way to the electrodes. A positive space-charge will thus be set up within the crystal near the electrodes; a negative charge will be induced on the surface of the electrodes, so that in the crystal near each electrode an electrical double layer will be formed. The result will be to lower the energy

† F. C. Nix, *Rev. Modern Physics*, 4, 742 (1932).
‡ W. Lehfeldt, *Göttinger Nachrichten*, Fachgruppe II, 1, 171 (1935).

of the conduction band for electrons situated in the interior of the crystal; the position of the energy levels will change from that shown in Fig. 74 (a) to that shown in Fig. 74 (b). The strength of the double layer could increase, under prolonged illumination, until the energy of the lowest conduction level sank to that of the surface of the

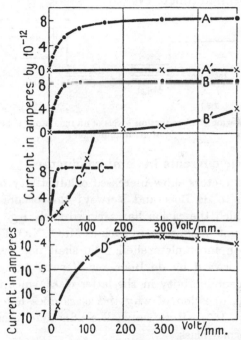

FIG. 73. Current-voltage curves for silver-chloride at −170° C. after various pre-illuminations. A, B, and C show the primary photoelectric current under illumination with $2 \times 10^9$ quanta per second of a wave-length of 4,050 A. A', B', C', and D' show the currents in the dark. A and A' are for a crystal that has been cooled in the dark, BB', CC', and D' after previous illumination with $2 \times 10^{13}$, $2 \times 10^{14}$, and $10^{17}$ quanta respectively

Fermi distribution in the metal; electrons could then come in from the metal and neutralize any further positive charge.

Prolonged illumination near the electrodes thus lowers the energy of the conduction band of levels relative to the energies of the electrons in the metallic electrodes. We thus see how a crystal which has been illuminated in the absence of a field can afterwards conduct in the dark under the influence of fairly strong fields; electrons can pass from the metal to the conduction levels of the crystal in the presence of a field much more easily when the electrical double layer already exists (Fig. 74 (b)) than when it does not.

The ease with which saturation of the primary current is obtained after previous field-free illumination must be ascribed to filling up of the traps by electrons released by the previous illumination; this has already been discussed (Chap. IV, § 5).

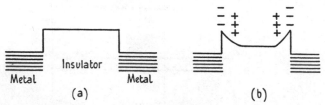

FIG. 74. Showing the conduction levels of an insulator (a) before, and (b) after, illumination

## 10. Photoelectric currents in semi-conductors

Many semi-conductors show increased conductivity on exposure to light. According to de Boer and Verwey† this occurs only in semi-conductors in which the cation has a closed shell, e.g. in $Cu_2O$, $CuI$, $ZnO$, $Ag_2S$, and not in substances such as $MnO$, $NiO$, $Fe_2O_3$, in which the cation has an incomplete shell. We shall not discuss here the hypothesis put forward by de Boer and Verwey to account for the absence of photoconductivity in the latter class, since it is bound up with the difficult question of why this class does not show metallic conduction (cf. p. 167). Here we shall confine our discussion to substances of the former class.

We shall have to consider both normal and deficit conductors. In the former we may say that the mechanism is similar to that in insulators; electrons are raised into the conduction band by the absorption of light. The differences are that the conduction band already contains some electrons which have been raised into it by thermal agitation, and that the photoelectrons, like the thermally excited electrons, end their careers by falling back into one of the levels from which they came originally. Although electron traps are present in the crystal, there is no question of the photocurrent being limited by them; deep traps will be filled up, and shallow traps will be too unstable to affect the behaviour of the electrons.

A deficit semi-conductor has impurity centres with vacant electronic levels lying above the full band. These provide a different mechanism

† J. H. de Boer and E. J. W. Verwey, *Proc. Phys. Soc.* **49**, extra part, 59 (1937).

of photoconduction; for the absorption of a quantum of light may throw an electron up from the full band into one of these impurity levels, creating thereby a mobile positive hole which moves off with a velocity determined by the $h\nu$ which has been absorbed. The kinetic energy with which this positive hole is thrown off will be great or small according as light of shorter or longer wave-length has been responsible. By the absorption of light of still longer wave-lengths, when an electron is thrown up into the vacant centre, the positive hole may have insufficient energy to escape from the electrostatic attraction of the electron; but if the positive hole is now released by the thermal vibrations, photoconductivity will result.

We may now attempt to apply these ideas to the interpretation of the absorption spectra of semi-conductors. The absorption due to the ions of the lattice will usually lie in the ultra-violet; or, if the crystal is an intrinsic semi-conductor, it may lie in the visible region. For excitation of the impurity centres, on the other hand, we must always expect the absorption to lie in the infra-red, for the following reason. A substance will only be a semi-conductor at room temperatures if the energy $E$ for thermal activation of the impurity centres is a fraction of an electron-volt. Now although the optical activation energy is always greater than the thermal activation energy, and may be twice as great, this still leaves an $h\nu$ corresponding to a wave-length in the infra-red. In both kinds of semi-conductor the excitation of an impurity centre may be followed by thermal dissociation, yielding either a free electron or else a mobile positive hole.

Experimental data on the absorption spectra of semi-conductors are meagre. Cuprous oxide is opaque in the visible region, and absorbs also in the infra-red, as shown by the experiments of Schönwald,[†] illustrated on p. 162. He found a wave limit for the inner photoelectric effect at $0.26$ eV.; and his maximum at $0.6$ eV. corresponds well with the thermal activation energy $2\epsilon = 0.7$, as pointed out by Engelhard.[‡]

Turning next to the absorption of $Cu_2O$ in the visible region, this might be due to absorption either by the impurity centres or by the ions of the lattice.

1. If it arises from the impurity centres, it must correspond to processes in which the positive holes are released directly with considerable kinetic energy. But even when the initial velocity of the positive hole is large, it will almost immediately be reduced to thermal

† B. Schönwald, *Ann. d. Physik*, **15**, 395 (1932).
‡ E. Engelhard, ibid. **17**, 501 (1933).

values; 100 mean free paths,† equivalent to a total distance of $10^{-4}$ cm., should be sufficient. This is an extremely small fraction of the path covered by a positive hole before capture (see estimate, below); consequently, for very nearly the whole of their lifetime these positive holes released by the light would have thermal energies and would be indistinguishable from the thermally excited positive holes which make the substance a conductor in the dark.

2. Perhaps the absorption coefficient of cuprous oxide is too high to be attributed in this way to a small concentration of impurity. Then the absorption in the visible may be the long-wave-length tail of the characteristic absorption of the pure material. An electron from the full band is thrown, not into an empty impurity centre but into the empty conduction band. In this case the light produces free electrons as well as mobile positive holes. We can show, however, that these photoelectrons are so quickly captured that they do not add appreciably to the conductivity. The corresponding remark may be made about normal semi-conductors, which in the dark contain no mobile positive holes; if under illumination mobile positive holes are created, these will be so quickly captured that they make no appreciable contribution to the conductivity. To prove these statements we must consider the numerical magnitudes.

In normal conductors we shall need an estimate of the time that a photoelectron remains in the conduction band before recombining with a vacant impurity centre. In a deficit conductor we shall need the time that a positive hole remains mobile in the full band before being captured by an impurity centre. In Chapter IV, § 5, we made an estimate of the total length of the Brownian track which would be covered by a photoelectron in a crystal containing a certain number of trapping centres. A semi-conductor with a resistivity of $10^6$ ohm/cm. will have $10^{11}$ electrons per cm.$^3$ in the conduction band if their mobility is 100 cm./sec. per volt/cm. There are thus $10^{11}$ vacant centres per cm.$^3$ with which an electron can recombine. Assuming a cross-section of $10^{-15}$ cm.$^2$ for recombination,‡ we see that an electron will cover a total distance

$$\frac{1}{10^{11} \times 10^{-15}} = 10^4 \text{ cm.}$$

before recapture. Its time in the conduction band will be of the order of $10^{-3}$ sec. The time spent by a positive hole before recapture will be of the same order of magnitude.

† Cf. Chap. III, § 12.                    ‡ Cf. Chap. IV, § 5.

In contrast to this consider the career of a photoelectron released by light in a deficit conductor, such as $Cu_2O$. The electron may be captured by any one of the ordinary vacant impurity centres, of which there may be $10^{18}$ per cm.$^3$ in the crystal. Thus the time that the photoelectron remains in the conduction band will be $10^7$ times *less* than the normal lifetime of a mobile positive hole in the crystal.

Both mechanisms suggest then that the effect of the light will be to increase the number of either electrons or holes, but not to change their sign or mean energy. This is in agreement with results of Engelhard,[†] who measured the conductivity $\sigma$ and Hall constant $R$ in the dark and under illumination. Some of his results are shown in Table 25.

TABLE 25. *Conductivity $\sigma$ (in cm.$^{-1}$ ohm$^{-1}$) and Hall Constant $R$ (in cm.$^3$/amp. sec.) for a Pair of Specimens of* $Cu_2O$

| Specimen | In the dark | | | Under Illumination | | |
|---|---|---|---|---|---|---|
| | $\sigma$ | $R$ | $\sigma R$ | $\sigma$ | $R$ | $\sigma R$ |
| 1 | $2 \cdot 23 \times 10^{-7}$ | $5 \cdot 63 \times 10^8$ | 126 | $1 \cdot 15 \times 10^{-6}$ | $1 \cdot 10 \times 10^8$ | 126 |
| 2 | $3 \cdot 30 \times 10^{-7}$ | $4 \cdot 38 \times 10^8$ | 145 | $1 \cdot 55 \times 10^{-6}$ | $9 \cdot 56 \times 10^7$ | 148 |

It will be seen that $R\sigma$ is unaffected by illumination, within the limits of experimental error. $R\sigma$ is a measure of the mobility of the carriers, so these results show that the photoelectrons are indistinguishable from those thermally excited.

To judge from the behaviour of $F$-centres, the true continuous absorption band of impurity centres is weak, and we think that process (2) is the more likely to occur in, for instance, cuprous oxide. Moreover, as we shall see in the next section, it gives a simple explanation of the action of oxide photocells.

Finally, we shall give an estimate of the change in conductivity produced by a given intensity of light.

Considering the case of a normal semi-conductor, suppose that, of the impurity centres in the crystal, $N$ per unit volume are unoccupied at $T = 0$.[‡] Then if $n$ electrons per unit volume have energies in the conduction band, let the probability that a given electron recombines with an impurity centre be $B(n+N)$.

Further, let $A$ electrons per second be ejected from the impurity levels by the heat motion of the surrounding atoms. Then if $n_0$ is the number of conduction electrons for the semi-conductor in the dark,

$$A = Bn_0(n_0+N). \tag{35}$$

† E. Engelhard, *Ann. d. Physik*, **17**, 539 (1933).                    ‡ Cf. § 2.

Now suppose that, on illumination, $I$ electrons are freed per second per unit volume. The number $n$ of electrons in the conduction band will now be given by

$$I+A = Bn(n+N).$$

Since, as we have seen, the conductivity is proportional to $n$, we have for the ratio of the conductivity under illumination to the conductivity in the dark

$$\frac{\sigma}{\sigma_0} = \frac{n}{n_0} = \frac{\sqrt{\{N^2+4(I+A)/B\}}-N}{\sqrt{(N^2+4A/B)}-N}.$$

For deficit conductors the same expression will be obtained. If $\sigma-\sigma_0 \ll \sigma_0$, i.e. for low intensities of illumination, this may be written

$$\frac{\sigma-\sigma_0}{\sigma_0} = \frac{I}{A},$$

so that a linear increase of conductivity is to be expected; for high intensities, on the other hand,

$$\frac{\sigma}{\sigma_0} = \text{const. } \sqrt{I}.$$

It will be noticed that, if $N = 0$,

$$\frac{\sigma}{\sigma_0} = \left(1+\frac{I}{A}\right)^{\frac{1}{2}},$$

so that the linear increase in $\sigma$ extends only to small values of $(\sigma-\sigma_0)/\sigma_0$. If, however, $N \gg n_0$, it will extend to values large compared with unity.

The numerical value of $A$ should be given by (35) on p. 191; $B$, as we have seen, is given by

$B =$ velocity of electrons $\times$ area for capture of each centre

$\sim 10^7$ cm./sec. $\times 10^{-15}$ cm.$^2$,

so, if $n_0 \sim 10^{11}$ at the temperature considered,

$$A \sim 10^{14} \text{ cm.}^{-3} \text{ sec.}^{-1}$$

## 11. The photovoltaic effect and the properties of oxide photocells

On illuminating certain semi-conducting substances which show also photoconductivity a potential difference is set up between different parts of the surface. The illuminated area is usually charged positively with respect to the dark area. The phenomenon was first observed by Coblentz,[†] and discovered afresh by Dember,[‡] and has since been

---

[†] W. W. Coblentz, *Sci. Papers Bureau of Standards*, 1919–21.
[‡] H. Dember, *Phys. Zeits.* **32**, 554 and 856 (1931); **33**, 207 (1932).

investigated by a number of authors (for references cf. Joffé).† One of the best-known effects of this type is the electromotive force set up in a copper-cuprous oxide rectifier when the contact is illuminated.‡

Theoretical discussions of the effect have been given by Joffé,‖ by Teichmann,†† by Fröhlich,‡‡ and by Landau and Lifshitz.‖‖ As the last-named authors have pointed out, earlier authors have been mistaken in assuming that an electromotive force is a *necessary* consequence of an increase in the number of free electrons near one electrode due to the absorption there of radiation.

The earlier argument was as follows. A crystal is mounted between two electrodes and illuminated in the neighbourhood of one electrode $A$. Let the field in the crystal at a distance $x$ from the electrode $A$ be $E(x)$, and the density of electrons $n(x)$. Then if no current is flowing, we must have

$$nvE(x) - D\frac{dn(x)}{dx} = 0, \tag{36}$$

where $v$ is the mobility and $D$ the diffusion coefficient of an electron. Making use of the Einstein relation (p. 63) between $v$ and $D$, we have on integrating (36) across the crystal

$$-\int E\,dx = \frac{kT}{e}\log\frac{n(0)}{n(L)},$$

where $L$ is the thickness of the crystal. The left-hand side represents the potential difference between the two ends of the crystal; the right-hand side may be written

$$\frac{kT}{e}\log\frac{\sigma_{\text{ill}}}{\sigma_{\text{dark}}}, \tag{37}$$

where $\sigma_{\text{ill}}$ and $\sigma_{\text{dark}}$ are the conductivities under illumination and in the dark respectively.

Up to this point the argument is correct; it is, however, incorrect to argue that the electromotive force (37) will be observed in the circuit. As a matter of fact *no* electromotive force should appear with this model, because the change in contact potential between the semi-conductor and the metal due to the excess density of electrons in the latter exactly balances the term (37), provided that the photoelectrons, like the

† A. Joffé and A. F. Joffé, *Phys. Zeits. d. Sowjetunion*, **7**, 347 (1935).

‡ Cf., for instance, L. O. Grondahl, *Rev. Modern Physics*, **5**, 162 (1933), where a list of references is given.

‖ Loc. cit.  †† H. Teichmann, *Proc. Roy. Soc.* (A), **139**, 105 (1933).

‡‡ H. Fröhlich, *Phys. Zeits. d. Sowjetunion*, **8**, 501 (1935).

‖‖ L. Landau and E. Lifshitz, ibid. **9**, 477 (1936).

thermally excited electrons, have a Maxwell distribution. This may easily be shown by the methods used in § 7 to obtain formula (28).

Landau and Lifshitz point out that an electromotive force can only occur if the photoelectrons do not have a Maxwell distribution, or if they are in a different band of energy levels from the thermally excited electrons (the two cases considered on p. 189). They give formulae for the e.m.f. to be expected in these cases, but we do not know of any attempt to compare their rather complicated results with experiment.

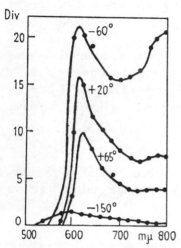

FIG. 75. Spectral sensitivity curve of an oxide photo-cell

From the theoretical point of view the electromotive force at a rectifying contact of the type discussed in § 8 appears especially simple, and we shall reproduce here a theoretical discussion due to Mott.†

In copper-cuprous oxide cells the following facts have been established:

1. Schottky, by assuming a source of e.m.f. located in the illuminated area and by considering the remainder of the cell as a shunt resistance which shunts the external load, has shown that the source of electrons is at the boundary between the copper and the cuprous oxide.

2. The flow of electrons is in all cases across the illuminated boundary from oxide to metal, and thus in the direction of high resistance.

3. The short-circuit current is directly proportional to the intensity of illumination. The e.m.f. is not directly proportional, owing to the variation with voltage of the resistance of the rectifying contact.‡

4. The number of electrons contributing to the effect is quite high, as much as 50 per cent. of the number of quanta absorbed.

5. The long-wave limit of the effect is about $1 \cdot 4 \mu$, and the short-wave limit about $0 \cdot 6 \mu$, as shown in Fig. 75 (due to Lange).‖ In § 10 we stated that the long-wave limit of the inner photo-effect was $5 \mu$, probably corresponding to the work required to remove an electron from the full band into an empty impurity level. We also suggested

† N. F. Mott, *Proc. Roy. Soc.* (A), **171**, 281 (1939).
‡ F. C. Nix, *Rev. Modern Physics*, **4**, 723 (1932).
‖ B. Lange, *Phys. Zeits.* **32**, 850 (1931).

(p. 191) that for wave-lengths in the visible most of the light absorbed removes electrons from the full band into the empty band characteristic of the pure material. The theoretical considerations mentioned above suggest that only for wave-lengths short enough to cause this second process will a photo-e.m.f. be observed, and this assumption gives a theoretical meaning to the fact that the inner photo-effect and the photo-e.m.f. have different long-wave limits.

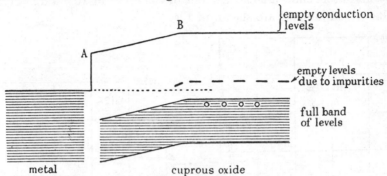

FIG. 76. The energy levels in cuprous oxide in contact with copper. The small circles represent the positive holes in the full band. The points $A$ and $B$ mark the boundaries of the blocking layer

With this assumption, then, in order to obtain a photoelectromotive force it is necessary to illuminate in the long-wave-length tail of the characteristic absorption band. Perhaps the sharp drop at 5,600 A shown in Fig. 75 is due to the increase of the absorption coefficient to values so large that the light cannot penetrate the material.

We now discuss how the photo-e.m.f. is set up. Fig. 76 shows the energy levels for electrons in oxygen-rich cuprous oxide separated from the copper by the usual blocking layer of pure material. Following the considerations of § 8, but for a defect- instead of for an excess-conductor, we see that the impurity levels nearest to the copper *capture* electrons from the metal, so the field set up in the blocking layer, which hinders positive holes from moving to the metal, helps electrons to do so

Thus almost every electron raised from the full band to the empty conduction band *in* the blocking layer where there are no impurity centres will find its way to the metal. If no current is flowing, an equal number of holes must flow across the contact from oxide to metal. Thus if $N$ electrons are released per cm.$^2$ per second, the contact potential across the blocking layer will be

$$V = Ne\rho, \tag{38}$$

where $\rho$ is the resistance of the contact.

The theory thus accounts for the order of magnitude and the direction of the observed current. There may also be an e.m.f. set up in the semi-conducting material, but owing to the large values of $\rho$ for the contact we should guess that (38) is the predominant term.

## 12. Conduction in very strong fields

For fields below the breakdown field, of the order of $10^6$ volts/cm., many insulators show a small current of the order of $10^{-9}$ amp. Some results of von Hippel[†] are shown in Fig. 77.

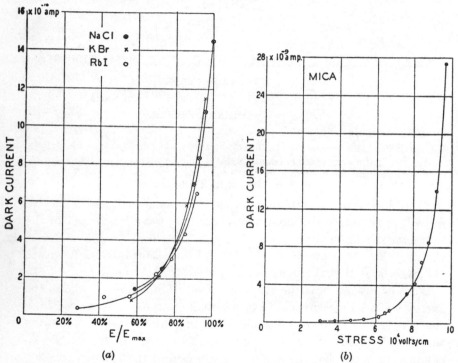

$(a)$ $\hspace{6cm}$ $(b)$

FIG. 77. Dark currents in $(a)$ alkali-halides (thickness $120\mu$) and $(b)$ mica (thickness $6\cdot5\mu$). The alkali-halides are shown on a reduced voltage scale, $E_{max}$ being the break-down voltage (p. 201) in each case

Von Hippel accounts for these results by strong-field emission from the cathode. If this explanation is the correct one, the current should depend on the work function of the cathode (cf. § 6).

Frenkel,[‡] on the other hand, believes that the field helps the thermal vibrations of the solid to eject electrons from impurity centres. He points out that the fields used are not great enough to remove electrons

† A. von Hippel, *Phys. Rev.* **54**, 1096 (1938).

‡ J. Frenkel, *Techn. Phys., U.S.S.R.*, **5**, 685 (1938).

directly from the full band into the conduction band, a process treated theoretically by Zener.†

It seems at present only possible to say with certainty that the currents are electronic in nature.‡

We may mention also the results of Klarmann and Mühlenpfordt,‖ who have measured the conductivity of quartz films with a thickness of 0·1 to 0·2 $\mu$ evaporated on silver, a silver electrode being evaporated on to the quartz. Currents of the order of $5 \times 10^{-9}$ amp. were obtained between electrodes of 3 mm.$^2$ area with a potential difference of 2 volts. The resistance decreased slightly with increasing voltage.

## 13. Dielectric breakdown

Our present ideas on dielectric breakdown are due mainly to the experiments and theoretical ideas of von Hippel,†† to the detailed theoretical work of Fröhlich,‡‡ and to the experimental work in the laboratory of the British Electrical Research Association‖‖ undertaken with a view to testing the theory of Fröhlich.

Above a critical temperature $T_0$, usually of the order 100° C., the breakdown field decreases very rapidly with temperature, and breakdown takes place some seconds after the application of the field. In this case it is well known††† that the breakdown is due to Joule heat generated by ionic conduction, which causes local melting. For temperatures below $T_0$, on the other hand, breakdown takes place in a very much shorter time, of the order of‡‡‡ $10^{-8}$ sec.; and the breakdown strength is independent of temperature or even decreases as the temperature is lowered. The phenomenon in this case is referred to as electric breakdown, any local melting being ruled out by the short times involved.

A detailed investigation of the dielectric strengths of the alkalihalides has been made by von Hippel (loc. cit.), who has established the following facts:

The breakdown strengths vary from 1·5 to 0·5 million volts per centimetre for the sodium, potassium, and rubidium halides.

---

† C. Zener, *Proc. Roy. Soc.* (A), **145**, 523 (1934).

‡ W. Pruschinina-Granowskaja, *Phys. Zeits. d. Sowjetunion*, **11**, 369 (1937).

‖ H. Klarmann and J. Mühlenpfordt, *Zeits. f. Elektrochem.* **44**, 603 (1938).

†† A. von Hippel, *Zeits. f. Physik*, **75**, 145 (1932); *Ergeb. d. exakt. Naturwiss.* **14**, 79 (1935).

‡‡ H. Fröhlich, *Proc. Roy. Soc.* (A), **160**, 230 (1937).

‖‖ A. E. W. Austen and W. Hackett, *Nature*, **143**, 637 (1939).

††† Cf. S. Whitehead, *Dielectric Phenomena* (London, 1932), p. 226.

‡‡‡ W. Rogowski, 'Probleme der modernen Physik', *Sommerfeld-Festschrift*, p. 189 (Leipzig, 1928).

Breakdown always takes place in the (110) direction, and the projection of the field in the (110) direction at the breakdown point is independent of the direction of the field.

The breakdown strengths of a series of mixed crystals of KCl and RbCl which form a continuous range of solid solutions are greater for the mixed crystals than for the pure salts, as shown in Fig. 78.

Austen and Hackett (loc. cit.) have shown that the breakdown strength of KBr drops from about 0·8 million volts per cm. at room temperature to 0·25 at the temperature of liquid air.†

To explain his results von Hippel proposes the following mechanism: In a high electric field there will be, as we know from the evidence of the last section, a few electrons in the conduction band of a crystal. If these electrons can gain enough energy from the field to remove electrons from the ions of the lattice, the number of free electrons and hence the current will increase very rapidly; an 'electron avalanche' will take place, similar to that in a spark in gases.

Two attempts have been made to give a quantitative development based on wave mechanics of von Hippel's ideas, that of Fröhlich,‡ and that of Seeger and Teller.‖ In both papers it is recognized that the condition for breakdown is that electrons shall gain energy from the field more rapidly than they lose it in the form of heat to the lattice vibrations; Seeger and Teller assume that the field must be strong enough to accelerate *all* electrons in the conduction band, while Fröhlich believes that the field need only accelerate those electrons which already have energy *nearly* large enough to produce secondaries.††

Until a thorough investigation has been made of the conditions under which a steady current can exist in a crystal, we cannot be absolutely certain which is the correct hypothesis. The fact that breakdown in alkali-halides takes place in the (110) direction suggests, however, that we have to do with fast electrons; as emphasized in Chapter III, § 3, electrons with thermal energies can move equally easily in all directions, which seems to rule out a criterion for breakdown which demands that the field shall be strong enough to accelerate the slowest electrons. We shall therefore discuss Fröhlich's theory only.

† See also A. von Hippel, *Phys. Rev.* **56**, 941 (1939), who obtains similar results.
‡ H. Fröhlich, *Proc. Roy. Soc.* (A), **160**, 230 (1937).
‖ R. J. Seeger and E. Teller, *Phys. Rev.* **54**, 515 (1938).
†† According to H. Fröhlich (*Phys. Rev.* **56**, 349 (1939)), the fact that Seeger and Teller get values similar to his for the breakdown strength is due to mistakes in their calculation of the rate of loss of energy.

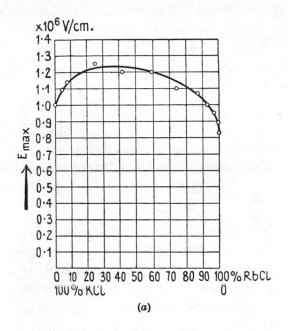

*(a)*

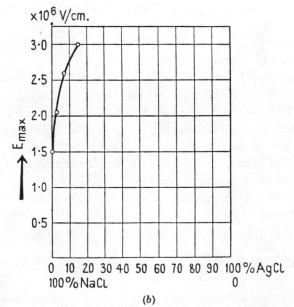

*(b)*

FIG. 78. Breakdown strength $E_{max}$ of mixed crystals (from A. von Hippel, *Zeits. f. Physik*, **75**, 145 (1932)).

If an electron is drifting in the direction of a field $F$ with velocity $u$, it gains energy at a rate $eFu$. The velocity of drift $u$ will be given by

$$u = \frac{e}{m}\tau(E)F,$$

where $\tau(E)$ is the time of relaxation of an electron with energy $E$. Thus the rate at which the electron gains energy from the field is

$$\frac{e^2 F^2}{m}\tau(E).$$

The rate of loss of energy in the form of heat $(dE/dt)_{heat}$ will be independent of $F$. According to Fröhlich, a steady current can exist if

$$-\left(\frac{dE}{dt}\right)_{heat} > \frac{e^2 F^2}{m}\tau(E)$$

for all energies $E$ less than the energy $I$ required to produce a secondary. The condition for breakdown is then

$$\left(\frac{dE}{dt}\right)_{heat} = \frac{e^2 F^2}{m}\tau(E) \quad (E = I).$$

Since $\tau(E)$ is proportional to the mean free path, we see at once that any influence which shortens the mean free path increases the breakdown strength. Since according to the considerations of Chapter III, §12, the mean free path increases as the temperature is lowered, we expect a lower breakdown strength at low temperatures, in agreement with the results of Austen and Hackett.

In the same way we may account for the high breakdown strength found by von Hippel in mixed crystals. In a mixed crystal the lattice field will be irregular and the mean free path shorter than in a perfect crystal, for exactly the same reason as in a metal.[†] Fröhlich has been able to give a quantitative discussion of the effect.[‡]

It has not yet been possible to give a satisfactory explanation of the fact that breakdown occurs in the (110) direction.

Using the methods described in Chapter III to obtain the mean free path and the rate of loss of energy, Fröhlich obtains the following formula for the breakdown field in a crystal of the alkali-halide type,

$$F = 1{\cdot}64 \times 10^5 \left(\frac{\rho}{G}\right)^{\frac{1}{3}} \frac{\lambda_0}{\lambda_1^{\frac{3}{4}}}\left(\frac{m^*}{m}\right)^{\frac{1}{2}}(\kappa - \kappa_0)\left\{1 + \frac{2}{e^{\theta/T}-1}\right\}^{-\frac{1}{2}} \text{volt/cm.}$$

---

† Cf. N. F. Mott and H. Jones, *Theory of the Properties of Metals and Alloys*, p. 286 (Oxford, 1936).

‡ H. Fröhlich, *Proc. Roy. Soc.* (A) (in press).

Here $\rho$ is the density, $G$ the molecular weight, $\lambda_0$, $\lambda_1$ the wave-lengths in angstroms of the first ultra-violet absorption band and the infra-red absorption line respectively, $\kappa$ and $\kappa_0$ the two dielectric constants, $\theta = hc/k\lambda_1$, and $m^*$ the effective mass of an electron in the conduction band with energy near $hc/\lambda_0$. Formulae for more complicated crystals are given in Fröhlich's paper.

The breakdown strengths calculated from this formula with $m^*/m = 1$ agree remarkably well with those measured by von Hippel, as the following table shows:

TABLE 26.  *Breakdown Strength in the* (100) *Direction in* $volts/cm. \times 10^5$ *at* $300°K.$

|          | NaCl | NaBr | NaI | KCl | KBr | KI  | RbCl | RbBr | RbI |
|----------|------|------|-----|-----|-----|-----|------|------|-----|
| Theory   | 15   | 13   | 14  | 8·9 | 7·3 | 6·3 | 8·4  | 5·4  | 4·7 |
| Observed | 15   | 10   | 8   | 8   | 7   | 6   | 7    | 6    | 5   |

The very good agreement must be partly fortuitous, since several approximations are made in the theory, e.g. that the frequency of the short longitudinal polarization waves responsible for the scattering is that of the optically active transverse vibrations.

The results do, however, suggest that the effective mass $m^*$ of an electron with an energy of several electron volts moving in the (110) direction is of the order $m$, i.e. that of a free electron.

### Note added February 1948

During the war years there have been certain additions to the theory of semi-conductors; in addition, we should like to mention the work of Schottky on rectifying contacts, which was not sufficiently known to the authors at the time of writing. Schottky's theory of rectification can be considered an extension of that given on p. 179 of this book; the difference is that Schottky considers the case where the boundary layer is not denuded of space charge. Formulae very similar to those of p. 184 are obtained; but the capacity of the blocking layer now depends on the field across it. For simple derivations of these results, cf. H. Henisch, *Metal Rectifiers*, Oxford 1948; N. F. Mott and I. N. Sneddon, *Wave Mechanics and its Applications*, Oxford 1948, p. 230.

Other important work is that of G. Busch and H. Labhart (*Helv. Phys. Acta*, **19**, 463 (1946)), who have made measurements of the temperature dependence of the conductivity of silicon carbide up to temperatures where most of the electrons are in the conduction band, and the conductivity drops because of the drop in the mean free path. Also an interesting paper by J. Bardeen (*Phys. Rev.* **71**, 717 (1947)), discusses the effect of surface levels on semi-conductors and on their rectifying properties. These are of profound importance for contacts between semi-conductors such as silicon or germanium and a metal probe; but not for semi-conductors formed chemically on the metal (e.g. $Cu_2O$ on copper).

# LUMINESCENCE AND THE DISSIPATION OF ENERGY

## 1. Introduction

IN earlier chapters we have already paid attention to phenomena which follow when an atom or ion of a solid is ionized by the absorption of a quantum of light. In Chapter IV we were mainly concerned with crystals to which an electric field had been applied; and many of the phenomena which we shall now discuss are closely connected with the photoconductivity which was treated there.

Consider, then, a crystal in which an atom or ion has been raised to an excited state, or ionized, by the absorption of light, or by an α-particle, or in some other way. Unless a photochemical reaction takes place, resulting in a permanent change in the state of the solid, the solid must return finally to its original state, and the energy which it has absorbed must be dissipated in some way.

The purpose of this chapter is to discuss the ways in which the solid gets rid of this energy. In nearly all cases some or all of the energy is dissipated as heat. In certain cases, however, some of the energy is re-emitted as radiation. The substance is then said to show luminescence. It is the existence of luminescent materials which lends the chief interest to the problems discussed in this chapter.

There is a very large amount of experimental material on the subject of luminescence in solids.† At present very little of this seems susceptible to theoretical interpretation. In this chapter we shall not attempt any general review of the experimental material. We shall only attempt to describe the theoretical concepts appropriate to the problem, and to apply them to a few selected experimental facts.

The problems which we have to investigate are the following:

1. Under what conditions a substance is luminescent at all. For this purpose we have to discuss the role of impurities in phosphors, and the mechanism by which non-luminescent materials get rid of the energy which they absorb.

2. The absorption and emission spectra.

3. The intensity and after-glow. If a phosphor is illuminated with a light or cathode-ray source of which the intensity varies with time as shown in Fig. 79 (a), the emitted radiation has an intensity varying

---

† Cf., for instance, P. Pringsheim, *Fluorescenz und Phosphorescenz* (Berlin, 1928); E. Hirschlaff, *Fluorescence and Phosphorescence* (London, 1938).

with time as in Fig. 79 (*b*). We are interested both in the *equilibrium* intensity of emission $I_{max}$, which may be expressed as the number of quanta emitted per quantum absorbed, and in the after-glow.

The after-glow, as we shall see, may last for a time of the order of minutes or for less than a microsecond. Materials with a long after-glow are said to show phosphorescence. The re-emission of radiation

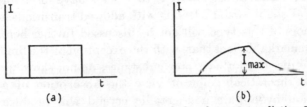

(a)                              (b)

FIG. 79. (*b*) shows the fluorescent and phosphorescent radiation from a light source (*a*)

during illumination is called fluorescence. We use luminescence as a general term including both sets of phenomena.

Both the time during which the after-glow takes place and $I_{max}$ may vary with temperature.

Phosphors may be divided into those which show luminescence in the pure state and those whose behaviour depends on the presence of an activating impurity. From the point of view of a theoretical discussion, 'pure' substances whose luminescence depends on previous heat treatment must be included in the latter class. Pure zinc sulphide activated by heat treatment is an example; the luminescence appears to be due to a stoichiometric excess of zinc, and thus to zinc atoms in interstitial positions.†

A discussion due to Randall‡ suggests that a substance will only fluoresce in the pure state if each unit cell of the crystal contains an ion or coordination group in which there is an incomplete shell of electrons fairly completely screened from its surroundings. This incomplete shell will then behave somewhat like a free atom. We expect fairly sharp emission and absorption lines, and no photoconductivity associated with the luminescence. In a list of phosphors of this type given by Randall are included manganous halides, salts of the rare earths, platino-cyanides, tungstates and molybdates, and uranyl salts. The sharpness of the emission spectra observed varies considerably from one substance to another; cf. Fig. 80, (*b*) and (*c*). The uranyl salts give

† F. Seitz, *J. Chem. Phys.* **6**, 454 (1938).
‡ J. T. Randall, *Trans. Faraday Soc.* **35**, 2 (1939).

sharp lines, while the platino-cyanides of barium and magnesium give diffuse emission. The uranyl salts[†] show no photoconductivity under strong ultra-violet illumination.

It is probable that in most of these substances we are dealing with forbidden transitions (quadripole or higher order). In that case the after-glow should be of the order $10^{-4}$ sec. In tungstates, on the other hand, very short after-glows ($< 10^{-5}$ sec.) have been observed by Strange.[‡] Possibly we are dealing with allowed transitions here.

Phosphors of this type will not be discussed further here.

It is a remarkable fact that, with the exception of the limited class of substances discussed above, pure substances do not show luminescence. From the theoretical point of view the absorption of a quantum of radiation by a pure non-metallic crystal will produce either an electron and a free positive hole or else an exciton (cf. Chap. III, § 6), in other words an electron and a positive hole which are still bound to each other by their electrostatic attraction. It appears then that the electron and hole recombine, in general, without the emission of radiation, except in special cases where they are screened from disturbance by the lattice vibrations. In most cases they must communicate their energy, of the order of 3 electron volts, to the lattice in the form of heat.

This fact enables us to understand to some extent the role of the impurity centres in impurity-activated phosphors. The impurity centre acts as a place where the electron and positive hole can recombine *with* emission of radiation; in some way which we do not at present understand completely, in the impurity centre they are more screened than elsewhere from the influence of the lattice vibrations and less likely to give up their energy to the surrounding atoms in the form of heat.

In impurity-activated phosphors the emission spectra and hence the colour of the fluorescence depend on the nature of the activating impurity. Some typical examples are shown in Fig. 80 (a), obtained for ultra-violet excitation. The emission spectrum is almost the same for cathode-ray excitation.[||] In zinc-sulphide phosphors activated by manganese the emission bands are narrow, while for those activated by copper the band extends over most of the visible spectrum.

The colour of the fluorescent radiation is green for copper-activated phosphors; if the phosphor is activated by manganese, it is yellow.[††] It appears therefore that each quantum of light is *emitted* by an electron

† J. T. Randall and M. H. F. Wilkins, *Proc. Roy. Soc.* (A) (in the press).
‡ J. W. Strange, *Trans. Faraday Soc.* **35**, 95 (1939).
|| S. T. Henderson, *Proc. Roy. Soc.* (A) **173**, 323 (1939).
†† F A. Kröger, *Physica*, **6**, 369 (1939); S. Rothschild, *Zeits. f. Phys.* **108**, 24 (1937).

in a centre.† It is not always *absorbed* by the centre, however. We may distinguish two cases:

1. The light is absorbed by the impurity centres.

2. The light is absorbed by atoms of the perfect lattice, or perhaps by atoms at the surfaces of cracks (Herzfeld absorption, Chap. III, § 9).

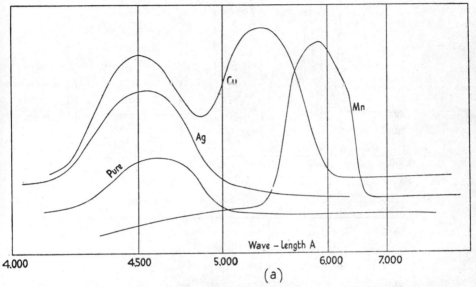

Fig. 80. (a) Emission spectra of zinc-sulphide phosphors activated by Cu, Ag, Mn, and of the pure sulphide activated by heat treatment‡

If the introduction of the impurity into the crystal leads to a new absorption band, not present in the pure substance, then illumination in the new absorption band will clearly give rise to an excitation or ionization of the impurity centres only (cf. Chap. III, § 9). Examples of crystals with absorption bands due to impurities are alkali-halides with $F$-centres (Chap. IV, § 3), or with $U$-centres (Chap. IV, § 9), and alkali-halide phosphors activated by thallium.

Reference to Fig. 81 will remind the reader of the type of absorption to be expected from an impurity centre. A quantum of light will lift

† We use the term 'centre' to describe the impurity atom and those of the surrounding atoms whose absorption spectrum is affected by it. We do not mean that the emission spectrum is the same as it would be if the centre were taken out of the crystal.

Probably each centre discussed in this chapter is either an interstitial atom (Chap. IV, § 1), as in zinc-sulphide phosphors, or a foreign ion replacing an ion of the lattice (e.g. thallium ions replacing alkali-metal ions in alkali-halide phosphors).

‡ We are grateful to Dr. J. T. Randall for providing us with the curves shown in Figs. 80(a), (b) and (c).

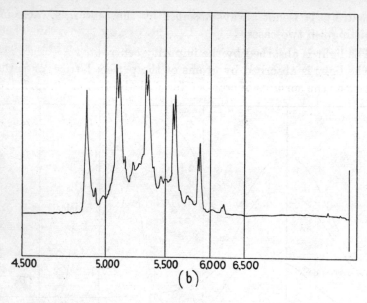

4,500    5,000    5,500    6,000  6,500

(b)

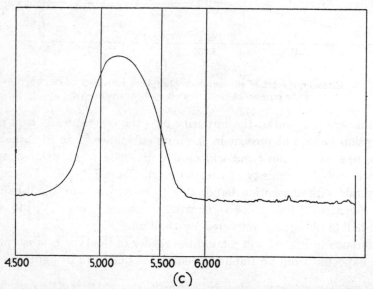

4,500        5,000        5,500        6,000

(c)

Fig. 80. Emission spectra of pure phosphors: (b) photometer curve of spectrum of uranyl nitrate. (c) photometer curve of spectrum of BaPt(CN₄)4H₂O

an electron either into an excited state, where it is still bound to the corresponding positive charge, or else directly into the conduction band.

For such substances as pure silver-halides or zinc-sulphide the correct interpretation of the ultra-violet absorption spectrum is at present in doubt (cf. Chap. III, § 8, and Chap. IV, § 6). We are not certain whether the wave-lengths which stimulate photoconductivity and fluorescence are wave-lengths absorbed by ions of the perfect lattice, or only by ions specially situated at the surfaces of cracks or by atoms in interstitial positions.† There is no general agreement, also, as to whether the absorption spectrum in this region depends on the activating impurity.

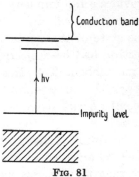

FIG. 81

There is fortunately at least one class of experiment in which one can be sure that the energy is absorbed by the atoms of the perfect lattice; we refer to the production of luminescence or photoconductivity by bombardment with α- or β-rays, cathode rays, or by illumination with X-rays. In these cases it is certain that all the atoms play their part in the absorption of the energy of the incident particles. The fact that specially situated atoms or ions can absorb rather smaller quanta of energy than can the atoms or ions of the perfect lattice will not give them any special advantage.

Of particular interest is the fluorescence of copper-activated zinc-sulphide phosphors under α-ray bombardment. These crystals contain about one copper atom per 10,000 molecules of ZnS. Their emission spectrum, whether excited by light or by α-particles, is quite different from that of pure luminescent zinc-sulphide, the colours being green and blue respectively. Thus the light must be emitted by the impurity centres. On the other hand, when the fluorescence is excited by α-particles, it is certain that in the first instance very nearly all the energy is absorbed by ions of the perfect lattice, and not by the impurity centres at all. In spite of this the efficiency of the luminescence is very high; Riehl‡ and his co-workers claim that at room temperature as much as 80 per cent. of the energy of an α-particle can be emitted as radiation.‖ There must thus exist a highly efficient mechanism by which the energy can be transferred from the absorbing ion to the copper atom.

The α-particle will lose nearly all its energy by producing electrons

† For a discussion of the last hypothesis, cf. F. Seitz, loc. cit. and *Trans. Faraday Soc.* **35**, 74 (1939). Cf. also the footnote on p. 209.
‡ N. Riehl, *Ann. d. Physik*, **29**, 640 (1937).
‖ For excitation by cathode rays the efficiency is also high, of the order of 10 per cent.; cf. F. Seitz, *Trans. Faraday Soc.* **35**, 84 (1939).

having energies up to 500 volts or more; the faster of these in their turn will lose most of their energy in producing secondaries. Thus most of the energy of the $\alpha$-particle is used up in producing free electrons in the conduction band and positive holes in the full band. We may expect that both are mobile; if, however, a positive hole moving through the crystal encounters an interstitial copper atom, which provides a full impurity level above the top of the full band (Fig. 81), an electron will drop from the impurity level into the full band. The state of the crystal is now just what it would have been if the electron had been ejected from the impurity centre; the vacant level is not mobile. The electrons thrown into the conduction band by the $\alpha$-particle will eventually find these empty impurity centres, and recombine with them, emitting radiation characteristic of the impurity centre.

Absorption of energy by an ion of the lattice can thus lead to the observed emission by the impurity centre. And we can now go on to say that this process may take place whether the energy has been absorbed from an incident $\alpha$-particle, as here, or from incident ultra-violet radiation. In order that an impurity centre should be ionized by the incident light, it is not necessary that a quantum should be absorbed by the centre. If the incident radiation creates a positive hole in the lattice, ionization of an impurity centre will ensue, provided that (1) the positive hole is mobile, and (2) an electron in the centre has an energy lying above the band in which the positive hole moves.

Various authors† have assumed that energy can be carried from the point where a quantum is absorbed to the radiating centre by an 'exciton' (cf. Chap. III, § 6). An atom of the crystal absorbs a quantum of radiation of insufficient energy to ionize it; although the positive and negative charges are not separated, the energy can be transferred from one atom to the next by a process similar to the familiar 'collision of the second kind'. Although this process is certainly possible in principle, we do not think it can be mainly responsible for the behaviour of zinc-sulphide phosphors bombarded by $\alpha$-particles, because the energy of the $\alpha$-particle will be mainly used up in producing free electrons in the crystal.

Actually in zinc-sulphide phosphors excited by ultra-violet light it may well be that a large part of the absorption is due to the centres

† Cf., for example, J. Franck and E. Teller, *J. Chem. Phys.* **6**, 861 (1938); C. F. Goodeve and J. A. Kitchener, *Trans. Faraday Soc.* **34**, 907 (1938); F. Seitz, ibid. **35**, 84 (1939).

themselves. According to Seitz† these centres are responsible for the long-wave-length tail of the absorption band. The foregoing argument shows, however, that energy can also be transferred from the lattice to the centre.

## 2. The decay of the after-glow

As a result of the discussion in the last section, we may divide the luminescence shown by impurity-activated phosphors into two types. These are

1. Luminescence in which the impurity centres are excited, but not ionized, by the incident radiation.

2. Luminescence in which the electron is removed from the centre, either directly by the absorption of light, or by the indirect process described above. Since we are discussing substances which undergo no permanent photochemical change on illumination, the electron must eventually return to its original centre or to another, and be recaptured. It will probably first be captured into an excited state, and then return to the ground state.

An electron may fall from the excited state in two ways:

(a) By the emission of radiation,

(b) By transferring all its energy to the thermal vibrations of the surrounding atoms. In materials which do not show luminescence or any photochemical reaction, (b) must happen in every case. In § 3 we discuss the relative probabilities of the two processes. In the remainder of this section we shall suppose that (a) takes place, either in every case, or with a certain probability which we denote by $P$.

Our main purpose in this section is to discuss the decay of the radiation emitted by impurity-activated phosphors after the exciting radiation is cut off. The variation of $P$ with temperature does not affect the decay law, but only the total intensity.

For luminescence of type (1), which in an applied field is not accompanied by photoconductivity, we may say at once that after the exciting radiation is cut off the emitted intensity will decay according to the law

$$I = I_0 e^{-\alpha t}.$$

For an allowed transition, $\alpha$ will be of the order $10^8$ sec.$^{-1}$, for a forbidden transition of the order‡ $10^4$ sec.$^{-1}$, and independent of the temperature

† F. Seitz, *J. Chem. Phys.* **6**, 454 (1938). The photoconductivity for zinc-sulphide activated by copper was investigated by B. Gudden and R. W. Pohl (*Zeits. f. Physik*, **2**, 181 (1920)); they found that the absorption peaks for stimulating luminescence and photoconductivity are practically identical, and lie entirely in the near ultra-violet.

‡ As for the uranyl salts; cf. J. T. Randall and M. H. F. Wilkins, loc. cit.

in either case. In certain special cases, to be discussed in § 4.1, $\alpha$ may be much smaller and dependent on temperature.

We turn now to luminescence of type (2), which in an applied field is accompanied by photoconductivity; the luminescence of zinc-sulphide phosphors is an important example.† Taking the simplest case first, we suppose that the crystal contains a certain number of impurity centres from which electrons can be ejected‡ and that an electron must return to one of the centres which has lost an electron in order to emit radiation. Then, if there are $n$ electrons per unit volume in the conduction band, there are also $n$ vacant impurity levels, and we may denote the probability per time $dt$ that a given electron, returning to an impurity centre, falls to the ground state with emission of radiation|| by

$$An\,dt, \qquad (1)$$

where $A$ is a constant which we shall discuss later. The number of electrons in the conduction band will then decay at the rate

$$\frac{dn}{dt} = -An^2,$$

which gives on integration

$$\frac{1}{n} = At + \text{const.},$$

or

$$n = \frac{n_0}{n_0 At + 1}, \qquad (2)$$

where $n_0$ is the value of $n$ at time $t = 0$. The number $N_q$ of quanta emitted per second per unit volume of the material is thus†† given by

$$N_q = An^2 = \frac{An_0^2}{(n_0 At + 1)^2}. \qquad (3)$$

Thus if $I$ is the intensity of the emitted radiation, $1/I^{\frac{1}{2}}$ is a linear function of the time, viz.

$$\frac{1}{\sqrt{I}} = \frac{1}{\sqrt{I_0}}(1 + An_0 t). \qquad (3.1)$$

In a similar way we may calculate the rise of the intensity of the

† Probably zinc-sulphide activated by manganese belongs to class (1); cf. note on p. 226.

‡ They may be ejected either by the direct absorption of energy or by the mechanism discussed in the last section.

|| Before radiating the electron will have already been captured into an excited state of the impurity centre (see below).

†† To allow for conversion of energy into heat, the factor $P$ must be introduced. The following formulae are given for the case $P = 1$.

emitted radiation after the exciting radiation is turned on. If $p$ electrons per second are raised into the conduction band, we now have

$$\frac{dn}{dt} = p - An^2,$$

giving

$$n = \sqrt{\frac{p}{A}} \tanh\{\sqrt{(Ap)}t\}.$$

One point about the bimolecular law (3) may be noted. The time taken for the intensity to decay by a factor 2, namely

$$(\sqrt{2}-1)/n_0 A,$$

depends on $n_0$ and hence on the initial intensity $I_0$ ($= An_0^2$), so that

$$t_0 = (\sqrt{2}-1)/\sqrt{(I_0 A)}.$$

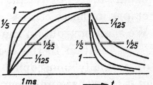

FIG. 82. Emitted intensities from a zinc-sulphide copper phosphor, the wave-length of the exciting radiation being 3,700 A. The intensity scales are adjusted to fit at the point on the time scale where the radiation was cut off. The figures show the relative intensities of the exciting radiation

High intensities thus give a rapid decay. An effect of this type has been found, for instance, by Antonow-Romanowsky[†] and by de Groot[‡] with copper-activated zinc-sulphide phosphors. De Groot's results are shown in Fig. 82.

De Groot finds also that the decay is more rapid with exciting radiation of short wave-length (3,150 A) than for a longer wave-length (3,700 A). He suggests that this is because the radiation of short wave-length is absorbed in a smaller thickness of material; thus the intensity of radiation emitted per unit volume of radiating material is greater for short wave-lengths.

On account of the different densities of electrons in different parts of the crystal, we may expect a more generalized form for the decay than (3),

$$N_q = \sum_r \frac{v_r A n_r^2}{(n_r At+1)^2},$$

where $v_r$ is the fraction of the crystal in which the density is $n_r$. For large $t$ this gives, however,

$$N_q = \text{const.}/At^2.$$

Under certain circumstances a bimolecular law of type (3) is not to be expected in photoconducting phosphors. If the impurity centres

† W. W. Antonow-Romanowsky, *Phys. Zeits. d. Sowjetunion*, 7, 366 (1935).
‡ W. de Groot, *Physica*, 6, 275 (1939).

are due to a stoichiometric excess of either constituent, then, as we have seen in our discussion of semi-conductors,† there may be some impurity centres which are *not* normally occupied by an electron. For instance, it has been suggested‡ that in 'pure' zinc-sulphide phosphors the impurity centres are interstitial zinc atoms, or in other words electrons trapped in the field of an interstitial zinc ion. We may expect that at room temperature a zinc-sulphide crystal will contain also a certain number of 'frozen-in' zinc ions in interstitial positions, with an equal number of vacant lattice points. The former will be the normally empty impurity centres. In such a case (3) will be valid only for large $n$. We shall now obtain the decay law valid for this general case.

In addition to the ordinary impurity centres, let $\nu$ be the number of normally unoccupied impurity centres. Then the probability per unit time that any given electron will emit a quantum of radiation is

$$A(n+\nu),$$

so that equation (1) has to be replaced by

$$\frac{dn}{dt} = -An(n+\nu).$$

The solution is

$$n = \frac{\nu}{Be^{\nu At}-1}, \tag{4}$$

where

$$B = 1+\nu/n_0.$$

Thus after a sufficiently long time the number of electrons in the conduction band will decay exponentially so that

$$n = \frac{\nu}{B}e^{-\nu At},$$

and, since then $n \ll \nu$, the number of quanta emitted per second per unit volume will be

$$\frac{A\nu^2}{B}e^{-\nu At}. \tag{5}$$

Thus an exponential decay of the phosphorescent radiation is to be expected. Initially, however, if $n_0$ is great compared with $\nu$, (4) reduces to (2), and so the decay law will be given initially by (3). The formula comprising the complete range‖ is

$$N_q = An(n+\nu), \tag{6}$$

with $n$ given by (4).

---

† Cf. Chap. V, p. 156.   ‡ F. Seitz, *J. Chem. Phys.* **6**, 454 (1938).
‖ This formula was first given by S. J. Wawilow, *Phys. Zeits. d. Sowjetunion*, **5**, 369 (1934).

The duration of phosphorescence varies for different substances from less than one microsecond to some hours or days; and, as we shall see, the mechanism is usually complicated. This does not mean, however, that we must begin by altering the simple formulae, (3), (5), and (6); it merely means, in the first place, that the value of the coefficient $A$ depends on a number of factors which describe the state of the crystal.

When a photoelectron in the conduction band encounters an unoccupied impurity centre, it will in general be captured into an excited state, the small amount of excess energy being at the same time taken up as heat by the lattice. The considerations of Chapter IV, § 5, suggest that the probability of capture into an excited state, where there is not much energy to be got rid of, may be quite large; an electron is likely to be trapped by the first centre it encounters. At the same time, we have stressed the fact that, at room temperature, an electron in an excited state is often thrown into the conduction band by the thermal vibrations before it has time to radiate. It will be noticed that, with this in view, in the expression (1) above, the coefficient $A$ was defined as giving, not the probability of being captured, but the probability of radiating on capture. An electron is likely to be captured by many impurity centres before it stays in one long enough to radiate.

In Chapter IV, § 5, we have seen also that in all real crystals, even in the pure state, there are 'electron traps', i.e. places where an electron in the conduction band may be trapped. An impurity-activated phosphor will presumably contain electron traps which are similar to those in the pure crystal and are quite distinct from the impurity centres. The presence of these traps will be one of the factors which determine the value of $A$ in formulae (3) and (6).†

It is a well-known fact that, if a zinc-sulphide phosphor is irradiated at a low temperature, for example that of liquid air, and then allowed to warm up after the source of illumination has been removed, it shows a burst of luminescence. The cold phosphor stores up energy which is only re-emitted as radiation when the crystal returns to room temperature. The obvious interpretation is that the phosphor contains shallow electron traps; there are in the crystal places where the electron can be trapped, and where it is stable at low temperatures, but from which it will be freed at higher temperatures.

We believe that when any crystal of the class discussed here,‡ at

---

† The quantity $n$ in these formulae for the number of electrons in the conduction band includes the trapped electrons.

‡ i.e. phosphors which show photoconductivity.

any temperature, shows an after-glow lasting for several seconds, or more (long after-glows, $An \sim 1$ sec.$^{-1}$), this is in every case to be ascribed to the return to the luminescent centres of electrons which have been trapped elsewhere. The sooner the electrons leave the traps, the larger will be the value of $A$; we therefore expect $A$ to increase rapidly with temperature.[†]

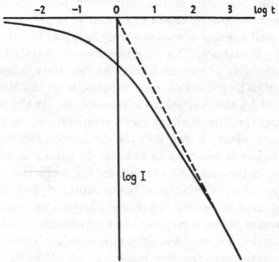

FIG. 83. Decay of a phosphor according to formula (3.1)

The slow decay of zinc-sulphide phosphors lasting for periods of the order of seconds or minutes, at room temperature and above, has been investigated mainly by the Russian school.[‡] These authors express their results by plotting $\log I$ against $\log t$. The type of curve to be expected according to formula (3.1) is shown in Fig. 83; the slope of the curve should tend to a constant value given by

$$\alpha = \frac{d(\log I)}{d(\log t)} = -2$$

for large $t$.

Antonow-Romanowsky found that the slope $\alpha$ approaches this value

[†] When a crystal is subjected to uniform exciting radiation, the character of the traps will govern the rate at which the luminescence approaches its maximum intensity. But, as soon as a steady state has been reached, the presence of traps can have no effect on the intensity of the emission.

[‡] W. W. Antonow-Romanowsky, *Phys. Zeits. d. Sowjetunion*, 7, 366 (1935); W. L. Lewschin, *Acta Physica Polonica*, 5, 301 (1936); S. J. Wawilow and W. L. Lewschin, *Zeits. f. Physik*, 35, 920 (1926); A. A. Schischlowski and S. J. Wawilow, *Phys. Zeits. d. Sowjetunion*, 5, 379 (1934); W. L. Lewschin and W. W. Antonow-Romanowsky, ibid. 5, 796 (1934).

for powders of large grain size ($\sim 50\,\mu$). For smaller grain size ($\sim 10\,\mu$) the slope may be as small as unity. Some of his results are shown in Fig. 85.

The apparent small slope for small grain size may perhaps be due to the existence of *two* kinds of trapping centre, e.g. Tamm surface levels (cf. Chap. III, § 5.2) and some other kind of level (cf. Chap. IV, § 5). If the two kinds of trap have slightly different depths, one will hold its electrons less firmly than the other type, and will thus lose its electrons first. As the phosphorescence progresses, then, the constant $A$ would *decrease*. Since

$$\log I \sim \log \frac{1}{A} - 2 \log t,$$

a decreasing value of $A$ would give an apparent slope less than 2, as Fig. 84 shows.

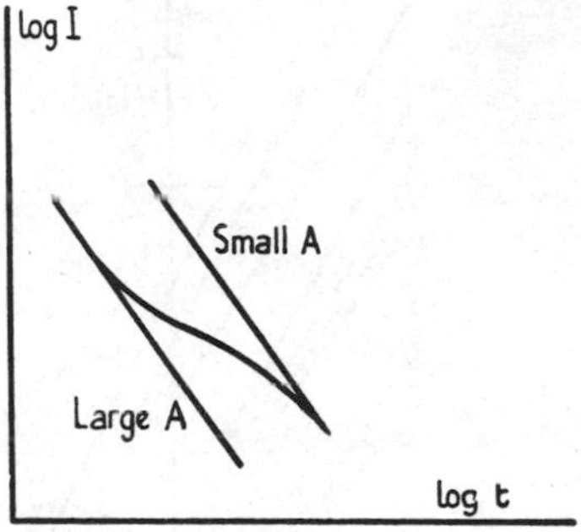

FIG. 84

The increase in the slope for very low intensities shown in Fig. 85 (*b*) may represent a breakdown in the bimolecular law due to frozen-in ions, of the kind described above.

The Russian workers find that $A$ increases with increasing temperature, as Fig. 85 shows.

Some results on the photoconductivity of zinc-sulphide are in agreement with the conclusions of the Russian authors. When a zinc-sulphide phosphor at $-196°$ C. has been illuminated with ultra-violet light, it will, under infra-red illumination at the same temperature, show an electrical conductivity, which decays slowly. Reimann[†] finds that the conductivity $\sigma$ dies away according to the law (cf. p. 126)

$$\sigma = \frac{\sigma_0}{1+\alpha t}.$$

Since the conductivity is proportional to the number of free electrons, his results are in agreement with formula (2).

This slow bimolecular decay of the type (3), found by the Russian investigators and supported by the experiments of Reimann, is not the only type of decay shown by this class of phosphors. The slow bimolecular decay may be preceded by a much more rapid decay. This behaviour is found after an intense stimulation of the crystal. Strange[‡] has made measurements of the decay of luminescence in zinc sulphides activated

[†] A. L. Reimann, *Nature*, **140**, 501 (1937).
[‡] J. W. Strange, *Trans. Faraday Soc.* **35**, 95 (1939).

by copper and silver and in tungstates after excitation by cathode rays. For very high intensities of the exciting radiation he found a very short *exponential* decay with a period of less than $10^{-6}$ sec. For lower intensities of the incident beam he found a longer decay period

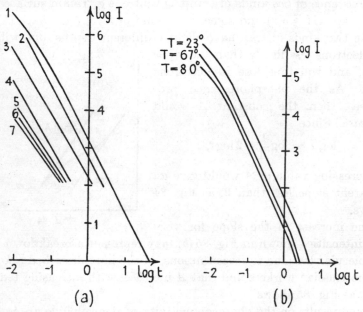

FIG. 85.† (a) Decay of a zinc-sulphide phosphor; the mean crystal size and slope of curve are shown below

| Phosphor | . | . | 1 | 2 | 3 | 4 | 5 | 6 | 7 |
|---|---|---|---|---|---|---|---|---|---|
| Crystal size ($\mu$) | . | | 69 | 54 | 27 | 17 | 14 | 12 | 10 |
| Slope . | . | . | 1·96 | 1·88 | 1·70 | 1·72 | 1·60 | 1·51 | 1·44 |

(b) Dependence of phosphorescence on temperature

| Temperature | 23° | 67° | 80° C. |
|---|---|---|---|
| Slope | 2·06 | 2·05 | 2·09 |

of the order $10^{-5}$ sec. Likewise for copper-activated zinc-sulphide phosphors, de Groot‡ found decay periods of the order one millisecond with very little dependence on temperature between 22° C. and 430° C. His results at room temperature have already been illustrated in Fig. 82, and the dependence on intensity suggests that the decay here follows the bimolecular law approximately.

† W. W. Antonow-Romanowsky, loc. cit., pp. 372, 375.
‡ W. de Groot, *Physica*, **6**, 275 (1939).

In this connexion we may remark that some photoconducting phosphors (but not all, cf. p. 223) give *during* illumination an emission which does not fall in intensity at low temperatures. The obvious interpretation is that under intense illumination the traps get filled up after a certain time, so that there is nothing to prevent the free electrons from returning rapidly to the luminescent centres.† We believe that, whereas the *tail-end* of the after-glow should always be slow, of the form given by (3) or (6) and very sensitive to temperature, for high incident intensities all the traps will become filled, so that the initial stages of the bimolecular decay are much more rapid. Decay of this type, then, will account for de Groot's results.

So long as electron traps are operative, it is impossible to predict a value for the constant $A$ in the formulae (3) and (6), until we have independent information as to the depth of the traps. On the other hand, as soon as these traps are filled, the crystal will behave like an ideal crystal with no traps; and we can at once discuss the value of $A$. Let the crystal have $N$ impurity centres, and let there be at any moment $n$ electrons per cm.³ in the conduction band. Let $u$ be the mean velocity of one of these electrons and $\sigma$ the cross-section for its capture into the excited state of an impurity centre. We obtain the upper limit to the value of $A$ by supposing that the thermal vibrations are insufficient to liberate the electron. Thus the electrons are captured and fall to the ground level at a rate given by (1) with

$$A \gtrsim \sigma u.$$

From the evidence of Chapter IV, § 5, we expect $\sigma$ to be of the order $10^{-15}$ cm.² With $u \sim 10^7$ cm./sec., this gives

$$A \gtrsim 10^{-8} \text{ cm.}^3/\text{sec.}$$

When the number of electrons initially in the conduction band is $n_0$, the time characteristic of the decay, $t_0$, is $1/A n_0$. It will be more convenient to express $t_0$ in terms of the initial intensity of emitted radiation $N_q$ (in quanta per cm.³/sec.), given by $N_q = A n_0^2$. We thus have
$$1/t_0 = \sqrt{(A N_q)} \gtrsim 10^{-4} \sqrt{N_q} \text{ sec.}^{-1}$$

If we subject the crystal to very great intensities of the exciting radiation, the number $n_0$ of free electrons with which the decay starts may ultimately reach values very nearly as great as $N$, the number

† In Chap. IV, § 5, we have shown how the filling up of the traps in a silver-bromide crystal can increase the primary photoelectric current in the crystal.

per cm.³ of impurity centres. If $N$ and $n_0$ are of the order $10^{18}$/cm.³, this would give a decay period $1/An_0$ of the order $10^{-10}$ sec.† This time, however, is less than the time which the electron would take to drop from the excited state to the ground state with the emission of radiation. Thus for sufficiently great intensities of the exciting radiation, the lifetime of the excited states of the individual centres

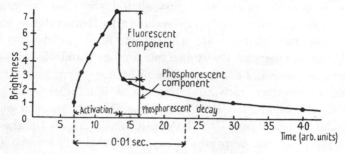

FIG. 86. Fast and slow decay, according to Beese, of an oxide phosphor

will determine the rate of decay. This will give a rapid *exponential* decay, $I = I_0 e^{-t/\tau}$. This we believe to be the explanation of the decay times less than a microsecond in Strange's experiments.

The time $\tau$ should be of the order (cf. Chap. III, §10) of $10^{-8}f^{-1}$ sec., where $f$ is the oscillator strength, a numerical constant less than unity. Decay periods of the order of a microsecond would suggest rather small values of $f$. These values are not impossible. $f$ is given by an expression of the type

$$f \propto \left| \int \psi_n x\psi_0 \, dx \right|^2,$$

where $\psi_n$, $\psi_0$ are the wave functions of the excited and normal states. In Chapter V, §4, we have emphasized that the radial extension especially of the excited states of impurity centres, is very large. If the radial extension of the excited state is much larger than that of the normal state, the oscillator strength is necessarily small.

We shall, then, sum up the type of decay to be expected from impurity-activated phosphors showing photoconductivity, as follows.

1. For very high emitted intensities, an exponential decay with a decay period of the order of a fraction of a microsecond, independent of temperature.

2. As the intensity decreases, this should change over to a rapid bimolecular decay, independent of temperature.

† If thermal vibrations repeatedly liberate the electron which has been captured into an excited state before it has time to radiate, the value of $1/An_0$ may be larger, say $10^{-8}$ sec.; but this is still small compared with a microsecond.

3. For still lower intensities, this should change to a slow bimolecular decay, with a value of $A$ strongly dependent on $T$.

4. Finally, the decay law may change over again to an exponential form, again dependent on temperature, due to the presence of frozen-in ions. This should only occur when the activating impurity is a stoichiometric excess of one constituent of the crystal.

The transition from fast to slow decay is shown by some results of Beese† on mixed ZnO and $SiO_2$+Mn phosphors, illustrated in Fig. 86.

## 3. Mechanisms for the dissipation of energy as heat; conditions for luminescence, and dependence of fluorescent radiation on temperature

We have seen that, in phosphorescent materials activated by some kind of impurity, an electron is either raised to an excited state in the neighbourhood of the impurity centre, or else it is ejected into the conduction band and then returns to the impurity centre after the lapse of an interval of time. It will then be captured into an excited state, and subsequently give up its energy. In either case, it may return to the lowest state in the impurity centre in two ways; *either* with the emission of radiation *or* by giving up its energy to the vibrational movement of the surrounding atoms, in which case the energy will be dissipated as heat. In order to understand which substances will act as phosphors, and the dependence of the intensity of the re-emitted radiation on temperature, it is important to have some idea of the factors determining the relative probabilities of the two processes. In § 2 the probability of emission has been denoted by $P$. The value of $P$, it may be emphasized, determines the efficiency of the phosphor, that is, the fraction of the absorbed energy which is re-emitted, but it does not affect the decay laws discussed in the last section.

We should expect the energy of the re-emitted quantum to be, in general, less than that of the absorbed quantum; in other words, the emission bands will lie to the long-wave-length side of the absorption bands (Stokes's law). This may be shown quite generally by a diagram of the type of Fig. 87 (due to Seitz‡ and to Von Hippel).|| In this diagram the energies of the normal and excited states of an impurity centre are plotted against *any* configurational coordinate—e.g. the displacement of any of the atoms in the neighbourhood of the centre or

---

† N. C. Beese, *J.O.S.A.* **29**, 28 (1939).
‡ F. Seitz, *Trans. Faraday Soc.* **35**, 74 (1939).
|| A. von Hippel, *Zeits. f. Physik*, **101**, 680 (1936).

of the centre itself. When the centre is in its state of lowest energy, the configurational coordinates will assume the values for which the energy is a minimum—i.e. the values represented by the point $A$. According to the Franck-Condon principle, in any optical transition the atomic nuclei remain at rest. Thus the impurity centre can absorb quanta of energy $h\nu_1$, equal to $AA'$ in Fig. 87. In general, however,

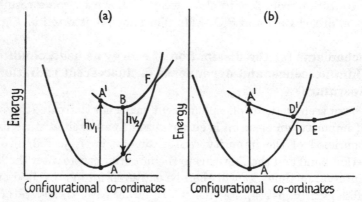

FIG. 87. Two possible arrangements of levels for normal and first excited states of an impurity centre†

when the electron of the centre is in its excited state, the values of the configurational coordinates will no longer remain the same as before; they will assume new values for which the energy of the excited state is a minimum (marked $B$ in Fig. 87 $(a)$), the energy $A'B$ being dissipated as heat. The quanta of energy re-emitted will have the energy $BC$, and finally the energy $CA$ will be turned into heat.

Seitz (loc. cit.) has suggested that the normal and excited energy levels may cross in certain cases (Fig. 87 $(b)$).‡ Actually, since two energy levels cannot cross unless the corresponding states are non-combining, the energy diagram would be as shown. In these cases the impurity centres would give no luminescence, all the energy being converted into heat. There are two possibilities. One is that the system after absorbing a quantum of radiation moves from $A'$ to $D'$, drops from $D'$ to $D$ with the emission of radiation in the far infra-red, and then moves from $D$ to $A$. The other is that the system, on reaching the point $D'$, has sufficient kinetic energy to 'jump' the gap $D'D$ and arrive at the point $E$, where it will remain until heat motion can lift it to $D$, whence it will return to $A$.

The first hypothesis would suggest that many apparently non-luminescent materials may fluoresce in the infra-red; the second suggests that at low temperatures, at which the heat motion would be insufficient to raise the system from $E$ to $D$, the absorbing centres would be 'used up' by prolonged illumination so that the absorption coefficient should change. We do not know of the existence of any such case.

Seitz suggests that the energy curves as shown in Fig. 87 (b) are typical for non-luminescent materials. Whether this is the case will be clearer when we consider the nature of the configurational coordinates. We may say at this stage, however, that it is quite possible that, even if the energy levels are as in Fig. 87 (a), a substance may be non-luminescent, because it is possible that an electron may make a transition such as from $B$ to $C$ without radiation by setting in vibration the surrounding atoms. The possibility of such a transition has been considered by Peierls,† but it is not yet possible to give any numerical estimate of its probability. At low temperatures, since a large number of vibrational quanta have to be absorbed at once, its probability may be quite small. Peierls finds that the probability of the process increases rapidly as the temperature is raised. We should thus expect, if this process actually takes place, that the efficiency of phosphors would drop as the temperature is raised.

It is, in fact, found that a large number of substances fluoresce at low temperatures which do not do so at room temperatures. For zinc-sulphide phosphors the drop in the intensity of the re-emitted radiation as the temperature is raised has been measured over a range of temperatures by Randall,‡ some of whose results are shown in Fig. 88 on p. 223.

Another mechanism‖ may be suggested whereby phosphors having energy curves as in Fig. 87 (a) may at high temperatures dissipate their energy as heat. If the direct transition $BC$, with the simultaneous excitation of a large number of vibrational quanta, is too improbable, it may be that the transition from one state to the other can take place easily if the system first absorbs enough energy to reach the point $F$ in Fig. 87 (a), where the energy curves are close together. The transition probability should then have the form $Ae^{-W/kT}$, where $W$ is the energy $BF$.

We now turn to a further consideration of the configurational co-

† R. Peierls, *Ann. d. Physik*, **13**, 905 (1932). See also J. Frenkel, *Phys. Rev.* **37**, 17 and 1276 (1931); *Phys. Zeits. d. Sowjetunion*, **9**, 158 (1936).

‡ J. T. Randall, *Proc. Phys. Soc.* **49** (extra part), 46 (1937).

‖ N. F. Mott, *Proc. Roy. Soc.* (A), **167**, 384 (1938).

ordinates. They are of two main types. The first measures the displacement of the surrounding ions towards or away from the centre. Consider, for instance, the case of an $F$-centre (an electron replacing a negative ion in the lattice). An $F$-centre is neutral, so outside the orbit of its electron the ions are not in any additional electrostatic field. When, however, the electron is raised into an excited state, it moves in a larger orbit; an additional electrostatic field now acts on the ions within this orbit. They will move into new positions of equilibrium; in other words, the medium here will become polarized (compare Chap. III, § 5, and Chap. V, § 3).

We do not believe that a displacement of this type can lead to any crossing of the energy levels, of the type illustrated in Fig. 87 (b).

If the impurity centre consists of an atom or ion in solid solution (e.g. H$^-$ ions replacing halogen ions in alkali-halides, Zn or Cu atoms dissolved interstitially in ZnS), then we have to consider also the displacement of the dissolved atom from its mean position. It is possible that in certain cases the energy of the central position is no longer a minimum, but a maximum, when the electron is excited. Consider, for instance, the case of hydrogen ions H$^-$ replacing halide ions in alkali-halides (Chap. IV, § 9). The absorption of a quantum of radiation removes an electron from the hydrogen ion to a *neighbouring* alkali ion, leaving a hydrogen atom. It is quite possible that there may be some kind of homopolar attraction between the hydrogen atom and the alkali atom, and that this would lead to a gain in the energy, if the H atom were displaced sideways. Moreover, since it would require much more work to displace the large H$^-$ ion than the small neutral atom, it is quite possible that the energies would cross as in Fig. 87 (b). Detailed calculations of the energy curves for some specific case would be of great interest.

A crossing of this type cannot happen, however, when the impurity centre is an electron (or positive hole) trapped at a vacant lattice point, and we are inclined to the opinion that such centres should always fluoresce at sufficiently low temperatures. We have given in Chap. IV, § 6.1, some indirect evidence that $F$-centres return to their normal state with emission of infra-red radiation.

As a result of the discussions of this section, we see that, in all types of phosphors, the effect of raising the temperature is to render the transference of the energy of excitation into heat more probable. We thus expect a drop in the intensity of the re-emitted radiation observed during irradiation either by ultra-violet light or by cathode rays, as the temperature is raised. Figs. 88 (*a*) and (*b*) show that such a drop is rather generally observed.

The cause of the drop at *low* temperatures in certain phosphors is

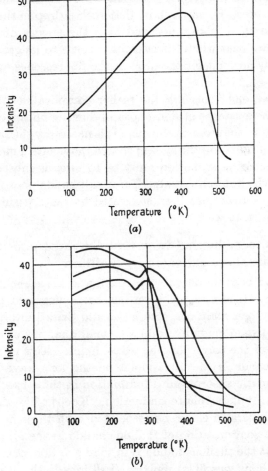

(*a*)

(*b*)

Fig. 88.   Intensity of fluorescent radiation as a function of the temperature in zinc-sulphide phosphors:† (*a*) impurities Mn, Mg, Ba, Si; (*b*) various specimens activated by Ag, Cu, Mg

uncertain. The only explanation which we can suggest is the following. The incident light in these cases is of a wave-length which produces only excitons in the lattice. At room temperature the thermal energy is sufficient to free the electron, producing at the same time a free positive hole. Ionization of an impurity centre then ensues by the mechanism

† From J. T. Randall, *Proc. Phys. Soc.* **49** (extra part), 52 (1937).

described on p. 135, and is followed by emission. But at low temperatures the thermal energy may be insufficient to dissociate the exciton. In Chapter IV, § 6, we have already used this mechanism to explain the rapid drop in the primary photoelectric current which is found in many substances. It may well be that such a drop in the photocurrent is present in these phosphors, and that the energy of the exciton is converted into heat when the electron returns to its ground state; this would clearly account for the drop in the fluorescence at low temperatures.

Finally, we must consider the rather complicated model necessary to explain the existence of non-photoconducting phosphors which show an after-glow of the order of seconds. It is necessary that after absorbing a quantum of radiation the system should move into a metastable state; but the effect of heat motion must be to raise it subsequently into a state from which it can radiate. For alkali-halide phosphors activated by thallium a model has been suggested by Seitz,† which will be discussed in the next section.

## 4. Non-photoconducting impurity-activated phosphors; alkali-halide phosphors activated by thallium

These have been investigated by Pohl and his school,‡ and a rather detailed theoretical interpretation has been suggested by Seitz.‖ We shall outline their main characteristics and Seitz's interpretation.

The crystals are made by adding a small quantity of thallous-halide to the melt of the corresponding alkali-halide. This gives rise to new absorption bands in the ultra-violet on the long-wave-length side of the characteristic absorption. Illumination in these bands gives rise to luminescence, but no photoconduction. Koch†† has shown that the number of dispersion electrons associated with these bands is proportional to the concentration of thallous-halide in the phosphor. This is evidence that the thallous-halide is in solid solution, and Seitz suggests that the thallous ions ($Tl^+$) replace alkali ions in the crystal lattice.

There are two possible transitions which may be responsible for these absorption bands. In the pure alkali-halides we have seen (Chap. III, § 7) that the absorption spectrum is due to the transition of an electron from a halide ion to an adjacent alkali ion; the work required to shift an electron on to a thallous ion from a neighbouring halide ion will be

---

† F. Seitz, *J. Chem. Phys.* **6**, 150 (1938).

‡ For references see, for instance, R. Hilsch, *Proc. Phys. Soc.* **49** (extra part), 40 (1937).

‖ F. Seitz, loc. cit.

†† W. Koch, *Zeits. f. Physik*, **57**, 638 (1929), and **59**, 378 (1930).

less because of the higher ionization potential of thallium (6·07 eV.) than that of any alkali metal (5·37 eV. for Li, 5·12 for Na). Such transitions will therefore give absorption lines on the long-wave-length side of the characteristic absorption. The second alternative is that the whole of the absorption is due to the thallous ion itself. Seitz favours the second alternative; his strongest evidence is the invariance of the

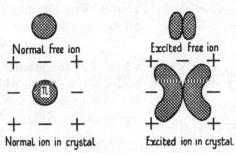

FIG. 89. Schematic representation of the space occupied by the normal and excited valence electron on the thallium ion[†]

absorption spectrum from one alkali-halide to another, and the absence of the doublet spectrum associated with absorption by the halogen ion (Chap. III, § 7). Seitz also gives a discussion of the way in which the absorption spectrum of the free thallous ion will differ from that of an ion replacing an alkali ion in the crystal. Briefly, one can say that the wave functions of the excited states of the ion will overlap the surrounding ions; the polarizability of the latter, or in other words the dielectric constant of the medium, will lead to a diminution in the restoring force pulling the electron back to its ion. As a consequence the radial extension of the wave functions is increased, as Fig. 89 (due to Seitz) shows; and also the energies of the excited states are crowded closer together.[‡]

As regards the emission spectra, the experimental facts are as follows. The phosphors have a number of broad emission bands, lying to the long-wave-length side of the absorption bands. The quantum efficiency at 50° and 150° C. is near to unity, in the sense that the number of quanta emitted in all the bands is about equal to the number of quanta absorbed.[||] At low concentrations of the activator (e.g. less than 0·0015 mol. per cent. in the crystal), fluorescence without phosphorescence is observed, the decay period being less than $5 \times 10^{-5}$ sec.

For high concentrations of activator, however, a phosphorescence occurs; the ratio of the total light sum of the phosphorescent emission

† F. Seitz, loc. cit.    ‡ Compare the arguments on pp. 84, 166, 218.
|| W. Bünger, Zeits. f. Physik, 66, 311 (1930).

to the absorption is roughly proportional to the concentration of thallium. Since the absorption itself is proportional to the concentration, it follows that the absorption leading to phosphorescence is proportional to the square of the concentration. Seitz deduces that it is due to pairs of thallium ions at adjacent lattice points. The phosphorescence follows an exponential decay

$$I = I_0 e^{-\alpha t},$$

where $I$ is the intensity of the light, and $\alpha$ is a constant which varies with the temperature according to the equation (for KCl),

$$\alpha = 2 \cdot 9 \times 10^9 e^{-0 \cdot 67 \, \text{eV.}/kT} \text{ sec.}^{-1}$$

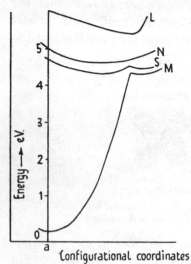

Fig. 90. Energy levels for a centre in which two Tl ions are neighbours, according to Seitz

Moreover, the release of phosphorescent light can be accelerated, at a given temperature, by irradiating the crystal with additional light of suitable wave-length.[†] The effectiveness of the stimulating light varies with wave-length; quanta with energy less than about 0·67 eV. are not effective.

To account for the phosphorescence from adjacent pairs of thallium ions, Seitz proposes a scheme of energy levels as shown in Fig. 90. The system, after absorbing a quantum of radiation, reaches the point $L$, and thence falls to the metastable state $M$. Seitz assumes that it will then be excited to $N$ by heat motion or by the accelerating radiation ($MN = 0.67$ eV.), so that it can then return to the ground state with emission of radiation. He suggests that, except at low temperatures, this may happen before the system reaches the saddle point on the same curve, because the system will have a small probability of finding this point out of a large region of multidimensional configurational space.

† W. Bünger and W. Flechsig, Zeits. f. Physik, 67, 42 (1931).

### Note of recent developments

In a recent paper (J. T. Randall and M. H. F. Wilkins, Proc. Roy. Soc. (A), in the press) it has been suggested that in most manganese-activated phosphors electrons are not ejected from the centres, and that the photo-conductivity observed is not connected with the luminescence.

# PHOTOCHEMICAL PROCESSES IN SILVER HALIDES AND THE PHOTOGRAPHIC LATENT IMAGE

## 1. The photochemical reduction of silver halides

THE main purpose of this chapter is to discuss the photolysis of silver halides, and in particular their decomposition into silver and halogen under the action of light. The process is one of great technical importance, because the behaviour of most photographic emulsions is based on it. Photographic emulsions will be discussed in detail in this chapter. We are interested both in using the theoretical concepts of the preceding chapters to make a theory of the action of light on a photographic plate; and, conversely, we regard the photographic plate as an instrument by which information can be gained about the action of light on polar salts.

In our discussion of the photographic plate, it is convenient to distinguish between exposures in which a visible amount of metallic silver is formed, so that the plate is darkened (the print-out effect), and the much smaller exposures of which the effect can only be detected by development. So far as we know, the print-out effect is not very structure-sensitive; the rate of formation of silver does not depend on the presence of small quantities of impurity. The sensitivity of an emulsion to small exposures with subsequent development is, however, very sensitive to small amounts of impurity; the removal of the surface silver and silver sulphide from the grains by treatment with acid permanganate may decrease the speed by 1,500 times.†

It will be convenient to deal with the print-out effect first. As shown by Fig. 91, a microphotograph of a partially printed-out emulsion, the silver is found after exposure in the form of colloidal particles, each containing many millions of atoms. In this respect the processes described in this chapter differ fundamentally from those of Chapter IV (e.g. formation of $F$-centres from $U$-centres), where the photochemical product remains dispersed in atomic form throughout the parent lattice.

The formation of colloidal particles of metallic silver may be observed in large single crystals as well as in photographic emulsions; it will be convenient to deal with the phenomena in single crystals first.

† Private communication from Dr. O. Bloch.

If a silver-halide crystal is illuminated *at room temperature*† it becomes coloured, a new absorption band appearing in the visible. This has been investigated by Hilsch and Pohl,‡ and is attributed to the formation of colloidal particles of metal. It differs from the type of absorption band due to $F$-centres in two ways:

1. The absorption is almost independent of temperature.
2. Monochromatic illumination in the new absorption band bleaches the band only in the neighbourhood of the wave-length used, instead of bleaching out the whole band as for $F$-centres (p. 112).

The nature of the absorption process and of the bleaching process will be discussed in § 10. Here we need only say that, as the correct interpretation of the absorption spectrum is uncertain, the amount of colloidal silver present cannot yet be determined optically from it.‖

## 2. The print-out effect

We now turn to the phenomena observed in photographic emulsions. In any ordinary photographic emulsion, the little silver-halide crystals, embedded in the gelatine, are of different sizes, but the majority of them usually have a diameter lying between $10^{-4}$ and $10^{-5}$ cm., and thus they contain between $10^{12}$ and $10^{11}$ ion pairs. These crystals are usually known as 'grains'. Under the action of light, specks of colloidal silver grow in these separate grains; and after prolonged illumination the total amount of metallic silver in the whole emulsion can be determined chemically, as, for instance, in the work of Eggert and Noddack.††

The following table gives some results:

### Agfa 'Reproduction' Emulsion

$\lambda = 4,360$ A; 11 per cent. of incident light estimated to be absorbed by the emulsion.

| No. of quanta incident, cm.$^{-2}$ ($\times 10^{16}$) | No. of quanta abs., cm.$^{-2}$ ($\times 10^{16}$) | No. of silver atoms formed, cm.$^{-2}$ ($\times 10^{16}$) | Quantum efficiency |
|:---:|:---:|:---:|:---:|
| 0·76 | 0·08 | 0·08 | 1·00 |
| 13 | 1·43 | 0·71 | 0·5 |

† Note that the experiments on photoconductivity in silver halides discussed in Chap. IV, § 5, were carried out at the temperature of liquid air. At room temperatures the photocurrent is obscured by the electrolytic conduction.

‡ R. Hilsch and R. W. Pohl, *Zeits. f. Physik*, **77**, 421 (1932).

‖ R. Hilsch and R. W. Pohl (ibid. **64**, 612 (1930)) obtained an estimate of the amount of silver on the assumption that it *was* dispersed atomically, but in a later paper (ibid. **77**, 421 (1932)) they came to the conclusion that it is present in colloidal form.

†† J. Eggert and W. Noddack, ibid. **20**, 299 (1923); *Handb. d. wissenschaftlichen u. angewandten Photographie*, **5**, 132 (1932).

For not too great exposures the quantum efficiency is near unity; thus for each quantum of radiation absorbed in a grain one atom of silver is added to a silver speck.

Fig. 91 shows a microphotograph of silver-bromide grains in an emulsion at various stages of the print-out process. It will be seen that here, as in the large single crystals, the silver is found in a relatively small number of specks of colloidal metal, each consisting, by the time it becomes visible under the microscope, of many millions of silver atoms.

In this process there are then three facts which we have to reconcile: in the first place, the quanta of light are incident at random over the grain and must be absorbed at random too; the silver is afterwards found localized in a relatively small number of specks; and yet nearly every quantum absorbed by the grain adds a silver atom to one or other of these specks. A theory of the process, then, must first explain how a quantum absorbed at a given point can add a silver atom to a speck located at a considerable distance.

In order to explain this we consider a crystal or grain of silver halide which already contains at least one small speck of metallic silver, and consider the growth of the speck under the action of light. The question of how a speck is first formed will be considered in a later section. The discussions of Chapter IV enable us to deduce from experiments on silver-bromide crystals the following:

1. Nearly every quantum of light absorbed by the silver bromide will liberate an electron, which can move through the lattice with energies lying in the conduction band of the crystal (p. 120).

2. Each electron, after wandering round for a certain time, will eventually find a particle of metal and be captured by it.†

This will happen to all the electrons only if the crystal contains a sufficiently large number of silver specks in relation to its size; otherwise some electrons may take such a long time to find a speck that they will have an appreciable chance of recombining first with one of the halogen atoms from which they came. We shall assume that the recombination is small.

It follows, then, that *for each quantum of radiation absorbed by the crystal, a negative charge e is added to one of the silver specks.*

It should be pointed out that the experiments on which these con-

---

† Before being captured it may be temporarily trapped at one or more places in the crystal before it finds the speck of metal (p. 240).

clusions were based were carried out at liquid-air temperature. There is, however, no reason to suppose that the conclusions are not valid at room temperature also.

At room temperatures pure silver halides are electrolytic conductors, the conductivity being due to the presence in thermal equilibrium of metal ions in interstitial positions, and to lattice points whence the metal ion is missing (Chap. II, §5). Thus, if the electrons are trapped on the specks, the electrostatic field set up in the halide crystal by their charge will lead to an electrolytic current; interstitial silver ions already present in the crystal will move up to the silver specks and adhere to them. If the illumination were ended, the process would continue until the charge on the silver speck was neutralized. During illumination, however, since the thermal agitation of the ions of the silver-halide crystal will supply new interstitial ions as fast as they are used up, the process can continue indefinitely.

This theory of the photolytic process, first given by Gurney and Mott,† enables one to understand why the silver is found as a few colloidal particles, and how the energy is transferred from the point where the quantum is absorbed to the point where the silver is found.‡ It explains also the high quantum efficiency of the process and also the agreement in spectral sensitivity between developed density of a blue-sensitive emulsion and photocurrent in single crystals of AgBr.‖ We shall now make some rather more tentative suggestions about the details of the process.

We have first to consider the geometry of the process. The conductivity of pure silver bromide may be due both to the motion of interstitial silver ions and to that of vacant lattice points normally occupied by silver ions. Only the first process can be effective in building up a silver speck. The flow of ions to the silver speck will cause it to increase in size. We imagine that it will be pushed bodily outwards, if it is being formed on the surface. Our picture suggests that a large silver speck could not be formed in the body of a crystal, because there would not be room for it, unless the whole crystal were split. It can only be formed at the surface, or at the surface of an internal crack.

---

† R. W. Gurney and N. F. Mott, *Proc. Roy. Soc.* (A), **164**, 151 (1938).

‡ It has been suggested (C. F. Goodeve and J. A. Kitchener, *Trans. Faraday Soc.* **34**, 902 (1938)) that the energy is carried by 'excitons'. Since, however, silver halides are photoconductors for just those wave-lengths for which they are light-sensitive, and the quantum efficiency of the production of photoelectrons is high, it seems to us much more likely that the energy is carried by electrons, as suggested here.

‖ F. C. Toy, *7th Internat. Cong. Phot. London*, p. 14 (1928).

The precipitation of silver along crystallographic planes sometimes observed in the photolysis of silver halides may be due to splitting along these planes due to nuclei formed within the crystal. In the crack so formed new silver can be precipitated.

We have next to consider how the halogen escapes from the halide crystal. According to our theory of this process, the halogen escapes from the surface of the halide crystal, not from the interface between metal and silver-halide. On the other hand, halide ions cannot move in the crystal; the halogen arrives at the surface in the following way.

The initial removal of an electron from a halide ion in the interior of the crystal will produce what has been termed a 'positive hole' in the full band of energy levels corresponding to the $4p$-state of an electron in a bromide ion. These positive holes must be assumed to diffuse to the surface, there forming halogen atoms. A positive hole will be attracted to the charged silver speck. It is fundamental to our theory that the speck should discharge more quickly by attracting silver ions from interstitial positions than by attracting the positive holes. We have unfortunately no *a priori* knowledge of the mobility of a positive hole. At liquid-air temperatures (cf. Chap. IV, § 5.1) they do not seem to be mobile at all. On the other hand, at room temperature we must postulate that they have some mobility, so that they can diffuse to the surface, forming halogen atoms there, which can escape from the crystal (cf. also Chap. VIII, § 2).

The silver-halide crystal in thermal equilibrium contains lattice points from which the silver ion is missing. These constitute negatively charged centres. The 'positive holes', i.e. points where the halide ion has lost an electron, will be attracted to them. It is possible that the two combine, so that we have a vacant metal lattice point next to a halogen atom. This forms a neutral centre,† which might diffuse to the surface as a whole.

The picture given here of the photochemical decomposition of salts can be applied to other salts as well as the silver halides (e.g. the metallic azides, p. 264). We recapitulate the assumptions made:

1. The crystal is an ionic conductor, metal ions being mobile.
2. Absorption of light produces electrons with high mobility which eventually are trapped by the metal already formed.
3. Absorption of light produces positive holes of very much smaller mobility, which after some time diffuse to the surface.

---

† Similar to the $F$-centres in alkali-halides, a vacant positive lattice point replacing the negative one, and a positive hole replacing the electron.

4. When a positive hole comes to the surface, converting a negative ion into an atom, the atom can escape.

We note that if the absorption of light is in an absorption band due to impurities the positive holes may not be mobile and we should not expect photochemical reduction to take place in general.

Alkali-halide crystals with $U$-centres (Chap. IV, § 9) are an exception, however, because the hydrogen atom formed when an electron is removed from a $U$-centre can itself diffuse through the crystal (transport of atoms instead of electrons). In this case, actually, neither free electrons nor positive holes are produced.

## 3. Rate of growth of a silver speck

Consider a silver speck on the surface of a halide crystal. If the speck carries a charge $ne$, the field at a distance $r$ from it will be $ne/\kappa r^2$, where $\kappa$ is the dielectric constant. Thus the total current due to the ions flowing towards it from all directions is, if the surface is plane,

$$\pi n \sigma e/\kappa,$$

where $\sigma$ is the electrolytic conductivity. Thus the number of ions per unit time which the silver speck collects is $\pi n \sigma/\kappa$.

If the speck has originally a charge, the time taken for this charge to be neutralized is of the order $\kappa/\pi\sigma$, or $(\kappa/\pi\sigma) \times 9 \times 10^{11}$ if $\sigma$ is measured in ohms. We give below some values of this quantity for AgBr ($\kappa \sim 12$).

### TABLE 27

| $T$ (degrees C.) | $-50$ | $0$ | $50$ | $100$ |
|---|---|---|---|---|
| $\sigma$ (cm.$^{-1}$ ohm$^{-1}$, obs.) | $10^{-11}$ | $3 \times 10^{-9}$ | $10^{-7}$ | $10^{-5}$ |
| $(\kappa/\pi\sigma) \times 9 \times 10^{11}$ (sec.) | $0.4$ | $10^{-3}$ | $4 \times 10^{-5}$ | $4 \times 10^{-7}$ |

Suppose now that a speck is growing at a constant rate, and receiving $p$ electrons per second. Then we equate $p$ to the number of ions received per second, so that
$$p = 2\pi n \sigma/\kappa.$$

This equation gives the mean charge $ne$ on the speck. But if this charge is too great, the speck will repel electrons which try to reach it and thus will not be able to trap an additional electron. The potential at the boundary of a spherical speck of radius $R$ is $ne/\kappa R$; as a rough measure we shall assume that a speck cannot trap an additional electron if
$$ne^2/\kappa R > kT,$$
and thus if
$$n > \kappa R k T/e^2.$$

It follows that a speck cannot grow at a rate greater than that given by
$$p = 2\pi\sigma R k T/e^2,$$

$p$ being the number of atoms added to the speck per second. If, then, a grain of silver halide contains $\Re$ metallic silver specks of mean radius $R$, each absorbed quantum will produce a silver atom if and only if the number of quanta absorbed per second does not exceed

$$\Re \sigma \pi R k T / e^2.$$

If the intensity of illumination is increased above this value, the additional electrons produced by the light cannot reach the specks and thus

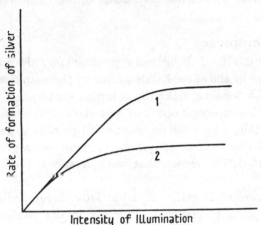

Fig. 92. Rate of formation of silver in a photographic emulsion, according to the theoretical ideas of this chapter: (1) high temperature; (2) low temperature

will eventually recombine with the halogen atoms from which they came. Thus in a photographic emulsion we expect the rate of formation of silver plotted against the intensity of illumination to appear as in Fig. 92. No very sharp bend of the curve is to be expected because of the varying size of the grains.

As an example of the orders of magnitude involved, we take $\Re = 10$ and $R = 5 \times 10^{-5}$ cm. Thus we have, for the maximum number of silver atoms which can be added to the already existing specks per second, the values given in the following table:†

TABLE 28

| $T$ | 20° C. | −100° C. |
|---|---|---|
| $\sigma$ (cm.$^{-1}$ ohm$^{-1}$) | $10^{-8}$ | $10^{-13}$ |
| $\Re \sigma \pi R k T / e^2$ (sec.$^{-1}$) | $2 \times 10^5$ | 2 |

† As shown in Chap. II, § 2, impurities in the silver bromide may give rise to vacant lattice points, and thus to an increased conductivity. These, however, will be eliminated in the early stages of the process, and we may therefore insert the value of the conductivity for pure silver bromide.

If a grain contains $2 \times 10^{10}$ ion pairs, it will thus according to this calculation take at least $10^5$ sec., or about a day, for complete reduction at room temperature. The times given by so simple a calculation may easily be in error by a factor 10 or more, however. At $-100°$ C. the time will be $10^{10}$ sec., or 300 years.

Berg and Mendelssohn[†] report that at liquid-air temperatures the rate at which the printing-out process proceeds is reduced by a factor $10^5$, but no investigation has been made of the variation with intensity of the light.

## 4. The latent image

The exposures used in ordinary photography do not produce any visible change in the silver-halide grains of the emulsion.

In this book we shall make the common assumption that the latent image is a submicroscopic speck of metallic silver, situated on the surface of the grain, where the developer will be able to get at it. A consideration of the number of quanta incident on a grain in ordinary exposures (10–1,000) shows that such a speck could hardly be of visible size.

In the silver-halide grains of a partially developed emulsion there are visible specks of colloidal silver (as in the partially printed-out emulsion, Fig. 91). During further development the growth of these silver specks at the surface of the grains can be observed, as is shown in Fig. 94. We know, then, that grains containing visible colloidal specks of silver are developable. It therefore seems reasonable to suppose that a submicroscopic speck will have the same effect.

A discussion, then, of the sensitivity of emulsions to ordinary photographic exposures with subsequent development resolves itself into a discussion of the conditions under which a silver speck can be formed and *start* to grow in a silver-halide grain. Let us, then, consider what will happen when an electron is released by the absorption of a quantum of light within a halide grain which does not contain any metallic silver. In order that a silver speck shall begin to form, it is necessary that the electron, which initially is free to move all over the halide grain, should be trapped at some point, which must lie on the surface of the grain. Then at this point a silver speck can begin to form. But we have seen (p. 132) that in pure crystals of silver bromide the trapping centres (interstitial silver ions?) active at liquid-air temperatures have a concentration of one in $10^{12}$ ion pairs, so many of the halide grains will

† W. F. Berg and K. Mendelssohn, *Proc. Phys. Soc.* **49** (extra part), 38 (1937).

not contain any such centre. Moreover, these trapping centres do not give rise to a stable position for an electron at room temperature. Thus in an emulsion of pure silver bromide at room temperature most of the electrons released by the light could not be trapped and would return to their original places.

The work of Sheppard† and his collaborators has shown that the grains of sensitive emulsions contain on the surface 'sensitivity specks'

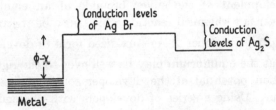

FIG. 93. Energy levels in silver halide, metallic silver, silver sulphide

(*Reifkeime*) formed during the ripening process.‡ The nature of the sensitivity specks is uncertain; they probably consist of crystalline specks of silver sulphide ($Ag_2S$) or of specks of metallic silver too small to act as a latent image. According to Sheppard, the function of these specks is to 'concentrate' the silver atoms formed by the light. From the point of view of the theory described here, their function will be to trap, at a point on the surface, the electrons released by the light. For this purpose a speck of any material would serve, provided only that its lowest conduction level lies below that of AgBr (Fig. 93). There is nothing unreasonable in the supposition that this is the case for $Ag_2S$. We imagine, then, that it is at these points that the latent image begins to form.

## 5. Chemical development

We have now to discuss the action of the developer on the halide grains, and how it discriminates between exposed and unexposed grains. In considering development we have two problems to consider: the mean time $\tau$ before visible development of each grain starts (the induction period) and the time $t$ occupied by the visible development of any grain which can be followed under the microscope. Under usual conditions of development the induction period is very much longer than $t$.

† S. E. Sheppard, A. P. H. Trivelli, and R. P. Loveland, *J. Franklin Inst.* **200**, 51 (1925).

‡ The ripening process consists in keeping the emulsion at an increased temperature for a considerable time, during which the grain size increases and the photographic sensitivity becomes greater.

The visible development of a single grain has been investigated by Rabinovitch[†] under conditions in which development extends from a single nucleus. Some of his results are shown in Fig. 94. He found that the radius of the developed region increased linearly with the time after growth had started. The mean time $t$ from the start of visible development of any given grain until its completion does not depend on the previous exposure.

The development of the silver bromide of an emulsion to form metallic silver is a chemical reaction which may be written

$$AgBr + developer \rightleftarrows Ag + oxidized\ form\ of\ developer.$$

In order that the equilibrium may lie well over to the right, the oxidation reduction potential of the developer solution must lie below a certain value. Using a series of developers with descending values of the redox potential, Reinders[‡] found that the development of exposed grains did not begin unless the redox potential lay 0·55 volt below that of a standard $Fe^{++}$—$Fe^{+++}$ electrode; this was within 0·1 volt of the value to be expected from the known free energies of AgBr and Ag. Reinders ascribes the discrepancy to the smallness of the silver speck which acts as a latent image. He thus suggests that a lower oxidation-reduction potential[||] is needed to start the reaction than to carry it on. Reinders, in fact, found that the oxidation-reduction potential necessary to complete the development, once it had begun, agreed well with the theoretical value.

As regards the kinetics of the process, there are two possibilities.[††] These are:

1. That the silver bromide dissolves in the developer, and that silver ions are brought from the bromide to the silver through the solution.

2. That the reaction takes place at the interface between the metal and the silver bromide, silver ions passing from the bromide to the silver without ever going into solution.

The present authors have suggested that if the reaction takes place at the interface it is unnecessary for any molecules of the developer to penetrate to the interface between the silver and the AgBr. A suitable developer will hand over electrons to the silver already deposited, thus setting up a potential difference between it and the silver bromide.

[†] A. J. Rabinovitch, *Trans. Faraday Soc.* **34**, 920 (1938).
[‡] W. Reinders, *J. Phys. Chem.* **38**, 784 (1934).
[||] The lower the oxidation-reduction potential, the greater is the reducing power.
[††] For references, cf. A. J. Rabinovitch, loc. cit.

This will cause a flow of interstitial silver ions to take place through the solid silver bromide directly to the interface with metallic silver. For this process to take place it is only necessary that molecules of the developer should come in contact with the silver.

The potential difference between the silver and the bromide will also cause a flow of ions through the developer solution; these ions will be deposited on the latent image. Thus the process of chemical development should be partly of type 1, partly of type 2. Owing, however, to the low solubility of AgBr, the process is probably mainly of type 1.†

If this is the case, the time $t$ from the beginning of visible development of any single grain until its completion should vary with the temperature in the same way as its electrolytic conductivity (Chap. II, § 4).

We shall examine next the conditions under which development will start in an exposed or unexposed grain, and hence the mean time $\tau$ before visible development starts. The redox potential of a developer solution is a measure of its tendency to set up an electrical double layer on the surface of any conductor with which it is in contact.‡ If the developer hands over electrons to the latent image, it will also have at least a small tendency to hand over electrons to the sensitivity specks on any unexposed grain. But since during normal development these sensitivity specks do not act as nuclei for development, we must assume that this tendency is negligibly small; this will be the case if the vacant electronic levels in the sensitivity specks lie rather above those in the metallic silver; if they lie a quarter of an electron-volt higher, the Boltzmann factor will introduce a ratio less than $10^{-4}$.

The condition that any speck may act as a nucleus for development, then, is that its vacant electronic levels shall be low enough to charge up negatively from the developer in use. This theory suggests that any singularity on the surface of a grain will act as a latent image if it provides a sufficiently deep potential hole. Both the work function $\phi$ of a metal speck and the electron affinity $\chi$ of $Ag_2S$ may be expected to decrease with decreasing size of the speck for very small particles of the order of 100 atoms or less. We thus see that a very small silver speck may act as a sensitivity speck but not as a latent image, and,

† The suggestion (cf. Reinders, loc. cit.) that a supersaturated solution of silver *atoms* forms in the developer, from which silver is deposited, seems to us inadmissible. The sublimation energy of silver is 2·9 eV. per atom. Hence, if we neutralize an ion in solution before depositing a neutral atom on the surface, we have raised the system to a state which is 2·9 eV. higher than necessary. Since, according to Reinders, the redox potential for development agrees with the theoretical one within 0·1 volt, this mechanism requires an activation energy of 2·8 eV., and will not occur.

‡ For the mechanism, cf. R. W. Gurney, *Ions in Solution*, p. 117 (Cambridge, 1936).

conversely, it is possible that a large speck of $Ag_2S$ may act as a latent image. It is, in fact, observed that prolonged ripening—and thus increase in size of sensitivity specks—increases the fog in an emulsion, and hence the number of grains developable without exposure.†

As is well known, over-exposure leads to a decrease in the developed density of the photographic image; the phenomenon is known as solarization. This is probably due to the formation of a layer of silver

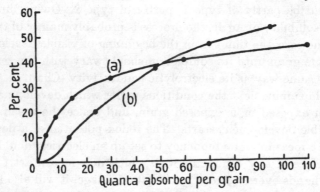

FIG. 95.‡ Number of quanta per grain which must be absorbed in order to make a given percentage of the grains of an emulsion developable: (a) fast emulsion; (b) slow emulsion

halide covering the latent image, which has been attacked by the halogen liberated in the reaction;‖ this layer would prevent the molecules of the developer from coming into contact with the latent image.

## 6. Size of the latent image

From experiments on single-layer plates, i.e. on emulsions in which very few grains overlap others, the number of quanta may be deduced which must be absorbed by a grain to make it developable. Fig. 95 shows the number of quanta which have to be absorbed per grain of two different emulsions (fast and slow) in order that a given percentage of the grains shall be developable. For both emulsions about 50 quanta must be absorbed per grain in order to make 50 per cent. of the grains developable. If we suppose that nearly all of these quanta have contributed to the growth of a silver speck lying on the surface of the grain, we shall conclude that the latent image in any grain is a speck of silver containing something in the neighbourhood of 50 atoms. This order of magnitude is supported by experiments on Lippmann emul-

---

† A. P. H. Trivelli, E. P. Wightman, and S. E. Sheppard, *Phot. Journal*, **65**, 138 (1925).

‡ The curves are plotted from data given in the *Handb. d. Photographie*, **5**, 263 (1932).

‖ J. M. Eder, *Zeits. f. phys. Chem.* **117**, 293 (1925).

sions (very fine-grain emulsions, the grains containing about $10^6$ molecules). Here the amount of silver in an emulsion exposed sufficiently to be about 50 per cent. developable can be determined chemically, and is of the order 50 to 100 atoms per grain.[†]

As Fig. 95 shows, a few of the grains in fast emulsions are sensitive to a much smaller number of quanta (one or two). We imagine that each of these grains already contains a sensitivity speck (silver or silver sulphide) which is nearly big enough to act as a latent image, and which by the addition of one or two silver atoms becomes quite big enough.

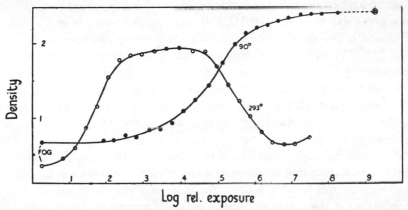

Fig. 96. Characteristic curves for a high-speed, blue-sensitive film at 293° and 90° K. The high fog values, particularly that at 90°, are caused by light scattered during the long exposures necessary. The highest point on the 90° curve was the result of a separate experiment

## 7. Effect of low temperatures on latent-image formation

In general the sensitivity of a photographic plate drops at low temperatures. Fig. 96 shows density-exposure curves for a photographic emulsion at 20° C. and at −183° C. The results are due to Berg;[‡] similar curves have been obtained by Webb and Evans,[||] who proposed the following explanation of the drop in sensitivity at low temperatures. At liquid-air temperatures the electrolytic conductivity of silver bromide has fallen to negligibly small values; at these temperatures electrons released by the light may travel to the sensitivity specks and be trapped there; but the latent image cannot form until the emulsion is warmed up, previously to immersion in the developer. Now a sensitivity

---

† Cf. *Handb. d. Photographie*, **5**, 266 (1932).
‡ W. F. Berg, *Trans. Faraday Soc.* **35**, 445 (1939).
|| J. H. Webb and C. H. Evans, *J.O.S.A.* **28**, 249 (1938).

speck cannot accommodate more than a small number of electrons; if we picture such a speck as a sphere of radius $r$, then $n$ electrons will give a potential on the boundary of $ne/\kappa r$, and, as we have seen, if this is much greater than $kT/e$, electrons cannot reach the speck. For values of $r$ up to about $10^{-6}$ cm., this ensures that not more than one or two electrons can be accommodated on the speck. Thus at low temperatures, however long the exposure, only a few electrons can be stored up in each grain; the rest will recombine with halogen atoms. And hence, on warming up, only those grains which are normally sensitive to a few quanta will become developable.

Webb and Evans found that much greater densities could be obtained for a given exposure at $-186°$ C. if the exposure was given in a number of separate flashes, and the emulsion warmed up between each flash (Fig. 97). The explanation proposed is that, on warming up, silver ions can move up to the sensitivity speck and neutralize the negative charge on it, so that during the next flash the speck can trap more electrons.

An alternative view (due to Berg†) is that all the electrons released on illumination at low temperatures are stored up in the grain at electron traps, perhaps of the same kind as those responsible for the finite range in single crystals. To account for the drop in the sensitivity, he assumes that the electrons are released on warming up before the temperature is high enough for ionic movement. Thus a certain proportion of the electrons would be lost by recombination, and the proportion would be greater if the number stored up were large.‡ The experiments of Webb and Evans with flashes are thus accounted for.

In support of the view that a single exposure at low temperatures can make available a very large number of electrons for latent-image formation, Berg cites the fact that at low temperatures even a slightly higher maximum density after chemical development can be obtained than that at room temperatures (Fig. 96).

The nature of the traps responsible for holding in a grain such a large number of electrons (several thousand?) is obscure. Their number must be much greater than the number of traps in single crystals. It is unlikely that electrons are trapped 'by digging their own holes',‖ since this does not happen in single crystals.†† Perhaps they are trapped in

---

† W. F. Berg, *Trans. Faraday Soc.* **35**, 445 (1939).

‡ Suppose that the time during which the electrons are free but the ionic conductivity is small is $t$. If there are $n_0$ free electrons initially, the rate of recombination is proportional to $n_0^2$, and, hence, by equation (2) on p. 210, the fraction lost is proportional to $n_0$.

‖ Chap. III, § 5.3.                                        †† Chap. IV, § 5.

Tamm levels at the grain surface. Alternatively, they may be trapped in the immediate neighbourhood of the halogen atom from which they came, by a process of the type discussed on p. 220.

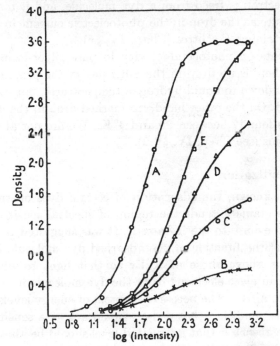

FIG. 97. Curves illustrating the effect on the sensitivity of a pure silver-bromide emulsion of an increased number of interruptions with warming-up periods between exposures (Webb and Evans)

| Curve | Temperature | Number of exposures | Time of each exposure (sec.) |
|-------|-------------|---------------------|------------------------------|
| A | 20° C. | 1 | 160 |
| B | −186° C. | 1 | 160 |
| C | −186° C. | 2 | 80 |
| D | −186° C. | 4 | 40 |
| E | −186° C. | 8 | 20 |

Emulsions B, C, D, E were warmed up to 20° C. between each exposure.

## 8. Effect of temperature on the primary process

The drop in the sensitivity of dye-sensitized panchromatic emulsions at low temperatures is much greater than that of blue-sensitive emulsions.† For instance, at 20° K. the sensitivity to red light of a panchro-

† S. E. Sheppard, E. P. Wightman, and R. F. Quirk, *J. Phys. Chem.* **38**, 817 (1934); W. F. Berg and K. Mendelssohn, *Proc. Phys. Soc.* **49** (extra part), 38 (1937).

matic emulsion drops to 0·02 per cent. of that at room temperature; as compared with 4 per cent. for an unsensitized emulsion. We believe this to be due to a drop in the efficiency of the primary process by which an electron is freed from a dye molecule, and it may be due to the same cause as the drop in the photoelectric current in alkali-halide crystals containing $F$-centres (Chap. IV, § 6).

Experiments on photoconductivity in pure silver-bromide crystals show that there is no drop in the efficiency of the primary process in the pure salt down to liquid-hydrogen temperatures, but suggest a drop below that.† On the other hand, no marked drop in the sensitivity of emulsions is found‡ between 20 and 4° K. We are not at present able to explain this (see Chap. IV, § 6.2).

## 9. Dye sensitization

As is well known, the adsorption of certain dyes on the surface of silver-halide grains extends the region of spectral sensitivity towards the red, and even into the infra-red. It was suggested by the present authors‖ that the function of the adsorbed dye molecule is to provide energy levels above those of AgBr so that light to which AgBr is insensitive can eject electrons from the dye molecule into the conduction levels of AgBr. The necessary system of energy levels is shown in Fig. 98. The condition that a dye should act as a sensitizer to light which it can absorb is that its excited level should be above the lowest conduction level of AgBr. Then each time that a dye molecule absorbs a quantum of radiation there will be a certain probability—which may well be of the order unity—that an electron will be transferred from the dye molecule to the conduction band of the AgBr grain.

Evidence has been given that each dye molecule can be instrumental in producing several silver atoms.†† The conclusion has been drawn that the dye molecule cannot lose its electron. We do not believe this conclusion to be correct. When a dye molecule has lost an electron it remains positively charged. It will consequently repel interstitial Ag⁺ ions and will attract vacant Ag⁺ lattice points from the interior of the crystal. Now the energy of the electron in a halide ion next to a missing silver ion (Fig. 99) is very substantially raised (owing to the absence of the adjacent positive charge); it may well be raised *above* the ground

† W. Lehfeldt, *Göttinger Nachrichten*, Fachgruppe II, **1**, 171 (1935).

‡ W. F. Berg and K. Mendelssohn, *Trans. Faraday Soc.* **35**, 457 (1939).

‖ R. W. Gurney and N. F. Mott, *Proc. Roy. Soc.* (A), **164**, 151 (1938).

†† W. Leszynski, *Zeits. f. wiss. Phot.* **24**, 261 (1926).

state of the ionized dye molecule. In that case an electron could be transferred from the halide ion to the dye molecule.

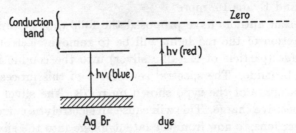

FIG. 98. Showing levels of an electron in a silver-halide grain and in a molecule of the sensitizing dye

Franck and Teller,† however, have suggested a mechanism by means of which dye molecules can sensitize an emulsion in the red without losing electrons on illumination. In order to raise an electron from the full band into the conduction band a quantum of blue light is necessary. After the absorption process both electron and positive hole may polarize the medium round them, i.e. become 'trapped by digging their own holes', in the sense of Chapter III, § 5.3. In this process a good deal of energy will be given out. Thus an electron and positive hole may be produced with the expenditure of less energy than $h\nu_{blue}$, if at the same time the surrounding ions are allowed to move into new positions of equilibrium. The authors

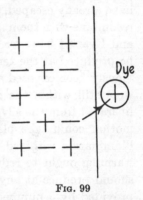

FIG. 99

quoted suggest that the excited dye molecule could hand over its energy, producing an electron and hole with polarized surroundings.

## 10. The Herschel effect

If an exposed but undeveloped photographic plate is exposed to red light for a considerable period, the effect of the previous exposure to blue light is partly erased; in other words, when the plate is developed, the density is less than it would have been without the exposure to red light. This is known as the Herschel effect. In some of the grains of the emulsion the latent image has been destroyed or rendered unsusceptible to the developer. The efficiency of the red light is extremely low at room temperature; the exposure necessary to give a marked

† J. Franck and E. Teller, *J. Chem. Phys.* **6**, 861 (1938).

effect is very much greater than the previous exposure to blue light. According to Tollert† some $10^{10}$ more quanta are necessary; according to Webb and Evans $10^6$ more.

The present authors have proposed the following explanation. The primary action of the red light will be to remove electrons from the latent image (particle of metallic silver) into the conduction band of the silver bromide. The spectral sensitivity of this process should be given by a curve of the type shown on p. 73. The silver speck then carries a positive charge. This will cause an electrolytic current, consisting of silver ions, to flow from the latent image into the silver-bromide crystal. This will take place either through the motion of vacant $Ag^+$ lattice points towards the latent image, or through ions leaving the latent image and moving into interstitial positions in the halide grain.

What happens next depends on whether in an exposed grain, containing a latent image or silver speck, the corresponding halogen atoms have already escaped. If they are still in the grain, the electrons could recombine with them and the crystal return to its original state. Webb and Evans,‡ however, have shown that no bleaching by red light can be produced at the temperature of liquid air, if the emulsion has previously been exposed at room temperature. Now if the halogen atoms were still within the grain, they could recombine with the electrons liberated from the silver even at liquid-air temperatures, and the ionic motion could take place when the emulsion was warmed up. Thus illumination with red light at liquid-air temperature with subsequent warming ought to reduce the latent image by at least one atom; this should produce at any rate some bleaching. A decisive test would be provided by a number of exposures to red light, with warming up in between.

If the halogen escapes as soon as the latent image is formed, the effect of subsequent Herschel illumination must be to separate electrons followed by ions from the latent image, which will afterwards recombine and form interstitial silver atoms dissolved in the silver bromide. We should expect that these silver atoms would condense and form a new silver speck. Perhaps, however, the speck would be formed at a new point, e.g. in the interior of the grain, where it cannot act as a latent image.

Evidence in favour of this view is provided by experiments with overexposed emulsions, where the silver of the latent image can be measured‖

---

† H. Tollert, *Z. Phys. Chem.* **140**, 355 (1929).

‡ J. H. Webb and C. H. Evans, *J.O.S.A.* **28**, 249 (1938).  ‖ H. Tollert, loc. cit.

by chemical methods. Exposure to red light does not decrease the silver content.

Webb and Evans† found that an emulsion exposed at liquid-air temperature can also be bleached at liquid-air temperature, *if the emulsion has not been warmed up in between the two exposures.* In this case, of course, no ionic motion ever takes place; the red light will remove an electron from the sensitivity speck, which will then have a chance to recombine with its original halogen atom before it finds the sensitivity speck again.

A similar effect has been observed by Berg,‡ who finds that the bleaching process at liquid air temperatures requires only 1/1000 of the exposure necessary to produce the same bleaching at room temperature.

The spectral sensitivity of the Herschel effect (at room temperatures) has been investigated in pure bromide and chloride emulsions by Bartelt and Klug‖ and by Carroll and Kretchmann.†† They find that in both emulsions the bleaching effect drops to zero for wave-lengths rather longer than 10,000 A; thus the energy required to remove an electron from the latent image into the conduction band is of the order 1 eV.

It is rather dangerous to assume that the energy required to remove an electron from a silver speck the size of the latent image is the same as that from a large speck of silver; if, however, we make that assumption we can obtain the energy $\chi$ of the lowest state of the conduction band, since

$$\phi - \chi \sim 1 \text{ eV.},$$

where $\phi$ is the work function of a clean silver surface. Since $\phi \sim 4 \cdot 6$ eV., $\chi$ must be of the order $3 \cdot 6$ eV.

We must emphasize, then, that the stability of the latent image at ordinary temperatures is due to the fact that *electrons* cannot get out of it into the conduction band of the crystal. There are plenty of mobile interstitial ions in the halide crystal, and silver ions can leave the latent image and go into these interstitial positions. What keeps them back is the charge that would be built up on the silver speck, since the electrons cannot follow them.

## 11. The breakdown of the reciprocity law

The developed density of a photographic emulsion is not in general a function of the product $It$ of the intensity of illumination $I$ and the

† J. H. Webb and C. H. Evans, loc. cit.

‡ W. F. Berg, *Trans. Faraday Soc.* **35**, 445 (1939).

‖ O. Bartelt and H. Klug, *Zeits. f. Physik,* **89**, 779 (1934).

†† B. H. Carroll and C. M. Kretchmann, *Bur. Stand. J. Res.* **10**, 449 (1933).

time of exposure $t$ only. For given exposure $It$ there is an optimum intensity of illumination. This optimum intensity depends on the temperature at which the exposure is made, shifting to lower intensities as the temperature is lowered. This is shown in Fig. 100, where are plotted the exposures $It$ necessary to give a given density, as a function of $I$, according to measurements by Webb.†

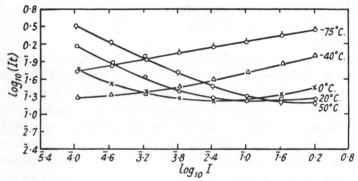

Fig. 100. Exposure $It$ required to give a developed density $I$ (from J. H. Webb, loc. cit.)

A possible explanation of the breakdown of the reciprocity law at high intensities is the following: We have seen (p. 240) that the sensitivity speck, or latent image, will never carry a charge greater than two or three times the charge on an electron, because the field round it then becomes too great to allow any more electrons to diffuse to the speck and be captured; also that a speck of silver will take a certain time to discharge by attracting positive ions. If the intensity of illumination is so great that electrons are produced in the grain more rapidly than the latent image can form, a concentration of free electrons will be built up within the grain. This may reduce the density in two ways:

1. By recombination of electrons with halogen atoms.

2. By causing the formation of several silver specks, some of them perhaps within the grain, or some perhaps too small to act as a latent image.‡ Under a high concentration of electrons a shallow trap, where an electron could only be trapped for a short time, might carry a sufficiently great mean charge for the formation of silver specks to begin. The Clayden effect (desensitization to subsequent exposure by an initial flash) suggests that high-intensity exposures form silver specks

† J. H. Webb, *J.O.S.A.* **26**, 367 (1936).

‡ H. Lüppo-Cramer, *Phot. Korr.* **72**, 1 (1936).

within the grain, the grain being thereby desensitized, since in a subsequent exposure many electrons would be wasted in building up the specks of silver within the grain.

Both explanations are compatible with the fact that the breakdown of the reciprocity law at high intensities is more marked at fairly low temperatures;† at low temperatures the ionic conductivity falls, and thus the time taken by a charged silver speck to discharge is longer (cf. p. 232).

For the breakdown of the reciprocity law at *low* intensities we suggest the following explanation.‡ We know from the Herschel effect that if electrons are released from the latent image by the absorption of red light, the latent image is dispersed, probably because ions follow the electrons. Since the latent image is stable at room temperature, it follows that the work $(\phi-\chi)$ necessary to eject an electron from the latent image into the conduction level of the salt is too great for this to happen owing to thermal agitation. This implies that $\phi-\chi$ must be greater than $\sim 0{\cdot}7$ eV., which agrees with our estimate of $\sim 1$ eV. from the spectral sensitivity of the Herschel effect.

The work necessary to release a trapped electron from the sensitivity speck, or to remove an electron from a very small silver speck of three or four atoms, may however be less. Thus for low intensities of illumination we may picture that the following happens: An electron is released by the light and travels to the sensitivity speck; an interstitial silver ion moves up to the sensitivity speck and adheres to it. Before the next electron comes along, however, the electron is released by thermal agitation of its surroundings. This may even happen several times, the electron being recaptured and released, and during the time that it is free it will have a chance to recombine with a halogen atom, and be wasted.

Clearly, as the temperature is lowered, the time taken for an electron to be released from the sensitivity speck will be increased, so that we have to go to lower intensities to observe the drop in sensitivity. This also is in agreement with experiment (Fig. 100).

At the temperature of liquid air, several investigators‖ have shown that the reciprocity law is actually satisfied. For exposures at these temperatures we have seen that ionic motion takes place only when

---

† At very low temperatures (that of liquid air) the reciprocity law is actually valid; this is discussed below.

‡ Cf. J. H. Webb and C. H. Evans, *J.O.S.A.* **28**, 249 (1938).

‖ W. F. Berg and K. Mendelssohn, *Proc. Roy. Soc.* (A), **168**, 168 (1938), and C. H. Evans and E. Hirschlaff, *J.O.S.A.* **29**, 164 (1939).

the emulsion is warmed up. At the low temperatures electrons are released which are trapped at centres which are stable at those temperatures. A breakdown in the reciprocity law is only to be expected if the time between the freeing of an electron and its trapping is comparable with the time of exposure; we might then expect a high concentration of free electrons to be formed in the grain, leading to some loss by recombination. Our ignorance of the mechanism of trapping, however, makes it impossible to estimate this time.

## Notes on recent developments

Berg has shown in a recent paper (*Proc. Roy. Soc.* (A) **174** (1940), 559) that for exposures of less than $\frac{1}{25,000}$ sec. no further loss of sensitivity occurs as the exposure is shortened; the rising curve shown in Fig. 100, for instance for $0°$ C., will flatten out and give a constant value of $It$ for still higher values of $I$, and hence shorter times $t$. He interprets this result as showing that the time taken for ions to move up to and neutralize the charge captured on a silver speck will be of this order. The time is in fair agreement with the estimate made on p. 232 (about $10^{-4}$ sec. at $25°$ C.). The exposure time at which the bend over occurs increases as the temperature is lowered, corresponding to the decreased mobility of the interstitial silver ions.

## Note added February 1948

Since the first edition of this book appeared, the following advances in the theory of the latent image may be noted:

1. The work of Hautot and his colleagues at Liége, published in a series of papers in the *Bull. Soc. Roy. Sci. Liége*, on the distribution of the internal latent image; a noteworthy fact is that red light increases the internal image while destroying the surface image.

2. The work of Carroll and West (*J. Chem. Phys.* in the press); they find that photographic emulsions, dye-sensitized or not, show under illumination a slight increase in conductivity for wave-lengths for which they are photographically sensitive.

3. A new theory of the action of dye-sensitizers according to which no electron is transferred from the dye molecule to the latent image; the adsorbed layer of dye acts by greatly strengthening any red sensitivity, due to whatever cause, which already exists (Mott, *J. de Physique*, **7**, 249 (1946); *Photographic Journal*, in press).

4. The model for development suggested at the bottom of p. 236 is supported by the photographs taken with the electron microscope (Mees, *Theory of the Photographic Process*, New York 1942, p. 312). These show that the silver is formed in filaments, as though it had been pushed out of the grain. On the other hand, the model is not accepted by all authorities, cf. James and Kornfeld *Chem. Rev.* **30**, 1 (1942).

5. A paper by Barshevski (*J. exp. and theor. Phys. U.S.S.R.* **16**, 815 (1946)) showing that films of silver halides $10^{-6}$ cm. thick have a maximum photoconduction for a wavelength of 3130 A.

## PROCESSES INVOLVING THE TRANSPORT OF BOTH IONS AND ELECTRONS

### 1. Oxidation of a metal; tarnishing reactions

IN the last chapter we have considered a particular process involving the motion through a solid of ions and electrons, namely, the photochemical reduction of silver halides. In this chapter we shall consider the more general problem of the reduction and oxidation of polar crystals. We shall, however, limit our discussion to reactions in which the motion of the ions and electrons takes place *within* the solid; we exclude reactions, such as the electrochemical corrosion of metals, in which a first stage in the reaction is the solution of the reacting substances in a solvent such as water.†

We shall discuss first the oxidation of a metal. Wagner‡ has introduced the term 'Anlaufvorgänge', which has been translated as 'tarnishing reactions', to describe reactions in which a solid metal is attacked by an electro-negative substance, usually in a gaseous or liquid state (e.g. oxygen, a halogen, or liquid sulphur) in such a way that a compact layer of the salt or reaction product is built up between the two reacting constituents. The reaction can only continue by transport of further material through this layer, which becomes progressively thicker. It is characteristic of tarnishing reactions, that either metal atoms must diffuse through the film to react with the electro-negative substance; or vice versa.

Examples are provided by the oxidation of metals on heating in air, or the formation of a layer of $Ag_2S$ on silver in contact with liquid sulphur.

In the next section we shall consider also the reverse reactions, the reduction of a salt to form a metal and an electro-negative constituent. In these reactions, as in the photochemical reactions already considered, the metal is formed in specks or nuclei distributed through the crystal and the electro-negative constituent escapes, for instance, as a gas. We shall have to study the conditions under which such nuclei can be formed, and the factors determining their rate of growth.

In the reactions to be discussed here, the first question which we must ask is, Which constituent diffuses through the salt, the metal or the electro-negative substance ? For the reaction of silver with liquid

---

† We have seen in Chap. VII, § 5, that it is not quite certain to which of these classes chemical development of photographic emulsions belongs.

‡ C. Wagner, *Zeits. f. phys. Chem.* (B), **21**, 25 (1933).

sulphur, this has been settled experimentally in the following way:[†]
Liquid sulphur was separated from metallic silver by *two* slabs of sulphide (Fig. 101). After the reaction had been allowed to progress for
some time, it was found that the upper slab II had increased in mass,
but not the lower slab I. This shows that the silver diffuses through
the sulphide and that the reaction takes place at the interface between
the sulphur and the silver sulphide. If the sulphur were able to diffuse

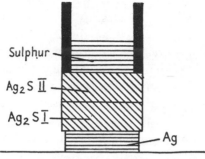

Fig. 101. Reaction of silver with sulphur

through the sulphide, the reaction would take place partly at the interface between silver and silver sulphide, and the mass of block I would
grow also.

In general, the constituent which diffuses is that which is found to
give rise to the ionic conductivity of the salt (Chap. II, § 5). In salts
in which ions of both kinds are mobile, both kinds of atom will be able
to diffuse.

The next question which concerns us is the rate of growth of the
layer of reaction product. There are two possibilities:

I. The rate of growth is controlled by the concentration gradient of
diffusing atoms; in that case, as we shall show, the thickness $x$ of the
film varies with the time according to the law

$$\frac{dx}{dt} = \frac{A}{x},$$
(1)

so that $\qquad x = \sqrt{(2At)}.$
(2)

The thickness thus varies as the square root of the time.

II. The rate of growth is controlled by the velocity of the reaction
at one of the interphase boundaries. In that case the rate of growth
is independent of the thickness, so that

$$\frac{dx}{dt} = B.$$
(3)

† C. Wagner, loc. cit.

Before discussing either of these types of reaction, we shall consider a salt placed in contact with one of its constituents only. When a salt is in contact with a metal and the whole system is in thermodynamical equilibrium, the salt will contain a small stoichiometric excess of metal (cf. Chap. IV, §§ 1, 8). For instance, if silver chloride is in contact with silver, it will contain a small number of additional silver atoms, nearly all of which dissociate into interstitial ions and electrons. Let the number per unit volume of these additional atoms (i.e. ions and electrons) be $n_1$. Similarly, we may consider a salt in contact with its electro-negative constituent, which we may take to be a gas at atmospheric pressure—for example, chlorine gas in contact with silver chloride. In this case, in the state of equilibrium a certain number of neutral chlorine atoms will have left the crystal, and will have paired to form diatomic molecules in the gas. The electrons from these chlorine ions and the corresponding positive ions will be left behind in the salt. No vacant lattice points will be formed in the crystal, if each of the corresponding silver ions goes into an interstitial position. The number of chlorine atoms which leave the crystal will depend on the pressure of the chlorine gas with which it is in contact. We denote by $n_2$ the concentration of excess metal ions in this case. Expressions for the values of $n_1$ and $n_2$ will be given below.

We see then that, whether the salt is in contact with its metallic or with its electro-negative constituent, in both cases it will contain, uniformly distributed through the crystal, an excess number of interstitial metallic ions and an equal number of free electrons in the conduction band.

This behaviour is shown by some substances, but in some others the reverse is the case. For instance, $Cu_2O$ in contact with oxygen contains excess oxygen (Chap. V, § 1).

We now return to the original question of a slab of salt or oxide separating its two constituents; on one side it is in contact with the metal, and on the other it is in contact with the electro-negative substance. In this case the distribution of interstitial atoms will not be uniform throughout the crystal, but there will be a concentration gradient, which will cause the slab to grow. We have seen that the rate of growth may follow either of two laws.

Case I will obtain, and the rate of growth will follow the parabolic law, under the following conditions: the concentration of excess atoms in the layer of salt adjacent to the metal, and likewise also in that adjacent to the electro-negative substance, is the same as it would be if the contact were in thermodynamical equilibrium. The concentrations are thus $n_1$, $n_2$ as defined above. In other words, it is assumed, as in the examples above, that the change in the free energy is zero on bringing an excess atom out of the metal into the salt, or on forming a new layer of salt at the free surface from interstitial atoms *near the surface* and chlorine gas. This will only be the case if there is a constant interchange of atoms at both surfaces; every atom, before it is finally built up into a layer of the salt, must be exchanged between salt and metal, or between salt and chlorine, a number of times.

This is certainly not true for all substances; in the case of a diatomic gas reacting with a metal, an activation energy may be necessary to break up the molecules into atoms before they can react. In that case the rate of the reaction, for not too large values of $x$, may well be determined by the rate at which the gas could be activated at the surface, and the rate of growth will follow (3). Another example is provided by the reverse of a tarnishing reaction, the reduction of a salt or oxide by heating *in vacuo*. The deficiency of (e.g.) oxygen in the surface layers of the oxide cannot be in equilibrium with the gas if the pressure of the gas is zero. The rate of reaction must be determined by the rate at which oxygen escapes from the surface. We shall return to these cases later on.

If both surfaces are in equilibrium, the rate of growth of the layer of salt should be given by an equation of the type (2), namely,

$$x = \text{const. } \sqrt{t}, \tag{4}$$

where $x$ is the thickness at a time $t$ after the reaction begins. For the concentrations at the two boundaries are independent of thickness, and hence the concentration gradient is inversely proportional to $x$. It follows that the flow of atoms and hence $dx/dt$ are inversely proportional to $x$:

$$\frac{dx}{dt} = \frac{A}{x}, \tag{5}$$

where $A$ is a constant. On integrating we obtain (4).†

If, on the other hand, the rate of reaction is determined by surface conditions, we should expect a constant value of $dx/dt$,

$$\frac{dx}{dt} = B, \tag{6}$$

and hence                    $x = Bt$.

We expect whichever rate is slower to determine the velocity of the reaction.

---

† The parabolic law of growth (4) was first obtained by G. Tammann, *Zeits. f. anorg. Chemie*, **111**, 78 (1920) and by N. B. Pilling and R. E. Bedworth, *J. Inst. of Metals*, **29**, 529 (1923).

These two types of reaction may be illustrated by some experiments of Wagner and Grünewald† on the oxidation of copper at $1,000°$ C.

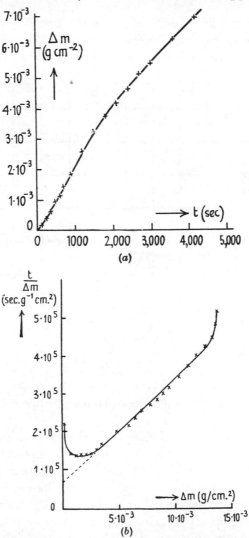

FIG. 102. Reaction of copper with oxygen ($O_2$). Mass $\Delta m$ of oxide per unit area deposited in time $t$. Pressure of $O_2$ is 0·23 mm. Hg in ($a$), 1·17 mm. Hg in ($b$)

Their results are shown in Fig. 102 ($a$), where the mass $\Delta m$ of oxide per cm.² of surface is plotted against time. $\Delta m$ is proportional to $x$. In Fig. 102 ($b$), $t/\Delta m$ is plotted against $\Delta m$. We see that, if the pressure

† C. Wagner and K. Grünewald, *Zeits. f. phys. Chem.* (B), **40**, 455 (1938).

is low, in the initial stages of the reaction $\Delta m$ increases as a power of $t$ higher than the first, probably owing to a slow nuclear formation; then comes a region in which $\Delta m$ is a linear function of $t$ ($\Delta m/t$ constant), followed by a region in which $\Delta m$ is proportional to $t^{\frac{1}{2}}$ ($\Delta m/t$ proportional to $\Delta m$). It follows that, once nuclei are formed, the rate is determined at first by the surface reaction (case II), then for greater thicknesses

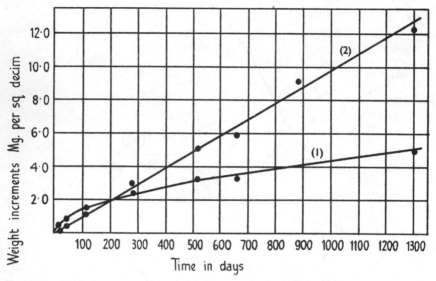

FIG. 103. Oxidation of copper at ordinary temperatures in a normal city atmosphere: (1) weight increment; (2) square of weight increment

for which the concentration gradient has dropped to a small value, by the gradient (case I).

The parabolic law is also followed in the slow oxidation of many metals in contact with the atmosphere at room temperatures.[†] Fig. 103 shows some results due to Vernon[‡] on the oxidation of copper at room temperature, exposed to the atmosphere in the basement of the Royal School of Mines. The parabolic law is obeyed quite accurately.

Other metals, notably aluminium, do not obey a parabolic law; when the film has a thickness of the order 50 to 100 A there is no further growth. This is discussed on p. 262.

Dunn[‖] has measured, for the oxidation of copper, the constant $A$

[†] For a number of examples, cf. H. Carpenter and J. M. Robertson, *Metals*, pp. 508 ff. (Oxford, 1939).

[‡] W. H. J. Vernon, *Trans. Faraday Soc.* **23**, 117 (1927).

[‖] J. S. Dunn, *Proc. Roy. Soc.* (A), **111**, 203 (1926).

occurring in formula (1). He finds, expressing the amount of oxidation as the mass increase $W$ per square decimetre of surface,

$$W^2 = At,$$

with

$$A = A_0 e^{-Q/RT}$$

and

$$Q \sim 40 \text{ kcals.}$$

We must now discuss the theoretical interpretation of the constants occurring in the formulae for the rate of reaction.

As regards numerical values of the constant $B$ in (6) very little theoretical work has been done. We shall return to the question of surface reactions in § 2. We turn now to a consideration of the constant $A$ in (5).

If the excess metal atoms in a salt do not dissociate into ions and electrons, the constant $A$ may be determined as follows. Let $n$ be the concentration of excess atoms at a distance $x$ from the metal surface, and $D$ the diffusion coefficient. Then the number $j$ of atoms crossing unit area per unit time is

$$j = -D\frac{dn}{dx}. \tag{7}$$

If we integrate across the layer of thickness $x_0$ of the salt, we obtain

$$jx_0 = D(n_1 - n_2).$$

Thus, if $\Omega$ is the volume of the salt per metal ion,

$$\frac{dx_0}{dt} = j\Omega = \frac{D(n_1 - n_2)\Omega}{x_0}. \tag{8}$$

Thus

$$A = \Omega D(n_1 - n_2). \tag{9}$$

If the additional atoms dissociate, a similar formula will be valid, provided that the crystal with stoichiometric composition is an insulator, so that the extra atoms alone can move. For $D$ we must now take the diffusion coefficient of the ions; the much more mobile electrons will be held back by the slow-moving ions. Moreover, as we shall see (eq. (13)), the dissociation introduces a factor 2 into the formula for $A$.

If, however, the substance is already an ionic conductor, even when of stoichiometric composition, so that when additional atoms are present the number of interstitial ions largely exceeds the number of electrons, the electrons will no longer be held back by the ions. The rate of reaction will be determined by the rate at which the electrons diffuse. An electron which enters at one surface of the layer will travel right across it. But the metal ion which it takes out with it, to form with the electro-negative constituent a new layer of salt, is by no means the same as the ion which entered the layer with it. The metal ions have diffused a much smaller distance.

In either case we may proceed as follows, assuming for simplicity that only the metal is mobile. We denote by $x$ the distance from the metal surface, and by $n_e(x)$, $n_i(x)$ the density of electrons and mobile (interstitial) ions. Let $v_e$, $v_i$ be their mobilities, and $D_e$, $D_i$ their diffusion coefficients. Let $F$ be the electrostatic field in the medium due to space-charges. Then the electronic current, expressed in units of $e$, will be

$$j_e = -D_e \frac{\partial n_e}{\partial x} + F n_e v_e$$

and the ionic current

$$-j_i = -D_i \frac{\partial n_i}{\partial x} - F n_i v_i.$$

In a steady state $j_e$ and $j_i$ must be equal and opposite; the number $j$ of atoms (electrons+ions) crossing unit area per unit time is thus, eliminating $F$ and using the equation† $D/v = kT/e$,

$$j \left[ \frac{1}{n_e v_e} + \frac{1}{n_i v_i} \right] = -\frac{kT}{e} \left[ \frac{\partial}{\partial x} \log(n_e n_i) \right]. \tag{10}$$

We may set        $e n_e v_e = \sigma_e, \qquad e n_i v_i = \sigma_i,$

where $\sigma_e$ and $\sigma_i$ are respectively the electronic and ionic contributions to the conductivity of the salt *at the point* $x$; as already emphasized, $\sigma_e$ especially is not necessarily the conductivity of the salt of stoichiometric composition and may be of a different order of magnitude. We may also write        $\sigma_e = \theta_e \sigma, \qquad \sigma_i = \theta_i \sigma,$

where $\sigma$ is the total conductivity, and $\theta_e$, $\theta_i$ are transport numbers.

Equation (10) then becomes

$$j = -\theta_e \theta_i \sigma \frac{kT}{e^2} \frac{\partial}{\partial x} \log(n_e n_i). \tag{11}$$

There are two special cases in which we can integrate these equations. The first is when the ionic conductivity is larger than the electronic, and may be taken as constant through the slab of salt. Then the equation (10) becomes

$$j = -\frac{kT}{e} v_e \frac{\partial n_e}{\partial x},$$

so that

$$A = \Omega v_e \frac{kT}{e} [(n_e)_1 - (n_e)_2]. \tag{12}$$

† Cf. Chap. II, § 9.

The second case is when $n_e = n_i$, i.e. when the product of the reaction is an insulator when of stoichiometric composition, but acquires an electronic and an ionic conductivity through the presence of excess atoms. In this case $\sigma_e \gg \sigma_i$. We may then write, with $n_e = n_i = n$,

$$j = -\frac{kT}{e} v_i \, 2 \frac{\partial n}{\partial x},$$

The factor 2 is to be noted. On integrating we obtain

$$A = 2\Omega v_i \frac{kT}{e} [n_1 - n_2]. \tag{13}$$

We note that according to (12) and (13) $A$ is proportional to either the electronic or the ionic conductivity, whichever is the *smaller*.

In most cases of tarnishing reactions the concentration of excess atoms at one boundary will be negligible compared with that at the other, so that, according to formulae (12) and (13), the reaction rate depends on the conditions at one boundary only. Wagner† has shown this in a recent paper on the rates of oxidation of zinc and of copper in oxygen. He finds that the rate of oxidation of copper increases with increasing pressure of oxygen, while the rate for zinc is practically independent of the pressure. Now it was shown in Chapter V that cuprous oxide is a conductor only if it contains an excess of oxygen, and that its conductivity increases with increasing pressure of oxygen in contact with the crystal. On the other hand, cuprous oxide in contact with copper is practically of stoichiometric composition. Thus in the tarnishing reaction $n_1 \ll n_2$, and the rate of reaction is determined by $n_2$, the concentration of excess oxygen at the free surface.

In zinc oxide the state of affairs is just the other way round. Zinc oxide is a conductor only if it contains excess zinc. In the tarnishing reaction the oxide in equilibrium with the metal contains excess zinc, but at the free surface the composition is nearly stoichiometric. Thus the rate of reaction is almost independent of the pressure of oxygen—provided that this is great enough to provide atoms to react with the zinc atoms which diffuse to the surface. At very low pressures we should, of course, expect a drop in the rate.

Fig. 104 illustrates the concentration gradients in the two cases.

Wagner and Grünewald show, moreover, that for the oxidation of copper the rate of reaction is proportional to $p^{1/7}$, where $p$ is the oxygen pressure. A similar dependence on pressure was found for the

† C. Wagner and K. Grünewald, *Zeits. f. phys. Chem.* (B), **40**, 455 (1938).

conductivity of cuprous oxide in oxygen at the same temperature†
(1,000° C.). For cuprous oxide, in which the number of mobile ions and
electrons is equal, the proportionality of conductivity and rate of
reaction follows from formula (13).

We see then that for a reaction to take place either $n_1$ or $n_2$ must
be appreciable, but not necessarily both. Thus ZnO will form on zinc
at pressures and temperatures at which the oxide in equilibrium with

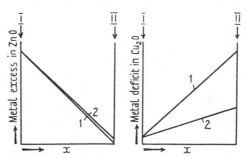

Fig. 104. Schematic representation‡ of the concentration gradient of Zn in ZnO and O in Cu$_2$O. I. Metal-
oxide surface; II. oxide-oxygen surface. (1) Pressure
of oxygen 1 atm.; (2) pressure of oxygen 0·1 atm.

oxygen has stoichiometric composition, and Cu$_2$O will form on copper
even at temperatures at which no copper dissolves in the oxide.

The process occurring during the oxidation of copper may be discussed in rather greater detail. At the surface between cuprous oxide
and oxygen, oxygen atoms are adsorbed on the surface, leaving a
number of unoccupied copper lattice points, together with 'positive
holes' in the full band of the oxide (cf. Chap. V, § 1). $n_i$ must therefore
refer to the number of vacant lattice points, and $n_e$ to the number of
positive holes. It is actually the copper ions which move in this case.

A similar process must take place in the reaction of silver with
chlorine or bromine at room temperature, since (Chap. VII, § 10) silver
is not soluble in the halide at room temperatures. Interesting information about this process may be obtained from the behaviour of photographic emulsions.

We have seen (Chap. VII, § 11) how in photographic emulsions an
exposure of short duration can produce in the *interior* of a grain a latent
image, whose presence can be revealed by dissolving the halide and
subsequent physical development. Now it is found that an internal

† J. Gundermann and C. Wagner, *Zeits. f. phys. Chem.* (B), **37**, 155 (1937).
‡ C. Wagner and K. Grünewald, loc. cit.

latent image of this kind can be bleached by applying an oxidizing agent, in particular a halogen. This is a typical tarnishing reaction. But we know that the silver of the latent image is not soluble in the halide of the grain, because red light is necessary to disperse it (Chap. VII, § 10). Thus no electron concentration exists in the grain round the metallic speck. We think rather that when the halogen is applied the halogen atoms adhere to the surface of the grain, and, by capturing an electron from a neighbour, give rise to a certain concentration of positive holes in the full band of the halide grain. The metallic speck then loses electrons by filling up the holes in the full band. Positive ions can then leave the speck and move into interstitial positions in the grain of silver halide in the usual way.†

We shall now calculate the respective concentrations $n_i$ and $n_e$ of ions and electrons of the salt in equilibrium with the metal and with a gas. The free energy of an electron gas may be written (cf. p. 157)

$$F_e(n_e) = -n_e kT\left[\log\left(\frac{2\pi mkT}{h^2}\right)^{\frac{3}{2}} + \log\frac{V}{n_e} + 1\right],$$

and the derivative is

$$F'_e(n_e) = -kT\left[\log\left(\frac{2\pi mkT}{h^2}\right)^{\frac{3}{2}} + \log\frac{V}{n_e}\right].$$

For the free energy of the interstitial ions we may write

$$F_i(n_i) = -kT\log\frac{N!}{n_i!\,(N-n_i)!},$$

where $N$ is the number of interstitial positions available.

Let $\Delta F_{\text{metal}}$ be the change in (free) energy when an atom is brought from the metal into an interstitial position in the salt, excluding the changes in $F_e$ and $F_i$. Let $\Delta F_{\text{gas}}$ be similarly the change in the free energy of the system when one atom is removed from the gas, and at the same time an interstitial metal atom is taken from the salt, and the two together are allowed to form a new ion pair of the salt.

When the salt is in equilibrium with metal or with gas, the free-energy change must be zero when an interstitial ion and an electron are taken from the salt and added to the metal or gas. This gives

$$\Delta F + F'_i(n_i) + F'_e(n_e) = 0,$$

or
$$\frac{n_i n_e}{VN} = \left(\frac{2\pi mkT}{h^2}\right)^{\frac{3}{2}} e^{-\Delta F/kT}. \tag{14}$$

To obtain a further relation between $n_i$ and $n_e$ we must know something about the number of vacant lattice points. Suppose, for instance,

† Similar conclusions about the mechanism of the reaction of silver with halogens have been obtained by C. Wagner, *Zeits. f. phys. Chem.* (B), **32**, 459 (1933).

that the pure salt is an ionic conductor only, so that all the electrons are due to excess atoms. Then the number of vacant lattice points is $n_i - n_e$. Since the free energy must be a minimum with respect to changes in the number of vacant lattice points, we have

$$F_i'(n_i) + F_i'(n_i - n_e) + W = 0,$$

where $W$ is the energy required to form a vacant lattice point and an interstitial ion. Thus

$$\frac{n_i(n_i - n_e)}{N^2} = e^{-W/kT}. \tag{15}$$

The quantity $\Delta F_{\text{metal}}$ is simply the energy required to bring an atom from the metal into an interstitial position in the crystal; or, if the interstitial atom dissociates, we may write

$$\Delta F_{\text{metal}} = W_i + W_e, \tag{16}$$

where $W_i$ is the work required to bring an ion from the metal into an interstitial position in the salt, and $W_e$ ($= \phi - \chi$, cf. Chap. III, §3) is the work to bring an electron from the metal into the conduction band of the salt.

The quantity $\Delta F_{\text{gas}}$ requires more careful consideration. If we take one molecule out of the gas, we may be able to form more than one interstitial atom. For instance, if the gas is oxygen ($O_2$) and the reaction product $Cu_2O$, for each molecule of oxygen we obtain two oxygen ions $O^{--}$, and thus *four* vacant metal points.[†]

Let, then, the gas contain $n_g$ molecules per unit volume, and let each of these give $s$ interstitial ions or similar singularities in the oxide. Then

$$s\Delta F_{\text{gas}} = -F'_{\text{gas}}(n_g) + E,$$

where $E$ is the energy required to dissociate the molecule and to form the interstitial atoms. Thus

$$\Delta F_{\text{gas}} = \frac{E}{s} + kT\left[\log\left(\frac{1}{n_g}\right)^{\frac{1}{s}} + \log\left(\frac{2\pi mkT}{h^2}\right)^{\frac{3}{2s}}\right].$$

Thus from (14)

$$\frac{n_i n_e}{VN} = \left(\frac{2\pi mkT}{h^2}\right)^{\frac{3}{2}\left(1+\frac{1}{s}\right)} n_g^{1/s}\, e^{-E/skT}. \tag{17}$$

Since $n_g$ is proportional to the pressure $p$ of the gas, it follows that $n_i n_e$ is proportional to $p^{1/s}$.

Wagner and Hammen[‡] have measured the concentration of oxygen in $Cu_2O$ at 1,000° C. for varying oxygen pressures. For this oxide, as

† Cf. p. 163.
‡ C. Wagner and H. Hammen, *Zeits. f. phys. Chem.* (B), **40**, 197 (1938).

already mentioned, there is very little ionic conductivity in the pure state, so that one may assume

$$n_i \simeq n_e.$$

We thus expect a concentration proportional to $p^{\frac{1}{4}}$. Wagner actually finds that the concentration varies approximately as $p^{\frac{1}{4}}$, and the electrical conductivity† as $p^{\frac{1}{4}}$. He ascribes this to incomplete dissociation, or rather to an incomplete disorder of ions and electrons in the sense of the Debye-Hückel theory of strong electrolytes.

If $\Delta F_{\text{metal}}$ and $\Delta F_{\text{gas}}$ are very nearly equal, so that $n_e$ and $n_i$ are almost constant through the crystal, formula (14) may be used to obtain a convenient estimate of the reaction constant in tarnishing reactions. Turning to formula (11) for the current, we may then assume $\theta_e$, $\theta_i$, $\sigma$ to be constants, and on integrating obtain

$$jx = \theta_e \theta_i \sigma \frac{kT}{e^2} \log \frac{(n_e n_i)_{\text{gas}}}{(n_e n_i)_{\text{metal}}}$$

$$= \frac{\theta_e \theta_i \sigma}{e^2} (\Delta F_{\text{metal}} - \Delta F_{\text{gas}}).$$

The value of the reaction constant is thus

$$\theta_e \theta_i \sigma \Omega \, \Delta F / e^2, \tag{18}$$

where $\Delta F$ is the free energy liberated in the reaction per metal atom.

For applications of this formula to actual reactions, reference may be made to Jost's book.‡

We shall next discuss those metals which do not tarnish on exposure to the atmosphere. Some metals, e.g. aluminium, become coated with a thin protective film—that is to say, an oxide layer is built up on the surface until it reaches a certain thickness, after which it shows no appreciable growth, provided that the layer is not injured (Fig. 105). Suppose, for the sake of argument, that the oxide layer is of the ZnO type (p. 258), that is to say that under normal pressures of oxygen it does not take up any excess oxygen. Then the reaction can only proceed, if at all, by the metal atoms going from the metal into solution in the oxide, diffusing through the oxide and reacting with the oxygen at the oxide-oxygen interface.

Now we have seen in formulae (14) and (16) that the concentration of interstitial atoms depends on the work $W_i + W_e$ required to bring an ion and an electron from the metal into the oxide. If $W_i + W_e$ is too large the solubility will be negligible and the oxide film cannot grow. It may be, however, that $W_e$ is larger than $W_i$, and that $W_i$ is small enough to allow ions to pass occasionally from the metal into interstitial positions

† J. Gundermann and C. Wagner, *Zeits. f. phys. Chem.* (B), **37**, 155 (1937).
‡ W. Jost, *Diffusion und chemische Reaktion in festen Stoffen*, chap. iv (Dresden, 1937).

in the oxide, but that $W_e$ is too large for there to be any appreciable thermionic emission from the metal to the oxide. In this case it has been suggested by Mott† that, while the oxide film is still thin enough, electrons can pass through it by quantum-mechanical tunnel effect; thus the necessary electrons can move from the metal to the oxide-oxygen interface without receiving any thermal energy of activation.

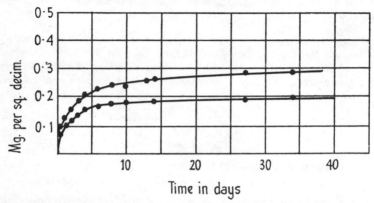

Fig. 105. Formation of aluminium oxide on sheet aluminium exposed to the atmosphere at room temperature (from W. H. J. Vernon, *Trans. Faraday Soc.* **23**, 113 (1927))

It may be shown that the maximum film thickness that electrons can penetrate by quantum-mechanical tunnel effect is about 40 A, if $W_e \sim 1$ eV. A film of this thickness would give a weight increase of 0·075 mg. per square decimetre for $Al_2O_3$. This is of the same order as the weight increase of 0·2 mg. observed; the difference may well be accounted for by the corrugated nature of the surface of a metal sheet.

We may note that a consequence of the theory is that the protective oxide films on metals are necessarily insulators for electronic currents flowing between the oxidized metal and an electrode in contact with the oxide film, for very small potential differences.

## 2. Reduction of ionic crystals

By reduction of a polar crystal we mean its decomposition into metal and electro-negative constituent. We have already considered two examples: the photochemical reduction of silver halides, and reduction of silver-halide grains by development. We shall in this section make a few very tentative remarks on the extension of these ideas to the reduction process in general.

† N. F. Mott, *Trans. Faraday Soc.* **35**, 1175 (1939) and **36**, 472 (1940).

We may distinguish several types of reducing agent, which we now enumerate:

I. Reduction of oxides by hydrogen. We believe that this takes place in the following way: the hydrogen reacts directly with the oxygen at the surface of the oxide forming water molecules; which escape. The metal ions and electrons which are left behind will form interstitial atoms of the usual type, which probably dissociate into ions and electrons and diffuse into the interior of the crystal. Thus a 'gas' of interstitial atoms will fill the solid oxide, and its density will gradually increase, until metallic nuclei form, at the surface or at internal cracks. These will grow as the surface atoms are gradually removed.

In any reaction where the primary process is the removal of surface atoms, leaving metal atoms behind, the rate of reaction should be proportional to the surface area, and independent of how much metal is formed, except in so far as the metallic deposits may split the crystal and form new surfaces.

II. If, however, the interface between the compound and the reducing agent is in equilibrium, in the sense discussed in the last section, the rate of reaction will depend on the amount of metal present. For let the crystal in equilibrium with the reducing agent contain $n_1$ interstitial atoms per cm.$^3$, and in equilibrium with the metal $n_2$. Consider a metallic nucleus; at a distance $r$ from it let the concentration of interstitial atoms be $n(r)$. Then the flow of atoms to the nucleus is, per second,

$$j = -4\pi r^2 D \frac{\partial n(r)}{\partial r},$$

where $D$ is the diffusion coefficient. If $r_0$ is the radius of the nucleus, we have, integrating from $r_0$ to infinity:

$$j/4\pi r_0 = D(n_1 - n_2).$$

Thus $j$, the number of atoms added to the nucleus per second, is

$$4\pi r_0 D(n_1 - n_2).$$

Thus the rate at which the reaction proceeds increases with the size of each nucleus and with the number of nuclei. The rate of growth of each nucleus is given by

$$\frac{dr_0}{dt} = \frac{D(n_1 - n_2)\Omega}{r_0},$$

which gives the parabolic law

$$r_0 = \text{const. } \sqrt{t}$$

for the rate of growth.

III. Reduction of halides by a developer. This has already been discussed. We believe that in these the primary action of the reducing agent is to give an electron to a metallic nucleus already present. Reducers of this type are to be contrasted with those of the type which attack the electro-negative constituent directly.

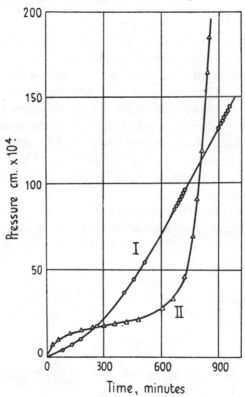

FIG. 106.† Pressure of nitrogen given off from potassium azide $KN_3$: (I) in a vacuum at 341° C.; (II) in potassium vapour at 249° C.

IV. Photochemical reduction. We have seen that for this to happen the light must free an electron *and* a positive hole. The electron drifts to a metal speck and attracts mobile interstitial ions to it; the positive hole drifts to the surface and turns a negative ion into an atom, which can then escape.

V. Reactions which are catalysed by the presence of metallic nuclei. The reduction of metallic azides by heat‡ ($\sim 100°$ C.) gives an example

† From W. E. Garner and D. J. B. Marke, *J. Chem. Soc.*, p. 657 (1936).

‡ Investigated notably by Garner and co-workers, cf., for example, W. E. Garner and I. Maggs, *Proc. Roy. Soc.* (A) **172**, 299 (1939), or W. E. Garner, *Science Progress*, **33**, 209 (1938).

of this type of reaction. On heating these substances there occurs at first a very slow evolution of nitrogen; then, after a certain period, metallic nuclei appear and the reaction is enormously accelerated (Fig. 106, curve II). In potassium azide the accelerated part of the reaction only appears if the experiment is carried out in potassium vapour;† otherwise the nuclei evaporate as fast as they are formed (curve I). This shows that the accelerated part of the reaction is due to

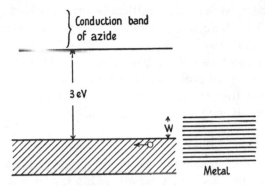

Fig. 107.  Energy levels of barium azide in contact
with metallic barium

the presence of metallic nuclei. In barium azide the rate of growth of the nuclei has been measured and obeys the equation

$$\frac{dr}{dt} = A,$$

where $A$ is a constant at given temperature and varies with $T$ according to the law
$$A = A_0 e^{-W/RT}, \qquad W \sim 23{,}000 \text{ cals.}$$

The metallic azides may be reduced by irradiation with ultra-violet light at room temperature, metallic nuclei being formed and nitrogen escaping.‡ We believe that the process here is exactly similar to that occurring in silver halides. If this is the case, the azides must be ionic conductors at room temperatures and *a fortiori* at 100° C. We may postulate also that it is the small metallic ions which are mobile.

As in the photochemical process, the thermal reaction will proceed if the metallic nuclei gain electrons, and if positive holes are formed which can diffuse to the surface. Both will happen at the metal-salt interface if the energy of the top of the full band is abnormally high, so that the activation energy $W$ in Fig. 107 required to bring an

† W. E. Garner and D. J. B. Marks, loc. cit.
‡ W. E. Garner and I. Maggs, *Proc. Roy. Soc.* (A) **172**, 299 (1939).

electron from the full band on to the metal is not too great. We may assume that this is so for the azides, where the negative ion is unstable.

Our process, then, is the following. At the metal-salt interface, an electron jumps from an azide ion ($N_3^-$) into the metal, the activation energy required corresponding to the 23 kcals. observed. The positive hole so formed escapes to the surface and removes an electron from an $N_3^-$ ion there, so that an $N_3$ radical is formed, which can escape and decompose. The charged metal speck attracts an interstitial metal ion and grows in that way.

Two things must be emphasized about all the five mechanisms of this section. They all postulate that the salt is an ionic conductor, and they all suggest that the electro-negative constituent escapes from the surface of the salt, and *not* from the metal-salt interface.

### 2.1. Formation of nuclei

The *formation* of metallic nuclei in the grains of photographic emulsions has been discussed in Chapter VII, §4, and it has been shown that it depends essentially on the presence of impurities ('sensitivity specks') on the surface. We have also given evidence that a latent image is more likely to form if the concentration of electrons in the grain reaches a certain value, because for low concentrations a very small nucleus (3 or 4 atoms) may dissolve as soon as it is formed—although the larger nuclei are quite stable.

The only other work on nuclei which seems susceptible to theoretical interpretation is that on the azides. For barium azide undergoing reduction by heat treatment the number $N$ of nuclei formed has been found† to vary as $t^3$. Thus

$$\frac{dN}{dt} = \text{const.} \, t^2. \tag{19}$$

The constant appears to be structure-sensitive; nuclei form in lines, presumably along cracks. Now before nuclear formation, or a long way from any nucleus, we expect that nitrogen will be driven off steadily, interstitial barium atoms being formed at a constant rate and diffusing into the body of the crystal. The law (19) suggests that whenever *two* of these atoms meet at some favoured spot on the surface, a nucleus is formed‡ which can then grow by the mechanism described above.

† A. Wischin, *Proc. Roy. Soc.* (A) **139**, 314 (1939).
‡ N. F. Mott, ibid. p. 326 (1939).

## Note added February 1948

*Oxidation of metals.* In § 1 of this chapter we have described the mechanism by which oxide films grow on metals according to the parabolic law valid at high temperatures; on pp. 261 and 262 we have suggested a mechanism to explain the formation of protective films on such metals as aluminium and chromium. While, as far as can be seen at present, the proposed mechanism is possible in theory, closer examination has shown that it is not the one which actually limits film growth on these metals. The growth of these oxide films is stopped by the difficulty in passing metal ions through the oxide. An analysis of the situation has been given by Mott[†] following earlier work by Verwey[‡]. This work is based on experiments by Gunterschultze and Betz[§] on the electrolytic formation of oxide films on aluminium. These authors find that the ionic current $J$ depends on the field $F$ (volts) in the oxide layer according to the equation

$$J = \alpha e^{\beta F}.$$

Here $\alpha^{-1} = 2 \cdot 75 \times 10^{16}$ if the current is measured in $\mu$. amp./cm.$^2$, or $0 \cdot 92 \times 10^{13}$ in e.s.u. If $F$ is in volt/cm., $\beta = 4 \cdot 2 \times 10^{-6}$. For small fields ($\beta F \sim 1$) the current is negligible. Modifying slightly Verwey's original explanation, Mott accounts for this as follows:

Suppose, to leave the metal and go into an interstitial position in the oxide, an aluminium ion must surmount a potential barrier of height $U$ at a distance $a$ from its position in the metal. Then in the presence of a field $F$ the height of the barrier becomes $U - qaF$, where $q$ is the charge on the ion. The current may thus be written

$$J = Nq\nu e^{-(U-qaF)/kT},$$

where $N$ is the number of atoms per unit area of aluminium surface and $\nu$ the frequency of atomic vibrations. Comparing this with the observed constants $\alpha$, $\beta$, we find

$$qa/kT = \beta, \qquad U = kT\log(Nq\nu/\alpha).$$

Taking $N \sim 10^{15}$ cm.$^{-2}$, $q = 3e$, $\nu = 10^{12}$ sec.$^{-1}$ and $kT = 0 \cdot 025$ eV., we find $U = 1 \cdot 8$ eV., $a = 3 \cdot 5 \times 10^{-8}$ cm.

These values seem reasonable.

Taking $\Omega$, the volume of oxide per aluminium ion, to be $2 \cdot 7 \times 10^{-23}$ cm.$^3$, it is easily seen that the growth rate of the oxide film is

$$dx/dt = N\Omega\nu e^{-U/kT}e^{aqF/kT} = 2 \times 10^{-26}e^{\beta F}$$

at room temperature.

The explanation given by Mott of the formation of protective films in air is based on the assumption that electrons can pass freely through these thin films, either by tunnel effect or by thermionic emission into the conduction band of the oxide, probably the former. These electrons will then combine with adsorbed oxygen atoms at the interface between oxide and air. A potential difference $V$, of the order of a few electron volts, will thus be set up across the oxide layer, and it is easily seen that $V$ is independent of the thickness $x$. Thus the field across the layer is $V/x$, and the rate of growth

$$dx/dt = N\Omega\nu e^{-U/kT}e^{aqV/kTx}.$$

---

† N. F. Mott, *Journal de Chimie-Physique* **44**, 172 (1947); *Trans. Faraday Soc.* **43**, 429 (1947).

‡ E. J. Verwey, *Physica*, **2**, 1059 (1935).

§ A. Gunterschultze and H. Betz, *Zeits. f. Physik*, **92**, 367 (1934).

The thickness of the stable film may be estimated as follows. Growth will be said to have stopped when one atomic layer is added in $10^5$ secs., so that $dx/dt \sim 10^{-13}$; $N\Omega\nu$ is of order $10^4$, so that $x$ will be given by

$$U - aqV/x \sim kT \log_e 10^{17}.$$

This gives at once for the critical film thickness

$$x = \frac{Vaq}{U - 39kT}.$$

All constants in this formula are known, except $V$. Measuring $V$ in volts, we find

$$x = 6 \times 10^{-8} V/(1 - T/530) \, \text{cm}.$$

At room temperature this gives a value of $V \times 10^{-7}$ cm., and if $V$ is, say, 3 volts, we obtain for $x$ the value 30 A, which is the most recent value obtained by Cabrera and Hamon[†] by an optical method for the thickness of the layer formed in dry air on an evaporated film. Cabrera, Terrien, and Hamon[‡] have also found that an increase of thickness of the order 50 per cent. could be produced by U.V. illumination. A possible explanation is that a photovoltaic effect increases $V$.

Cabrera and Hamon[§] have been able to verify roughly the temperature dependence of the thickness $x$ given by theory. They find that the limiting thickness increases with temperature, being at 100° C. about twice the value at 10° C.; while above 300° C. the rate of growth is rapid and seems to continue without limit.

It has been shown also by Gulbransen and Wysing[||] that, in the range 350°–450° C, the rate of oxidation follows a parabolic law, and, as we should expect, is independent of temperature.

The chief criticism of the theory as presented here is that we have taken for $N$ the number of metal atoms per unit area of surface. In fact, as layer after layer of metal atoms is peeled off, only certain favourably situated atoms will be in a position to move at any moment. Theoretical investigations at present in progress show that no formal alteration of the theory is required to take account of this, but that the interpretation of the activation energy $U$ is rather more complicated than that given here.

## Note on Chapter III

One of the most important predictions of the theory of light absorption in alkali halides is that absorption in the first U.V. band should produce excitons and hence no photoconduction; while absorption in the second band should release electrons and produce a current. This prediction of the theory has been verified by J. N. Ferguson (*Phys. Rev.* **66**, 220 (1944)), who finds that in sodium chloride the photocurrent begins at a wave-length of about 2800 A, which, as shown in Table 20 on p. 97, corresponds to the peak of the second band.

[†] N. Cabrera and J. Hamon, *C.R.* **224**, 1713 (1947).
[‡] N. Cabrera, N. Terrien, and J. Hamon, ibid. 1558.
[§] loc. cit.
[||] E. A. Gulbransen and W. S. Wysing, *J. Phys. and Colloid Chemistry*, **57**, 1087 (1947).

# APPENDIX

## *Conventional Ionic Radii, in cm.* $\times 10^{-8}$

THE values printed first are due to L. Pauling (*J. Am. Chem. Soc.* **49**, 765 (1927)), those printed below to V. M. Goldschmidt (*Norske Vid. Akad. Oslo Skr., Mat.-Nat. Kl.* (1926), No. 2; *Chem. Ber.* **60**, 1263 (1927)). Pauling's values are deduced by wave mechanics from certain observed constants of the ions, Goldschmidt's from the interionic distance in crystals, on the assumption that the ions behave like rigid spheres.

**(a)** *Ions with 8 or 2 outer electrons:*

| | | | | | | IV | V | VI | VII |
|---|---|---|---|---|---|---|---|---|---|
| | | | | | | IV | V | VI | VII |
| | | $H^-$ | $Li^+$ | $Be^{++}$ | $B^{+++}$ | C | N | O | F |
| | | 2·08 | 0·60 | 0·31 | 0·20 | 0·15 | 0·11 | 0·09 | 0·07 |
| | | 1·27 | 0·78 | 0·34 | .. | 0·2 | 0·1–0·2 | .. | .. |
| | | | | | | IV | V | VI | VII |
| $N^{---}$ | $O^{--}$ | $F^-$ | $Na^+$ | $Mg^{++}$ | $Al^{+++}$ | Si | P | S | Cl |
| 1·71 | 1·40 | 1·36 | 0·95 | 0·65 | 0·50 | 0·41 | 0·34 | 0·29 | 0·26 |
| .. | 1·32 | 1·33 | 0·98 | 0·78 | 0·57 | 0·39 | 0·03–0·4 | 0·34 | .. |
| | | | | | | IV | V | VI | VII |
| $P^{---}$ | $S^{--}$ | $Cl^-$ | $K^+$ | $Ca^{++}$ | $Sc^{+++}$ | Ti | V | Cr | Mn |
| 2·12 | 1·84 | 1·81 | 1·33 | 0·99 | 0·81 | 0·68 | 0·59 | 0·52 | 0·46 |
| .. | 1·74 | 1·81 | 1·33 | 1·06 | 0·83 | 0·64 | 0·4 | 0·3–0·4 | .. |
| | | | | | | IV | V | VI | VII |
| $As^{---}$ | $Se^{--}$ | $Br^-$ | $Rb^+$ | $Sr^{++}$ | $Y^{+++}$ | Zr | Nb | Mo | Ma |
| 2·22 | 1·98 | 1·95 | 1·48 | 1·13 | 0·93 | 0·80 | 0·70 | 0·62 | .. |
| .. | 1·91 | 1·96 | 1·49 | 1·27 | 1·06 | 0·87 | 0·69 | .. | .. |
| | | | | | | IV | | | |
| $Sb^{---}$ | $Te^{--}$ | $I^-$ | $Cs^+$ | $Ba^{++}$ | $La^{+++}$ | Ce | | | |
| 2·45 | 2·21 | 2·16 | 1·69 | 1·35 | 1·15 | 1·01 | | | |
| .. | 2·11 | 2·20 | 1·65 | 1·43 | 1·22 | 1·02 | | | |

**(b)** *Ions with 18 outer electrons:*

| | | | IV | V | VI | VII |
|---|---|---|---|---|---|---|
| | | | IV | V | VI | VII |
| $Cu^+$ | $Zn^{++}$ | $Ga^{+++}$ | Ge | As | Se | Br |
| 0·96 | 0·74 | 0·62 | 0·53 | 0·47 | 0·42 | 0·39 |
| .. | 0·83 | 0·62 | 0·44 | .. | 0·3–0·4 | .. |
| | | | IV | V | VI | VII |
| $Ag^+$ | $Cd^{++}$ | $In^{+++}$ | Sn | Sb | Te | I |
| 1·26 | 0·97 | 0·81 | 0·71 | 0·62 | 0·56 | 0·50 |
| 1·13 | 1·03 | 0·92 | 0·74 | .. | .. | .. |
| | | | IV | V | VI | |
| $Au^+$ | $Hg^{++}$ | $Tl^{+++}$ | Pb | Bi | Po | |
| 1·37 | 1·10 | 0·95 | 0·84 | 0·74 | .. | |
| .. | 1·12 | 1·05 | 0·84 | .. | .. | |

(c) *Ions with* $18 + 2$ *outer electrons:*

| $Tl^+$ | $Pb^{++}$ |
|---|---|
| 1·44 | 1·21 |
| 1·49 | 1·32 |

(d) *Ions of the transition elements:*

| $Mn^{++}$ | $Fe^{++}$ | $Co^{++}$ | $Ni^{++}$ | $Cu^{++}$ | $Cr^{+++}$ | $Fe^{+++}$ |
|---|---|---|---|---|---|---|
| 0·80 | 0·75 | 0·72 | 0·69 | .. | .. | .. |
| 0·91 | 0·83 | 0·82 | 0·78 | 1·01 | 0·65 | 0·67 |

# INDEX OF NAMES

# INDEX OF SUBJECTS

# CATALOG OF DOVER BOOKS

# BOOKS EXPLAINING SCIENCE AND MATHEMATICS

**THE COMMON SENSE OF THE EXACT SCIENCES, W. K. Clifford.** Introduction by James Newman, edited by Karl Pearson. For 70 years this has been a guide to classical scientific and mathematical thought. Explains with unusual clarity basic concepts, such as extension of meaning of symbols, characteristics of surface boundaries, properties of plane figures, vectors, Cartesian method of determining position, etc. Long preface by Bertrand Russell. Bibliography of Clifford. Corrected, 130 diagrams redrawn. 249pp. 5⅜ x 8.
TC1 Paperbound **$1.60**

**SCIENCE THEORY AND MAN, Erwin Schrödinger.** This is a complete and unabridged reissue of SCIENCE AND THE HUMAN TEMPERAMENT plus an additional essay: "What is an Elementary Particle?" Nobel Laureate Schrödinger discusses such topics as nature of scientific method, the nature of science, chance and determinism, science and society, conceptual models for physical entities, elementary particles and wave mechanics. Presentation is popular and may be followed by most people with little or no scientific training. "Fine practical preparation for a time when laws of nature, human institutions . . . are undergoing a critical examination without parallel," Waldemar Kaempffert, N. Y. TIMES. 192pp. 5⅜ x 8.
T428 Paperbound **$1.35**

**PIONEERS OF SCIENCE, O. Lodge.** Eminent scientist-expositor's authoritative, yet elementary survey of great scientific theories. Concentrating on individuals—Copernicus, Brahe, Kepler, Galileo, Descartes, Newton, Laplace, Herschel, Lord Kelvin, and other scientists—the author presents their discoveries in historical order adding biographical material on each man and full, specific explanations of their achievements. The clear and complete treatment of the post-Newtonian astronomers is a feature seldom found in other books on the subject. Index. 120 illustrations. xv + 404pp. 5⅜ x 8.
T716 Paperbound **$1.50**

**THE EVOLUTION OF SCIENTIFIC THOUGHT FROM NEWTON TO EINSTEIN, A. d'Abro.** Einstein's special and general theories of relativity, with their historical implications, are analyzed in non-technical terms. Excellent accounts of the contributions of Newton, Riemann, Weyl, Planck, Eddington, Maxwell, Lorentz and others are treated in terms of space and time, equations of electromagnetics, finiteness of the universe, methodology of science. 21 diagrams. 482pp. 5⅜ x 8.
T2 Paperbound **$2.00**

**THE RISE OF THE NEW PHYSICS, A. d'Abro.** A half-million word exposition, formerly titled THE DECLINE OF MECHANISM, for readers not versed in higher mathematics. The only thorough explanation, in everyday language, of the central core of modern mathematical physical theory, treating both classical and modern theoretical physics, and presenting in terms almost anyone can understand the equivalent of 5 years of study of mathematical physics. Scientifically impeccable coverage of mathematical-physical thought from the Newtonian system up through the electronic theories of Dirac and Heisenberg and Fermi's statistics. Combines both history and exposition; provides a broad yet unified and detailed view, with constant comparison of classical and modern views on phenomena and theories. "A must for anyone doing serious study in the physical sciences," JOURNAL OF THE FRANKLIN INSTITUTE. "Extraordinary faculty . . . to explain ideas and theories of theoretical physics in the language of daily life," ISIS. First part of set covers philosophy of science, drawing upon the practice of Newton, Maxwell, Poincaré, Einstein, others, discussing modes of thought, experiment, interpretations of causality, etc. In the second part, 100 pages explain grammar and vocabulary of mathematics, with discussions of functions, groups, series, Fourier series, etc. The remainder is devoted to concrete, detailed coverage of both classical and quantum physics, explaining such topics as analytic mechanics, Hamilton's principle, wave theory of light, electromagnetic waves, groups of transformations, thermodynamics, phase rule, Brownian movement, kinetics, special relativity, Planck's original quantum theory, Bohr's atom, Zeeman effect, Broglie's wave mechanics, Heisenberg's uncertainty, Eigen-values, matrices, scores of other important topics. Discoveries and theories are covered for such men as Alembert, Born, Cantor, Debye, Euler, Foucault, Galois, Gauss, Hadamard, Kelvin, Kepler, Laplace, Maxwell, Pauli, Rayleigh, Volterra, Weyl, Young, more than 180 others. Indexed. 97 illustrations. ix + 982pp. 5⅜ x 8.
T3 Volume 1, Paperbound **$2.00**
T4 Volume 2, Paperbound **$2.00**

**CONCERNING THE NATURE OF THINGS, Sir William Bragg.** Christmas lectures delivered at the Royal Society by Nobel laureate. Why a spinning ball travels in a curved track; how uranium is transmuted to lead, etc. Partial contents: atoms, gases, liquids, crystals, metals, etc. No scientific background needed; wonderful for intelligent child. 32pp. of photos, 57 figures. xii + 232pp. 5⅜ x 8.
T31 Paperbound **$1.35**

**THE UNIVERSE OF LIGHT, Sir William Bragg.** No scientific training needed to read Nobel Prize winner's expansion of his Royal Institute Christmas Lectures. Insight into nature of light, methods and philosophy of science. Explains lenses, reflection, color, resonance, polarization, x-rays, the spectrum, Newton's work with prisms, Huygens' with polarization, Crookes' with cathode ray, etc. Leads into clear statement or 2 major historical theories of light, corpuscle and wave. Dozens of experiments you can do. 199 illus., including 2 full-page color plates. 293pp. 5⅜ x 8.
S538 Paperbound **$1.85**

**FAMOUS PROBLEMS OF ELEMENTARY GEOMETRY, Felix Klein.** Expanded version of the 1894 Easter lectures at Göttingen. 3 problems of classical geometry, in an excellent mathematical treatment by a famous mathematician: squaring the circle, trisecting angle, doubling cube. Considered with full modern implications: transcendental numbers, pi, etc. Notes by R. Archibald. 16 figures. xi + 92pp. 5⅜ x 8. T348 Clothbound **$1.50**
T298 Paperbound **$1.00**

✳        ✳        ✳

**ELEMENTARY MATHEMATICS FROM AN ADVANCED STANDPOINT, Felix Klein.**

This classic text is an outgrowth of Klein's famous integration and survey course at Göttingen. Using one field of mathematics to interpret, adjust, illuminate another, it covers basic topics in each area, illustrating its discussion with extensive analysis. It is especially valuable in considering areas of modern mathematics. "Makes the reader feel the inspiration of . . . a great mathematician, inspiring teacher . . . with deep insight into the foundations and interrelations," BULLETIN, AMERICAN MATHEMATICAL SOCIETY.

**Vol. 1. ARITHMETIC, ALGEBRA, ANALYSIS.** Introducing the concept of function immediately, it enlivens abstract discussion with graphical and geometrically perceptual methods. Partial contents: natural numbers, extension of the notion of number, special properties, complex numbers. Real equations with real unknowns, complex quantities. Logarithmic, exponential functions, goniometric functions, infinitesimal calculus. Transcendence of e and pi, theory of assemblages. Index. 125 figures. ix + 274pp . 5⅜ x 8. S150 Paperbound **$1.75**

**Vol. 2. GEOMETRY.** A comprehensive view which accompanies the space perception inherent in geometry with analytic formulas which facilitate precise formulation. Partial contents: Simplest geometric manifolds: line segment, Grassmann determinant principles, classification of configurations of space, derivative manifolds. Geometric transformations: affine transformations, projective, higher point transformations, theory of the imaginary. Systematic discussion of geometry and its foundations. Indexes. 141 illustrations. ix + 214pp. 5⅜ x 8.
S151 Paperbound **$1.75**

*        *        *

**COORDINATE GEOMETRY, L. P. Eisenhart.** Thorough, unified introduction. Unusual for advancing in dimension within each topic (treats together circle, sphere; polar coordinates, 3-dimensional coordinate systems; conic sections, quadric surfaces), affording exceptional insight into subject. Extensive use made of determinants, though no previous knowledge of them is assumed. Algebraic equations of 1st degree, 2 and 3 unknowns, carried further than usual in algebra courses. Over 500 exercises. Introduction. Appendix. Index. Bibliography. 43 illustrations. 310pp. 5⅜ x 8. S600 Paperbound **$1.65**

**MONOGRAPHS ON TOPICS OF MODERN MATHEMATICS, edited by J. W. A. Young.** Advanced mathematics for persons who haven't gone beyond or have forgotten high school algebra. 9 monographs on foundation of geometry, modern pure geometry, non-Euclidean geometry, fundamental propositions of algebra, algebraic equations, functions, calculus, theory of numbers, etc. Each monograph gives proofs of important results, and descriptions of leading methods, to provide wide coverage. New introduction by Prof. M. Kline, N. Y. University. 100 diagrams. xvi + 416pp. 6⅛ x 9¼. S289 Paperbound **$2.00**

# MATHEMATICS, INTERMEDIATE TO ADVANCED

## Geometry

**THE FOUNDATIONS OF EUCLIDEAN GEOMETRY, H. G. Forder.** The first rigorous account of Euclidean geometry, establishing propositions without recourse to empiricism, and without multiplying hypotheses. Corrects many traditional weaknesses of Euclidean proofs, and investigates the problems imposed on the axiom system by the discoveries of Bolya and Lobatchefsky. Some topics discussed are Classes and Relations; Axioms for Magnitudes; Congruence and Similarity; Algebra of Points; Hessenberg's Theorem; Continuity; Existence of Parallels; Reflections; Rotations; Isometries; etc. Invaluable for the light it throws on foundations of math. Lists: Axioms employed, Symbols, Constructions. 295pp. 5⅜ x 8.
S481 Paperbound **$2.00**

**ADVANCED EUCLIDEAN GEOMETRY, R. A. Johnson.** For years the standard textbook on advanced Euclidean geometry, requires only high school geometry and trigonometry. Explores in unusual detail and gives proofs of hundreds of relatively recent theorems and corollaries, many formerly available only in widely scattered journals. Covers tangent circles, the theorem of Miquel, symmedian point, pedal triangles and circles, the Brocard configuration, and much more. Formerly "Modern Geometry." Index. 107 diagrams. xiii + 319pp. 5⅜ x 8.
S669 Paperbound **$1.65**

**NON-EUCLIDEAN GEOMETRY, Roberto Bonola.** The standard coverage of non-Euclidean geometry. It examines from both a historical and mathematical point of view the geometries which have arisen from a study of Euclid's 5th postulate upon parallel lines. Also included are complete texts, translated, of Bolyai's THEORY OF ABSOLUTE SPACE, Lobachevsky's THEORY OF PARALLELS. 180 diagrams. 431pp. 5⅜ x 8.                  S27 Paperbound **$1.95**

**ELEMENTS OF NON-EUCLIDEAN GEOMETRY, D. M. Y. Sommerville.** Unique in proceeding step-by-step, in the manner of traditional geometry. Enables the student with only a good knowledge of high school algebra and geometry to grasp elementary hyperbolic, elliptic, analytic non-Euclidean geometries; space curvature and its philosophical implications; theory of radical axes; homothetic centres and systems of circles; parataxy and parallelism; absolute measure; Gauss' proof of the defect area theorem; geodesic representation; much more, all with exceptional clarity. 126 problems at chapter endings provide progressive practice and familiarity. 133 figures. Index. xvi + 274pp. 5⅜ x 8.      S460 Paperbound **$1.50**

**HIGHER GEOMETRY: AN INTRODUCTION TO ADVANCED METHODS IN ANALYTIC GEOMETRY, F. S. Woods.** Exceptionally thorough study of concepts and methods of advanced algebraic geometry (as distinguished from differential geometry). Exhaustive treatment of 1-, 2-, 3-, and 4-dimensional coordinate systems, leading to n-dimensional geometry in an abstract sense. Covers projectivity, tetracyclical coordinates, contact transformation, pentaspherical coordinates, much more. Based on M.I.T. lectures, requires sound preparation in analytic geometry and some knowledge of determinants. Index. Over 350 exercises. References. 60 figures. x + 423pp. 5⅜ x 8.                         S737 Paperbound **$2.00**

**ELEMENTS OF PROJECTIVE GEOMETRY, L. Cremona.** Outstanding complete treatment of projective geometry by one of the foremost 19th century geometers. Detailed proofs of all fundamental principles, stress placed on the constructive aspects. Covers homology, law of duality, anharmonic ratios, theorems of Pascal and Brianchon, foci, polar reciprocal figures, etc. Only ordinary geometry necessary to understand this honored classic. Index. Over 150 fully worked out examples and problems. 252 diagrams. xx + 302pp. 5⅜ x 8.      S668 Paperbound **$1.75**

**A TREATISE ON THE DIFFERENTIAL GEOMETRY OF CURVES AND SURFACES, L. P. Eisenhart.** Introductory treatise especially for the graduate student, for years a highly successful textbook. More detailed and concrete in approach than most more recent books. Covers space curves, osculating planes, moving axes, Gauss' method, the moving trihedral, geodesics, conformal representation, etc. Last section deals with deformation of surfaces, rectilinear congruences, cyclic systems, etc. Index. 683 problems. 00 diagrams. vii + 474pp. 5⅜ x 8.
S667 Paperbound **$2.75**

**A TREATISE ON ALGEBRAIC PLANE CURVES, J. L. Coolidge.** Unabridged reprinting of one of few full coverages in English, offering detailed introduction to theory of algebraic plane curves and their relations to geometry and analysis. Treats topological properties, Riemann-Roch theorem, all aspects of wide variety of curves including real, covariant, polar, containing series of a given sort, elliptic, polygonal, rational, the pencil, two parameter nets, etc. This volume will enable the reader to appreciate the symbolic notation of Aronhold and Clebsch. Bibliography. Index. 17 illustrations. xxiv + 513pp. 5⅜ x 8.      S543 Paperbound **$2.45**

**AN INTRODUCTION TO THE GEOMETRY OF N DIMENSIONS, D. M. Y. Sommerville.** An introduction presupposing no prior knowledge of the field, the only book in English devoted exclusively to higher dimensional geometry. Discusses fundamental ideas of incidence, parallelism, perpendicularity, angles between linear space; enumerative geometry; analytical geometry from projective and metric points of view; polytopes; elementary ideas in analysis situs; content of hyper-spacial figures. Bibliography. Index. 60 diagrams. 196pp. 5⅜ x 8.
S494 Paperbound **$1.50**

**GEOMETRY OF FOUR DIMENSIONS, H. P. Manning.** Unique in English as a clear, concise introduction. Treatment is synthetic, and mostly Euclidean, although in hyperplanes and hyperspheres at infinity, non-Euclidean geometry is used. Historical introduction. Foundations of 4-dimensional geometry. Perpendicularity, simple angles. Angles of planes, higher order. Symmetry, order, motion; hyperpyramids, hypercones, hyperspheres; figures with parallel elements; volume, hypervolume in space; regular polyhedroids. Glossary. 78 figures. ix + 348pp. 5⅜ x 8.                          S182 Paperbound **$1.95**

**ELEMENTARY CONCEPTS OF TOPOLOGY, P. Alexandroff.** First English translation of the famous brief introduction to topology for the beginner or for the mathematician not undertaking extensive study. This unusually useful intuitive approach deals primarily with the concepts of complex, cycle, and homology, and is wholly consistent with current investigations. Ranges from basic concepts of set-theoretic topology to the concept of Betti groups. "Glowing example of harmony between intuition and thought," David Hilbert. Translated by A. E. Farley. Introduction by D. Hilbert. Index. 25 figures. 73pp. 5⅜ x 8.      S747 Paperbound **$1.00**

**THE WORKS OF ARCHIMEDES, edited by T. L. Heath.** All the known works of the great Greek mathematician are contained in this one volume, including the recently discovered Method of Archimedes. Contains: On Sphere & Cylinder, Measurement of a Circle, Spirals, Conoids, Spheroids, etc. This is the definitive edition of the greatest mathematical intellect of the ancient world. 186-page study by Heath discusses Archimedes and the history of Greek mathematics. Bibliography. 563pp. 5⅜ x 8.                  S9 Paperbound **$2.00**

**THE THIRTEEN BOOKS OF EUCLID'S ELEMENTS,** edited by **Sir Thomas Heath.** Definitive edition of one of the very greatest classics of Western world. Complete English translation of Heiberg text, together with spurious Book XIV. Detailed 150-page introduction discussing aspects of Greek and Medieval mathematics. Euclid, texts, commentators, etc. Paralleling the text is an elaborate critical apparatus analyzing each definition, proposition, postulate, covering textual matters, mathematical analysis, commentators of all times, refutations, supports, extrapolations, etc. This is the FULL EUCLID. Unabridged reproduction of Cambridge U. 2nd edition. 3 volumes. Total of 995 figures, 1426pp. 5⅜ x 8.
S88,89,90, 3 volume set, paperbound **$6.00**

**THE GEOMETRY OF RENE DESCARTES.** With this book Descartes founded analytical geometry. Excellent Smith-Latham translation, plus original French text with Déscartes' own diagrams. Contains Problems the Construction of Which Requires Only Straight Lines and Circles; On the Nature of Curved Lines; On the Construction of Solid or Supersolid Problems. Notes. Diagrams. 258pp. 5⅜ x 8.
S68 Paperbound **$1.50**

See also: **FOUNDATIONS OF GEOMETRY, B. Russell; THE PHILOSOPHY OF SPACE AND TIME, H. Reichenbach; FAMOUS PROBLEMS OF ELEMENTARY GEOMETRY, F. Klein; MONOGRAPHS ON TOPICS OF MODERN MATHEMATICS, ed. by J. W. Young.**

# Calculus and function theory, Fourier theory, real and complex functions, determinants

**A COLLECTION OF MODERN MATHEMATICAL CLASSICS,** edited by **R. Bellman.** 13 classic papers, complete in their original languages, by Hermite, Hardy and Littlewood, Tchebychef, Fejér, Fredholm, Fuchs, Hurwitz, Weyl, van der Pol, Birkhoff, Kellogg, von Neumann, and Hilbert. Each of these papers, collected here for the first time, triggered a burst of mathematical activity, providing useful new generalizations or stimulating fresh investigations. Topics discussed include classical analysis, periodic and almost periodic functions, analysis and number theory, integral equations, theory of approximation, non-linear differential equations, and functional analysis. Brief introductions and bibliographies to each paper. xii + 292pp. 6 x 9.
S730 Paperbound **$2.00**

**MATHEMATICS OF MODERN ENGINEERING, E. G. Keller** and **R. E. Doherty.** Written for the Advanced Course in Engineering of the General Electric Corporation, deals with the engineering use of determinants, tensors, the Heaviside operational calculus, dyadics, the calculus of variations, etc. Presents underlying principles fully, but purpose is to teach engineers to deal with modern engineering problems, and emphasis is on the perennial engineering attack of set-up and solve. Indexes. Over 185 figures and tables. Hundreds of exercises, problems, and worked-out examples. References. Two volume set. Total of xxxiii + 623pp. 5⅜ x 8.
S734 Vol I Paperbound **$1.65**
S735 Vol II Paperbound **$1.65**
The set **$3.30**

**MATHEMATICAL METHODS FOR SCIENTISTS AND ENGINEERS, L. P. Smith.** For scientists and engineers, as well as advanced math students. Full investigation of methods and practical description of conditions under which each should be used. Elements of real functions, differential and integral calculus, space geometry, theory of residues, vector and tensor analysis, series of Bessel functions, etc. Each method illustrated by completely-worked-out examples, mostly from scientific literature. 368 graded unsolved problems. 100 diagrams. x + 453pp. 5⅝ x 8⅜.
S220 Paperbound **$2.00**

**THEORY OF FUNCTIONS AS APPLIED TO ENGINEERING PROBLEMS,** edited by **R. Rothe, F. Ollendorff,** and **K. Pohlhausen.** A series of lectures given at the Berlin Institute of Technology that shows the specific applications of function theory in electrical and allied fields of engineering. Six lectures provide the elements of function theory in a simple and practical form, covering complex quantities and variables, integration in the complex plane, residue theorems, etc. Then 5 lectures show the exact uses of this powerful mathematical tool, with full discussions of problem methods. Index. Bibliography. 108 figures. x + 189pp. 5⅜ x 8.
S733 Paperbound **$1.35**

**ADVANCED CALCULUS, E. B. Wilson.** An unabridged reprinting of the work which continues to be recognized as one of the most comprehensive and useful texts in the field. It contains an immense amount of well-presented, fundamental material, including chapters on vector functions, ordinary differential equations, special functions, calculus of variations, etc., which are excellent introductions to these areas. For students with only one year of calculus, more than 1300 exercises cover both pure math and applications to engineering and physical problems. For engineers, physicists, etc., this work, with its 54 page introductory review, is the ideal reference and refresher. Index. ix + 566pp. 5⅜ x 8.
S504 Paperbound **$2.45**

**CALCULUS OF VARIATIONS, A. R. Forsyth.** Methods, solutions, rather than determination of weakest valid hypotheses. Over 150 examples completely worked-out show use of Euler, Legendre, Jacoby, Weierstrass tests for maxima, minima. Integrals with one original dependent variable; with derivatives of 2nd order; two dependent variables, one independent variable; double integrals involving 1 dependent variable, 2 first derivatives; double integrals involving partial derivatives of 2nd order; triple integrals; much more. 50 diagrams. 678pp. 5⅝ x 8⅜.                                                              S622 Paperbound **$2.95**

**LECTURES ON THE CALCULUS OF VARIATIONS, O. Bolza.** Analyzes in detail the fundamental concepts of the calculus of variations, as developed from Euler to Hilbert, with sharp formulations of the problems and rigorous demonstrations of their solutions. More than a score of solved examples; systematic references for each theorem. Covers the necessary and sufficient conditions; the contributions made by Euler, Du Bois Reymond, Hilbert, Weierstrass, Legendre, Jacobi, Erdmann, Kneser, and Gauss; and much more. Index. Bibliography. xi + 271pp. 5⅜ x 8.                                                            S218 Paperbound **$**

**A TREATISE ON THE CALCULUS OF FINITE DIFFERENCES, G. Boole.** A classic in the literature of the calculus. Thorough, clear discussion of basic principles, theorems, methods. Covers MacLaurin's and Herschel's theorems, mechanical quadrature, factorials, periodical constants, Bernoulli's numbers, difference-equations (linear, mixed, and partial), etc. Stresses analogies with differential calculus. 236 problems, answers to the numerical ones. viii + 336pp. 5⅜ x 8.                                                            S695 Paperbound **$1.85**

**THE ANALYTICAL THEORY OF HEAT, Joseph Fourier.** This book, which revolutionized mathematical physics, is listed in the Great Books program, and many other listings of great books. It has been used with profit by generations of mathematicians and physicists who are interested in either heat or in the application of the Fourier integral. Covers cause and reflection of rays of heat, radiant heating, heating of closed spaces, use of trigonometric series in the theory of heat, Fourier integral, etc. Translated by Alexander Freeman. 20 figures. xxii + 466pp. 5⅜ x 8.                                           S93 Paperbound **$2.00**

**AN INTRODUCTION TO FOURIER METHODS AND THE LAPLACE TRANSFORMATION, Philip Franklin.** Concentrates upon essentials, enabling the reader with only a working knowledge of calculus to gain an understanding of Fourier methods in a broad sense, suitable for most applications. This work covers complex qualities with methods of computing elementary functions for complex values of the argument and finding approximations by the use of charts; Fourier series and integrals with half-range and complex Fourier series; harmonic analysis; Fourier and Laplace transformations, etc.; partial differential equations with applications to transmission of electricity; etc. The methods developed are related to physical problems of heat flow, vibrations, electrical transmission, electromagnetic radiation, etc. 828 problems with answers. Formerly entitled "Fourier Methods." Bibliography. Index. x + 289pp. 5⅜ x 8.
                                                                   S452 Paperbound **$1.75**

**THE FOURIER INTEGRAL AND CERTAIN OF ITS APPLICATIONS, Norbert Wiener.** The only book-length study of the Fourier integral as link between pure and applied math. An expansion of lectures given at Cambridge. Partial contents: Plancherel's theorem, general Tauberian theorem, special Tauberian theorems, generalized harmonic analysis. Bibliography. viii + 201pp. 5⅜ x 8.                                                        S272 Paperbound **$1.50**

**INTRODUCTION TO THE THEORY OF FOURIER'S SERIES AND INTEGRALS, H. S. Carslaw.** 3rd revised edition. This excellent introduction is an outgrowth of the author's courses at Cambridge. Historical introduction, rational and irrational numbers, infinite sequences and series, functions of a single variable, definite integral, Fourier series, Fourier integrals, and similar topics. Appendixes discuss practical harmonic analysis, periodogram analysis, Lebesgues theory. Indexes. 84 examples, bibliography. xiii + 368pp. 5⅜ x 8.      S48 Paperbound **$2.00**

**FOURIER'S SERIES AND SPHERICAL HARMONICS, W. E. Byerly.** Continues to be recognized as one of most practical, useful expositions. Functions, series, and their differential equations are concretely explained in great detail; theory is applied constantly to practical problems, which are fully and lucidly worked out. Appendix includes 6 tables of surface zonal harmonics, hyperbolic functions, Bessel's functions. Bibliography. 190 problems, approximately half with answers. ix + 287pp. 5⅜ x 8.                               S536 Paperbound **$1.75**

**ASYMPTOTIC EXPANSIONS, A. Erdélyi.** The only modern work available in English, this is an unabridged reproduction of a monograph prepared for the Office of Naval Research. It discusses various procedures for asymptotic evaluation of integrals containing a large parameter and solutions of ordinary linear differential equations. Bibliography of 71 items. vi + 108pp. 5⅜ x 8.                                                             S318 Paperbound **$1.35**

**LINEAR INTEGRAL EQUATIONS, W. V. Lovitt.** Systematic survey of general theory, with some application to differential equations, calculus of variations, problems of math, physics. Partial contents: integral equation of 2nd kind by successive substitutions; Fredholm's equation as ratio of 2 integral series in lambda, applications of the Fredholm theory, Hilbert-Schmidt theory of symmetric kernels, application, etc. Neumann, Dirichlet, vibratory problems. Index. ix + 253pp. 5⅜ x 8.                                       S175 Clothbound **$3.50**
                                                                   S176 Paperbound **$1.60**

**ELLIPTIC INTEGRALS, H. Hancock.** Invaluable in work involving differential equations containing cubics or quartics under the root sign, where elementary calculus methods are inadequate. Practical solutions to problems that occur in mathematics, engineering, physics: differential equations requiring integration of Lamé's, Briot's, or Bouquet's equations; determination of arc of ellipse, hyperbola, lemiscate; solutions of problems in elastica; motion of a projectile under resistance varying as the cube of the velocity; pendulums; many others. Exposition is in accordance with Legendre-Jacobi theory and includes rigorous discussion of Legendre transformations. 20 figures. 5 place table. Index. 104pp. 5⅛ x 8.
S484 Paperbound **$1.25**

## FIVE VOLUME "THEORY OF FUNCTIONS" SET BY KONRAD KNOPP

This five-volume set, prepared by Konrad Knopp, provides a complete and readily followed account of theory of functions. Proofs are given concisely, yet without sacrifice of completeness or rigor. These volumes are used as texts by such universities as M.I.T., University of Chicago, N. Y. City College, and many others. "Excellent introduction . . . remarkably readable, concise, clear, rigorous," JOURNAL OF THE AMERICAN STATISTICAL ASSOCIATION.

**ELEMENTS OF THE THEORY OF FUNCTIONS, Konrad Knopp.** This book provides the student with background for further volumes in this set, or texts on a similar level. Partial contents: foundations, system of complex numbers and the Gaussian plane of numbers, Riemann sphere of numbers, mapping by linear functions, normal forms, the logarithm, the cyclometric functions and binomial series. "Not only for the young student, but also for the student who knows all about what is in it," MATHEMATICAL JOURNAL. Bibliography. Index. 140pp. 5⅜ x 8.
S154 Paperbound **$1.35**

**THEORY OF FUNCTIONS, PART I, Konrad Knopp.** With volume II, this book provides coverage of basic concepts and theorems. Partial contents: numbers and points, functions of a complex variable, integral of a continuous function, Cauchy's integral theorem, Cauchy's integral formulae, series with variable terms, expansion of analytic functions in power series, analytic continuation and complete definition of analytic functions, entire transcendental functions, Laurent expansion, types of singularities. Bibliography. Index. vii + 146pp. 5⅜ x 8.
S156 Paperbound **$1.35**

**THEORY OF FUNCTIONS, PART II, Konrad Knopp.** Application and further development of general theory, special topics. Single valued functions, entire, Weierstrass, Meromorphic functions. Riemann surfaces. Algebraic functions. Analytical configuration, Riemann surface. Bibliography. Index. x + 150pp. 5⅜ x 8.
S157 Paperbound **$1.35**

**PROBLEM BOOK IN THE THEORY OF FUNCTIONS, VOLUME 1, Konrad Knopp.** Problems in elementary theory, for use with Knopp's THEORY OF FUNCTIONS, or any other text, arranged according to increasing difficulty. Fundamental concepts, sequences of numbers and infinite series, complex variable, integral theorems, development in series, conformal mapping. 182 problems. Answers. viii + 126pp. 5⅜ x 8.
S158 Paperbound **$1.35**

**PROBLEM BOOK IN THE THEORY OF FUNCTIONS, VOLUME 2, Konrad Knopp.** Advanced theory of functions, to be used either with Knopp's THEORY OF FUNCTIONS, or any other comparable text. Singularities, entire & meromorphic functions, periodic, analytic, continuation, multiple-valued functions, Riemann surfaces, conformal mapping. Includes a section of additional elementary problems. "The difficult task of selecting from the immense material of the modern theory of functions the problems just within the reach of the beginner is here masterfully accomplished," AM. MATH. SOC. Answers. 138pp. 5⅜ x 8. S159 Paperbound **$1.35**

\* \* \*

**LECTURES ON THE THEORY OF ELLIPTIC FUNCTIONS, H. Hancock.** Reissue of the only book in English with so extensive a coverage, especially of Abel, Jacobi, Legendre, Weierstrasse, Hermite, Liouville, and Riemann. Unusual fullness of treatment, plus applications as well as theory, in discussing elliptic function (the universe of elliptic integrals originating in works of Abel and Jacobi), their existence, and ultimate meaning. Use is made of Riemann to provide the most general theory. 40 page table of formulas. 76 figures. xxiii + 498pp.
S483 Paperbound **$2.55**

**THE THEORY AND FUNCTIONS OF A REAL VARIABLE AND THE THEORY OF FOURIER'S SERIES, E. W. Hobson.** One of the best introductions to set theory and various aspects of functions and Fourier's series. Requires only a good background in calculus. Provides an exhaustive coverage of: metric and descriptive properties of sets of points; transfinite numbers and order types; functions of a real variable; the Riemann and Lebesgue integrals; sequences and series of numbers; power-series; functions representable by series sequences of continuous functions; trigonometrical series; representation of functions by Fourier's series; complete exposition (200pp.) on set theory; and much more. "The best possible guide," Nature. Vol. I: 88 detailed examples, 10 figures. Index. xv + 736pp. Vol. II: 117 detailed examples, 13 figures. Index. x + 780pp. 6⅛ x 9¼.
Vol. I: S387 Paperbound **$3.00**
Vol. II: S388 Paperbound **$3.00**

**ALMOST PERIODIC FUNCTIONS, A. S. Besicovitch.** This unique and important summary by a well-known mathematician covers in detail the two stages of development in Bohr's theory of almost periodic functions: (1) as a generalization of pure periodicity, with results and proofs; (2) the work done by Stepanoff, Wiener, Weyl, and Bohr in generalizing the theory. Bibliography. xi + 180pp. 5⅜ x 8.
S18 Paperbound **$1.75**

**THEORY OF FUNCTIONALS AND OF INTEGRAL AND INTEGRO-DIFFERENTIAL EQUATIONS, Vito Volterra.** Unabridged republication of the only English translation. An exposition of the general theory of the functions depending on a continuous set of values of another function, based on the author's fundamental notion of the transition from a finite number of variables to a continually infinite number. Though dealing primarily with integral equations, much material on calculus of variations is included. The work makes no assumption of previous knowledge on the part of the reader. It begins with fundamental material and proceeds to Generalization of Analytic Functions, Integro-Differential Equations, Functional Derivative Equations, Applications, Other Directions of Theory of Functionals, etc. New introduction by G. C. Evans. Bibliography and criticism of Volterra's work by E. Whittaker. Bibliography. Index of authors cited. Index of subjects. xxxx + 226pp. 5⅜ x 8.       S502 Paperbound **$1.75**

**AN ELEMENTARY TREATISE ON ELLIPTIC FUNCTIONS, A. Cayley.** Still the fullest and clearest text on the theories of Jacobi and Legendre for the advanced student (and an excellent supplement for the beginner). A masterpiece of exposition by the great 19th century British mathematician (creator of the theory of matrices and abstract geometry), it covers the addition-theory, Landen's theorem, the 3 kinds of elliptic integrals, transformations, the q-functions, reduction of a differential expression, and much more. Index. xii + 386pp. 5⅜ x 8.
S728 Paperbound **$2.00**

**THE APPLICATIONS OF ELLIPTIC FUNCTIONS, A. G. Greenhill.** Modern books forgo detail for sake of brevity—this book offers complete exposition necessary for proper understanding, use of elliptic integrals. Formulas developed from definite physical, geometric problems; examples representative enough to offer basic information in widely useable form. Elliptic integrals, addition theorem, algebraical form of addition theorem, elliptic integrals of 2nd, 3rd kind, double periodicity, resolution into factors, series, transformation, etc. Introduction. Index. 25 illus. xi + 357pp. 5⅜ x 8.       S603 Paperbound **$1.75**

**THE THEORY OF FUNCTIONS OF REAL VARIABLES, James Pierpont.** A 2-volume authoritative exposition, by one of the foremost mathematicians of his time. Each theorem stated with all conditions, then followed by proof. No need to go through complicated reasoning to discover conditions added without specific mention. Includes a particularly complete, rigorous presentation of theory of measure; and Pierpont's own work on a theory of Lebesgue integrals, and treatment of area of a curved surface. Partial contents, Vol. 1: rational numbers, exponentials, logarithms, point aggregates, maxima, minima, proper integrals, improper integrals, multiple proper integrals, continuity, discontinuity, indeterminate forms. Vol. 2: point sets, proper integrals, series, power series, aggregates, ordinal numbers, discontinuous functions, sub-, infra-uniform convergence, much more. Index. 95 illustrations. 1229pp. 5⅜ x 8.       S558-9, 2 volume set, paperbound **$4.90**

**FUNCTIONS OF A COMPLEX VARIABLE, James Pierpont.** Long one of best in the field. A thorough treatment of fundamental elements, concepts, theorems. A complete study, rigorous, detailed, with carefully selected problems worked out to illustrate each topic. Partial contents: arithmetical operations, real term series, positive term series, exponential functions, integration, analytic functions, asymptotic expansions, functions of Weierstrass, Legendre, etc. Index. List of symbols. 122 illus. 597pp. 5⅜ x 8.       S560 Paperbound **$2.45**

**ELEMENTS OF THE THEORY OF REAL FUNCTIONS, J. E. Littlewood.** Based on lectures given at Trinity College, Cambridge, this book has proved to be extremely successful in introducing graduate students to the modern theory of functions. It offers a full and concise coverage of classes and cardinal numbers, well-ordered series, other types of series, and elements of the theory of sets of points. 3rd revised edition. vii + 71pp. 5⅜ x 8.
S171 Clothbound **$2.85**
S172 Paperbound **$1.25**

**TRANSCENDENTAL AND ALGEBRAIC NUMBERS, A. O. Gelfond.** First English translation of work by leading Soviet mathematician. Thue-Siegel theorem, its p-adic analogue, on approximation of algebraic numbers by numbers in fixed algebraic field; Hermite-Lindemann theorem on transcendency of Bessel functions, solutions of other differential equations; Gelfond-Schneider theorem on transcendency of alpha to power beta; Schneider's work on elliptic functions, with method developed by Gelfond. Translated by L. F. Boron. Index. Bibliography. 200pp. 5⅜ x 8.       S615 Paperbound **$1.75**

**THEORY OF MAXIMA AND MINIMA, H. Hancock.** Fullest treatment ever written; only work in English with extended discussion of maxima and minima for functions of 1, 2, or n variables, problems with subsidiary constraints, and relevant quadratic forms. Detailed proof of each important theorem. Covers the Scheeffer and von Dantscher theories, homogeneous quadratic forms, reversion of series, fallacious establishment of maxima and minima, etc. Unsurpassed treatise for advanced students of calculus, mathematicians, economists, statisticians. Index. 24 diagrams. 39 problems, many examples. 193pp. 5⅜ x 8.       S665 Paperbound **$1.50**

**DICTIONARY OF CONFORMAL REPRESENTATIONS, H. Kober.** Laplace's equation in 2 dimensions solved in this unique book developed by the British Admiralty. Scores of geometrical forms & their transformations for electrical engineers, Joukowski aerofoil for aerodynamists. Schwartz-Christoffel transformations for hydrodynamics, transcendental functions. Contents classified according to analytical functions describing transformation. Twin diagrams show curves of most transformations with corresponding regions. Glossary. Topological index. 447 diagrams. 244pp. 6⅛ x 9¼.       S160 Paperbound **$2.00**

**THE TAYLOR SERIES, AN INTRODUCTION TO THE THEORY OF FUNCTIONS OF A COMPLEX VARIABLE, P. Dienes.** This book investigates the entire realm of analytic functions. Only ordinary calculus is needed, except in the last two chapters. Starting with an introduction to real variables and complex algebra, the properties of infinite series, elementary functions, complex differentiation and integration are carefully derived. Also biuniform mapping, a thorough two part discussion of representation and singularities of analytic functions, overconvergence and gap theorems, divergent series, Taylor series on its circle of convergence, divergence and singularities, etc. Unabridged, corrected reissue of first edition. Preface and index. 186 examples, many fully worked out. 67 figures. xii + 555pp. 5⅜ x 8.
S391 Paperbound **$2.75**

**INTRODUCTION TO BESSEL FUNCTIONS, Frank Bowman.** A rigorous self-contained exposition providing all necessary material during the development, which requires only some knowledge of calculus and acquaintance with differential equations. A balanced presentation including applications and practical use. Discusses Bessel Functions of Zero Order, of Any Real Order; Modified Bessel Functions of Zero Order; Definite Integrals; Asymptotic Expansions; Bessel's Solution to Kepler's Problem; Circular Membranes; much more. "Clear and straightforward . . . useful not only to students of physics and engineering, but to mathematical students in general," Nature. 226 problems. Short tables of Bessel functions. 27 figures. Index. x + 135pp. 5⅜ x 8.
S462 Paperbound **$1.35**

**MODERN THEORIES OF INTEGRATION, H. Kestelman.** Connected and concrete coverage, with fully-worked-out proofs for every step. Ranges from elementary definitions through theory of aggregates, sets of points, Riemann and Lebesgue integration, and much more. This new revised and enlarged edition contains a new chapter on Riemann-Stieltjes integration, as well as a supplementary section of 186 exercises. Ideal for the mathematician, student, teacher, or self-studier. Index of Definitions and Symbols. General Index. Bibliography. x + 310pp. 5⅜ x 8⅜.
S572 Paperbound **$2.00**

**A TREATISE ON THE THEORY OF DETERMINANTS, T. Muir.** Unequalled as an exhaustive compilation of nearly all the known facts about determinants up to the early 1930's. Covers notation and general properties, row and column transformation, symmetry, compound determinants, adjugates, rectangular arrays and matrices, linear dependence, gradients, Jacobians, Hessians, Wronskians, and much more. Invaluable for libraries of industrial and research organizations as well as for student, teacher, and mathematician; very useful in the field of computing machines. Revised and enlarged by W. H. Metzler. Index. 485 problems and scores of numerical examples. iv + 766pp. 5⅜ x 8.
S670 Paperbound **$2.95**

**THEORY OF DETERMINANTS IN THE HISTORICAL ORDER OF DEVELOPMENT, Sir Thomas Muir.** Unabridged reprinting of this complete study of 1,859 papers on determinant theory written between 1693 and 1900. Most important and original sections reproduced, valuable commentary on each. No other work is necessary for determinant research: all types are covered—each subdivision of the theory treated separately; all papers dealing with each type are covered; you are told exactly what each paper is about and how important its contribution is. Each result, theory, extension, or modification is assigned its own identifying numeral so that the full history may be more easily followed. Includes papers on determinants in general, determinants and linear equations, symmetric determinants, alternants, recurrents, determinants having invariant factors, and all other major types. "A model of what such histories ought to be," NATURE. "Mathematicians must ever be grateful to Sir Thomas for his monumental work," AMERICAN MATH MONTHLY. Four volumes bound as two. Indices. Bibliographies. Total of lxxxiv + 1977pp. 5⅜ x 8.
S672-3 The set, Clothbound **$10.00**

**A COURSE IN MATHEMATICAL ANALYSIS, Edouard Goursat. Trans. by E. R. Hedrick, O. Dunkel.** Classic study of fundamental material thoroughly treated. Exceptionally lucid exposition of wide range of subject matter for student with 1 year of calculus. Vol. 1: Derivatives and Differentials, Definite Integrals, Expansion in Series, Applications to Geometry. Problems. Index. 52 illus. 556pp. Vol. 2, Part I: Functions of a Complex Variable, Conformal Representations, Doubly Periodic Functions, Natural Boundaries, etc. Problems. Index. 38 illus. 269pp. Vol. 2, Part 2: Differential Equations, Cauchy-Lipschitz Method, Non-linear Differential Equations, Simultaneous Equations, etc. Problems. Index. 308pp. 5⅜ x 8.
Vol. 1 S554 Paperbound **$2.25**
Vol. 2 part 1 S555 Paperbound **$1.65**
Vol. 2 part 2 S556 Paperbound **$1.65**
3 vol. set **$5.00**

**INFINITE SEQUENCES AND SERIES, Konrad Knopp.** First publication in any language! Excellent introduction to 2 topics of modern mathematics, designed to give the student background to penetrate farther by himself. Sequences & sets, real & complex numbers, etc. Functions of a real & complex variable. Sequences & series. Infinite series. Convergent power series. Expansion of elementary functions. Numerical evaluation of series. Bibliography. v + 186pp. 5⅜ x 8.
S152 Clothbound **$3.50**
S153 Paperbound **$1.75**

**TRIGONOMETRICAL SERIES, Antoni Zygmund.** Unique in any language on modern advanced level. Contains carefully organized analyses of trigonometric, orthogonal, Fourier systems of functions, with clear adequate descriptions of summability of Fourier series, proximation theory, conjugate series, convergence, divergence of Fourier series. Especially valuable for Russian, Eastern European coverage. Bibliography. 329pp. 5⅜ x 8.
S290 Paperbound **$1.50**

**COLLECTED WORKS OF BERNHARD RIEMANN.** This important source book is the first to contain the complete text of both 1892 Werke and the 1902 supplement, unabridged. It contains 31 monographs, 3 complete lecture courses, 15 miscellaneous papers, which have been of enormous importance in relativity, topology, theory of complex variables, and other areas of mathematics. Edited by R. Dedekind, H. Weber, M. Noether, W. Wirtinger. German text. English introduction by Hans Lewy. 690pp. 5⅜ x 8.                                      S226 Paperbound **$2.85**

See also: **A HISTORY OF THE CALCULUS, C. B. Boyer; CALCULUS REFRESHER FOR TECHNICAL MEN, A. A. Klaf; MONOGRAPHS ON TOPICS OF MODERN MATHEMATICS, ed. by J. W. A. Young; THE CONTINUUM AND OTHER TYPES OF SERIAL ORDER, E. V. Huntington.**

## Symbolic logic

**AN INTRODUCTION TO SYMBOLIC LOGIC, Susanne K. Langer.** Probably the clearest book ever written on symbolic logic for the philosopher, general scientist and layman. It will be particularly appreciated by those who have been rebuffed by other introductory works because of insufficient mathematical training. No special knowledge of mathematics is required. Starting with the simplest symbols and conventions, you are led to a remarkable grasp of the Boole-Schroeder and Russell-Whitehead systems clearly and quickly. PARTIAL CONTENTS: Study of forms, Essentials of logical structure, Generalization, Classes, The deductive system of classes, The algebra of logic, Abstraction of interpretation, Calculus of propositions, Assumptions of PRINCIPIA MATHEMATICA, Logistics, Logic of the syllogism, Proofs of theorems. "One of the clearest and simplest introductions to a subject which is very much alive. The style is easy, symbolism is introduced gradually, and the intelligent non-mathematician should have no difficulty in following the argument," MATHEMATICS GAZETTE. Revised, expanded second edition. Truth-value tables. 368pp. 5⅜ x 8.
                                      S164 Paperbound **$1.75**

**THE ELEMENTS OF MATHEMATICAL LOGIC, Paul Rosenbloom.** First publication in any language. This book is intended for readers who are mature mathematically, but have no previous training in symbolic logic. It does not limit itself to a single system, but covers the field as a whole. It is a development of lectures given at Lund University, Sweden, in 1948. Partial contents: Logic of classes, fundamental theorems, Boolean algebra, logic of propositions, logic of propositional functions, expressive languages, combinatory logics, development of mathematics within an object language, paradoxes, theorems of Post and Goedel, Church's theorem, and similar topics. iv + 214pp. 5⅜ x 8.        S227 Paperbound **$1.45**

**A SURVEY OF SYMBOLIC LOGIC: THE CLASSIC ALGEBRA OF LOGIC, C. I. Lewis.** Classic survey of the field, comprehensive and thorough. Indicates content of major systems, alternative methods of procedure, and relation of these to the Boole-Schroeder algebra and to one another. Contains historical summary, as well as full proofs and applications of the classic, or Boole-Schroeder, algebra of logic. Discusses diagrams for the logical relations of classes, the two-valued algebra, propositional functions of two or more variables, etc. Chapters 5 and 6 of the original edition, which contained material not directly pertinent, have been omitted in this edition at the author's request. Appendix. Bibliography. Index. viii + 352pp. 5⅝ x 8⅜.
                                      S643 Paperbound **$2.00**

**INTRODUCTION TO SYMBOLIC LOGIC AND ITS APPLICATIONS, R. Carnap.** One of the clearest, most comprehensive, and rigorous introductions to modern symbolic logic by perhaps its greatest living master. Symbolic languages are analyzed and one constructed. Applications to math (symbolic representation of axiom systems for set theory, natural numbers, real numbers, topology, Dedekind and Cantor explanations of continuity), physics (the general analysis of concepts of determination, causality, space-time-topology, based on Einstein), biology (symbolic representation of an axiom system for basic concepts). "A masterpiece," Zentralblatt für Mathematik und ihre Grenzgebiete. Over 300 exercises. 5 figures. Bibliography. Index. xvi + 241pp. 5⅜ x 8.                       S453 Paperbound **$1.85**
                                      Clothbound **$4.00**

**SYMBOLIC LOGIC, C. I. Lewis, C. H. Langford.** Probably the most cited book in symbolic logic, this is one of the fullest treatments of paradoxes. A wide coverage of the entire field of symbolic logic, plus considerable material that has not appeared elsewhere. Basic to the entire volume is the distinction between the logic of extensions and of intensions. Considerable emphasis is placed on converse substitution, while the matrix system presents the supposition of a variety of non-Aristotelian logics. It has especially valuable sections on strict limitations, existence of terms, 2-valued algebra and its extension to propositional functions, truth value systems, the matrix method, implication and deductibility, general theory of propositions, propositions of ordinary discourse, and similar topics. "Authoritative, most valuable," TIMES, London. Bibliography. 506pp. 5⅜ x 8.        S170 Paperbound **$2.00**

**THE LAWS OF THOUGHT, George Boole.** This book founded symbolic logic some hundred years ago. It is the 1st significant attempt to apply logic to all aspects of human endeavour. Partial contents: derivation of laws, signs & laws, interpretations, eliminations, conditions of a perfect method, analysis, Aristotelian logic, probability, and similar topics. xviii + 424pp. 5⅜ x 8.                                            S28 Paperbound **$2.00**

**THE PRINCIPLES OF SCIENCE, A TREATISE ON LOGIC AND THE SCIENTIFIC METHOD, W. S. Jevons.** Treating such topics as Inductive and Deductive Logic, the Theory of Number, Probability, and the Limits of Scientific Method, this milestone in the development of symbolic logic remains a stimulating contribution to the investigation of inferential validity in the natural and social sciences. It significantly advances Boole's logic, and contains a detailed introduction to the nature and methods of probability in physics, astronomy, everyday affairs, etc. In his introduction, Ernest Nagel of Columbia University says, "[Jevons] continues to be of interest as an attempt to articulate the logic of scientific inquiry." Index. liii + 786pp. 5⅜ x 8.                                    S446 Paperbound **$2.98**

## Group theory, algebra, sets

**LECTURES ON THE ICOSAHEDRON AND THE SOLUTION OF EQUATIONS OF THE FIFTH DEGREE, Felix Klein.** The solution of quintics in terms of rotation of a regular icosahedron around its axes of symmetry. A classic & indispensable source for those interested in higher algebra, geometry, crystallography. Considerable explanatory material included. 230 footnotes, mostly bibliographic. 2nd edition. xvi + 289pp. 5⅜ x 8.                         S314 Paperbound **$1.85**

**LINEAR GROUPS, WITH AN EXPOSITION OF THE GALOIS FIELD THEORY, L. E. Dickson.** The classic exposition of the theory of groups, well within the range of the graduate student. Part I contains the most extensive and thorough presentation of the theory of Galois Fields available, with a wealth of examples and theorems. Part II is a full discussion of linear groups of finite order. Much material in this work is based on Dickson's own contributions. Also includes expositions of Jordan, Lie, Abel, Betti-Mathieu, Hermite, etc. "A milestone in the development of modern algebra," W. Magnus, in his historical introduction to this edition. Index. xv + 312pp. 5⅜ x 8.                                   S482 Paperbound **$1.95**

**INTRODUCTION TO THE THEORY OF GROUPS OF FINITE ORDER, R. Carmichael.** Examines fundamental theorems and their application. Beginning with sets, systems, permutations, etc., it progresses in easy stages through important types of groups: Abelian, prime power, permutation, etc. Except 1 chapter where matrices are desirable, no higher math needed. 783 exercises, problems. Index. xvi + 447pp. 5⅜ x 8.              S299 Clothbound **$3.95**
                                                              S300 Paperbound **$2.00**

**THEORY OF GROUPS OF FINITE ORDER, W. Burnside.** First published some 40 years ago, this is still one of the clearest introductory texts. Partial contents: permutations, groups independent of representation, composition series of a group, isomorphism of a group with itself, Abelian groups, prime power groups, permutation groups, invariants of groups of linear substitution graphical representation, etc. 45pp. of notes. Indexes. xxiv + 512pp. 5⅜ x 8.
                                                              S38 Paperbound **$2.45**

**THEORY AND APPLICATIONS OF FINITE GROUPS, G. A. Miller, H. F. Blichfeldt, L. E. Dickson.** Unusually accurate and authoritative work, each section prepared by a leading specialist: Miller on substitution and abstract groups, Blichfeldt on finite groups of linear homogeneous transformations, Dickson on applications of finite groups. Unlike more modern works, this gives the concrete basis from which abstract group theory arose. Includes Abelian groups, prime-power groups, isomorphisms, matrix forms of linear transformations, Sylow groups, Galois' theory of algebraic equations, duplication of a cube, trisection of an angle, etc. 2 Indexes. 267 problems. xvii + 390pp. 5⅜ x 8.                               S216 Paperbound **$2.00**

**CONTINUOUS GROUPS OF TRANSFORMATIONS, L. P. Eisenhart.** Intensive study of the theory and geometrical applications of continuous groups of transformations; a standard work on the subject, called forth by the revolution in physics in the 1920's. Covers tensor analysis, Riemannian geometry, canonical parameters, transitivity, imprimitivity, differential invariants, the algebra of constants of structure, differential geometry, contact transformations, etc. "Likely to remain one of the standard works on the subject for many years . . . principal theorems are proved clearly and concisely, and the arrangement of the whole is coherent," MATHEMATICAL GAZETTE. Index. 72-item bibliography. 185 exercises. ix + 301pp. 5⅜ x 8.
                                                              S781 Paperbound **$1.85**

**THE THEORY OF GROUPS AND QUANTUM MECHANICS, H. Weyl.** Discussions of Schroedinger's wave equation, de Broglie's waves of a particle, Jordan-Hoelder theorem, Lie's continuous groups of transformations, Pauli exclusion principle, quantization of Maxwell-Dirac field equations, etc. Unitary geometry, quantum theory, groups, application of groups to quantum mechanics, symmetry permutation group, algebra of symmetric transformation, etc. 2nd revised edition. Bibliography. Index. xxii + 422pp. 5⅜ x 8.           S268 Clothbound **$4.50**
                                                              S269 Paperbound **$1.95**

**ALGEBRAIC THEORIES, L. E. Dickson.** Best thorough introduction to classical topics in higher algebra develops theories centering around matrices, invariants, groups. Higher algebra, Galois theory, finite linear groups, Klein's icosahedron, algebraic invariants, linear transformations, elementary divisors, invariant factors; quadratic, bi-linear, Hermitian forms, singly and in pairs. Proofs rigorous, detailed; topics developed lucidly, in close connection with their most frequent mathematical applications. Formerly "Modern Algebraic Theories." 155 problems. Bibliography. 2 indexes. 285pp. 5⅜ x 8.             S547 Paperbound **$1.50**

**ALGEBRAS AND THEIR ARITHMETICS, L. E. Dickson.** Provides the foundation and background necessary to any advanced undergraduate or graduate student studying abstract algebra. Begins with elementary introduction to linear transformations, matrices, field of complex numbers; proceeds to order, basal units, modulus, quaternions, etc.; develops calculus of linear sets, describes various examples of algebras including invariant, difference, nilpotent, semi-simple. "Makes the reader marvel at his genius for clear and profound analysis," Amer. Mathematical Monthly. Index. xii + 241pp. 5⅜ x 8.           S616 Paperbound $1.35

**THE THEORY OF EQUATIONS WITH AN INTRODUCTION TO THE THEORY OF BINARY ALGEBRAIC FORMS, W. S. Burnside and A. W. Panton.** Extremely thorough and concrete discussion of the theory of equations, with extensive detailed treatment of many topics curtailed in later texts. Covers theory of algebraic equations, properties of polynomials, symmetric functions, derived functions, Horner's process, complex numbers and the complex variable, determinants and methods of elimination, invariant theory (nearly 100 pages), transformations, introduction to Galois theory, Abelian equations, and much more. Invaluable supplementary work for modern students and teachers. 759 examples and exercises. Index in each volume. Two volume set. Total of xxiv + 604pp. 5⅜ x 8.         S714 Vol I Paperbound $1.85
                                                                     S715 Vol II Paperbound $1.85
                                                                     The set $3.70

**COMPUTATIONAL METHODS OF LINEAR ALGEBRA, V. N. Faddeeva,** translated by **C. D. Benster.** First English translation of a unique and valuable work, the only work in English presenting a systematic exposition of the most important methods of linear algebra—classical and contemporary. Shows in detail how to derive numerical solutions of problems in mathematical physics which are frequently connected with those of linear algebra. Theory as well as individual practice. Part I surveys the mathematical background that is indispensable to what follows. Parts II and III, the conclusion, set forth the most important methods of solution, for both exact and iterative groups. One of the most outstanding and valuable features of this work is the 23 tables, double and triple checked for accuracy. These tables will not be found elsewhere. Author's preface. Translator's note. New bibliography and index. x + 252pp. 5⅜ x 8.              S424 Paperbound $1.95

**ALGEBRAIC EQUATIONS, E. Dehn.** Careful and complete presentation of Galois' theory of algebraic equations; theories of Lagrange and Galois developed in logical rather than historical form, with a more thorough exposition than in most modern books. Many concrete applications and fully-worked-out examples. Discusses basic theory (very clear exposition of the symmetric group); isomorphic, transitive, and Abelian groups; applications of Lagrange's and Galois' theories; and much more. Newly revised by the author. Index. List of Theorems. xi + 208pp. 5⅜ x 8.              S697 Paperbound $1.45

**THEORY OF SETS, E. Kamke.** Clearest, amplest introduction in English, well suited for independent study. Subdivision of main theory, such as theory of sets of points, are discussed, but emphasis is on general theory. Partial contents: rudiments of set theory, arbitrary sets and their cardinal numbers, ordered sets and their order types, well-ordered sets and their cardinal numbers. Bibliography. Key to symbols. Index. vii + 144pp. 5⅜ x 8.
                                                                     S141 Paperbound $1.35

# Number theory

**INTRODUCTION TO THE THEORY OF NUMBERS, L. E. Dickson.** Thorough, comprehensive approach with adequate coverage of classical literature, an introductory volume beginners can follow. Chapters on divisibility, congruences, quadratic residues & reciprocity, Diophantine equations, etc. Full treatment of binary quadratic forms without usual restriction to integral coefficients. Covers infinitude of primes, least residues, Fermat's theorem, Euler's phi function, Legendre's symbol, Gauss's lemma, automorphs, reduced forms, recent theorems of Thue & Siegel, many more. Much material not readily available elsewhere. 239 problems. Index. J figure. viii + 183pp. 5⅜ x 8.              S342 Paperbound $1.65

**ELEMENTS OF NUMBER THEORY, I. M. Vinogradov.** Detailed 1st course for persons without advanced mathematics; 95% of this book can be understood by readers who have gone no farther than high school algebra. Partial contents: divisibility theory, important number theoretical functions, congruences, primitive roots and indices, etc. Solutions to both problems and exercises. Tables of primes, indices, etc. Covers almost every essential formula in elementary number theory! Translated from Russian. 233 problems, 104 exercises. viii + 227pp. 5⅜ x 8.              S259 Paperbound $1.60

**THEORY OF NUMBERS and DIOPHANTINE ANALYSIS, R. D. Carmichael.** These two complete works in one volume form one of the most lucid introductions to number theory, requiring only a firm foundation in high school mathematics. "Theory of Numbers," partial contents: Eratosthenes' sieve, Euclid's fundamental theorem, G.C.F. and L.C.M. of two or more integers, linear congruences, etc "Diophantine Analysis": rational triangles, Pythagorean triangles, equations of third, fourth, higher degrees, method of functional equations, much more. "Theory of Numbers": 76 problems. Index. 94pp. "Diophantine Analysis": 222 problems. Index. 118pp. 5⅜ x 8.              S529 Paperbound $1.35

**CONTRIBUTIONS TO THE FOUNDING OF THE THEORY OF TRANSFINITE NUMBERS, Georg Cantor.** These papers founded a new branch of mathematics. The famous articles of 1895-7 are translated, with an 82-page introduction by P. E. B. Jourdain dealing with Cantor, the background of his discoveries, their results, future possibilities. Bibliography. Index. Notes. ix + 211 pp. 5⅜ x 8. S45 Paperbound **$1.25**

See also: **TRANSCENDENTAL AND ALGEBRAIC NUMBERS, A. O. Gelfond.**

## Probability theory and information theory

**A PHILOSOPHICAL ESSAY ON PROBABILITIES, Marquis de Laplace.** This famous essay explains without recourse to mathematics the principle of probability, and the application of probability to games of chance, natural philosophy, astronomy, many other fields. Translated from the 6th French edition by F. W. Truscott, F. L. Emory, with new introduction for this edition by E. T. Bell. 204pp. 5⅜ x 8. S166 Paperbound **$1.35**

**MATHEMATICAL FOUNDATIONS OF INFORMATION THEORY, A. I. Khinchin.** For the first time mathematicians, statisticians, physicists, cyberneticists, and communications engineers are offered a complete and exact introduction to this relatively new field. Entropy as a measure of a finite scheme, applications to coding theory, study of sources, channels and codes, detailed proofs of both Shannon theorems for any ergodic source and any stationary channel with finite memory, and much more are covered. Bibliography. vii + 120pp. 5⅜ x 8. S434 Paperbound **$1.35**

**SELECTED PAPERS ON NOISE AND STOCHASTIC PROCESS,** edited by **Prof. Nelson Wax,** U. of Illinois. 6 basic papers for newcomers in the field, for those whose work involves noise characteristics. Chandrasekhar, Uhlenbeck & Ornstein, Uhlenbeck & Ming, Rice, Doob. Included is Kac's Chauvenet-Prize winning Random Walk. Extensive bibliography lists 200 articles, up through 1953. 21 figures. 337pp. 6⅛ x 9¼. S262 Paperbound **$2.35**

**THEORY OF PROBABILITY, William Burnside.** Synthesis, expansion of individual papers presents numerous problems in classical probability, offering many original views succinctly, effectively. Game theory, cards, selections from groups; geometrical probability in such areas as suppositions as to probability of position of point on a line, points on surface of sphere, etc. Includes methods of approximation, theory of errors, direct calculation of probabilities, etc. Index. 136pp. 5⅜ x 8. S567 Paperbound **$1.00**

## Vector and tensor analysis, matrix theory

**VECTOR AND TENSOR ANALYSIS, A. P. Wills.** Covers the entire field of vector and tensor analysis from elementary notions to dyads and non-Euclidean manifolds (especially detailed), absolute differentiation, the Lamé operator, the Riemann-Christoffel and Ricci-Einstein tensors, and the calculation of the Gaussian curvature of a surface. Many illustrations from electrical engineering, relativity theory, astro-physics, quantum mechanics. Presupposes only a good working knowledge of calculus. Exercises at end of each chapter. Intended for physicists and engineers as well as pure mathematicians. 44 diagrams. 114 problems. Bibliography. Index. xxxii + 285pp. 5⅜ x 8. S454 Paperbound **$1.75**

**APPLICATIONS OF TENSOR ANALYSIS, A. J. McConnell.** (Formerly APPLICATIONS OF THE ABSOLUTE DIFFERENTIAL CALCULUS.) An excellent text for understanding the application of tensor methods to familiar subjects such as dynamics, electricity, elasticity, and hydrodynamics. Explains the fundamental ideas and notation of tensor theory, the geometrical treatment of tensor algebra, the theory of differentiation of tensors, and includes a wealth of practical material. Bibliography. Index. 43 illustrations. 685 problems. xii + 381pp. 5⅜ x 8. S373 Paperbound **$1.85**

**VECTOR AND TENSOR ANALYSIS, G. E. Hay.** One of the clearest introductions to this increasingly important subject. Start with simple definitions, finish the book with a sure mastery of oriented Cartesian vectors, Christoffel symbols, solenoidal tensors, and their applications. Complete breakdown of plane, solid, analytical, differential geometry. Separate chapters on application. All fundamental formulae listed & demonstrated. 195 problems, 66 figures. viii + 193pp. 5⅜ x 8. S109 Paperbound **$1.75**

**VECTOR ANALYSIS, FOUNDED UPON THE LECTURES OF J. WILLARD GIBBS,** by **E. B. Wilson.** Still a first-rate introduction and supplementary text for students of mathematics and physics. Based on the pioneering lectures of Yale's great J. Willard Gibbs, can be followed by anyone who has had some calculus. Practical approach, stressing efficient use of combinations and functions of vectors. Worked examples from geometry, mechanics, hydrodynamics, gas theory, etc., as well as practice examples. Covers basic vector processes, differential and integral calculus in relation to vector functions, and theory of linear vector functions, forming an introduction to the study of multiple algebra and matrix theory. While the notation is not always modern, it is easily followed. xviii + 436pp. 5⅜ x 8. S656 Paperbound **$2.00**

**PROBLEMS AND WORKED SOLUTIONS IN VECTOR ANALYSIS, L. R. Shorter.** More pages of fully-worked-out examples than any other text on vector analysis. A self-contained course for home study or a fine classroom supplement. 138 problems and examples begin with fundamentals, then cover systems of coordinates, relative velocity and acceleration, the commutative and distributive laws, axial and polar vectors, finite displacements, the calculus of vectors, curl and divergence, etc. Final chapter treats applications in dynamics and physics: kinematics of a rigid body, equipotential surfaces, etc. "Very helpful . . . very comprehensive. A handy book like this . . . will fill a great want," MATHEMATICAL GAZETTE. Index. List of 174 important equations. 158 figures. xiv + 356pp. 5⅜ x 8. S135 Paperbound **$2.00**

**THE THEORY OF DETERMINANTS, MATRICES, AND INVARIANTS, H. W. Turnbull.** 3rd revised, corrected edition of this important study of virtually all the salient features and major theories of the subject. Covers Laplace identities, linear equations, differentiation, symbolic and direct methods for the reduction of invariants, seminvariants, Hilbert's Basis Theorem, Clebsch's Theorem, canonical forms, etc. New appendix contains a proof of Jacobi's lemma, further properties of symmetric determinants, etc. More than 350 problems. New references to recent developments. xviii + 374pp. 5⅜ x 8. S699 Paperbound **$2.00**

# Differential equations, ordinary and partial, and integral equations

**INTRODUCTION TO THE DIFFERENTIAL EQUATIONS OF PHYSICS, L. Hopf.** Especially valuable to the engineer with no math beyond elementary calculus. Emphasizing intuitive rather than formal aspects of concepts, the author covers an extensive territory. Partial contents: **Law** of causality, energy theorem, damped oscillations, coupling by friction, cylindrical and spherical coordinates, heat source, etc. Index. 48 figures. 160pp. 5⅜ x 8.
S120 Paperbound **$1.25**

**INTRODUCTION TO THE THEORY OF LINEAR DIFFERENTIAL EQUATIONS, E. G. Poole.** Authoritative discussions of important topics, with methods of solution more detailed than usual, for students with background of elementary course in differential equations. Studies existence theorems, linearly independent solutions; equations with constant coefficients; with uniform analytic coefficients; regular singularities; the hypergeometric equation; conformal representation; etc. Exercises. Index. 210pp. 5⅜ x 8. S629 Paperbound **$1.65**

**DIFFERENTIAL EQUATIONS FOR ENGINEERS, P. Franklin.** Outgrowth of a course given 10 years at M. I. T. Makes most useful branch of pure math accessible for practical work. Theoretical basis of D.E.'s; solution of ordinary D.E.'s and partial derivatives arising from heat flow, steady-state temperature of a plate, wave equations; analytic functions; convergence of Fourier Series. 400 problems on electricity, vibratory systems, other topics. Formerly "Differential Equations for Electrical Engineers." Index. 41 illus. 307pp. 5⅜ x 8.
S601 Paperbound **$1.65**

**DIFFERENTIAL EQUATIONS, F. R. Moulton.** A detailed, rigorous exposition of all the non-elementary processes of solving ordinary differential equations. Several chapters devoted to the treatment of practical problems, especially those of a physical nature, which are far more advanced than problems usually given as illustrations. Includes analytic differential equations; variations of a parameter; integrals of differential equations; analytic implicit functions; problems of elliptic motion; sine-amplitude functions; deviation of formal bodies; Cauchy-Lipschitz process; linear differential equations with periodic coefficients; differential equations in infinitely many variations; much more. Historical notes. 10 figures. 222 problems. Index. xv + 395pp. 5⅜ x 8. S451 Paperbound **$2.00**

**LECTURES ON CAUCHY'S PROBLEM, J. Hadamard.** Based on lectures given at Columbia, Rome, this discusses work of Riemann, Kirchhoff, Volterra, and the author's own research on the hyperbolic case in linear partial differential equations. It extends spherical and cylindrical waves to apply to all (normal) hyperbolic equations. Partial contents: Cauchy's problem, fundamental formula, equations with odd number, with even number of independent variables; method of descent. 32 figures. Index. iii + 316pp. 5⅜ x 8. S105 Paperbound **$1.75**

**PARTIAL DIFFERENTIAL EQUATIONS OF MATHEMATICAL PHYSICS, A. G. Webster.** A keystone work in the library of every mature physicist, engineer, researcher. Valuable sections on elasticity, compression theory, potential theory, theory of sound, heat conduction, wave propagation, vibration theory. Contents include: deduction of differential equations, vibrations, normal functions, Fourier's series, Cauchy's method, boundary problems, method of Riemann-Volterra. Spherical, cylindrical, ellipsoidal harmonics, applications, etc. 97 figures. vii + 440pp. 5⅜ x 8. S263 Paperbound **$2.00**

**ORDINARY DIFFERENTIAL EQUATIONS, E. L. Ince.** A most compendious analysis in real and complex domains. Existence and nature of solutions, continuous transformation groups, solutions in an infinite form, definite integrals, algebraic theory, Sturmian theory, boundary problems, existence theorems, 1st order, higher order, etc. "Deserves the highest praise, a notable addition to mathematical literature," BULLETIN, AM. MATH. SOC. Historical appendix. Bibliography. 18 figures. viii + 558pp. 5⅜ x 8. S349 Paperbound **$2.55**

**THEORY OF DIFFERENTIAL EQUATIONS, A. R. Forsyth.** Out of print for over a decade, the complete 6 volumes (now bound as 3) of this monumental work represent the most comprehensive treatment of differential equations ever written. Historical presentation includes in 2500 pages every substantial development. Vol. 1, 2: EXACT EQUATIONS, PFAFF'S PROBLEM; ORDINARY EQUATIONS, NOT LINEAR: methods of Grassmann, Clebsch, Lie, Darboux; Cauchy's theorem; branch points; etc. Vol. 3, 4: ORDINARY EQUATIONS, NOT LINEAR; ORDINARY LINEAR EQUATIONS: Zeta Fuchsian functions, general theorems on algebraic integrals, Brun's theorem, equations with uniform periodic coffiecients, etc. Vol. 4, 5: PARTIAL DIFFERENTIAL EQUATIONS: 2 existence-theorems, equations of theoretical dynamics, Laplace transformations, general transformation of equations of the 2nd order, much more. Indexes. Total of 2766pp. 5⅜ x 8.               S576-7-8 Clothbound. the set $15.00

**DIFFERENTIAL AND INTEGRAL EQUATIONS OF MECHANICS AND PHYSICS (DIE DIFFERENTIAL- UND INTEGRALGLEICHUNGEN DER MECHANIK UND PHYSIK), edited by P. Frank and R. von Mises.** Most comprehensive and authoritative work on the mathematics of mathematical physics available today in the United States: the standard, definitive reference for teachers, physicists, engineers, and mathematicians—now published (in the original German) at a relatively inexpensive price for the first time! Every chapter in this 2,000-page set is by an expert in his field: Caratheodory, Courant, Frank, Mises, and a dozen others. Vol. I, on mathematics, gives concise but complete coverages of advanced calculus, differential equations, integral equations, and potential, and partial differential equations. Index. xxiii + 916pp. Vol. II (physics): classical mechanics, optics, continuous mechanics, heat conduction and diffusion, the stationary and quasi-stationary electromagnetic field, electromagnetic oscillations, and wave mechanics. Index. xxiv + 1106pp. Two volume set. Each volume available separately. 5⅝ x 8⅜.                S787 Vol I Clothbound **$7.50**
S788 Vol II Clothbound **$7.50**
The set **$15.00**

**MATHEMATICAL ANALYSIS OF ELECTRICAL AND OPTICAL WAVE-MOTION, Harry Bateman.** Written by one of this century's most distinguished mathematical physicists, this is a practical introduction to those developments of Maxwell's electromagnetic theory which are directly connected with the solution of the partial differential equation of wave motion. Methods of solving wave-equation, polar-cylindrical coordinates, diffraction, transformation of coordinates, homogeneous solutions, electromagnetic fields with moving singularities, etc. Index. 168pp. 5⅜ x 8.                S14 Paperbound **$1.60**

See also: **THE ANALYTICAL THEORY OF HEAT, J. Fourier; INTRODUCTION TO BESSEL FUNCTIONS, F. Bowman.**

# Statistics

**ELEMENTARY STATISTICS, WITH APPLICATIONS IN MEDICINE AND THE BIOLOGICAL SCIENCES, F. E. Croxton.** A sound introduction to statistics for anyone in the physical sciences, assuming no prior acquaintance and requiring only a modest knowledge of math. All basic formulas carefully explained and illustrated; all necessary reference tables included. From basic terms and concepts, the study proceeds to frequency distribution, linear, non-linear, and multiple correlation, skewness, kurtosis, etc. A large section deals with reliability and significance of statistical methods. Containing concrete examples from medicine and biology, this book will prove unusually helpful to workers in those fields who increasingly must evaluate, check, and interpret statistics. Formerly titled "Elementary Statistics with Applications in Medicine." 101 charts. 57 tables. 14 appendices. Index. iv + 376pp. 5⅜ x 8.                S506 Paperbound **$1.95**

**METHODS OF STATISTICS, L. H. C. Tippett.** A classic in its field, this unusually complete systematic introduction to statistical methods begins at beginner's level and progresses to advanced levels for experimenters and poll-takers in all fields of statistical research. Supplies fundamental knowledge of virtually all elementary methods in use today by sociologists, psychologists, biologists, engineers, mathematicians, etc. Explains logical and mathematical basis of each method described, with examples for each section. Covers frequency distributions and measures, inference from random samples, errors in large samples, simple analysis of variance, multiple and partial regression and correlation, etc. 4th revised (1952) edition. 16 charts. 5 significance tables. 152-item bibliography. 96 tables. 22 figures. 395pp. 6 x 9.                S228 Clothbound **$7.50**

**STATISTICS MANUAL, E. L. Crow, F. A. Davis, M. W. Maxfield.** Comprehensive collection of classical, modern statistics methods, prepared under auspices of U. S. Naval Ordnance Test Station, China Lake, Calif. Many examples from ordnance will be valuable to workers in all fields. Emphasis is on use, with information on fiducial limits, sign tests, Chi-square runs, sensitivity, quality control, much more. "Well written . . . excellent reference work," Operations Research. Corrected edition of NAVORD Report 3360 NOTS 948. Introduction. Appendix of 32 tables, charts. Index. Bibliography. 95 illustrations. 306pp. 5⅜ x 8.                S599 Paperbound **$1.55**

**ANALYSIS & DESIGN OF EXPERIMENTS, H. B. Mann.** Offers a method for grasping the analysis of variance and variance design within a short time. Partial contents: Chi-square distribution and analysis of variance distribution, matrices, quadratic forms, likelihood ration tests and tests of linear hypotheses, power of analysis, Galois fields, non-orthogonal data, interblock estimates, etc. 15pp. of useful tables. x + 195pp. 5 x 7⅜.                S180 Paperbound **$1.45**


# Numerical analysis, tables

**PRACTICAL ANALYSIS, GRAPHICAL AND NUMERICAL METHODS, F. A. Willers.** Translated by R. T. Beyer. Immensely practical handbook for engineers, showing how to interpolate, use various methods of numerical differentiation and integration, determine the roots of a single algebraic equation, system of linear equations, use empirical formulas, integrate differential equations, etc. Hundreds of shortcuts for arriving at numerical solutions. Special section on American calculating machines, by T. W. Simpson. 132 illustrations. 422pp. 5⅜ x 8.
                                                                        S273 Paperbound **$2.00**

**NUMERICAL SOLUTIONS OF DIFFERENTIAL EQUATIONS, H. Levy & E. A. Baggott.** Comprehensive collection of methods for solving ordinary differential equations of first and higher order. All must pass 2 requirements: easy to grasp and practical, more rapid than school methods. Partial contents: graphical integration of differential equations, graphical methods for detailed solution. Numerical solution. Simultaneous equations and equations of 2nd and higher orders. "Should be in the hands of all in research in applied mathematics, teaching," NATURE. 21 figures. viii + 238pp. 5⅜ x 8.                                S168 Paperbound **$1.75**

**NUMERICAL INTEGRATION OF DIFFERENTIAL EQUATIONS, Bennett, Milne & Bateman.** Unabridged republication of original monograph prepared for National Research Council. New methods of integration of differential equations developed by 3 leading mathematicians: THE INTERPOLATIONAL POLYNOMIAL and SUCCESSIVE APPROXIMATIONS by A. A. Bennett; STEP-BY-STEP METHODS OF INTEGRATION by W. W. Milne; METHODS FOR PARTIAL DIFFERENTIAL EQUATIONS by H. Bateman. Methods for partial differential equations, transition from difference equations to differential equations, solution of differential equations to non-integral values of a parameter will interest mathematicians and physicists. 288 footnotes, mostly bibliographic; 235-item classified bibliography. 108pp. 5⅜ x 8.            S305 Paperbound **$1.35**

**INTRODUCTION TO RELAXATION METHODS, F. S. Shaw.** Fluid mechanics, design of electrical networks, forces in structural frameworks, stress distribution, buckling, etc. Solve linear simultaneous equations, linear ordinary differential equations, partial differential equations, Eigen-value problems by relaxation methods. Detailed examples throughout. Special tables for dealing with awkwardly-shaped boundaries. Indexes. 253 diagrams. 72 tables. 400pp. 5⅜ x 8.                                                            S244 Paperbound **$2.45**

**TABLES OF INDEFINITE INTEGRALS, G. Petit Bois.** Comprehensive and accurate, this orderly grouping of over 2500 of the most useful indefinite integrals will save you hours of laborious mathematical groundwork. After a list of 49 common transformations of integral expressions, with a wide variety of examples, the book takes up algebraic functions, irrational monomials, products and quotients of binomials, transcendental functions, natural logs, etc. You will rarely or never encounter an integral of an algebraic or transcendental function not included here; any more comprehensive set of tables costs at least $12 or $15. Index. 2544 integrals. xii + 154pp. 6⅛ x 9¼.                                                S225 Paperbound **$1.65**

**A TABLE OF THE INCOMPLETE ELLIPTIC INTEGRAL OF THE THIRD KIND, R. G. Selfridge, J. E. Maxfield.** The first complete 6 place tables of values of the incomplete integral of the third kind, prepared under the auspices of the Research Department of the U.S. Naval Ordnance Test Station. Calculated on an IBM type 704 calculator and thoroughly verified by echo-checking and a check integral at the completion of each value of **a**. Of inestimable value in problems where the surface area of geometrical bodies can only be expressed in terms of the incomplete integral of the third and lower kinds; problems in aero-, fluid-, and thermodynamics involving processes where nonsymmetrical repetitive volumes must be determined; various types of seismological problems; problems of magnetic potentials due to circular current; etc. Foreword. Acknowledgment. Introduction. Use of table. xiv + 805pp. 5⅝ x 8⅜.                                                          S501 Clothbound **$7.50**

**MATHEMATICAL TABLES, H. B. Dwight.** Unique for its coverage in one volume of almost every function of importance in applied mathematics, engineering, and the physical sciences. Three extremely fine tables of the three trig functions and their inverse functions to thousandths of radians; natural and common logarithms; squares, cubes; hyperbolic functions and the inverse hyperbolic functions; $(a^2 + b^2)$ exp. ½a; complete elliptic integrals of the 1st and 2nd kind; sine and cosine integrals; exponential integrals $Ei(x)$ and $Ei(-x)$; binomial coefficients; factorials to 250; surface zonal harmonics and first derivatives; Bernoulli and Euler numbers and their logs to base of 10; Gamma function; normal probability integral; over 60 pages of Bessel functions; the Riemann Zeta function. Each table with formulae generally used, sources of more extensive tables, interpolation data, etc. Over half have columns of differences, to facilitate interpolation. Introduction. Index. viii + 231pp. 5⅜ x 8.
                                                                        S445 Paperbound **$1.75**

**TABLES OF FUNCTIONS WITH FORMULAE AND CURVES, E. Jahnke & F. Emde.** The world's most comprehensive 1-volume English-text collection of tables, formulae, curves of transcendent functions. 4th corrected edition, new 76-page section giving tables, formulae for elementary functions—not in other English editions. Partial contents: sine, cosine, logarithmic integral; factorial function; error integral; theta functions; elliptic integrals, functions; Legendre, Bessel, Riemann, Mathieu, hypergeometric functions, etc. Supplementary books. Bibliography. Indexed. "Out of the way functions for which we know no other source," SCIENTIFIC COMPUTING SERVICE, Ltd. 212 figures. 400pp. 5⅜ x 8.                                     S133 Paperbound **$2.00**

**JACOBIAN ELLIPTIC FUNCTION TABLES, L. M. Milne-Thomson.** An easy to follow, practical book which gives not only useful numerical tables, but also a complete elementary sketch of the application of elliptic functions. It covers Jacobian elliptic functions and a description of their principal properties; complete elliptic integrals; Fourier series and power series expansions; periods, zeros, poles, residues, formulas for special values of the argument; transformations, approximations, elliptic integrals, conformal mapping, factorization of cubic and quartic polynomials; application to the pendulum problem; etc. Tables and graphs form the body of the book: Graph, 5 figure table of the elliptic function sn (u m); cn (u m); dn (u m). 8 figure table of complete elliptic integrals K, K', E, E', and the nome q. 7 figure table of the Jacobian zeta-function Z(u). 3 figures. xi + 123pp. 5⅜ x 8.
                                                                                   S194 Paperbound **$1.35**

# PHYSICS

## General physics

**FOUNDATIONS OF PHYSICS, R. B. Lindsay & H. Margenau.** Excellent bridge between semi-popular works & technical treatises. A discussion of methods of physical description, construction of theory; valuable for physicist with elementary calculus who is interested in ideas that give meaning to data, tools of modern physics. Contents include symbolism, mathematical equations; space & time foundations of mechanics; probability; physics & continua; electron theory; special & general relativity; quantum mechanics; causality. "Thorough and yet not overdetailed. Unreservedly recommended," NATURE (London). Unabridged, corrected edition. List of recommended readings. 35 illustrations. xi + 537pp. 5⅜ x 8.
                                                                                   S377 Paperbound **$2.45**

**FUNDAMENTAL FORMULAS OF PHYSICS, ed. by D. H. Menzel.** Highly useful, fully inexpensive reference and study text, ranging from simple to highly sophisticated operations. Mathematics integrated into text—each chapter stands as short textbook of field represented. Vol. 1: Statistics, Physical Constants, Special Theory of Relativity, Hydrodynamics, Aerodynamics, Boundary Value Problems in Math. Physics; Viscosity, Electromagnetic Theory, etc. Vol. 2: Sound, Acoustics, Geometrical Optics, Electron Optics, High-Energy Phenomena, Magnetism, Biophysics, much more. Index. Total of 800pp. 5⅜ x 8.                     Vol. 1 S595 Paperbound **$2.00**
                                                                          Vol. 2 S596 Paperbound **$2.00**

**MATHEMATICAL PHYSICS, D. H. Menzel.** Thorough one-volume treatment of the mathematical techniques vital for classic mechanics, electromagnetic theory, quantum theory, and relativity. Written by the Harvard Professor of Astrophysics for junior, senior, and graduate courses, it gives clear explanations of all those aspects of function theory, vectors, matrices, dyadics, tensors, partial differential equations, etc., necessary for the understanding of the various physical theories. Electron theory, relativity, and other topics seldom presented appear here in considerable detail. Scores of definitions, conversion factors, dimensional constants, etc. "More detailed than normal for an advanced text . . . excellent set of sections on Dyadics, Matrices, and Tensors," JOURNAL OF THE FRANKLIN INSTITUTE. Index. 193 problems, with answers. x + 412pp. 5⅜ x 8.                         S56 Paperbound **$2.00**

**THE SCIENTIFIC PAPERS OF J. WILLARD GIBBS.** All the published papers of America's outstanding theoretical scientist (except for "Statistical Mechanics" and "Vector Analysis"). Vol I (thermodynamics) contains one of the most brilliant of all 19th-century scientific papers—the 300-page "On the Equilibrium of Heterogeneous Substances," which founded the science of physical chemistry, and clearly stated a number of highly important natural laws for the first time; 8 other papers complete the first volume. Vol II includes 2 papers on dynamics, 8 on vector analysis and multiple algebra, 5 on the electromagnetic theory of light, and 6 miscellaneous papers. Biographical sketch by H. A. Bumstead. Total of xxxvi + 718pp. 5⅝ x 8⅜.
                                                                          S721 Vol I Paperbound **$2.00**
                                                                         S722 Vol II Paperbound **$2.00**
                                                                                   The set **$4.00**

# Relativity, quantum theory, nuclear physics

**THE PRINCIPLE OF RELATIVITY, A. Einstein, H. Lorentz, M. Minkowski, H. Weyl.** These are the 11 basic papers that founded the general and special theories of relativity, all translated into English. Two papers by Lorentz on the Michelson experiment, electromagnetic phenomena. Minkowski's SPACE & TIME, and Weyl's GRAVITATION & ELECTRICITY. 7 epoch-making papers by Einstein: ELECTROMAGNETICS OF MOVING BODIES, INFLUENCE OF GRAVITATION IN PROPAGATION OF LIGHT, COSMOLOGICAL CONSIDERATIONS, GENERAL THEORY, and 3 others. 7 diagrams. Special notes by A. Sommerfeld. 224pp. 5⅜ x 8.
S81 Paperbound **$1.75**

**SPACE TIME MATTER, Hermann Weyl.** "The standard treatise on the general theory of relativity," (Nature), written by a world-renowned scientist, provides a deep clear discussion of the logical coherence of the general theory, with introduction to all the mathematical tools needed: Maxwell, analytical geometry, non-Euclidean geometry, tensor calculus, etc. Basis is classical space-time, before absorption of relativity. Partial contents: Euclidean space, mathematical form, metrical continuum, relativity of time and space, general theory. 15 diagrams. Bibliography. New preface for this edition. xviii + 330pp. 5⅜ x 8.
S267 Paperbound **$1.85**

**PRINCIPLES OF QUANTUM MECHANICS, W. V. Houston.** Enables student with working knowledge of elementary mathematical physics to develop facility in use of quantum mechanics, understand published work in field. Formulates quantum mechanics in terms of Schroedinger's wave mechanics. Studies evidence for quantum theory, for inadequacy of classical mechanics, 2 postulates of quantum mechanics; numerous important, fruitful applications of quantum mechanics in spectroscopy, collision problems, electrons in solids; other topics. "One of the most rewarding features . . . is the interlacing of problems with text," Amer. J. of Physics. Corrected edition. 21 illus. Index. 296pp. 5⅜ x 8.    S524 Paperbound **$1.85**

**PHYSICAL PRINCIPLES OF THE QUANTUM THEORY, Werner Heisenberg.** A Nobel laureate discusses quantum theory; Heisenberg's own work, Compton, Schroedinger, Wilson, Einstein, many others. Written for physicists, chemists who are not specialists in quantum theory, only elementary formulae are considered in the text; there is a mathematical appendix for specialists. Profound without sacrifice of clarity. Translated by C. Eckart, F. Hoyt. 18 figures. 192pp. 5⅜ x 8.    S113 Paperbound **$1.25**

**SELECTED PAPERS ON QUANTUM ELECTRODYNAMICS, edited by J. Schwinger.** Facsimiles of papers which established quantum electrodynamics, from initial successes through today's position as part of the larger theory of elementary particles. First book publication in any language of these collected papers of Bethe, Bloch, Dirac, Dyson, Fermi, Feynman, Heisenberg, Kusch, Lamb, Oppenheimer, Pauli, Schwinger, Tomonoga, Weisskopf, Wigner, etc. 34 papers in all, 29 in English, 1 in French, 3 in German, 1 in Italian. Preface and historical commentary by the editor. xvii + 423pp. 6⅛ x 9¼.    S444 Paperbound **$2.45**

**THE FUNDAMENTAL PRINCIPLES OF QUANTUM MECHANICS, WITH ELEMENTARY APPLICATIONS, E. C. Kemble.** An inductive presentation, for the graduate student or specialist in some other branch of physics. Assumes some acquaintance with advanced math; apparatus necessary beyond differential equations and advanced calculus is developed as needed. Although a general exposition of principles, hundreds of individual problems are fully treated, with applications of theory being interwoven with development of the mathematical structure. The author is the Professor of Physics at Harvard Univ. "This excellent book would be of great value to every student . . . a rigorous and detailed mathematical discussion of all of the principal quantum-mechanical methods . . . has succeeded in keeping his presentations clear and understandable," Dr. Linus Pauling, J. of the American Chemical Society. Appendices: calculus of variations, math. notes, etc. Indexes. 611pp. 5⅜ x 8.
S472 Paperbound **$2.95**

**ATOMIC SPECTRA AND ATOMIC STRUCTURE, G. Herzberg.** Excellent general survey for chemists, physicists specializing in other fields. Partial contents: simplest line spectra and elements of atomic theory, building-up principle and periodic system of elements, hyperfine structure of spectral lines, some experiments and applications. Bibliography. 80 figures. Index. xii + 257pp. 5⅜ x 8.    S115 Paperbound **$1.95**

**THE THEORY AND THE PROPERTIES OF METALS AND ALLOYS, N. F. Mott, H. Jones.** Quantum methods used to develop mathematical models which show interrelationship of basic chemical phenomena with crystal structure, magnetic susceptibility, electrical, optical properties. Examines thermal properties of crystal lattice, electron motion in applied field, cohesion, electrical resistance, noble metals, para-, dia-, and ferromagnetism, etc. "Exposition . . . clear . . . mathematical treatment . . . simple," Nature. 138 figures. Bibliography. Index. xiii + 320pp. 5⅜ x 8.    S456 Paperbound **$1.85**

**FOUNDATIONS OF NUCLEAR PHYSICS, edited by R. T. Beyer.** 13 of the most important papers on nuclear physics reproduced in facsimile in the original languages of their authors: the papers most often cited in footnotes, bibliographies. Anderson, Curie, Joliot, Chadwick, Fermi, Lawrence, Cockcroft, Hahn, Yukawa. UNPARALLELED BIBLIOGRAPHY. 122 double-columned pages, over 4,000 articles, books classified. 57 figures. 288pp. 6⅛ x 9¼.
S19 Paperbound **$1.75**

**MESON PHYSICS, R. E. Marshak.** Traces the basic theory, and explicitly presents results of experiments with particular emphasis on theoretical significance. Phenomena involving mesons as virtual transitions are avoided, eliminating some of the least satisfactory predictions of meson theory. Includes production and study of $\pi$ mesons at nonrelativistic nucleon energies, contrasts between $\pi$ and $\mu$ mesons, phenomena associated with nuclear interaction of $\pi$ mesons, etc. Presents early evidence for new classes of particles and indicates theoretical difficulties created by discovery of heavy mesons and hyperons. Name and subject indices. Unabridged reprint. viii + 378pp. 5⅜ x 8.     S500 Paperbound **$1.95**

See also: **STRANGE STORY OF THE QUANTUM,** B. Hoffmann; **FROM EUCLID TO EDDINGTON,** E. Whittaker; **MATTER AND LIGHT, THE NEW PHYSICS,** L. de Broglie; **THE EVOLUTION OF SCIENTIFIC THOUGHT FROM NEWTON TO EINSTEIN,** A. d'Abro; **THE RISE OF THE NEW PHYSICS,** A. d'Abro; **THE THEORY OF GROUPS AND QUANTUM MECHANICS,** H. Weyl; **SUBSTANCE AND FUNCTION, & EINSTEIN'S THEORY OF RELATIVITY,** E. Cassirer; **FUNDAMENTAL FORMULAS OF PHYSICS,** D. H. Menzel.


# Hydrodynamics

**HYDRODYNAMICS, H. Dryden, F. Murnaghan, Harry Bateman.** Published by the National Research Council in 1932 this enormous volume offers a complete coverage of classical hydrodynamics. Encyclopedic in quality. Partial contents: physics of fluids, motion, turbulent flow, compressible fluids, motion in 1, 2, 3 dimensions; viscous fluids rotating, laminar motion, resistance of motion through viscous fluid, eddy viscosity, hydraulic flow in channels of various shapes, discharge of gases, flow past obstacles, etc. Bibliography of over 2,900 items. Indexes. 23 figures. 634pp. 5⅜ x 8.     S303 Paperbound **$2.75**

**A TREATISE ON HYDRODYNAMICS, A. B. Basset.** Favorite text on hydrodynamics for 2 generations of physicists, hydrodynamical engineers, oceanographers, ship designers, etc. Clear enough for the beginning student, and thorough source for graduate students and engineers on the work of d'Alembert, Euler, Laplace, Lagrange, Poisson, Green, Clebsch, Stokes, Cauchy, Helmholtz, J. J. Thomson, Love, Hicks, Greenhill, Besant, Lamb, etc. Great amount of documentation on entire theory of classical hydrodynamics. Vol I: theory of motion of frictionless liquids, vortex, and cyclic irrotational motion, etc. 132 exercises. Bibliography. 3 Appendixes. xii + 264pp. Vol II: motion in viscous liquids, harmonic analysis, theory of tides, etc. 112 exercises. Bibliography. 4 Appendixes. xv + 328pp. Two volume set. 5⅜ x 8.

    S724 Vol I Paperbound **$1.75**
    S725 Vol II Paperbound **$1.75**
    The set **$3.50**

**HYDRODYNAMICS, Horace Lamb.** Internationally famous complete coverage of standard reference work on dynamics of liquids & gases. Fundamental theorems, equations, methods, solutions, background, for classical hydrodynamics. Chapters include Equations of Motion, Integration of Equations in Special Gases, Irrotational Motion, Motion of Liquid in 2 Dimensions, Motion of Solids through Liquid-Dynamical Theory, Vortex Motion, Tidal Waves, Surface Waves, Waves of Expansion, Viscosity, Rotating Masses of liquids. Excellently planned, arranged; clear, lucid presentation. 6th enlarged, revised edition. Index. Over 900 footnotes, mostly bibliographical. 119 figures. xv + 738pp. 6⅛ x 9¼.     S256 Paperbound **$2.95**

See also: **FUNDAMENTAL FORMULAS OF PHYSICS,** D. H. Menzel; **THEORY OF FLIGHT,** R. von Mises; **FUNDAMENTALS OF HYDRO- AND AEROMECHANICS,** L. Prandtl and O. G. Tietjens; **APPLIED HYDRO- AND AEROMECHANICS,** L. Prandtl and O. G. Tietjens; **HYDRAULICS AND ITS APPLICATIONS,** A. H. Gibson; **FLUID MECHANICS FOR HYDRAULIC ENGINEERS,** H. Rouse.


# Acoustics, optics, electromagnetics

**ON THE SENSATIONS OF TONE, Hermann Helmholtz.** This is an unmatched coordination of such fields as acoustical physics, physiology, experiment, history of music. It covers the entire gamut of musical tone. Partial contents: relation of musical science to acoustics, physical vs. physiological acoustics, composition of vibration, resonance, analysis of tones by sympathetic resonance, beats, chords, tonality, consonant chords, discords, progression of parts, etc. 33 appendixes discuss various aspects of sound, physics, acoustics, music, etc. Translated by A. J. Ellis. New introduction by Prof. Henry Margenau of Yale. 68 figures. 43 musical passages analyzed. Over 100 tables. Index. xix + 576pp. 6⅛ x 9¼.
    S114 Paperbound **$2.95**

**THE THEORY OF SOUND, Lord Rayleigh.** Most vibrating systems likely to be encountered in practice can be tackled successfully by the methods set forth by the great Nobel laureate, Lord Rayleigh. Complete coverage of experimental, mathematical aspects of sound theory. Partial contents: Harmonic motions, vibrating systems in general, lateral vibrations of bars, curved plates or shells, applications of Laplace's functions to acoustical problems, fluid friction, plane vortex-sheet, vibrations of solid bodies, etc. This is the first inexpensive edition of this great reference and study work. Bibliography. Historical introduction by R. B. Lindsay. Total of 1040pp. 97 figures. 5⅜ x 8.

S292, S293, Two volume set, paperbound, **$4.00**

**THE DYNAMICAL THEORY OF SOUND, H. Lamb.** Comprehensive mathematical treatment of the physical aspects of sound, covering the theory of vibrations, the general theory of sound, and the equations of motion of strings, bars, membranes, pipes, and resonators. Includes chapters on plane, spherical, and simple harmonic waves, and the Helmholtz Theory of Audition. Complete and self-contained development for student and specialist; all fundamental differential equations solved completely. Specific mathematical details for such important phenomena as harmonics, normal modes, forced vibrations of strings, theory of reed pipes, etc. Index. Bibliography. 86 diagrams. viii + 307pp. 5⅜ x 8.  S655 Paperbound **$1.50**

**WAVE PROPAGATION IN PERIODIC STRUCTURES, L. Brillouin.** A general method and application to different problems: pure physics, such as scattering of X-rays of crystals, thermal vibration in crystal lattices, electronic motion in metals; and also problems of electrical engineering. Partial contents: elastic waves in 1-dimensional lattices of point masses. Propagation of waves along 1-dimensional lattices. Energy flow. 2 dimensional, 3 dimensional lattices. Mathieu's equation. Matrices and propagation of waves along an electric line. Continuous electric lines. 131 illustrations. Bibliography. Index. xii + 253pp. 5⅜ x 8.

S34 Paperbound **$1.85**

**THEORY OF VIBRATIONS, N. W. McLachlan.** Based on an exceptionally successful graduate course given at Brown University, this discusses linear systems having 1 degree of freedom, forced vibrations of simple linear systems, vibration of flexible strings, transverse vibrations of bars and tubes, transverse vibration of circular plate, sound waves of finite amplitude, etc. Index. 99 diagrams. 160pp. 5⅜ x 8.  S190 Paperbound **$1.35**

**LOUD SPEAKERS: THEORY, PERFORMANCE, TESTING AND DESIGN, N. W. McLachlan.** Most comprehensive coverage of theory, practice of loud speaker design, testing; classic reference, study manual in field. First 12 chapters deal with theory, for readers mainly concerned with math. aspects; last 7 chapters will interest reader concerned with testing, design. Partial contents: principles of sound propagation, fluid pressure on vibrators, theory of moving coil principle, transients, driving mechanisms, response curves, design of horn type moving coil speakers, electrostatic speakers, much more. Appendix. Bibliography. Index. 165 illustrations, charts. 411pp. 5⅜ x 8.  S588 Paperbound **$2.25**

**MICROWAVE TRANSMISSION, J. S. Slater.** First text dealing exclusively with microwaves, brings together points of view of field, circuit theory, for graduate student in physics, electrical engineering, microwave technician. Offers valuable point of view not in most later studies. Uses Maxwell's equations to study electromagnetic field, important in this area. Partial contents: infinite line with distributed parameters, impedance of terminated line, plane waves, reflections, wave guides, coaxial line, composite transmission lines, impedance matching, etc. Introduction. Index. 76 illus. 319pp. 5⅜ x 8.

S564 Paperbound **$1.50**

**THE ANALYSIS OF SENSATIONS, Ernst Mach.** Great study of physiology, psychology of perception, shows Mach's ability to see material freshly, his "incorruptible skepticism and independence." (Einstein). Relation of problems of psychological perception to classical physics, supposed dualism of physical and mental, principle of continuity, evolution of senses, will as organic manifestation, scores of experiments, observations in optics, acoustics, music, graphics, etc. New introduction by T. S. Szasz, M. D. 58 illus. 300-item bibliography. Index. 404pp. 5⅜ x 8.  S525 Paperbound **$1.75**

**APPLIED OPTICS AND OPTICAL DESIGN, A. E. Conrady.** With publication of vol. 2, standard work for designers in optics is now complete for first time. Only work of its kind in English; only detailed work for practical designer and self-taught. Requires, for bulk of work, no math above trig. Step-by-step exposition, from fundamental concepts of geometrical, physical optics, to systematic study, design, of almost all types of optical systems. Vol. 1: all ordinary ray-tracing methods; primary aberrations; necessary higher aberration for design of telescopes, low-power microscopes, photographic equipment. Vol. 2: (Completed from author's notes by R. Kingslake, Dir. Optical Design, Eastman Kodak.) Special attention to high-power microscope, anastigmatic photographic objectives. "An indispensable work," J., Optical Soc. of Amer. "As a practical guide this book has no rival," Transactions, Optical Soc. Index. Bibliography. 193 diagrams. 852pp. 6⅛ x 9¼.  Vol. 1 T611 Paperbound **$2.95**
Vol. 2 T612 Paperbound **$2.95**

**THE THEORY OF OPTICS, Paul Drude.** One of finest fundamental texts in physical optics, classic offers thorough coverage, complete mathematical treatment of basic ideas. Includes fullest treatment of application of thermodynamics to optics; sine law in formation of images, transparent crystals, magnetically active substances, velocity of light, apertures, effects depending upon them, polarization, optical instruments, etc. Introduction by A. A. Michelson. Index. 110 illus. 567pp. 5⅜ x 8.  S532 Paperbound **$2.45**

**OPTICKS, Sir Isaac Newton.** In its discussions of light, reflection, color, refraction, theories of wave and corpuscular theories of light, this work is packed with scores of insights and discoveries. In its precise and practical discussion of construction of optical apparatus, contemporary understandings of phenomena it is truly fascinating to modern physicists, astronomers, mathematicians. Foreword by Albert Einstein. Preface by I. B. Cohen of Harvard University. 7 pages of portraits, facsimile pages, letters, etc. cxvi + 414pp. 5⅜ x 8.
S205 Paperbound **$2.00**

**OPTICS AND OPTICAL INSTRUMENTS: AN INTRODUCTION WITH SPECIAL REFERENCE TO PRACTICAL APPLICATIONS, B. K. Johnson.** An invaluable guide to basic practical applications of optical principles, which shows how to set up inexpensive working models of each of the four main types of optical instruments—telescopes, microscopes, photographic lenses, optical projecting systems. Explains in detail the most important experiments for determining their accuracy, resolving power, angular field of view, amounts of aberration, all other necessary facts about the instruments. Formerly "Practical Optics." Index. 234 diagrams. Appendix. 224pp. 5⅜ x 8.
S642 Paperbound **$1.65**

**PRINCIPLES OF PHYSICAL OPTICS, Ernst Mach.** This classical examination of the propagation of light, color, polarization, etc. offers an historical and philosophical treatment that has never been surpassed for breadth and easy readability. Contents: Rectilinear propagation of light. Reflection, refraction. Early knowledge of vision. Dioptrics. Composition of light. Theory of color and dispersion. Periodicity. Theory of interference. Polarization. Mathematical representation of properties of light. Propagation of waves, etc. 279 illustrations, 10 portraits. Appendix. Indexes. 324pp. 5⅜ x 8.
S178 Paperbound **$1.75**

**FUNDAMENTALS OF ELECTRICITY AND MAGNETISM, L. B. Loeb.** For students of physics, chemistry, or engineering who want an introduction to electricity and magnetism on a higher level and in more detail than general elementary physics texts provide. Only elementary differential and integral calculus is assumed. Physical laws developed logically, from magnetism to electric currents, Ohm's law, electrolysis, and on to static electricity, induction, etc. Covers an unusual amount of material; one third of book on modern material: solution of wave equation, photoelectric and thermionic effects, etc. Complete statement of the various electrical systems of units and interrelations. 2 Indexes. 75 pages of problems with answers stated. Over 300 figures and diagrams. xix +669pp. 5⅜ x 8.
S745 Paperbound **$2.75**

**THE ELECTROMAGNETIC FIELD, Max Mason & Warren Weaver.** Used constantly by graduate engineers. Vector methods exclusively: detailed treatment of electrostatics, expansion methods, with tables converting any quantity into absolute electromagnetic, absolute electrostatic, practical units. Discrete charges, ponderable bodies, Maxwell field equations, etc. Introduction. Indexes. 416pp. 5⅜ x 8.
S185 Paperbound **$2.00**

**ELECTRICAL THEORY ON THE GIORGI SYSTEM, P. Cornelius.** A new clarification of the fundamental concepts of electricity and magnetism, advocating the convenient m.k.s. system of units that is steadily gaining followers in the sciences. Illustrating the use and effectiveness of his terminology with numerous applications to concrete technical problems, the author here expounds the famous Giorgi system of electrical physics. His lucid presentation and well-reasoned, cogent argument for the universal adoption of this system form one of the finest pieces of scientific exposition in recent years. 28 figures. Index. Conversion tables for translating earlier data into modern units. Translated from 3rd Dutch edition by L. J. Jolley. x + 187pp. 5½ x 8¾.
S909 Clothbound **$6.00**

**THEORY OF ELECTRONS AND ITS APPLICATION TO THE PHENOMENA OF LIGHT AND RADIANT HEAT, H. Lorentz.** Lectures delivered at Columbia University by Nobel laureate Lorentz. Unabridged, they form a historical coverage of the theory of free electrons, motion, absorption of heat, Zeeman effect, propagation of light in molecular bodies, inverse Zeeman effect, optical phenomena in moving bodies, etc. 109 pages of notes explain the more advanced sections. Index. 9 figures. 352pp. 5⅜ x 8.
S173 Paperbound **$1.85**

**TREATISE ON ELECTRICITY AND MAGNETISM, James Clerk Maxwell.** For more than 80 years a seemingly inexhaustible source of leads for physicists, mathematicians, engineers. Total of 1082pp. on such topics as Measurement of Quantities, Electrostatics, Elementary Mathematical Theory of Electricity, Electrical Work and Energy in a System of Conductors, General Theorems, Theory of Electrical Images, Electrolysis, Conduction, Polarization, Dielectrics, Resistance, etc. "The greatest mathematical physicist since Newton," Sir James Jeans. 3rd edition. 107 figures, 21 plates. 1082pp. 5⅜ x 8.
S636-7, 2 volume set, paperbound **$4.00**

See also: FUNDAMENTAL FORMULAS OF PHYSICS, D. H. Menzel; MATHEMATICAL ANALYSIS OF ELECTRICAL & OPTICAL WAVE MOTION, H. Bateman.

## Mechanics, dynamics, thermodynamics, elasticity

**MECHANICS VIA THE CALCULUS, P. W. Norris, W. S. Legge.** Covers almost everything, from linear motion to vector analysis: equations determining motion, linear methods, compounding of simple harmonic motions, Newton's laws of motion, Hooke's law, the simple pendulum, motion of a particle in 1 plane, centers of gravity, virtual work, friction, kinetic energy of rotating bodies, equilibrium of strings, hydrostatics, sheering stresses, elasticity, etc. 550 problems. 3rd revised edition. xii + 367pp. 6 x 9.
S207 Clothbound **$3.95**

**MECHANICS, J. P. Den Hartog.** Already a classic among introductory texts, the M.I.T. professor's lively and discursive presentation is equally valuable as a beginner's text, an engineering student's refresher, or a practicing engineer's reference. Emphasis in this highly readable text is on illuminating fundamental principles and showing how they are embodied in a great number of real engineering and design problems: trusses, loaded cables, beams, jacks, hoists, etc. Provides advanced material on relative motion and gyroscopes not usual in introductory texts. "Very thoroughly recommended to all those anxious to improve their real understanding of the principles of mechanics." MECHANICAL WORLD. Index. List of equations. 334 problems, all with answers. Over 550 diagrams and drawings. ix + 462pp. 5⅜ x 8.
S754 Paperbound **$2.00**

**THEORETICAL MECHANICS: AN INTRODUCTION TO MATHEMATICAL PHYSICS, J. S. Ames, F. D. Murnaghan.** A mathematically rigorous development of theoretical mechanics for the advanced student, with constant practical applications. Used in hundreds of advanced courses. An unusually thorough coverage of gyroscopic and baryscopic material, detailed analyses of the Coriolis acceleration, applications of Lagrange's equations, motion of the double pendulum, Hamilton-Jacobi partial differential equations, group velocity and dispersion, etc. Special relativity is also included. 159 problems. 44 figures. ix + 462pp. 5⅜ x 8.
S461 Paperbound **$2.00**

**THEORETICAL MECHANICS: STATICS AND THE DYNAMICS OF A PARTICLE, W. D. MacMillan.** Used for over 3 decades as a self-contained and extremely comprehensive advanced undergraduate text in mathematical physics, physics, astronomy, and deeper foundations of engineering. Early sections require only a knowledge of geometry; later, a working knowledge of calculus. Hundreds of basic problems, including projectiles to the moon, escape velocity, harmonic motion, ballistics, falling bodies, transmission of power, stress and strain, elasticity, astronomical problems. 340 practice problems plus many fully worked out examples make it possible to test and extend principles developed in the text. 200 figures. xvii + 430pp. 5⅜ x 8.
S467 Paperbound **$2.00**

**THEORETICAL MECHANICS: THE THEORY OF THE POTENTIAL, W. D. MacMillan.** A comprehensive, well balanced presentation of potential theory, serving both as an introduction and a reference work with regard to specific problems, for physicists and mathematicians. No prior knowledge of integral relations is assumed, and all mathematical material is developed as it becomes necessary. Includes: Attraction of Finite Bodies; Newtonian Potential Function; Vector Fields, Green and Gauss Theorems; Attractions of Surfaces and Lines; Surface Distribution of Matter; Two-Layer Surfaces; Spherical Harmonics; Ellipsoidal Harmonics; etc. "The great number of particular cases . . . should make the book valuable to geophysicists and others actively engaged in practical applications of the potential theory," Review of Scientific Instruments. Index. Bibliography. xiii + 469pp. 5⅜ x 8.          S486 Paperbound **$2.25**

**THEORETICAL MECHANICS: DYNAMICS OF RIGID BODIES, W. D. MacMillan.** Theory of dynamics of a rigid body is developed, using both the geometrical and analytical methods of instruction. Begins with exposition of algebra of vectors, it goes through momentum principles, motion in space, use of differential equations and infinite series to solve more sophisticated dynamics problems. Partial contents: moments of inertia, systems of free particles, motion parallel to a fixed plane, rolling motion, method of periodic solutions, much more. 82 figs. 199 problems. Bibliography. Indexes. xii + 476pp. 5⅜ x 8.          S641 Paperbound **$2.00**

**MATHEMATICAL FOUNDATIONS OF STATISTICAL MECHANICS, A. I. Khinchin.** Offering a precise and rigorous formulation of problems, this book supplies a thorough and up-to-date exposition. It provides analytical tools needed to replace cumbersome concepts, and furnishes for the first time a logical step-by-step introduction to the subject. Partial contents: geometry & kinematics of the phase space, ergodic problem, reduction to theory of probability, application of central limit problem, ideal monatomic gas, foundation of thermo-dynamics, dispersion and distribution of sum functions. Key to notations. Index. viii + 179pp. 5⅜ x 8.
S147 Paperbound **$1.35**

**ELEMENTARY PRINCIPLES IN STATISTICAL MECHANICS, J. W. Gibbs.** Last work of the great Yale mathematical physicist, still one of the most fundamental treatments available for advanced students and workers in the field. Covers the basic principle of conservation of probability of phase, theory of errors in the calculated phases of a system, the contributions of Clausius, Maxwell, Boltzmann, and Gibbs himself, and much more. Includes valuable comparison of statistical mechanics with thermodynamics: Carnot's cycle, mechanical definitions of entropy, etc. xvi + 208pp. 5⅜ x 8.          S707 Paperbound **$1.45**

**THE DYNAMICS OF PARTICLES AND OF RIGID, ELASTIC, AND FLUID BODIES; BEING LECTURES ON MATHEMATICAL PHYSICS, A. G. Webster.** The reissuing of this classic fills the need for a comprehensive work on dynamics. A wide range of topics is covered in unusually great depth, applying ordinary and partial differential equations. Part I considers laws of motion and methods applicable to systems of all sorts; oscillation, resonance, cyclic systems, etc. Part 2 is a detailed study of the dynamics of rigid bodies. Part 3 introduces the theory of potential; stress and strain, Newtonian potential functions, gyrostatics, wave and vortex motion, etc. Further contents: Kinematics of a point; Lagrange's equations; Hamilton's principle; Systems of vectors; Statics and dynamics of deformable bodies; much more, not easily found together in one volume. Unabridged reprinting of 2nd edition. 20 pages of notes on differential equations and the higher analysis. 203 illustrations. Selected bibliography. Index. xi + 588pp. 5⅜ x 8.          S522 Paperbound **$2.35**

**A TREATISE ON DYNAMICS OF A PARTICLE, E. J. Routh.** Elementary text on dynamics for beginning mathematics or physics student. Unusually detailed treatment from elementary definitions to motion in 3 dimensions, emphasizing concrete aspects. Much unique material important in recent applications. Covers impulsive forces, rectilinear and constrained motion in 2 dimensions, harmonic and parabolic motion, degrees of freedom, closed orbits, the conical pendulum, the principle of least action, Jacobi's method, and much more. Index. 559 problems, many fully worked out, incorporated into text. xiii + 418pp. 5⅜ x 8.

S696 Paperbound **$2.25**

**DYNAMICS OF A SYSTEM OF RIGID BODIES (Elementary Section), E. J. Routh.** Revised 7th edition of this standard reference. This volume covers the dynamical principles of the subject, and its more elementary applications: finding moments of inertia by integration, foci of inertia, d'Alembert's principle, impulsive forces, motion in 2 and 3 dimensions, Lagrange's equations, relative indicatrix, Euler's theorem, large tautochronous motions, etc. Index. 55 figures. Scores of problems. xv + 443pp. 5⅜ x 8.

S664 Paperbound **$2.35**

**DYNAMICS OF A SYSTEM OF RIGID BODIES (Advanced Section), E. J. Routh.** Revised 6th edition of a classic reference aid. Much of its material remains unique. Partial contents: moving axes, relative motion, oscillations about equilibrium, motion. Motion of a body under no forces, any forces. Nature of motion given by linear equations and conditions of stability. Free, forced vibrations, constants of integration, calculus of finite differences, variations, precession and nutation, motion of the moon, motion of string, chain, membranes. 64 figures. 498pp. 5⅜ x 8.

S229 Paperbound **$2.35**

**DYNAMICAL THEORY OF GASES, James Jeans.** Divided into mathematical and physical chapters for the convenience of those not expert in mathematics, this volume discusses the mathematical theory of gas in a steady state, thermodynamics, Boltzmann and Maxwell, kinetic theory, quantum theory, exponentials, etc. 4th enlarged edition, with new material on quantum theory, quantum dynamics, etc. Indexes. 28 figures. 444pp. 6⅛ x 9¼.

S136 Paperbound **$2.45**

**FOUNDATIONS OF POTENTIAL THEORY, O. D. Kellogg.** Based on courses given at Harvard this is suitable for both advanced and beginning mathematicians. Proofs are rigorous, and much material not generally avaialable elsewhere is included. Partial contents: forces of gravity, fields of force, divergence theorem, properties of Newtonian potentials at points of free space, potentials as solutions of Laplace's equations, harmonic functions, electrostatics, electric images, logarithmic potential, etc. One of Grundlehren Series. ix + 384pp. 5⅜ x 8.

S144 Paperbound **$1.98**

**THERMODYNAMICS, Enrico Fermi.** Unabridged reproduction of 1937 edition. Elementary in treatment; remarkable for clarity, organization. Requires no knowledge of advanced math beyond calculus, only familiarity with fundamentals of thermometry, calorimetry. Partial Contents: Thermodynamic systems; First & Second laws of thermodynamics; Entropy; Thermodynamic potentials: phase rule, reversible electric cell; Gaseous reactions: van't Hoff reaction box, principle of LeChatelier; Thermodynamics of dilute solutions: osmotic & vapor pressures, boiling & freezing points; Entropy constant. Index. 25 problems. 24 illustrations. x + 160pp. 5⅜ x 8

S361 Paperbound **$1.75**

**THE THERMODYNAMICS OF ELECTRICAL PHENOMENA IN METALS and A CONDENSED COLLECTION OF THERMODYNAMIC FORMULAS, P. W. Bridgman.** Major work by the Nobel Prizewinner: stimulating conceptual introduction to aspects of the electron theory of metals, giving an intuitive understanding of fundamental relationships concealed by the formal systems of Onsager and others. Elementary mathematical formulations show clearly the fundamental thermodynamical relationships of the electric field, and a complete phenomenological theory of metals is created. This is the work in which Bridgman announced his famous "thermomotive force" and his distinction between "driving" and "working" electromotive force. We have added in this Dover edition the author's long unavailable tables of thermodynamic formulas, extremely valuable for the speed of reference they allow. Two works bound as one. Index. 33 figures. Bibliography. xviii + 256pp. 5⅜ x 8. S723 Paperbound **$1.65**

**REFLECTIONS ON THE MOTIVE POWER OF FIRE, by Sadi Carnot,** and other papers on the 2nd law of thermodynamics by E. Clapeyron and R. Clausius. Carnot's "Reflections" laid the groundwork of modern thermodynamics. Its non-technical, mostly verbal statements examine the relations between heat and the work done by heat in engines, establishing conditions for the economical working of these engines. The papers by Clapeyron and Clausius here reprinted added further refinements to Carnot's work, and led to its final acceptance by physicists. Selections from posthumous manuscripts of Carnot are also included. All papers in English. New introduction by E. Mendoza. 12 illustrations. xxii + 152pp. 5⅜ x 8.

S661 Paperbound **$1.50**

**TREATISE ON THERMODYNAMICS, Max Planck.** Based on Planck's original papers this offers a uniform point of view for the entire field and has been used as an introduction for students who have studied elementary chemistry, physics, and calculus. Rejecting the earlier approaches of Helmholtz and Maxwell, the author makes no assumptions regarding the nature of heat, but begins with a few empirical facts, and from these deduces new physical and chemical laws. 3rd English edition of this standard text by a Nobel laureate. xvi + 297pp. 5⅜ x 8.

S219 Paperbound **$1.75**

**THE THEORY OF HEAT RADIATION, Max Planck.** A pioneering work in thermodynamics, providing basis for most later work. Nobel Laureate Planck writes on Deductions from Electrodynamics and Thermodynamics, Entropy and Probability, Irreversible Radiation Processes, etc. Starts with simple experimental laws of optics, advances to problems of spectral distribution of energy and irreversibility. Bibliography. 7 illustrations, xiv + 224pp. 5⅜ x 8.
S546 Paperbound **$1.50**

**A HISTORY OF THE THEORY OF ELASTICITY AND THE STRENGTH OF MATERIALS, I. Todhunter and K. Pearson.** For over 60 years a basic reference, unsurpassed in scope or authority. Both a history of the mathematical theory of elasticity from Galileo, Hooke, and Mariotte to Saint Venant, Kirchhoff, Clebsch, and Lord Kelvin and a detailed presentation of every important mathematical contribution during this period. Presents proofs of thousands of theorems and laws, summarizes every relevant treatise, many unavailable elsewhere. Practically a book apiece is devoted to modern founders: Saint Venant, Lame, Boussinesq, Rankine, Lord Kelvin, F. Neumann, Kirchhoff, Clebsch. Hundreds of pages of technical and physical treatises on specific applications of elasticity to particular materials. Indispensable for the mathematician, physicist, or engineer working with elasticity. Unabridged, corrected reprint of original 3-volume 1886-1893 edition. Three volume set. Two indexes. Appendix to Vol. I. Total of 2344pp. 5⅜ x 8⅜.
S914–916 The set, Clothbound **$12.50**

**THE MATHEMATICAL THEORY OF ELASTICITY, A. E. H. Love.** A wealth of practical illustration combined with thorough discussion of fundamentals—theory, application, special problems and solutions. Partial Contents: Analysis of Strain & Stress, Elasticity of Solid Bodies, Elasticity of Crystals, Vibration of Spheres, Cylinders, Propagation of Waves in Elastic Solid Media, Torsion, Theory of Continuous Beams, Plates. Rigorous treatment of Volterra's theory of dislocations, 2-dimensional elastic systems, other topics of modern interest. "For years the standard treatise on elasticity," AMERICAN MATHEMATICAL MONTHLY. 4th revised edition. Index. 76 figures. xviii + 643pp. 6⅛ x 9¼.
S174 Paperbound **$2.95**

**RAYLEIGH'S PRINCIPLE AND ITS APPLICATIONS TO ENGINEERING, G. Temple & W. Bickley.** Rayleigh's principle developed to provide upper and lower estimates of true value of fundamental period of a vibrating system, or condition of stability of elastic systems. Illustrative examples; rigorous proofs in special chapters. Partial contents: Energy method of discussing vibrations, stability. Perturbation theory, whirling of uniform shafts. Criteria of elastic stability. Application of energy method. Vibrating systems. Proof, accuracy, successive approximations, application of Rayleigh's principle. Synthetic theorems. Numerical, graphical methods. Equilibrium configurations, Ritz's method. Bibliography. Index. 22 figures. ix + 156pp. 5⅜ x 8.
S307 Paperbound **$1.50**

**INVESTIGATIONS ON THE THEORY OF THE BROWNIAN MOVEMENT, Albert Einstein.** Reprints from rare European journals. 5 basic papers, including the Elementary Theory of the Brownian Movement, written at the request of Lorentz to provide a simple explanation. Translated by A. D. Cowper. Annotated, edited by R. Fürth. 33pp. of notes elucidate, give history of previous investigations. Author, subject indexes. 62 footnotes. 124pp. 5⅜ x 8.
S304 Paperbound **$1.25**

See also: **FUNDAMENTAL FORMULAS OF PHYSICS, D. H. Menzel.**

# ENGINEERING

**THEORY OF FLIGHT, Richard von Mises.** Remains almost unsurpassed as balanced, well-written account of fundamental fluid dynamics, and situations in which air compressibility effects are unimportant. Stressing equally theory and practice, avoiding formidable mathematical structure, it conveys a full understanding of physical phenomena and mathematical concepts. Contains perhaps the best introduction to general theory of stability. "Outstanding," Scientific, Medical, and Technical Books. New introduction by K. H. Hohenemser. Bibliographical, historical notes. Index. 408 illustrations. xvi + 620pp. 5⅜ x 8⅜.
S541 Paperbound **$2.85**

**THEORY OF WING SECTIONS, I. H. Abbott, A. E. von Doenhoff.** Concise compilation of subsonic aerodynamic characteristics of modern NASA wing sections, with description of their geometry, associated theory. Primarily reference work for engineers, students, it gives methods, data for using wing-section data to predict characteristics. Particularly valuable: chapters on thin wings, airfoils; complete summary of NACA's experimental observations, system of construction families of airfoils. 350pp. of tables on Basic Thickness Forms, Mean Lines, Airfoil Ordinates, Aerodynamic Characteristics of Wing Sections. Index. Bibliography. 191 illustrations. Appendix. 705pp. 5⅜ x 8.
S558 Paperbound **$2.95**

**SUPERSONIC AERODYNAMICS, E. R. C. Miles.** Valuable theoretical introduction to the supersonic domain, with emphasis on mathematical tools and principles, for practicing aerodynamicists and advanced students in aeronautical engineering. Covers fundamental theory, divergence theorem and principles of circulation, compressible flow and Helmholtz laws, the Prandtl-Busemann graphic method for 2-dimensional flow, oblique shock waves, the Taylor-Maccoll method for cones in supersonic flow, the Chaplygin method for 2-dimensional flow, etc. Problems range from practical engineering problems to development of theoretical results. "Rendered outstanding by the unprecedented scope of its contents . . . has undoubtedly filled a vital gap," AERONAUTICAL ENGINEERING REVIEW. Index. 173 problems, answers. 106 diagrams. 7 tables. xii + 255pp. 5⅜ x 8.
S214 Paperbound **$1.45**

**WEIGHT-STRENGTH ANALYSIS OF AIRCRAFT STRUCTURES, F. R. Shanley.** Scientifically sound methods of analyzing and predicting the structural weight of aircraft and missiles. Deals directly with forces and the distances over which they must be transmitted, making it possible to develop methods by which the minimum structural weight can be determined for any material and conditions of loading. Weight equations for wing and fuselage structures. Includes author's original papers on inelastic buckling and creep buckling. "Particularly successful in presenting his analytical methods for investigating various optimum design principles," AERONAUTICAL ENGINEERING REVIEW. Enlarged bibliography. Index. 199 figures. xiv + 404pp. 5⅝ x 8⅜.
S660 Paperbound **$2.45**

**INTRODUCTION TO THE STATISTICAL DYNAMICS OF AUTOMATIC CONTROL SYSTEMS, V. V. Solodovnikov.** First English publication of text-reference covering important branch of automatic control systems—random signals; in its original edition, this was the first comprehensive treatment. Examines frequency characteristics, transfer functions, stationary random processes, determination of minimum mean-squared error, of transfer function for a finite period of observation, much more. Translation edited by J. B. Thomas, L. A. Zadeh. Index. Bibliography. Appendix. xxii + 308pp. 5⅜ x 8.
S420 Paperbound **$2.25**

**TENSORS FOR CIRCUITS, Gabriel Kron.** A boldly original method of analysing engineering problems, at center of sharp discussion since first introduced, now definitely proved useful in such areas as electrical and structural networks on automatic computers. Encompasses a great variety of specific problems by means of a relatively few symbolic equations. "Power and flexibility . . . becoming more widely recognized," Nature. Formerly "A Short Course in Tensor Analysis." New introduction by B. Hoffmann. Index. Over 800 diagrams. xix + 250pp. 5⅜ x 8.
S534 Paperbound **$1.85**

**DESIGN AND USE OF INSTRUMENTS AND ACCURATE MECHANISM, T. N. Whitehead.** For the instrument designer, engineer; how to combine necessary mathematical abstractions with independent observation of actual facts. Partial contents: instruments & their parts, theory of errors, systematic errors, probability, short period errors, erratic errors, design precision, kinematic, semikinematic design, stiffness, planning of an instrument, human factor, etc. Index. 85 photos, diagrams. xii + 288pp. 5⅜ x 8.
S270 Paperbound **$1.95**

**APPLIED ELASTICITY, J. Prescott.** Provides the engineer with the theory of elasticity usually lacking in books on strength of materials, yet concentrates on those portions useful for immediate application. Develops every important type of elasticity problem from theoretical principles. Covers analysis of stress, relations between stress and strain, the empirical basis of elasticity, thin rods under tension or thrust, Saint Venant's theory, transverse oscillations of thin rods, stability of thin plates, cylinders with thin walls, vibrations of rotating disks, elastic bodies in contact, etc. "Excellent and important contribution to the subject, not merely in the old matter which he has presented in new and refreshing form, but also in the many original investigations here published for the first time," NATURE. Index. 3 Appendixes. vi + 672pp. 5⅜ x 8.
S726 Paperbound **$2.95**

**STRENGTH OF MATERIALS, J. P. Den Hartog.** Distinguished text prepared for M.I.T. course, ideal as introduction, refresher, reference, or self-study text. Full clear treatment of elementary material (tension, torsion, bending, compound stresses, deflection of beams, etc.), plus much advanced material on engineering methods of great practical value: full treatment of the Mohr circle, lucid elementary discussions of the theory of the center of shear and the "Myosotis" method of calculating beam deflections, reinforced concrete, plastic deformations, photoelasticity, etc. In all sections, both general principles and concrete applications are given. Index. 186 figures (160 others in problem section). 350 problems, all with answers. List of formulas. viii + 323pp. 5⅜ x 8.
S755 Paperbound **$1.95**

**PHOTOELASTICITY: PRINCIPLES AND METHODS, H. T. Jessop, F. C. Harris.** For the engineer, for specific problems of stress analysis. Latest time-saving methods of checking calculations in 2-dimensional design problems, new techniques for stresses in 3 dimensions, and lucid description of optical systems used in practical photoelasticity. Useful suggestions and hints based on on-the-job experience included. Partial contents: strained and stress-strain relations, circular disc under thrust along diameter, rectangular block with square hole under vertical thrust, simply supported rectangular beam under central concentrated load, etc. Theory held to minimum, no advanced mathematical training needed. Index. 164 illustrations. viii + 184pp. 6⅛ x 9¼.
S137 Clothbound **$3.75**

**MECHANICS OF THE GYROSCOPE, THE DYNAMICS OF ROTATION, R. F. Deimel,** Professor of Mechanical Engineering at Stevens Institute of Technology. Elementary general treatment of dynamics of rotation, with special application of gyroscopic phenomena. No knowledge of vectors needed. Velocity of a moving curve, acceleration to a point, general equations of motion, gyroscopic horizon, free gyro, motion of discs, the damped gyro, 103 similar topics. Exercises. 75 figures. 208pp. 5⅜ x 8.
S66 Paperbound **$1.65**
S144 Paperbound **$1.98**

**A TREATISE ON GYROSTATICS AND ROTATIONAL MOTION: THEORY AND APPLICATIONS, Andrew Gray.** Most detailed, thorough book in English, generally considered definitive study. Many problems of all sorts in full detail, or step-by-step summary. Classical problems of Bour, Lottner, etc.; later ones of great physical interest. Vibrating systems of gyrostats, earth as a top, calculation of path of axis of a top by elliptic integrals, motion of unsymmetrical top, much more. Index. 160 illus. 550pp. 5⅜ x 8.
S589 Paperbound **$2.75**

**FUNDAMENTALS OF HYDRO- AND AEROMECHANICS, L. Prandtl and O. G. Tietjens.** The well-known standard work based upon Prandtl's lectures at Goettingen. Wherever possible hydrodynamics theory is referred to practical considerations in hydraulics, with the view of unifying theory and experience. Presentation is extremely clear and though primarily physical, mathematical proofs are rigorous and use vector analysis to a considerable extent. An Enginering Society Monograph, 1934. 186 figures. Index. xvi + 270pp. 5⅜ x 8.
S374 Paperbound **$1.85**

**APPLIED HYDRO- AND AEROMECHANICS, L. Prandtl and O. G. Tietjens.** Presents, for the most part, methods which will be valuable to engineers. Covers flow in pipes, boundary layers, airfoil theory, entry conditions, turbulent flow in pipes, and the boundary layer, determining drag from measurements of pressure and velocity, etc. "Will be welcomed by all students of aerodynamics," NATURE. Unabridged, unaltered. An Engineering Society Monograph, 1934. Index. 226 figures, 28 photographic plates illustrating flow patterns. xvi + 311pp. 5⅜ x 8.
S375 Paperbound **$1.85**

**HYDRAULICS AND ITS APPLICATIONS, A. H. Gibson.** Excellent comprehensive textbook for the student and thorough practical manual for the professional worker, a work of great stature in its area. Half the book is devoted to theory and half to applications and practical problems met in the field. Covers modes of motion of a fluid, critical velocity, viscous flow, eddy formation, Bernoulli's theorem, flow in converging passages, vortex motion, form of effluent streams, notches and weirs, skin friction, losses at valves and elbows, siphons, erosion of channels, jet propulsion, waves of oscillation, and over 100 similar topics. Final chapters (nearly 400 pages) cover more than 100 kinds of hydraulic machinery: Pelton wheel, speed regulators, the hydraulic ram, surge tanks, the scoop wheel, the Venturi meter, etc. A special chapter treats methods of testing theoretical hypotheses: scale models of rivers, tidal estuaries, siphon spillways, etc. 5th revised and enlarged (1952) edition. Index. Appendix. 427 photographs and diagrams. 95 examples, answers. xv + 813pp. 6 x 9.
S791 Clothbound **$8.00**

**FLUID MECHANICS FOR HYDRAULIC ENGINEERS, H. Rouse.** Standard work that gives a coherent picture of fluid mechanics from the point of view of the hydraulic engineer. Based on courses given to civil and mechanical engineering students at Columbia and the California Institute of Technology, this work covers every basic principle, method, equation, or theory of interest to the hydraulic engineer. Much of the material, diagrams, charts, etc., in this self-contained text are not duplicated elsewhere. Covers irrotational motion, conformal mapping, problems in laminar motion, fluid turbulence, flow around immersed bodies, transportation of sediment, general charcteristics of wave phenomena, gravity waves in open channels, etc. Index. Appendix of physical properties of common fluids. Frontispiece + 245 figures and photographs. xvi + 422pp. 5⅜ x 8.
S729 Paperbound **$2.25**

**THE MEASUREMENT OF POWER SPECTRA FROM THE POINT OF VIEW OF COMMUNICATIONS ENGINEERING, R. B. Blackman, J. W. Tukey.** This pathfinding work, reprinted from the "Bell System Technical Journal," explains various ways of getting practically useful answers in the measurement of power spectra, using results from both transmission theory and the theory of statistical estimation. Treats: Autocovariance Functions and Power Spectra; Direct Analog Computation; Distortion, Noise, Heterodyne Filtering and Pre-whitening; Aliasing; Rejection Filtering and Separation; Smoothing and Decimation Procedures; Very Low Frequencies; Transversal Filtering; much more. An appendix reviews fundamental Fourier techniques. Index of notation. Glossary of terms. 24 figures. XII tables. Bibliography. General index. 192pp. 5⅜ x 8.
S507 Paperbound **$1.85**

**MICROWAVE TRANSMISSION DESIGN DATA, T. Moreno.** Originally classified, now rewritten and enlarged (14 new chapters) for public release under auspices of Sperry Corp. Material of immediate value or reference use to radio engineers, systems designers, applied physicists, etc. Ordinary transmission line theory; attenuation; capacity; parameters of coaxial lines; higher modes; flexible cables; obstacles, discontinuities, and injunctions; tuneable wave guide impedance transformers; effects of temperature and humidity; much more. "Enough theoretical discussion is included to allow use of data without previous background," Electronics. 324 circuit diagrams, figures, etc. Tables of dielectrics, flexible cable, etc., data. Index. Ix + 248pp. 5⅜ x 8.
S459 Paperbound **$1.50**

**GASEOUS CONDUCTORS: THEORY AND ENGINEERING APPLICATIONS, J. D. Cobine.** An indispensable text and reference to gaseous conduction phenomena, with the engineering viewpoint prevailing throughout. Studies the kinetic theory of gases, ionization, emission phenomena; gas breakdown, spark characteristics, glow, and discharges; engineering applications in circuit interrupters, rectifiers, light sources, etc. Separate detailed treatment of high pressure arcs (Suits); low pressure arcs (Langmuir and Tonks). Much more. "Well organized, clear, straightforward," Tonks, Review of Scientific Instruments. Index. Bibliography. 83 practice problems. 7 appendices. Over 600 figures. 58 tables. xx + 606pp. 5⅜ x 8.
S442 Paperbound **$2.85**

See also: **BRIDGES AND THEIR BUILDERS,** D. Steinman, S. R. Watson; **A DIDEROT PICTORIAL ENCYCLOPEDIA OF TRADES AND INDUSTRY; MATHEMATICS IN ACTION,** O. G. Sutton; **THE THEORY OF SOUND,** Lord Rayleigh; **RAYLEIGH'S PRINCIPLE AND ITS APPLICATION TO ENGINEERING,** G. Temple, W. Bickley; **APPLIED OPTICS AND OPTICAL DESIGN,** A. E. Conrady; **HYDRODYNAMICS,** Dryden, Murnaghan, Bateman; **LOUD SPEAKERS,** N. W. McLachlan; **HISTORY OF THE THEORY OF ELASTICITY AND OF THE STRENGTH OF MATERIALS,** I. Todhunter,

K. Pearson; THEORY AND OPERATION OF THE SLIDE RULE, J. P. Ellis; DIFFERENTIAL EQUATIONS FOR ENGINEERS, P. Franklin; MATHEMATICAL METHODS FOR SCIENTISTS AND ENGINEERS, L. P. Smith; APPLIED MATHEMATICS FOR RADIO AND COMMUNICATIONS ENGINEERS, C. E. Smith; MATHEMATICS OF MODERN ENGINEERING, E. G. Keller, R. E. Doherty; THEORY OF FUNCTIONS AS APPLIED TO ENGINEERING PROBLEMS, R. Rothe, F. Ollendorff, K. Pohlhausen.

# CHEMISTRY AND PHYSICAL CHEMISTRY

**ORGANIC CHEMISTRY, F. C. Whitmore.** The entire subject of organic chemistry for the practicing chemist and the advanced student. Storehouse of facts, theories, processes found elsewhere only in specialized journals. Covers aliphatic compounds (500 pages on the properties and synthetic preparation of hydrocarbons, halides, proteins, ketones, etc.), alicyclic compounds, aromatic compounds, heterocyclic compounds, organophosphorus and organometallic compounds. Methods of synthetic preparation analyzed critically throughout. Includes much of biochemical interest. "The scope of this volume is astonishing," INDUSTRIAL AND ENGINEERING CHEMISTRY. 12,000-reference index. 2387-item bibliography. Total of x + 1005pp. 5⅜ x 8. Two volume set.
S700 Vol I Paperbound **$2.00**
S701 Vol II Paperbound **$2.00**
The set **$4.00**

**THE PRINCIPLES OF ELECTROCHEMISTRY, D. A. MacInnes.** Basic equations for almost every subfield of electrochemistry from first principles, referring at all times to the soundest and most recent theories and results; unusually useful as text or as reference. Covers coulometers and Faraday's Law, electrolytic conductance, the Debye-Hueckel method for the theoretical calculation of activity coefficients, concentration cells, standard electrode potentials, thermodynamic ionization constants, pH, potentiometric titrations, irreversible phenomena, Planck's equation, and much more. "Excellent treatise," AMERICAN CHEMICAL SOCIETY JOURNAL. "Highly recommended," CHEMICAL AND METALLURGICAL ENGINEERING. 2 Indices. Appendix. 585-item bibliography. 137 figures. 94 tables. ii + 478pp. 5⅝ x 8⅜.
S52 Paperbound **$2.35**

**THE CHEMISTRY OF URANIUM: THE ELEMENT, ITS BINARY AND RELATED COMPOUNDS, J. J. Katz and E. Rabinowitch.** Vast post-World War II collection and correlation of thousands of AEC reports and published papers in a useful and easily accessible form, still the most complete and up-to-date compilation. Treats "dry uranium chemistry," occurrences, preparation, properties, simple compounds, isotopic composition, extraction from ores, spectra, alloys, etc. Much material available only here. Index. Thousands of evaluated bibliographical references. 324 tables, charts, figures. xxi + 609pp. 5⅜ x 8.
S757 Paperbound **$2.95**

**KINETIC THEORY OF LIQUIDS, J. Frenkel.** Regarding the kinetic theory of liquids as a generalization and extension of the theory of solid bodies, this volume covers all types of arrangements of solids, thermal displacements of atoms, interstitial atoms and ions, orientational and rotational motion of molecules, and transition between states of matter. Mathematical theory is developed close to the physical subject matter. 216 bibliographical footnotes. 55 figures. xi + 485pp. 5⅜ x 8.
S94 Clothbound **$3.95**
S95 Paperbound **$2.45**

**POLAR MOLECULES, Pieter Debye.** This work by Nobel laureate Debye offers a complete guide to fundamental electrostatic field relations, polarizability, molecular structure. Partial contents: electric intensity, displacement and force, polarization by orientation, molar polarization and molar refraction, halogen-hydrides, polar liquids, ionic saturation, dielectric constant, etc. Special chapter considers quantum theory. Indexed. 172pp. 5⅜ x 8.
S64 Paperbound **$1.50**

**ELASTICITY, PLASTICITY AND STRUCTURE OF MATTER, R. Houwink.** Standard treatise on rheological aspects of different technically important solids such as crystals, resins, textiles, rubber, clay, many others. Investigates general laws for deformations; determines divergences from these laws for certain substances. Covers general physical and mathematical aspects of plasticity, elasticity, viscosity. Detailed examination of deformations, internal structure of matter in relation to elastic and plastic behavior, formation of solid matter from a fluid, conditions for elastic and plastic behavior of matter. Treats glass, asphalt, gutta percha, balata, proteins, baker's dough, lacquers, sulphur, others. 2nd revised, enlarged edition. Extensive revised bibliography in over 500 footnotes. Index. Table of symbols. 214 figures. xviii + 368pp. 6 x 9¼.
S385 Paperbound **$2.45**

**THE PHASE RULE AND ITS APPLICATION, Alexander Findlay.** Covering chemical phenomena of 1, 2, 3, 4, and multiple component systems, this "standard work on the subject," (NATURE, London), has been completely revised and brought up to date by A. N. Campbell and N. O. Smith. Brand new material has been added on such matters as binary, tertiary liquid equilibria, solid solutions in ternary systems, quinary systems of salts and water. Completely revised to triangular coordinates in ternary systems, clarified graphic representation, solid models, etc. 9th revised edition. Author, subject indexes. 236 figures. 505 footnotes, mostly bibliographic. xii + 494pp. 5⅜ x 8.
S91 Paperbound **$2.45**

**TERNARY SYSTEMS: INTRODUCTION TO THE THEORY OF THREE COMPONENT SYSTEMS, G. Masing.** Furnishes detailed discussion of representative types of 3-components systems, both in solid models (particularly metallic alloys) and isothermal models. Discusses mechanical mixture without compounds and without solid solutions; unbroken solid solution series; solid solutions with solubility breaks in two binary systems; iron-silicon-aluminum alloys; allotropic forms of iron in ternary system; other topics. Bibliography. Index. 166 illustrations. 178pp. 5⅝ x 8⅜. S631 Paperbound **$1.45**

**THE STORY OF ALCHEMY AND EARLY CHEMISTRY, J. M. Stillman.** An authoritative, scholarly work, highly readable, of development of chemical knowledge from 4000 B.C. to downfall of phlogiston theory in late 18th century. Every important figure, many quotations. Brings alive curious, almost incredible history of alchemical beliefs, practices, writings of Arabian Prince Oneeyade, Vincent of Beauvais, Geber, Zosimos, Paracelsus, Vitruvius, scores more. Studies work, thought of Black, Cavendish, Priestley, Van Helmont, Bergman, Lavoisier, Newton, etc. Index. Bibliography. 579pp. 5⅜ x 8. S628 Paperbound **$2.45**

See also: **ATOMIC SPECTRA AND ATOMIC STRUCTURE, G. Herzberg; INVESTIGATIONS ON THE THEORY OF THE BROWNIAN MOVEMENT, A. Einstein; TREATISE ON THERMODYNAMICS, M. Planck.**

# ASTRONOMY AND ASTROPHYSICS

**AN ELEMENTARY SURVEY OF CELESTIAL MECHANICS, Y. Ryabov.** Elementary exposition of gravitational theory and celestial mechanics. Historical introduction and coverage of basic principles, including: the elliptic, the orbital plane, the 2- and 3-body problems, the discovery of Neptune, planetary rotation, the length of the day, the shapes of galaxies, satellites (detailed treatment of Sputnik I), etc. First American reprinting of successful Russian popular exposition. Elementary algebra and trigonometry helpful, but not necessary; presentation chiefly verbal. Appendix of theorem proofs. 58 figures. 165pp. 5⅜ x 8.
T756 Paperbound **$1.25**

**THE SKY AND ITS MYSTERIES, E. A. Beet.** One of most lucid books on mysteries of universe; deals with astronomy from earliest observations to latest theories of expansion of universe, source of stellar energy, birth of planets, origin of moon craters, possibility of life on other planets. Discusses effects of sunspots on weather; distances, ages of several stars; master plan of universe; methods and tools of astronomers; much more. "Eminently readable book," London Times. Extensive bibliography. Over 50 diagrams. 12 full-page plates, fold-out star map. Introduction. Index, 238pp. 5¼ x 7½. T627 Clothbound **$3.00**

**THE REALM OF THE NEBULAE, E. Hubble.** One of the great astronomers of our time records his formulation of the concept of "island universes," and its impact on astronomy. Such topics are covered as the velocity-distance relation; classification, nature, distances, general field of nebulae; cosmological theories; nebulae in the neighborhood of the Milky Way. 39 photos of nebulae, nebulae clusters, spectra of nebulae, and velocity distance relations shown by spectrum comparison. "One of the most progressive lines of astronomical research," The Times (London). New introduction by A. Sandage. 55 illustrations. Index. iv + 201pp. 5⅜ x 8. S455 Paperbound **$1.50**

**OUT OF THE SKY, H. H. Nininger.** A non-technical but comprehensive introduction to "meteoritics", the young science concerned with all aspects of the arrival of matter from outer space. Written by one of the world's experts on meteorites, this work shows how, despite difficulties of observation and sparseness of data, a considerable body of knowledge has arisen. It defines meteors and meteorites; studies fireball clusters and processions, meteorite composition, size, distribution, showers, explosions, origins, craters, and much more. A true connecting link between astronomy and geology. More than 175 photos, 22 other illustrations. References. Bibliography of author's publications on meteorites. Index. viii + 336pp. 5⅜ x 8. T519 Paperbound **$1.85**

**SATELLITES AND SCIENTIFIC RESEARCH, D. King-Hele.** Non-technical account of the manmade satellites and the discoveries they have yielded up to the spring of 1959. Brings together information hitherto published only in hard-to-get scientific journals. Includes the life history of a typical satellite, methods of tracking, new information on the shape of the earth, zones of radiation, etc. Over 60 diagrams and 6 photographs. Mathematical appendix. Bibliography of over 100 items. Index. xii + 180pp. 5⅜ x 8½. T703 Clothbound **$4.00**

**HOW TO MAKE A TELESCOPE, Jean Texereau.** Enables the most inexperienced to choose, design, and build an f/6 or f/8 Newtonian type reflecting telescope, with an altazimuth Couder mounting, suitable for lunar, planetary, and stellar observation. A practical step-by-step course covering every operation and every piece of equipment. Basic principles of geometric and physical optics are discussed (though unnecessary to construction), and the merits of reflectors and refractors compared. A thorough discussion of eyepieces, finders, grinding, installation, testing, using the instrument, etc. 241 figures and 38 photos show almost every operation and tool. Potential errors are anticipated as much as possible. Foreword by A. Couder. Bibliography and sources of supply listing. Index. xiii + 191pp. 6¼ x 10. T464 Clothbound **$3.50**

**PRINCIPLES OF STELLAR DYNAMICS, S. Chandrasekhar.** A leading astrophysicist here presents the theory of stellar dynamics as a branch of classical dynamics, clarifying the fundamental issues and the underlying motivations of the theory. He analyzes the effects of stellar encounters in terms of the classical 2-body problem, and investigates problems centering about Liouville's theorem and the solutions of the equations of continuity. This edition also includes 4 important papers by the author published since "Stellar Dynamics," and equally indispensable for all workers in the field: "New Methods in Stellar Dynamics" and "Dynamical Friction," Parts I, II, and III. Index. 3 Appendixes. Bibliography. 50 illustrations. x + 313pp. 5⅜ x8.
S659 Paperbound **$2.00**

**A SHORT HISTORY OF ASTRONOMY, A. Berry.** Popular standard work for over 50 years, this thorough and accurate volume covers the science from primitive times to the end of the 10th century. After the Greeks and the Middle Ages, individual chapters analyze Copernicus, Brahe, Galileo, Kepler, and Newton, and the mixed reception of their discoveries. Post-Newtonian achievements are then discussed in unusual detail: Halley, Bradley, Lagrange, Laplace, Herschel, Bessel, etc. 2 Indexes. 104 illustrations, 9 portraits. xxxi + 440pp. 5⅜ x 8.
T210 Paperbound **$2.00**

**THREE COPERNICAN TREATISES, translated with notes by Edward Rosen.** 3 papers available nowhere else in English: "The Commentariolus" and "Letter against Werner" of Copernicus; the "Narratio prima" of Rheticus. The "Commentariolus" is Copernicus's most lucid exposition of his system. The "Letter against Werner" throws light on development of Copernicus's thought. The "Narratio prima" is earliest printed presentation of the new astronomy. "Educational and enjoyable," Astrophysical Journal. Corrected edition. Biographical introduction. 877-item bibliography of virtually every book, article, on Copernicus published 1939-1958. Index. 19 illustrations. 218pp. 5⅜ x 8.
S585 Paperbound **$1.75**

# EARTH SCIENCES

**PRINCIPLES OF STRATIGRAPHY, A. W. Grabau.** Classic of 20th century geology, unmatched in scope and comprehensiveness. Nearly 600 pages cover the structure and origins of every kind of sedimentary, hydrogenic, oceanic, pyroclastic, atmoclastic, hydroclastic, marine hydroclastic, and bioclastic rock; metamorphism; erosion; etc. Includes also the constitution of the atmosphere; morphology of oceans, rivers, glaciers; volcanic activities; faults and earthquakes; and fundamental principles of paleontology (nearly 200 pages). New introduction by Prof. M. Kay, Columbia U. 1277 bibliographical entries. 264 diagrams. Tables, maps, etc. Two volume set. Total of xxxii + 1185pp. 5⅜ x 8.
S686 Vol I Paperbound **$2.50**
S687 Vol II Paperbound **$2.50**
The set **$5.00**

**THE GEOLOGICAL DRAMA, H. and G. Termier.** Unusual work by 2 noted French geologists: not the usual survey of geological periods, but general principles; continent formation, the influence of ice-ages and earth movements in shaping the present-day land masses, the creation and advance of life, the position of man. Readable and authoritative survey for the layman; excellent supplement for the student of geology; important collection of recent European theories for the American geologist. Much material appears here for the first time in a non-technical work. Index. 30 photographs, 5 diagrams. 5 maps. 144pp. 6 x 9.
T702 Clothbound **$3.95**

**THE EVOLUTION OF THE IGNEOUS ROCKS, N. L. Bowen.** Invaluable serious introduction applies techniques of physics and chemistry to explain igneous rock diversity in terms of chemical composition and fractional crystallization. Discusses liquid immiscibility in silicate magmas, crystal sorting, liquid lines of descent, fractional resorption of complex minerals, petrogenesis, etc. Of prime importance to geologists & mining engineers, also to physicists, chemists working with high temperatures and pressures. "Most important," TIMES, London. 3 indexes. 263 bibliographic notes. 82 figures. xviii + 334pp. 5⅜ x 8.
S311 Paperbound **$1.85**

**INTERNAL CONSTITUTION OF THE EARTH, edited by Beno Gutenberg.** Completely revised. Brought up-to-date, reset. Prepared for the National Research Council this is a complete & thorough coverage of such topics as earth origins, continent formation, nature & behavior of the earth's core, petrology of the crust, cooling forces in the core, seismic & earthquake material, gravity, elastic constants, strain characteristics and similar topics. "One is filled with admiration . . . a high standard . . . there is no reader who will not learn something from this book," London, Edinburgh, Dublin, Philosophic Magazine. Largest bibliography in print: 1127 classified items. Indexes. Tables of constants. 43 diagrams. 439pp. 6⅛ x 9¼.
S414 Paperbound **$2.45**

**HYDROLOGY, edited by Oscar E. Meinzer.** Prepared for the National Research Council. Detailed complete reference library on precipitation, evaporation, snow, snow surveying, glaciers, lakes, infiltration, soil moisture, ground water, runoff, drought, physical changes produced by water, hydrology of limestone terranes, etc. Practical in application, especially valuable for engineers. 24 experts have created "the most up-to-date, most complete treatment of the subject," AM. ASSOC. of PETROLEUM GEOLOGISTS. Bibliography. Index. 165 illustrations. xi + 712pp. 6⅛ x 9¼.
S191 Paperbound **$2.95**

**THE BIRTH AND DEVELOPMENT OF THE GEOLOGICAL SCIENCES, F. D. Adams.** Most thorough history of the earth sciences ever written. Geological thought from earliest times to the end of the 19th century, covering over 300 early thinkers & systems: fossils & their explanation, vulcanists vs. neptunists, figured stones & paleontology, generation of stones, dozens of similar topics. 91 illustrations, including medieval, renaissance woodcuts, etc. Index. 632 footnotes, mostly bibliographical. 511pp. 5⅜ x 8. **T5 Paperbound $2.00**

**DE RE METALLICA, Georgius Agricola.** 400-year old classic translated, annotated by former President Herbert Hoover. The first scientific study of mineralogy and mining, for over 200 years after its appearance in 1556, it was the standard treatise. 12 books, exhaustively annotated, discuss the history of mining, selection of sites, types of deposits, making pits, shafts, ventilating, pumps, crushing machinery; assaying, smelting, refining metals; also salt, alum, nitre, glass making. Definitive edition, with all 289 16th century woodcuts of the original. Biographical, historical introductions, bibliography, survey of ancient authors. Indexes. A fascinating book for anyone interested in art, history of science, geology, etc. Deluxe edition. 289 illustrations. 672pp. 6¾ x 10¾. Library cloth. **S6 Clothbound $10.00**

**GEOGRAPHICAL ESSAYS, William Morris Davis.** Modern geography & geomorphology rest on the fundamental work of this scientist. 26 famous essays presenting most important theories, field researches. Partial contents: Geographical Cycle, Plains of Marine and Subaerial Denudation, The Peneplain, Rivers and Valleys of Pennsylvania, Outline of Cape Cod, Sculpture of Mountains by Glaciers, etc. "Long the leader & guide," ECONOMIC GEOGRAPHY. "Part of the very texture of geography . . . models of clear thought," GEOGRAPHIC REVIEW. Index. 130 figures. vi + 777pp. 5⅜ x 8. **S383 Paperbound $2.95**

**A HISTORY OF ANCIENT GEOGRAPHY, E. H. Bunbury.** Standard study, in English, of ancient geography; never equalled for scope, detail. First full account of history of geography from Greeks' first world picture based on mariners, through Ptolemy. Discusses every important map, discovery, figure, travel, expedition, war, conjecture, narrative, bearing on subject. Chapters on Homeric geography, Herodotus, Alexander expedition, Strabo, Pliny, Ptolemy, would stand alone as exhaustive monographs. Includes minor geographers, men not usually regarded in this context: Hecataeus, Pythea, Hipparchus, Artemidorus, Marinus of Tyre, etc. Uses information gleaned from military campaigns such as Punic wars, Hannibal's passage of Alps, campaigns of Lucullus, Pompey, Caesar's wars, the Trojan war. New introduction by W. H. Stahl, Brooklyn College. Bibliography. Index. 20 maps. 1426pp. 5⅜ x 8. **T570-1, clothbound, 2 volume set $12.50**

**URANIUM PROSPECTING, H. L. Barnes.** For immediate practical use, professional geologist considers uranium ores, geological occurrences, field conditions, all aspects of highly profitable occupation. Index. Bibliography. x + 117pp. 5⅜ x 8. **T309 Paperbound $1.00**

DATE DUE